Old English is a companion to Old English studies and to historical studies of early English in general. It is also an introduction to Indo-European studies in the particular sense in which they underpin the history of English. Professor Roger Lass makes accessible in a linguistically up-to-date and readable form the Indo-European and Germanic background to Old English, as well as what can be reconstructed about the resulting state of Old English itself. His book is a bridge between the more elementary Old English grammars and the major philological grammars and recent interpretations of the Old English data.

A further and important aim of *Old English* is to encourage a view of the language as emerging from and implicated in a complex and ancient background, carrying in its structure relics of a long history. The phonology, morphology, morphophonology and some aspects of its syntax are, therefore, viewed from a wide historical perspective. The features of the language are seen partly as backward-looking to Indo-European and German, partly as forward-looking to later stages of English, as well as constituting the synchronic structure of Old English itself.

In *Old English*, Roger Lass assumes a basic knowledge of synchronic linguistic theory (phonetics, phonology, morphology and syntax), and at least an introductory acquaintance with historical linguistics. An extensive glossary gives definitions of the major technical terms used.

Old English

Old English

A historical linguistic companion

Roger Lass
University of Cape Town

CAMBRIDGE
UNIVERSITY PRESS

Published by the Press Syndicate of the University of Cambridge
The Pitt Building, Trumpington Street, Cambridge CB2 1RP
40 West 20th Street, New York, NY 10011–4211, USA
10 Stamford Road, Oakleigh, Melbourne 3166, Australia

First published 1994
Reprinted 1995, 1997, 1998

Printed in the United Kingdom at the University Press, Cambridge

A catalogue record for this book is available from the British Library

Library of Congress cataloguing in publication data

Lass, Roger.
Old English: a historical linguistic companion / Roger Lass.
    p.   cm.
Includes bibliographical references and index.
ISBN 0 521 43087 9 (hardback); 0 521 45848 X (paperback)
1. English language – Old English, ca. 450-1100 – Grammar,
Historical. I. Title
PE 125.L37 1993
429 – dc20 93-18182   CIP

ISBN 0 521 43087 9 hardback
ISBN 0 521 45848 X paperback

For Sue and René, whose fault this book is, whether or not they intended it

Biology is more like history than it is like physics. You have to know the past to understand the present. And you have to know it in exquisite detail. There is as yet no predictive theory of biology, just as there is not yet a predictive theory of history. The reasons are the same: both subjects are still too complicated for us.

Carl Sagan, Cosmos

. . . the search for explicative laws in natural facts proceeds in a tortuous fashion. In the face of some inexplicable facts you must try to imagine many general laws, whose connection with the facts escapes you. Then suddenly, in the unexpected connection of a result, a specific situation, and one of those laws, you perceive a line of reasoning that seems more convincing than the others.

Umberto Eco, The name of the rose

'Therefore you don't have a simple answer to your questions?'
'Adso, if I did I would teach theology in Paris.'
'In Paris do they always have the true answer?'
'Never,' Williams said, 'but they are very sure of their errors.'
'And you,' I said with childish impertinence, 'never commit errors?'
'Often,' he answered. 'But instead of conceiving only one, I imagine many, so I become the slave of none.'

Umberto Eco, The name of the rose

Contents

Preface

This is an approximation to the book I wish had existed when, more years ago than I like to remember, I embarked on the serious linguistic study of Old English. I felt a great need then for something to bridge the gap between elementary Old English grammars and the standard 'philological' handbooks (Campbell, Sievers-Brunner, Luick); as well as a source of background for making proper use of the etymological dictionaries like Holthausen, or even the *OED*. (Why is Skr *lúbhyati* given as a cognate for OE *lufian*, but Skr *śaptá* for *seofon*? Are there 'two kinds' of OE categories spelled <f>, and if so, why?)

The closest thing to the sort of book I wanted is still, as it was in the 1960s, the invaluable Moore & Knott, *Elements of Old English* (1955); this does provide a lot of the necessary background, if in an old-fashioned and 'pre-structural' way. It explores the major sound changes in both Germanic and Old English, and gives an overall view of the morphology – but not in enough detail to make an approach to the Big Boys very easy, and not in a sophisticated enough way to help in the transition to the 'new' OE scholarship: the tradition of 'linguistic' rather than 'philological', but still historically based work beginning with Stockwell and others in the 1950s, and still going on, more vigorously than ever. (Some of these problems are now taken care of by Alfred Bammesberger's *English etymology* (1984), but this has a much wider coverage, and is not dedicated to Old English in detail.) And neither of these books (nor most of the standard grammars) has anything much to say about syntax or suprasegmentals.

This guide sets out in the first instance to bridge the historical gap by supplying the most important Indo-European and Germanic background, conceptual, substantive, and terminological; it also approaches things in a reasonably modern way, in terms of systems and contrasts and the interrelatedness of linguistic levels rather than atomistically, and with a basis in the theoretical developments that inform much of the current scholarly literature.

Traditional IE and Germanic courses are thin on the ground these days; it's not easy now for students to get up the kind of background that was still (if fadingly) available in the 1960s, when a few of the Last Neogrammarians, as it were, could still be found teaching rigorous philological courses in some universities. This was the kind of training I had at Yale under the late Helge Kökeritz (who was also a linguist and phonetician); a combination of this with a certain amount of modern linguistics and 'revisionist' analysis seems to be what's needed. Students, even very bright and motivated ones, have trouble contextualizing in the traditional historical way. I have for instance seen no relatively introductory grammar that gives the sort of account of IE Ablaut and its Germanic reflexes that would make it clear why the present, preterite singular, and preterite plural of strong verbs have the shapes they do (or why indeed the classes are called 'ablaut series'); or why OE *byrþen* is regularly related to the verb *beran* (or more properly its past participle *boren*). Or, to take a wider view, why *cunnan* and *cnāwan* and *cūþe* and *cȳþan*, all sharing some sense like 'know', should be related and look the way they do.

This book is designed in the first instance to help students approach the handbooks and dictionaries with something of the kind of background the authors seem to have assumed, and which much of the modern literature also assumes, and to do it in a reasonably (but not excessively or trendily) modern framework, providing a contemporary eye to cast on the older works, and a traditional eye for the modern.

But I have something else in mind as well, perhaps just as important. This is to encourage a view of Old English not in a synchronic vacuum, nor on the other hand as a state of affairs interesting merely as a precursor of Modern English. Rather to see it as a (set of) system(s) emerging from and still implicated in a complex and ancient background, carrying in its structure relics of its long history. The idea is to set Old English (its phonology, morphology, morphophonology and some aspects of its syntax) in a wide historical perspective, stressing both its Indo-Europeanness and Germanicness, seeing it partly as backward-looking (a collection of lineages of ancient date), and partly as forward-looking (in terms of what it was to turn into) – as well of course as a language in itself.

There is a certain self-indulgence here, a pandering to my own fascination with historical inertia, the way languages, despite, or with no concern with, their speakers can maintain a strong and systematic connectivity over great ranges of time and space. There are certain classes of relation that are often not stressed, and ought to be – both for the sake of historical background and synchronic coherence. One example may illustrate the sort of concern that dominates much of this book.

The *-ne* in the pronouns *hine* and *hwone*, and in the 'article' *þone*, as well as the masculine accusative singular strong adjective, are structurally 'the same thing'. But they are also historically/comparatively 'the same thing' as the -*n* in the Greek masculine accusative singular article *tón*, and this in turn is the 'same thing' as the -*m* in Sanskrit *tam*. Synchronically, then, there is justification for segmenting *hi-ne*, *hwo-ne*, *þo-ne*. Historically, the *þ-* in *þone* represents the same IE deictic base */t-/ as the /t/ in *tón*, *tam* (which in turn we can now see as *t-ó-n*, *t-a-m*); and the *h-* in *hine* represents the deictic base */k-/ (L *c-is*), and the *hw-* in *hwone* the interrogative */kʷ-/ (Skr *k-am*, L *qu-em* with a different grade of the root). And so on.

I know that there is a post-Saussurean (pseudo-) problem about the status of historical 'sames' and 'continuations'; but historians can quite properly neglect this, and students ought to learn to see the larger picture, the essential conservativeness of linguistic structure even under massive transformation. Languages show a kind of 'persistence of memory', transformed morphs echoing Dali's melted watches. At least I tend to see things this way, and so did many of my predecessors. This rather nineteenth-century frame of mind is due for a revival, if not as the centre of linguistic inquiry, then certainly as a major part of the enterprise.

Another way of putting it is that (of course) a good deal of the structure of OE 'belongs to' OE in a systematic way; but a lot of it also does not, it's there as a matter of historical contingency. In part OE looks the way it does not because it is a functioning system of a particular kind, but because it happens to have had the ancestors it does. My nose, with its particular shape and size, is (of course) 'mine' in a synchronic biological sense; but it's also not mine, because it continues the nasomorphy (if I may) of my mother and father, and my maternal and paternal grand-fathers, and probably who knows who how far back. As Elizabeth Traugott once remarked in a lecture, synchrony in one sense is 'a way station along the path of history'.

The level of preparation I assume is what would be supplied by an elementary Old English course, in addition to or in the context of a good first-year general linguistics or linguistically sophisticated English Lan-guage course. That is, a basic knowledge of phonetics and phonology, the elements of syntactic and morphological theory, and an introduction to historical linguistics. For the student with less linguistic preparation, the services of a teacher, or guidance in the direction of useful elementary accounts of problem areas, will probably make this guide usable. I have refrained, for reasons of space, from building in a mini-course in linguistics as well, though I've supplied fairly extensive explanations of difficult matters in the text, and a glossary, which provides at least a working definition of the major technical terms used.

The reader will note a certain disproportion in the amount of space allotted to particular areas; there is more on phonology than anything else, with vocabulary perhaps running a close second; inflectional morphology

is treated in somewhat less detail, and the syntax chapter is restricted to
only two major topics. To a certain degree this reflects my own interests
and competence; but it also reflects both the traditional concerns of the
field (there is simply more information available on some topics than on
others), and the susceptibility of certain areas to the kind of historical
study I am pursuing here. Chapter 9 is more a sketch for a particular kind
of historical syntax than a thoroughgoing treatment of it; there are topics
that could probably have been treated but have not been (e.g. relativiza-
tion, general patterns of clause-joining, etc.). I am not entirely clear on the
best way to handle some of these additional topics in the chosen
framework; I thought it better simply to treat two exemplary ones than to
try a more fragmented approach to more.

Much of the content is quite traditional, in substance if not in
statement; some on the other hand is untraditional, even idiosyncratic. I
am indebted for both aspects of my approach especially to work by and
conversations over the years with John Anderson (the impress of Lass &
Anderson 1975 will be apparent), Fran Colman, Charles Jones, and
Richard Hogg, all of whose footprints will be visible to the *cognoscenti*:
both through pinched ideas, and suggestions of theirs that I've rejected,
often at my peril. The total range of indebtedness will be apparent from
the bibliography and notes. I am particularly grateful to Dieter Kastovsky
and Fran Colman for reading various drafts and commenting in excruciat-
ing detail, and giving me an enormous amount of extra work. It was
probably not very bright of me to disregard some of their suggestions, but
just as this book is mine, so in the end are all the mistakes; I can't blame
my pratfalls on my friends who tried to keep me standing. I am also
grateful to Judith Ayling of CUP for having faith in this perhaps somewhat
odd project, being constantly encouraging, and sweating over many a hot
fax in the course of getting this thing on the road.

Last but not at all least, my gratitude to René van der Westhuizen and
Sue Watermeyer, for wanting to do a course that included this sort of
stuff, and being interested in the kind of arcane things that I like. This was
originally written for them: altruistically, to serve the purposes outlined
above; more cynically, so I could use them as guinea pigs. They were nice
about it all.

Conventions, symbols and abbreviations

1   Citation of orthographic forms

If a language has a conventional roman orthography, this will be used except where phonetic or phonemic representation is appropriate. If the original alphabet is non-roman (as in Sanskrit, Greek, Old Church Slavic, Gothic, or the language of Germanic runic inscriptions), I use the normal transliterations, with diacritics for length and (where relevant) accent. I will comment below on special conventions for some of the more exotic languages.

2   Length

Long vowels are marked with a macron <¯> in all languages except Old Icelandic, where length is conventionally indicated by an acute: OE *gōd*, OIc *góðr* 'good'. Consonant length will (inconsistent though this is) be marked generally by double letters, as in the orthographies. In general, where length is marked (as in OE, Latin, Greek, etc.) short vowels will be left unmarked: except when the shortness itself is of importance, in which case a breve <˘> will be used: L *stă-tus* vs. *stā-re*.

3   Accent

Except in certain contexts (e.g. chapter 4), accented syllables, where it is necessary to mark them, will be indicated with an acute <´> over the vowel; if primary vs. secondary accent is at issue, the distinction will be <´> vs. <`>. Acutes and graves are used elsewhere in different senses (see above on length in OIc, and below on Sanskrit, Greek, Lithuanian). The context should make it clear what's being indicated.

4   Special conventions for particular languages

  (i) *Proto-Indo-European*: *[m̥, n̥, l̥, r̥] are syllabic consonants; */H/, with or without subscript numerals, represents a largyngeal.

 (ii) *Sanskrit*: <ṭ, ḍ, ṇ, ṣ, ḷ, r> are retroflex; <ś> = /ʃ/; <c> = a palatal
      stop or affricate; <ñ> is a palatal nasal; <ḥ> = [h]; <h> = voiced
      glottal fricative [ɦ]; <bh, dh, gh> are breathy-voiced stops:
      <ṁ> = nasal with the same place of articulation as a following
      consonant; <ṛ, ḷ> are syllabic; <ˊ> marks an accented high-tone
      vowel.
(iii) *Ancient Greek*: <ˊ> = accent (high tone); <ˆ> = accent (com-
      pound tone, rise-fall); <ˋ> = accent (low tone); <ph> etc. are
      aspirated stops.
 (iv) *Lithuanian*: <ˉ> = rising pitch; <ˊ> = falling pitch; <ˋ> = ac-
      cented short vowel; /y/ = /iː/.
  (v) *Old Church Slavic*: <ĭ, ŭ> = 'overshort' vowels; a hook under a
      vowel symbol as in <ą> = nasalization; <ě> = /jɛ/, <š, č> = /ʃ,
      tʃ/, <y> = /ɨ/.
 (vi) *Gothic*: <aí, aú> = [ɛ, ɔ]; otherwise <ai, au> = /ɑi, ɑu/;
      <gg> = [ŋg], <gq> = [ŋk].

5   *Morphological representations*

If morphological structure is relevant, the boundaries between elements
will generally be marked with a hyphen: OE {luf-od-e} 'he loved'.

6   *Other symbols*

*	In historical contexts, reconstructed item; in nonhistor-ical contexts, ungrammatical or nonoccurring item.
>	becomes
<	derives from
[ ]	phonetic representation
/ /	phonemic representation
{ }	morphemic representation
s	strong (accented) syllable or constituent
w	weak (unaccented) syllable or constituent
σ	syllable
σ̆	light syllable
σ̄	heavy syllable
σ̿	superheavy syllable
v̄	long vowel
v, v̆	short vowel

7　Phonetic symbols

(a) Vowels: −R = unrounded, +R = rounded

	FRONT		CENTRAL		BACK	
	−R	+R	−R	+R	−R	+R
HIGH close	i	y	ɨ	ʉ		u
half-close	e	ø				o
MID half-open	ɛ	œ			ʌ	ɔ
raised-open	æ					
LOW open	a				ɑ	

[˜] over a vowel symbol = nasalization

(b) Consonants: −V = voiceless, +V = voiced

L = Labial,　D = Dental,　A = Alveolar,　PA = Palato-alveolar,
P = Palatal, V = Velar, U = Uvular, G = Glottal, Fric = Fricative

	L	D	A	PA	P	V	U	G
Stop, −V	p		t		c	k	q	ʔ
Stop, +V	b		d		ɟ	g	G	
Fric, −V	f	θ	s	ʃ	ç	x	χ	h
Fric, +V	v	ð	z	ʒ	j	ɣ		
Nasal, +V	m		n			ŋ		
Liquid, +V	w		r, l		j	w		

Palato-alveolar affricates: −V [tʃ], +V [dʒ]; [ɫ] is a velarized ('dark') /l/. There is some likelihood that OE /t, d, n, l/ were dental; I will often use the term 'dental' to mean 'dental or alveolar', where no distinction is at issue. The grouping of [j, w] as liquids is nonconventional (but see Lass & Anderson 1975: Preliminaries); these are more commonly called 'glides' or 'semivowels'. I have listed [w] under two places of articulation, since it has two components, labial and velar.

ABBREVIATIONS

1　Languages

Afr Afrikaans; **Angl** Anglian; **Da** Danish; **Du** Dutch; **e** early; **E** East(ern); **EGmc** East Germanic; **F** French; **Fi** Finnish; **Fri** Frisian; **G** German; **Gmc** Germanic; **Go** Gothic; **Gr** Greek (Ancient); **IE** Indo-European; **Kt** Kentish; **l** late; **L** Latin; **Li** Lithuanian; **M** Middle; **ME** Middle English;

Merc Mercian; **ML** Midland(s); **Mod** Modern; **ModE** Modern English; **N** North(ern); **NGmc** North Germanic; **NWGmc** Northwest Germanic; **Nth** Northumbrian; **O** Old; **OCS** Old Church Slavic; **OE** Old English; **OF** Old French; **OFri** Old Frisian; **OHG** Old High German; **OIc** Old Icelandic (= 'Old Norse'); **OIr** Old Irish; **OLF** Old Low Franconian; **OPr** Old Prussian; **OS** Old Saxon; **OSc** Old Scandinavian; **PIE** Proto-Indo-European; **PGmc** Proto-Germanic; **S** South(ern); **Skr** Sanskrit; **Toch** Tocharian; **W** West(ern); **WGmc** West Germanic; **WS** West Saxon

2   Grammatical terms, sound changes etc.

abl ablative; **Adj** Adjective; **acc** accusative; **AFB** Anglo-Frisian Brightening; **aor** aorist; **art** article; **C** consonant; **cl** class; **comp** complementizer, comparative; **CSR** Compound Stress Rule; **DHH** Diphthong Height Harmony; **DO** direct object; **def** definite; **du** dual; **f** feminine; **gen** genitive; **GL** Grimm's Law; **GSR** Germanic Stress Rule; **imp** imperative; **ind** indicative; **indef** indefinite; **inf** infinitive; **inst** instrumental; **IO** indirect object; **IU** *i*-umlaut; **loc** locative; **m** masculine; **neg** negative; **N** noun; **n** neuter; **no** number; **NP** noun phrase; **nom** nominative; **O** object; **obl** oblique; **part** participle; **pl** plural; **pp** past participle; **pres** present; **prp** preposition; **pret** preterite; **rel** relative marker; **S** subject; **sg** singular; **subj** subjunctive; **T** theme; **tns** tense; **V** verb, vowel; **VL** Verner's Law; **voc** vocative; **WGG** West Germanic Gemination

Introduction and caveats: the notion 'Old English'

Though the great song return no more
There's keen delight in what we have:
The rattle of pebbles on the shore
Under the receding wave.

W. B. Yeats, 'The Nineteenth Century and After'

This book, as the title indicates, is largely about the historical background of Old English. The term 'Old English' itself, however, is not unproblematical. There is no single or uniform corpus of Old English, but rather a collection of texts from about the seventh to the eleventh centuries, representing dialects spread out from the North of England to the West Country and Kent.[1] This collection is extremely heterogeneous, as the range suggests: runic OE of the seventh century is in many ways as different from 'classical' literary OE of the eleventh as Chaucer's language is from Shakespeare's. Mercian OE of the ninth century is at least as different from West Saxon of the same period as the local dialects of Staffordshire now are from those of Hampshire or Dorset.

This is bad enough when one is looking backward; looking forward, as we must in trying to construct a coherent historical picture, we find that there is no OE textual tradition directly ancestral to any variety of modern standard English, of the kinds presumably native to most users of this book, or learned as a second language. There is a problem then in defining what we mean by the language name identifying our object of inquiry, and some apparently serious difficulties in talking, as we will a good deal, about 'ancestry'. What for instance is the status of a claim like 'OE /y/ as in *cyning* becomes ModE /ɪ/ as in *king*'? We say things like this all the time, but the remarks in the first paragraph suggest they must be either very sloppy or close to meaningless.

---

[1] For a detailed survey of the major OE sources, arranged by dialect, see Steponavičius (1987: ch. 2). Old English dialectology is not as straightforward as it might seem: see the discussion in Hogg (1988).

1

Sloppy they are, but in a rather benign way. There is first of all enough of a 'common core' in the vast corpus we call 'OE' to let us make certain kinds of general statements safely; and there are also many (often implicit) guidelines for preventing the worst kinds of intellectual abuses. This background is rarely made explicit, but it can be; and it is important enough to go into, even at the risk of tedium. Let me try then to unpack the mini-etymology of *king* above, to give some idea of what is (or ought to be) really intended by the conventional jargon of language historians. Saying that OE /y/ > ModE /ɪ/, or that OE *cyning* > ModE *king*, we really mean pretty much all of the following:

(i) All OE dialects (except later Kentish) had a vowel spelled <y>, which descends from what we reconstruct as West Germanic */u/, followed by /i/ or /j/ in the next syllable. The phonetic/phonological substance represented in spelling by <cyning> goes back to something that can be represented as */kuninɣ-α-z/. (For some support, note Finnish *kuningas*, an early Germanic loan, and OHG *kuning*.)

(ii) For all dialects, this vowel is systematically high, front, rounded, and short; it is a member of a quality system in which it is opposed to say /e, æ/ by highness, /u, o, α/ by frontness, /i, e, æ, α/ by roundness, /i:, y:, . . . / by length, etc.

(iii) This phonological characterization, on which all available good evidence converges, is assumed to have had as its phonetic realization a vowel in the vicinity of what the IPA writes as [y], making the notations /y/, [y] reasonable.

(iv) We have no idea whether or not there were any significant differences in its pronunciation from dialect to dialect. There probably were, if modern experience of 'the same' category across dialects or languages is anything to go by. We therefore use symbols like [y] with a certain latitude, as we generally do with modern languages. E.g. Dutch and Afrikaans /y/ are rather different phonetically, the former having protruded lip-rounding and the latter lip-compression; both are distinct from /i/ in both languages. And both in turn are different from Finnish /y/, which is opener and more strongly rounded than either.

Still, it is not irresponsible to say that these three languages each 'have a phoneme /y/'; the same thinking goes for Old English. That is, we believe that the realizations of this unit lay in that area of the vowel space ('high front corner, with some lip-rounding') that can be designated [y]; it was not open enough to be called [ø], was too rounded to be called [i], and so on.

(v) In all modern standard varieties of English, what we assume to be the 'continuation' of this element (except when interfered with by special developments like lengthening, which can usually be filtered out) lies in the area that by the criteria in (iv) we could responsibly designate [ɪ]. Therefore ModE (virtually all varieties) 'has /ɪ/' in the same sense that OE 'has /y/'; dialectal specification and microphonetic detail are not germane in the modern case, and unattainable for Old English.

Now the later history of English is complex; the emerging London standard of the fifteenth to seventeenth centuries (on which all modern non-Scottish standard and standard-like varieties are ultimately based) is itself a confluence of East Midland (Mercian), Southwestern (West Saxon) and Southeastern (Kentish) lineages, if with Mercian most prominent. But there is enough unity and continuity so that we can say – loosely, and with hedges – that 'OE *cyning* > ModE *king*' (in terms of word-identity), and 'OE /kyning/ > ModE /kɪŋ/' (in terms of phoneme-sequence ancestry), and finally that 'OE /y/ > ModE /ɪ/'.

We might add too that backward projections (into the Indo-European and Germanic past) rest on much the same kind of infrastructure. Only here our information is scantier, and assumption and argument play a correspondingly larger part. For instance, the entities we call 'West Germanic' or 'Proto-Germanic' must have been complexes of dialects, not uniform, invariant speech types; they could not in principle have been all that different from the complexes we label 'Old English' or 'Modern English'. So the same kinds of arguments apply to a construct like 'West Germanic */u/' as to 'ModE /ɪ/'; and this is the sense in which all such labels are to be construed.

This has been rather a lot of ammunition flung at a very small target; but the principle is important. The historian's craft is a tricky one, and the simplified ways we talk are strategies for avoiding having to say things like this every time we say anything at all. But such networks of converging justificatory argument, theoretical basis and assumption do lie (ideally) behind the individual 'shorthand' statements we make. This is not really a problem: anything a historian claims is corrigible by new evidence, better use of old evidence, or critical argument; and this is in the end what scholarship is about, not the propagation of dogma.

History however is in some ways harder than other kinds of disciplines; the evidence is often more tenuous, the craft of doing history is often itself the source of the 'data' that the subject is about. (Any reconstructed item is both a historian's product and data for further history.) I say this all here to defuse the dogmatic tone that will often creep in – not by intention, but through limitation of space. It's impossible to make all one's assumptions and underlying arguments explicit, because nobody wants a ten-volume encyclopedia as an introduction to a subject. But where these hidden underpinnings are of particular importance or interest, I will uncover them in some detail.

Virtually all standard handbooks, grammars and introductions to Old English are dialectally biased; the same is true of the texts the beginning student is normally exposed to. The bias is toward the 'literary language': the ninth-century variety of the Alfredian prose corpus, the 'classical' OE of later prose-writers like Ælfric, the 'poetic language' of the great works like *Beowulf*, *The Seafarer*, and so on. All these are written (more or less) in some form of West Saxon. So, because of the preoccupations of the university tradition of Old English study, with its skewing toward texts of 'literary value' rather than glossaries, charters, herbals, inscriptions, etc., what has come to be taken as 'Old English' pure and simple is actually a regionally, temporally and stylistically restricted subset of the existing texts.[2]

This book is designed as a support for the linguistic end of OE studies as normally conducted, and its readers' acquaintance with the language probably derives from this tradition; it therefore shares this bias to some extent. It is based largely on the norms of the texts most likely to be familiar, and the dialect types most emphasized in the grammars and handbooks. Personally I think it's a serious mistake to teach the history of a language (or the structure of any stage of it) primarily in terms of texts chosen for 'literary merit'. In many ways, as any historian knows, a shopping-list or scribbled private letter may be much more informative about the state of the language than a poem, a bad poem or clumsy piece of prose than good ones. Highly crafted language is the exception rather than the norm, and is parasitic on ordinary, inartistic language. Linguists by and large are (properly) more interested in language in general than very specialized minority varieties. This is not to downgrade literary language or texts; only to say that they represent a very small and by no means privileged fraction of all the things language does, and of the texts that survive from early periods; and they cannot even be properly understood at all without reference to the inartistic and the non-literary.

This said, there is still reason for following tradition to some extent, and focussing on West Saxon varieties. Where these are very different from others, or where the histories of others are crucial to understanding later developments or earlier texts, the latter will be invoked. This will be the practice particularly for the earlier stages, since developments obscured in 'standard' (WS) OE are still clear in other dialects. For instance, the fact that two vowels have merged is not apparent from WS *cēne* 'keen' and *fēng* 'he seized'; but the latter is always spelled with <e>, whereas the former

---

[2] In fact the phonology usually referred to in the handbooks is that of the ninth to tenth centuries, but the morphology and syntax is that of the tenth to eleventh! (I am reminded of this curious paradox by Dieter Kastovsky.)

occurs in early texts as *coene*. Conversely, when the elementary grammars say that the ending of the infinitive was *-an* 'in Old English' (e.g. WS *wesan* 'be'), we must be aware that this was not the case in Northumbrian, which has *wesa*, *woesa*. And knowing that such reduced forms existed already in the North, we are less surprised to find, in Middle English times, that erosion of morphology is advanced in northern dialects; and that while the North has zero infinitives quite early, in the fourteenth century Chaucer still has a good number in *-en*. Points like this will be brought up where relevant.

This excursus should suggest why the historical story-telling bogs down in places, and why there may be more exemplification of different varieties than at first conduces to easy digestion. With luck, it should all be reasonably clear in the end. It is also a warning that the world of the handbooks is much more complex than that of introductory texts, and that there is a lot more to Old English than may be apparent at first. So much in fact that it's still a viable proposition to be a historian of Old English, and promises to be so for a long time to come. If anything in this book manages to whet an appetite, I'll be pleased and feel that I've done my job.

A note on handbooks

This book is not (and is not intended to be) a 'complete' grammar or even historical grammar of Old English. It is rather a treatment of major topics from a primarily historical point of view. Given the extent of coverage (e.g. word-formation, syntax, and the details of Indo-European ancestry, which are not generally included in the usual so-called 'standard handbooks'), I cannot give here the enormous amount of detail found in the major 'philological' grammars.

Because of this I will often refer my somewhat briefer or more linguistically oriented discussions to the detailed treatments in the massive historical grammars of OE, Germanic, Indo-European, and English in general. Fortunately for the anglophone reader, at least some of these are available in English. For general older Germanic matters (at least phonology and inflectional morphology), the classic is still probably Prokosch's *Comparative Germanic grammar* (1938); this is of course somewhat dated, and – like all great books – idiosyncratic and eccentric in places. It is however the best general book on Old Germanic, and repays careful reading. On a more modern (if again often eccentric) note, there is a very useful collection of essays by various hands in van Coetsem & Kufner, *Towards a grammar of Proto-Germanic* (1972) (though this is not a 'handbook' in the strict sense).

For the more remote IE background, there is unfortunately nothing really adequate in English; Lockwood's *Indo-European philology* (1966) gives an outline of the family, and some useful information, but is linguistically primitive; Baldi's *An introduction to the Indo-European languages* (1983) is better, but is lacking in extensive linguistic detail. The best general book on Indo-European (phonology and morphology, but no syntax) available is Szemerényi's *Einführung in die vergleichende Sprachwissenschaft* (1989); this again is idiosyncratic, and very technical and difficult, but linguistically sophisticated and full of insight; it also has one of the most copious bibliographies imaginable. Slightly simpler, but to my mind a bit too dogmatic and short on argumentation rather than assertion, there is Beekes' *Vergelijkende taalwetensschap* (1990), which is particularly good on the languages in the family and their attestation, and on the noun and verb categories, but not always reliable on technical matters.

Up until 1992, the standard handbook for Old English itself (phonology and morphology) has been Campbell's *Old English grammar* (1959). Linguistically it leaves much to be desired, but it is full of data and interesting discussion, and I will refer to it frequently. As far as phonology goes, Campbell has now been 'superseded' by Richard Hogg's *Old English grammars* (1992b); with its linguistic sophistication combined with traditional 'philological' skill and care, this will surely become the new standard work. Only vol. I, Phonology, has so far appeared; and since this was published too late to take account of in this text, the reader should consult it on all phonological matters (it is keyed to Campbell as well, which should make it extremely easy to use). Another classic handbook is Brunner's *Altenglische Grammatik* (1965), a major revision of Sievers' *Angelsächsische Grammatik*; if you read German it would be useful to compare Brunner, Campbell and Hogg on major issues. Germanic and Old English phonology are also treated extensively in vol. I of Luick's massive *Historische Grammatik der englischen Sprache* (1914/41).

For detailed and up-to-date studies of the structure and history of Old English, as well as its subsequent fate, from a number of different points of view, the first two volumes of The *Cambridge History of the English Language* (Hogg 1992a on Old English and Blake 1992 on Middle English) are now available, and indispensable; the relevant chapters will be useful additions (and often correctives, or at least alternatives) to those in this book.

It is certainly advisable to have at least one of the standard OE handbooks available for reference, since this book is designed to be both complementary to them, and an introduction to some of their more technical concerns.

Part I:

Historical prelude

So grew the Romaine Empire by degree,
Till that Barbarian hands it quite did spill,
And left of it but these olde markes to see
. . .
As they which gleane, the reliques vse to gather,
Which th'husbandman behind him chanst to scater.

Spenser, *The ruines of Rome*, 3

1   Background and origins

1.1   History in linguistic description

It should never be necessary to 'justify' a particular kind of study; a subject is intrinsically interesting and so worth pursuing, or it's not. But it is sometimes worthwhile to show why a particular study is useful or informative or 'relevant' (to use a piece of debased coinage) in reference to some other, where it fits in the larger picture.

Any serious student of Old English is presumably engaged in this pursuit because it somehow appeals; and anybody interested in the subsequent history of English of course needs to know Old English, since it is the input to that history. Crudely, the plural of *mouse* is *mice* because OE *mūs* had the nom/acc plural *mȳs*, and OE /y:/ comes down into modern English as /aɪ/.

Knowledge of antecedents provides a special sort of understanding, different from the kind that comes from knowledge of structure: what we might call genetic or genealogical understanding. Historically evolved systems are not continually made afresh; they contain remnants of earlier stages, sometimes fully functional, sometimes reduced and functionless, sometimes just marginal. Understanding a system involves knowing where these things come from and what they used to do, how their current functions (if any) relate to their old ones. To take an example from another field, we all know that there are three little bones in the middle ear that transmit sound from the eardrum to the cochlea, and we can understand easily how they work and what they do. But our understanding is richer if we know that two of these bones were once part of the architecture of the reptilian jaw, and that the ancient transition from reptile to mammal (indeed, a crucial part of the structural definition of 'mammal') is the migration of these bones to the ear, and their linking up in a sound-transmitting chain.

Linguistic systems are multilayered and complex, and there are always interactions of many kinds among their subsystems. One subsystem can change while others remain static, one can keep its function but change its structure, and so on. Along these lines, today's 'irregularities' may reflect yesterday's regularities. The nouns *bit, burden* for instance are reminiscences of a once productive process by which nouns could be formed from the root corresponding to the plural or past participle stems of strong verbs (thus they are related to *bitten, born*). And the verbs *set, rear* reflect an old process whereby causative verbs could be formed from the past singular stems of strong verbs: *set* (= 'cause to sit') is from the ancestor of *sat, rear* (= 'cause to rise') from that of *rose*. To take another case, *was* and *were* (OE *wæs, wǣron*) are related by a general rule that has major effects on OE morphology generally, and cannot be understood without some knowledge of Indo-European and early Germanic accentuation, the development of the IE voiceless stops, and other matters (see §§2.3–4 below). This text aims to provide the kind of background and linkage that will make these relations clear, and give some idea of how complex systems evolve.

1.2   Indo-European and Germanic

Old English is a member of the Germanic family (specifically its western branch), and Germanic is in turn a subgroup of the larger Indo-European (IE) family. To say that a language is a 'member of a family' is, like the same kind of statement about a person, to make a claim about ancestry; 'belonging-to' in this context is a genealogical, not a typological concept. That is, whatever one happens to look like, one belongs to a family by virtue of ancestry, not appearance. If both my biological parents are dark-eyed and dark-haired, and I am blonde and blue-eyed, I belong to the family just as much as my dark-eyed brunette sister (I just happened to get two copies of a recessive gene). And I belong on strictly genetic grounds, and these only. If I happen to have 'my father's nose' as well, this might serve as further corroboration, and counteract my unexpected eyes and hair, but it is not a proof of relationship.

Similarly, membership in a language family, while not 'genetic' in the biological sense, is still a matter of descent; English is Germanic not by virtue of any structural characters (though it shares many of these with its sister languages), but on the pure historical grounds of being the product of unbroken transmission (though with massive change) from a remote, unattested ancestor called **Proto-Germanic** (PGmc), which in turn is a descendant of an even more remote ancestor called **Proto-Indo-European** (PIE). The metaphors 'family', 'descent', etc. refer to transmission of a language from generation to generation by cultural means, rather than by being encoded in DNA; but the image is still a good one.

The IE family probably originated, a number of millenia BC, in the general region of the Caspian Sea;[1] over the centuries speakers spread as far east as India, as far west as the Americas, as far north as northern Russia and as far south as the southern tip of Africa. During their travels their languages changed continuously and independently, but regularly enough so that by means of standard reconstructive techniques we can show their relatedness, and extrapolate much of the history that happens not to be preserved in documents.

Germanic is specifically a northwestern IE group: it shares a number of major affinities with Slavic (Russian, Polish, Czech, etc.), Baltic (Latvian, Lithuanian), Celtic (Irish, Scots Gaelic, Welsh) and Italic (Latin and its descendants, e.g. French, Spanish, Italian).[2] The major IE subgroups are as follows († indicates an extinct language; the listings are exemplary, not exhaustive):[3]

   (i) INDO-IRANIAN: Indic: †Sanskrit, Hindi, Gujerati
       Iranian: †Avestan, Persian, Kurdish
  (ii) ARMENIAN: †Classical Armenian, Modern Armenian
 (iii) ALBANIAN: Albanian
 (iv) ANATOLIAN: †Hittite, †Luwian
  (v) HELLENIC: †Mycenean (Linear B), †Ancient Greek, Modern Greek
 (vi) ITALIC: Osco-Umbrian: †Oscan, †Umbrian
      Latin-Faliscan: †Faliscan, †Latin, French, Italian, Rumanian
 (vii) CELTIC: Brythonic: †Cornish, Welsh, Breton
      Goidelic: †Old Irish, Irish, Scots Gaelic
(viii) BALTIC: †Old Prussian, Lithuanian, Latvian
 (ix) SLAVIC: East Slavic: Russian, Ukrainian
      West Slavic: Polish, Czech
      South Slavic: †Old Church Slavic, Bulgarian, Serbo-Croatian
  (x) GERMANIC: East Germanic: †Gothic, †Crimean Gothic
      North Germanic: †Old Icelandic, Icelandic, Faroese, Danish, Swedish, Norwegian

[1] On the complex and controversial issue of the Indo-European homeland, see Szemerényi (1985), and the papers in the special issue of *Transactions of the Philological Society* (87.2, 1988) on linguistic and cultural change devoted to this matter. An important conflicting view posits a common 'Proto-Indo-Hittite' family originally based in Anatolia, which later broke up into Anatolian and non-Anatolian (Dolgopolsky 1989); an Anatolian homeland is also argued for (on rather different grounds, primarily non-linguistic) by Renfrew (1988).
[2] On the position of Germanic within the IE family, see Polomé (1972), Nielsen (1989: chs. 1–2).
[3] For a rather simple overall survey of the IE family see Lockwood (1966: ch. 3); a much more detailed one is available in Beekes (1990), in Dutch.

West Germanic: †Old English, †Old High German, Yiddish, English, Dutch, Afrikaans, Frisian

The rest of this treatment will concentrate on Old English and its relatives, but other IE languages will be an important historical and comparative resource.

1.3   The attestation of Germanic

The earliest Germanic texts are runic inscriptions, the oldest dating from about the third century AD.[4] These remains are fragmentary, sometimes unintelligible, and very short; but they give us an idea of what Germanic looked like in the early days. One of the earliest is that on the Nøvling clasp (North Jutland, Denmark), dating from about AD 200. This is in Northwest Germanic (see §1.4), and runs as follows (transliteration of the runes underneath):

(1.1)

ᛒ ᛁ ᛗ ᚨ ᚹ ᚨ ᚱ ᛁ ᛜ ᚨ ᛉ ᛏ ᚨ ᛚ ᚷ ᛁ ᛗ ᚨ ᛁ

b   i   d   a   w   a   r   i   j   a   z   t   a   l   g   i   d   a   i

Separating it into words and roughly translating:

(1.2)   bida-warijaz   talgidai
          Bida-Warijaz   carved (this)

Analysing the forms, to uncover the structure:

(1.3)   b i d -   a - w a r -   ija -z
          covenant-   T - protector - T - nom sg
          talg - i - d -   ai
          carve - T - past - 1st person, sg

T = 'theme' or 'thematic element', a morphological connective between a lexical root and endings; we will return to this when we deal with OE morphology (see especially §6.1.1). This short inscription can be made to show its Germanic and IE connections quite clearly:

(i) *bid-*: in Gmc this root (OE *bīdan* 'wait', OIc *bíða*) usually has the sense 'await, bide'; its cognates (words of the same ultimate ancestry) in

---

[4] These inscriptions are conveniently collected (in transliteration, with linguistic commentary) in Antonsen (1975). For general introductions to runes see Elliott (1963), Page (1987).

other IE dialects have the sense shown in L *fīdus* 'faithful', *foedus* 'covenant', Albanian *bē* 'oath'. The correspondence Gmc /b/ = L /f/ is regular: OE *brecan* 'break', L *fragilis* 'fragile', OE *brōþor*, L *frāter* 'brother', etc.

(ii) *war-*: cf. OE *werian* < */war-j-an/ 'to protect', OIc *verja* 'ward off', Skr *varuta* 'protector'.

(iii) *talg-*: OIc *telgia* 'to carve', L *dolāre* 'hew', Skr *dal-á-ya-ti* 'he splits'.

The phonological connections will be more apparent after a reading of chapter 2. Morphologically the ending *-a-z* (nom sg) = L *-u-s*, and of course the past tense *-d-* is recognizable as the modern past marker in weak verbs (*wound-e-d*, etc.).

There are a few earlier attestations, mainly names and scattered words cited by Greek and Roman historians. Caesar for instance (*Gallic wars*) cites *ūrus* 'aurochs, European bison', and in later Germanic we find OHG *ūrohso*, OE *ūr*; and Tacitus (*Germania*, AD 98) gives *glæsum* 'amber' (= OHG *glās*, OE *glǽr* 'amber, resin'). There are also very early loans into languages with which the Germanic peoples came into contact in northern Europe; these often show extremely conservative shapes, in some cases more archaic than anything actually attested in Germanic remains proper. So Finnish *kuningas* (see 'Introduction' above) looks very like what we would reconstruct as the ancestor of OE *cyning*, OHG *kuning*, etc., and the same for other loans into Finnish like *rengas* 'ring' (cf. OIc *hring-r*, OE *hring*), *ruhtinas* 'price' (cf. OE *dryhten*, OS *druhtin*). Finnish simplifies the initial clusters, but leaves the old suffixes intact: even without this evidence we would reconstruct forms that look very like the Finnish ones.[5]

Written texts in the Roman and other non-runic alphabets do not appear until the sixth century (Gothic); Old High German begins about the seventh century, and OE in the late seventh or eighth; Old Saxon and Old Low Franconian are known from the ninth century, but extensive Scandinavian texts do not begin until the twelfth, and Dutch and Frisian start, along with Low German, in the thirteenth.

1.4 Classification of the Germanic languages

The conventional classification recognizes three major groups: East, North and West Germanic. Recently however it has become clear that this is probably a secondary split: the bulk of the older runic inscriptions appear to be in a dialect distinct from East Germanic, and ancestral to

[5] There is an excellent discussion of Germanic loans (of all ages) into Balto-Finnic in Laanest (1975: ch. 5).

North and West Germanic, which is now called Northwest Germanic (NWGmc).[6] The overall family tree then is:

(1.4)

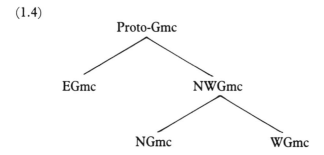

Many of the NWGmc inscriptions are actually later than the first texts in NGmc and WGmc; there is some likelihood that NWGmc was used for some time as a 'classical' language by speakers of its own descendants (as in the liturgical use of Latin by Romance-speaking Catholics, etc.). We will be concerned in this chapter only with the internal genealogy of West Germanic; on NWGmc see the next chapter.

According to Tacitus, the western Germanic peoples were divided into three major tribal groups, *Ingvaeones, Istvaeones*, and *Erminones*. It is not clear just what these names correspond to – ethnic, cultural or linguistic groupings, or a bit of all three; but they do serve to mark out some important geographical distributions that correspond to later dialect groups. The Ingvaeonic dialects are those spoken along the North Sea coast (the term 'North Sea Germanic' is also used); the Istvaeonic dialects are central (e.g. the Rhine basin), and these seem to have played a large part in the genesis of Dutch; and the Erminonic are mainly associated with modern High German (only 'Ingvaeonic' is currently in use).

The Ingvaeonic group (for its linguistic features see chapter 3) can be divided into Anglo-Frisian (English and Frisian) and Low German (Old Saxon and its descendants, Middle Low German and modern Low German dialects).[7] Dutch is a bit of a hybrid: it appears to continue both Ingvaeonic and non-Ingvaeonic lineages, primarily the latter. In the WGmc family tree below, the labels in inverted commas are entities of uncertain status: they are probably not 'protolanguages' in the usual sense, but *Sprachbünde* ('language associations'), clusters of dialects with high-intensity mutual contact and borrowing, and a certain amount of common

---

[6] On the grouping of the Germanic languages, see Lehmann (1966), Kufner (1972), Nielsen (1989). The latter is perhaps the best general introduction to Germanic available. On the particular relations of Old English, Nielsen (1985).
[7] For a detailed historical treatment of Ingvaeonic, see Markey (1976: vff).

innovation. At the very earliest periods of the evolution of WGmc, the situation was probably rather like that of the present-day English or Scottish dialects, or the German or Dutch dialect-continua, rather than mutually (relatively) incomprehensible and fully distinct 'different languages'.

The whole WGmc family, including the modern languages:

(1.5)

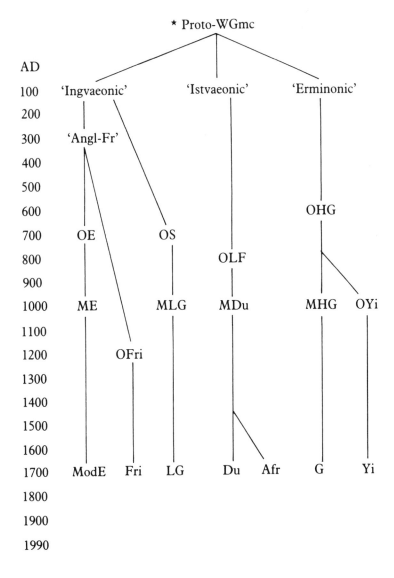

The dates along the left-hand margin do not represent (except perhaps for Afrikaans) the 'actual emergences' of the languages; they indicate rather (for OE and later languages) the dates of the first good textual evidence, or the times when a continuing tradition begins to look radically new.

2   Indo-European to Proto-Germanic to West Germanic[1]

2.1   Germanic: an innovation cluster

In the conventional model of language relationships, as in the family trees in the previous chapter, the growth of linguistic diversity, the origin of 'new' languages, is imaged as a process of branching. The tree has one ultimate 'mother' node, and the rest of the languages in the family arise by successive splits. Genealogical trees of this kind are familiar from biology and other fields; in linguistic history however the parent-offspring relations are most often parthenogenetic (only one parent per child!). Multiple parentage (except in the case of pidgins and creoles) is supposed to be relatively rare; though some 'normal' languages, like Dutch, may well be examples of something of the sort. There are problems in an oversimple interpretation of genealogical trees for languages (e.g. straight-line developments may be interrupted by diffusion of features from one dialect to another, etc.); but the metaphor is useful, is usually reasonably consistent with the facts, both linguistic and historical, and for most families is a useful organizing device.

Linguistically, 'branching' can be defined more or less as it is in biology: we propose a split in a lineage when one subgroup becomes different enough to merit being assigned to a new class. In other words, branchings are dialect splits; they represent the emergence of one or more structural innovations that are striking enough to make us give a new name to the innovating group. In many cases there is contoversy over whether an innovation is important enough to merit a new name; but normally there is fairly good agreement.

[1] The best treatment in English of the topics covered in this chapter (the IE/Gmc transition and earlier, pre-textual Germanic) is still Prokosch (1938), which though dated is well worth reading. Other standard handbooks are Streitberg (1963) and Krahe (1963). The material is also treated in some detail in Campbell (1959: chs. 3–4, 8–9). There is an excellent (if highly technical) collection of papers on Proto-Germanic in van Coetsem & Kufner (1972). For a more modern, if still reasonably elementary treatment, which differs in many details from the views presented here, see Steponavičius (1987: ch. 4).

Germanic is a relatively simple case, as the number of innovations, and the massiveness of their structural effects, clearly define a coherent new IE subgroup, quite different-looking from the other ancient languages. The innovations are: (a) a set of major vowel mergers; (b) a nearly complete transformation of the obstruent system; (c) restructuring of the accent system; (d) some important consonant developments connected with the accent; and (e) a reorganization of the verb system on a new basis. We will consider only the phonological innovations in this chapter; the changes in the verb system will be taken up in chapter 7.

2.2   Formation of the PGmc vowel system

On a conservative view,[2] the parent IE language had a vowel system of this general type:

(2.1)   i   u   i: u:
          e   o   e: o:
             α   α:
           ei   oi   αi
           eu   ou   αu

The PGmc system derives from a set of mergers, extensively reducing the original:

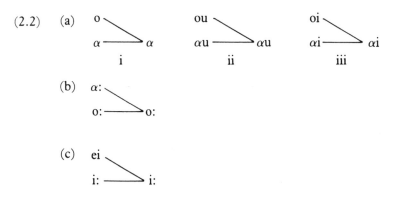

Mergers (a.i–iii) are of course all functions of */o/ > */α/. Illustrations of the vowel mergers:

[2] The sense of 'conservative' will be clearer in §5.3, where we consider proposals for larger systems (including */ɔ/) and smaller ones – even a system with only one vowel, */e/. But this is relevant only for very early PIE; the variety that concerns us here is 'Later Western PIE' (Dolgopolsky 1989), which is the input to PGmc.

(a.i)   L *octō* 'eight', *ager* 'field' = Go *ahtau, akkrs.*
(a.ii) L *rūfus* 'red' < */roudh-o-s/, *augeō* 'increase' = Go *raups, aukan.*
(a.iii) OLat *oinos* (later *ūnus*) 'one', *aes* /ais/ 'brass' = Go *ains, aiz.*
(b)   L *māter* 'mother', Gr (Doric) *pôs* 'foot' = OE *mōdor*, Go *fōtus.*
(c)   Gr *steíkhō* 'go', L *su-īnus* 'belonging to a pig' = OE *stīgan* 'ascend',
        swīn 'swine'.

The result is an asymmetrical and reduced PGmc system:

(2.3)   i   u   i: u:
        e   □   e: o:
            α   □
                  αi αu   eu

We will see later how the short /o/ and long /α:/ slots were refilled, and what happened to the diphthongs.

2.3   The IE consonants: Grimm's Law

The conventional reconstruction of the IE consonant system is:

(2.4)   p   t   k k^w
        b   d   g g^w
        bh   dh   gh g^wh
                  s
        m
             n
             r,l j   w

*/bh/ etc. are traditionally called 'voiced aspirates'; they were probably breathy-voiced stops as in modern Hindi and other Indic languages. There was also a set of 'laryngeals', rather mysterious consonants of uncertain type but with profound effects on phonological development. It is however unlikely that they survived into PGmc, and I will not treat them here.[3]

---

[3] On the laryngeals see §§5.3–4 and references. There are more serious challenges to this reconstruction, involving a complete recasting of the articulatory characterization of the obstruents. These challenges come under the heading of 'glottalic theory', and involve *inter alia* the claim that rather than the traditional voiced vs. voiceless vs. breathy-voiced opposition claimed here, the original voiced aspirated stops were in fact glottalic egressive (ejective). The arguments are complex and to my mind not convincing; for the original proposals see e.g. Gamkrelidze & Ivanov (1973), Hopper (1973); for critical (and I think devastating) counterargument, Szemerényi (1985, 1989a: §VI.9). The problems are well discussed (with some interesting additional proposals) in Joseph (1985), Bomhard (1986), and Hock (1991: ch. 19).

There was also a set of syllabic 'resonants', i.e. syllabic versions of the nasals and liquids, *[m̩, n̩, r̩, l̩]; their phonological status is uncertain, but their historical independence is clear, as we will see later.

Perhaps the major defining feature of PGmc is a massive transformation of the obstruent system, generally called the **First Sound Shift** (G *erste Lautverschiebung*) or **Grimm's Law**.[4] It consisted of three articulatory shifts (*/kʷ/ etc. omitted for simplicity, but see below):

(2.5)   *Grimm's Law*

A.	p,	t,	k	>	f,	θ,	x	
B.	b,	d,	g	>	p,	t,	k	
C.	bh,	dh,	gh	>	β,	ð,	γ	(later b, d, g)

The order of these changes in unclear, except that A must precede B – otherwise */b, d, g/ would emerge as /f, θ, x/ just like original */p, t, k/. */s/, the only fricative, is unaffected. Note that the number of contrasts remains the same: only the manner of articulation changes. (In other IE groups */bh/ etc. fell together with */b/, leaving a two-series system.) Illustrations of Grimm's Law:

A. */p/: L *pater*, Gr *patér* 'father' = Go *fader* OE *fæder*;
   */t/: L *trēs*, Gr *treîs* 'three' = OE *þrēo*, Oic *þrír*;
   */k/: L *cord-*, Gr *kardíā* 'heart' = Go *haírtō*, OE *heorte*;
B. */b/: Li *dubùs* 'deep' = Go *diups*, OE *dēop*;
   */d/: L *edō*, Gr *édō* 'eat' = Go *itan*, OE *etan*;
   */g/: L *ego*, Gr *egó* 'I' = Go *ik*, OE *ic*;
C. */bh/: Skr *bhrātar-* 'brother' = Go *brōþar*, OE *brōþor*;
   */dh/: Gr *thugátēr-* (Gr /th/ < */dh/) 'daughter' = Go *daúhtar*, OE *dohtor*;
   */gh/: Skr *haṁsa* < */ghαns-/ 'goose' = OHG *gans*, OE *gōs*.

The 'labiovelars' (better labial-velars) */kʷ/, etc. more or less followed Grimm's Law, but their developments are complicated by a tendency for the complex articulation to 'disintegrate', giving rise either to labials or velars. For this reason the cognate forms in the other IE languages are not as obvious as for the simple stops. Some illustrations:

A. */kʷ/ > /xw/ as predicted: L *quod* 'what' (neuter nom/acc sg) = OIc *hvat*, OE *hwæt*.

---

[4] The literature on Grimm's Law is enormous; for some idea of the issues involved, see Prokosch (1938: §§15–24), Moulton (1972).

B. $*/g^w/ > /kw/$ as predicted: Skr *gám-*, Gr *baínō* 'come' $< */g^w$em-/ = Go *qiman* /kwimɑn/, OHG *queman*, OE *cuman* (but cf. alternative OE preterite *cwōm*, retaining the labial element).

C. $*/g^wh/ > /\gamma w/$ after nasals: Gr *omphḗ* 'voice' $< */song^w$hɑ/, cf. Go *siggwan*, OIc *syngva* 'sing'; $> /\gamma/$ before back vowels and consonants: IE $*/g^w$hn̥t-/ 'battle', cf. OCS *gonǔ* 'hunting', Skr *hánti* 'he strikes' = OHG *gund* 'battle', OIc *gunnr*; $> /w/$ otherwise: Skr *gharmáḥ* 'heat, glow' = OIc *varmr*, OE *wearm* 'warm, hot'.

The results of Grimm's Law were more complex than (2.5) and the subsequent discussion suggests; in particular, */bh, dh, gh/ first became fricatives except after nasals and possibly liquids; here they became stops. So the PGmc results were at first /β, ð, γ/, with [b, d, g] as post-nasal allophones. By the time OE had emerged as an independent dialect (if not earlier), they had become stops in nearly all positions. The only exception is the ancestors of Dutch, where the reflexes of */gh/ never became stops except after nasals and liquids, and the old allophony remains: so Afr *berg* /bɛrx/ 'mountain' is phonetically [bɛrx], the pl *berge* is /bɛrxə/, but phonetic [bɛrgə]. (See §3.9 for details.)

2.4   The Accent Shift and Verner's Law

Another great defining change is the **Accent Shift**, leading to the development of what may be called the **Germanic Stress Rule** (GSR). In Indo-European, accent was by and large 'free'; it could occur on any syllable of the word, depending on morphological and other conditions. For instance there were initial-accented stems like */gómbh-o-/ 'peg' (Skr *jámbha-*, Gr *gómph-os*), and suffix-accented ones like */som-ó-/ 'same' (Skr *samá-*, Gr *hom-ós*). And there were accent-alterations within paradigms: e.g. nominative and accusative often had root-accent while other case forms of the noun had suffix accent. So Sanskrit 'light':

(2.6)   NOM SG   rúk   DAT SG ruk-é
        NOM/ACC PL rúc-aḥ   DAT PL rug-bhyáḥ

There were also contrasts within the verb, and in derivational morphology: Sanskrit fourth-class verbs with unaccented -ya- suffix (*kúp-ya-ti* 'he is angry') vs. derived verbs with accented -yá-(*vadhar* 'weapon', *vadhar-yá-ti* 'he hurls a weapon').

Germanic substituted for this a system in which (with certain exceptions to be discussed in chapter 4) the word-accent always fell on the first syllable of the lexical root, ignoring prefixes – regardless of word-length, syllable-structure, part of speech, etc. The accent rule will be discussed in detail in chapter 4; for now we will simply assume the informal prose description above.

We do not know when the accent shift took place, but we do know – for quite interesting reasons – that it must have occurred after the Grimm's Law change */p, t, k/ > /f, θ, x/. The story behind this is methodologically interesting and historically of great importance, as its elucidation is one of the foundation-stones of modern historical method. It all hinges on the explication of 'irregular' developments: in this case apparent 'exceptions' to Grimm's Law.

A simple example: Grimm's Law A says that IE voiceless stops become Gmc voiceless fricatives (L *piscis*: OE *fisc* 'fish', L *trēs*: OE *þrēo* 'three', etc.). But there are cases where Grimm's Law apparently 'fails', i.e. where instead of the expected voiceless fricatives we get something different. We find this in simplex words like OE *mōdor* 'mother'; given L *māter* we would expect *mōþor*. But – more significantly, because this is the source of the solution – we also find the 'wrong' reflexes within morphological paradigms. For instance the OE strong verb *weorþan* 'become':

(2.7) PRES 1 SG   PRET 1 SG   PRET PL   PAST PART
       weorþe   wearþ   wurdon   -worden

This verb has an IE root in */-t-/: Skr *várt-a-mi* 'I turn', L *uert-ō*, OCS *vrŭt-ĕ-ti* 'he turns', etc. All the Germanic forms therefore ought to have root-final /-θ/, like the OE present and preterite singular. If sound changes are regular (as in essence they must be, or we wouldn't have the sets of correspondences we do), where does the OE /d/ come from? The answer was supplied in a paper by the Danish linguist Karl Verner (1875),[5] who (to simplify) pointed out that the 'odd' developments could in fact be predicted from the position of the IE accent (and hence were not 'irregular'). If we compare the OE forms above with their closest Sanskrit equivalents (Sanskrit largely keeps the original IE accentuation, and indicates it in some texts), we find:

[5] Verner's paper is available in an English translation in Lehman (1967). It is elegant and tightly argued, and the general methodology is now standard for issues of this sort. Nobody with an interest in historical linguistics ought to be allowed not to have read it. For a quite different account of the Germanic accent, Grimm's Law, and the VL allophony, see Bennett (1972).

(2.8)

	OE		Skr
PRES 1 SG	weorþ-e	PRES 1 SG	várt-a-mi
PRET 1 SG	wearþ	PERF 1 SG	va-várt-a
PRET PL	wurd-on	PERF 1 PL	va-vr̥t-i-má
PAST PART	-word-en	VERBAL N	va-vr̥t-a-ná

The expected /θ/ <þ> occurs except where the IE accent did not immediately precede the */t/. So Verner's discovery is: the fricatives from Grimm's Law A come down as voiced stops in Germanic if and only if the accent in IE did not immediately precede them. (Actually they came down as voiced fricatives in the first instance, and only later became stops: see §3.9 below.) Essentially, the fricatives /f, θ, x/ < IE */p, t, k/ by Grimm's Law A, as well as original */s/ (see below) voice where there is an accented suffix in the ancestral form: this is shown clearly in the Sanskrit items above.

Post-voicing changes alter the original output in various ways. When the accent shift occurs, the conditions for voicing are of course lost, and the distinctions are no longer predictable but phonemic. This voicing is known as **Verner's Law**. To outline the history of two contrasting parts of this verb (exact vowel qualities in suffixes left unspecified):

(2.9)

	PRET SG	PAST PART
Pre-Gmc IE	wɑ́rt-	wr̥t-V́n-
Grimm's Law A	wɑ́rθ-	wr̥θ-V́n-
r̥ > ur	–	wurθ-V́n-
Verner's Law	–	wurð-V́n-
Accent Shift	–	wúrð-Vn-
ð > d	–	wúrd-Vn-

These changes form a neat and crucially ordered sequence in the history of Germanic; each one feeds the next (though the last could come before the Accent Shift), and the final results are inexplicable except as the result of the sequence.

Other common Verner's law cases involve the velars: so OE *slēan* 'slay', pret sg *slōh* pp *-slegen*, *wrēon* 'cover', pret sg *wrāh*, pp *-wrigen*. Verner's Law plus a later change takes care of another troublesome anomaly: the appearance of what ought to be unchanged IE */s/ as /r/. This is a striking property of a number of strong verbs: *cēosan* 'choose', pret sg *cēas*, pret pl *curon*, pp *-coren*, or the pret sg/pl of *wesan* 'be', *wæs* vs. *wǣron*. Here */s/ > [z] by Verner's Law, and a later change, **Rhotacism**, turns [z] to [r]. Rhotacism occurs in other IE dialects as well: cf. L *flōs* 'flower' (nom sg), gen sg *flōris* < *[flo:zis] < *[flo:sis]. It is now usual to conflate the voicing, the change of fricatives to stops, and rhotacism under 'Verner's Law'; the /r/ in *wǽron* is simply said to be an instance of Verner's Law, and we will stick to this loose but traditional way of speaking.

Verner's Law has largely retreated under analogical pressure to regularize paradigms; but aside from *was*, *were*, relics survive in *birth/burden*, *sodden* (originally the past participle of *seethe*), and *(for)lorn*, originally from *forlēosan* 'abandon'.

2.5   Recapitulation: PGmc phonological systems

After the vowel mergers and Grimm's Law, PGmc would have had the following phonological systems, which served as the basis for the individual developments in the later dialects:

(2.10) p t k   i u   i: u:
        f θ x   e   e: o:
        β ð γ   α
          s   αi αu eu
      m n
       r l j w

Some of the consonants showed a long/short contrast as well, but this was sporadic: see below.

2.6   Further remarks on PGmc phonology

A number of changes of early date show up in the later Gmc dialects; their status however (living processes or fossils?) in the protolanguage is hard to define. But they are important for explaining aspects of word-shape and phoneme distributions in later times.

(i) Pre-nasal raising. IE */eNC/ > /iNC/: */bhendh-/ 'bind' > Gmc /βinð-/: L *(of)fendimentum* 'fetter' (*/bh/ > L /f/), OE *bindan*, OHG *bintan* 'bind'. This means in effect that any later Gmc sequence /eNC/ (as in OE *menn* 'men') must (if not a loan) derive from some other vowel (in this case < */mann-i-/: see §3.8 below).

(ii) Early umlaut. **Umlaut**[6] is regressive or leftward vowel-harmony: a vowel is influenced by another vowel or vowel-like segment to its right. For PGmc we assume a general raising of */e/ before high vowels and */j/: PGmc */mið-jα-z/ 'middle' < IE */medh-jo-s/, L *medius*, OIc *miðr*. This

---

[6] *Umlaut* is from G *um* 'around' + *Laut* 'sound', i.e., 'turning about' of sounds. The term was coined, like so many standard Germanist ones, by Jacob Grimm.

leads to later alternations in the verb, e.g. OE *beran* 'bear', pres 3 sg *bir(e)ð* < */βer-ɑn-, βer-iθ-/. In the following section and chapter 3 we will consider later umlauts, including the most important of all, *i*-umlaut (as in *menn* above).

(iii) Nasal loss and compensatory lengthening. In certain cases [ŋ], the allophone of /n/ before velars, dropped before */x/, and the preceding vowel lengthened: *[-Vŋx-] > *[-V:x-]. This accounts for the odd preterites of certain weak verbs like *bring*, *think*. So *think*, infinitive *[θɑŋk-jɑ-n], pret 1 sg *[θɑŋx-to:] > *[θɑ:x-to:]: OE *þencan*, *þōhte*. (The vowel changes are due to other processes.) This lengthening of */ɑ/ and loss of */x/ are of considerable systemic importance: they are a major source of phonemic /ɑ:/ in the later dialects.

(iv) Developments in weak syllables. There is a tendency in Germanic for contrasts to be obscured in weak (unaccented) position, even to the extent of segment loss. For example, the earliest runic inscriptions show forms like acc sg *horna* 'horn' < */xorn-ɑn/, which in turn derives from neutralization of the word-final /m/:/n/ contrast (cf. L acc *-um*). Weak */ɑ, e/ were also lost finally: IE */woid-ɑ, woid-e/ 'I have seen'> PGmc/wɑit/ (Gr *oîd-a*, Go *wait* 'I know'). Vowels were also generally deleted in third syllables: Go *baíriþ* 'he bears' < */bher-e-ti/ (on this and related processes see chapter 4).

(v) Assimilation and geminates. Clusters of non-identical consonants often assimilated, giving rise to **geminates** (long consonants, identical clusters: cf. L *gemini* 'twins'). Compare Li *pìlnas* 'full' with Go *fulls*, OIc *full-r*, OE *full*; the same phenomenon occurs in other IE dialects, and also shows up in Germanic in e.g. L *stella* 'star' < */ste:rlɑ/, OE *steorra*. This leads to a fairly large stock of geminates, beyond what we'd expect as the IE heritage; in West Germanic this was added to even more, to the extent that there was a system-wide length contrast for most consonants (cf. §3.2 below).[7]

2.7   Features of Northwest Germanic

If PGmc is (partly) defined as a separate daughter of PIE by Grimm's Law, etc., NWGmc is defined by its own series of innovations. The most important are:

(i) PGmc */e:/ > /ɑ:/. PGmc */e:/ lowered and retracted to /ɑ:/ in NWGmc, as illustrated by EGmc (Gothic) *lētan* 'let' vs. NGmc (OIc) *lāta*,

---

[7] There is also a stock of what are sometimes called 'expressive' geminates: nicknames (OHG *Otto* < *Odoberht*), deformations of animal names (OHG *snecco* 'snail', cf. OE *snægel*), and 'intensive' changes, e.g. OIc *gjalla*, OE *giellan* 'yell' vs. OIc *gala*, OE *galan* 'sing': so *yell* < *giellan*, (*nightin*)*gale* < (*nihte*)*gala*.

WGmc (OHG) *lāzzan*. (OE *lǣtan* reflects a later development: see §3.4.)
This produces a large number of items with /ɑ:/, thus firmly establishing a
new phoneme in the long low back vowel slot (see (2.3) above). The nature
of this change (among other things) has led some authorities to argue that
what I have been representing as PGmc */e:/ was in fact a much opener
vowel, say */ɛ:/ or */æ:/. This would be the result of lowering of IE */e:/,
and would be a more natural precursor of /ɑ:/ than a higher vowel. Under
this interpretation, there were two nonhigh long front vowels in PGmc:
*/æ:/, sometimes called '*ē¹*', which comes down as NWGmc */ɑ:/, and a
rather sparsely distributed closer vowel '*ē²*', which occurs mainly in strong
verb past plurals, and is /e:/. The arguments pro and con are extremely
complex, but on balance there is probably not enough evidence to support
a PGmc */æ:/ -- though this is a likely transition value on the way to /ɑ:/.[8]

(ii) *a*-Umlaut. This, like the earlier /e/ > [i] (§2.5) is harmonization of a
root vowel to a following (usually suffixal) one. PGmc */u/, and sporadically */i/, lower to [o, e] before */o, ɑ/ (hence 'nonhigh umlaut' would be a
better name). Thus IE */wir-o-s/ 'man' > PGmc */wir-ɑ-z/ > NWGmc
*[wer-ɑ-z]: L *uir* vs. OE *wer*, OIc *ver-r*. This is the only item in which all
the dialects agree in /e/ for earlier */i/. The real importance of this change
is the uniform lowering of */u/ to [o], which first adds short [o] to the
system as an allophone of */u/. Later, when the suffixes that triggered the
change were lost or changed to higher vowels, the new quality became
phonemic, adding /o/ to the inventory. So IE */jug-o-m/ 'joke' > PGmc
*/juk-ɑ-m/ > NWGmc *[jok-ɑ-n]: L *jugum*, Go *juk* vs. OE *geoc*, OIc *ok*.

After */e:/ is lost by lowering and retraction, its slot is filled – at first
somewhat marginally – by special developments in the strong verb preterite, described above as '*ē²*'. A new type in /e:/ replaces the older
reduplicating one (see §7.1.3): OIc *heita* 'be called', pret sg *hét*, OE *hatan*,
pret sg *hēt* vs. Go *haitan*, pret sg *haí-hait*. (In OE, the incidence of /e:/ is
later increased, in most dialects, by the unrounding of /ø(:)/ < /o(:)/ by
i-umlaut, as in *fēt* 'feet': < */fø:t-iz/ < */fo:t-iz/: see §3.8.2.) At this stage
then a symmetrical long/short system, like that of IE (see (2.1)) is again
produced.

The phonologization of *a*-umlaut had consequences not only for the
phonemic system itself, but for aspects of morphology: for instance both
the preterite plural and past participle of class II strong verbs had
historical */u/ in the root, but this differentiated into /u/ vs. /o/ in
NWGmc, through changes to the suffixes. Consider the verb 'offer' (Go
-*biudan*, OE *bēodan*):

---

[8] See Steponavičius (1987: 101–7) for details. His account is different in a number of details
from mine, especially with regard not only to PGmc */e:/, but also the question of whether
there was an */e/:*/i/ contrast.

(2.11)   PRET PL   PAST PART
       Gothic   bud-um   bud-a-ns
       OE   bud-on   bod-en

Gothic retains the original height contrast in the suffix vowels, with no effect on the root; OE lowers the original high suffix vowel and raises the low one, but has a lowered root vowel where the suffix had */α/.

(iii) Rhotacism. This is the change whereby *[z] < */s/ by Verner's Law (§2.4) became [r], and fell in with original */r/. The verb 'choose' is a good illustration of the process and its morphophonemic effects:

(2.12)   INF   PRET SG   PRET PL   PP
       pre-Verner   *kéus-αn-   *kαus   *kus-ún-   *kus-ǻn-
       Gothic   kius-an   kaus   kus-um   kus-αn-s
       OIc   kjós-a   kaus   kør-um   kør-inn
       OE   cēos-an   cēas   cur-on   cor-en

Verner's Law (the voicing rule) survives marginally in some IE */s/ instances in Gothic: e.g. *maiza* 'more' (OE *māra*, OIc *meire*).

(iv) NWGmc is also distinguished by a number of minor changes at various linguistic levels, such as:

(a) A new demonstrative formation with /-se/ added to an existing stem: OIc *þes-se* 'this', OE *þēo-s*, OHG *des-se*.
(b) Loss of the old mediopassive conjugation (< IE middle voice), relatively intact only in Gothic.
(c) Loss of the third-person imperative, again attested only in Gothic.
(d) A sporadic change of PGmc */x/ > /f/ in certain environments: Go *auhns* 'oven' vs. OHG *ofan*, OIc *ofn*, OE *ofen*. The original IE velar can be seen in Skr *úkhas* 'cooking pot'; and a trace of it remains in the OIc alternative form *ogn*.

2.8   West Germanic

NWGmc is (oversimply) 'PGmc + /e:/-lowering + Rhotacism . . . '; keeping this style, WGmc is (equally oversimply) 'NWGmc + . . . '. To a certain extent WGmc is rather conservative; NGmc underwent many more early changes, so that the medieval Scandinavian languages are in some ways much less like NWGmc than OE, OHG, etc. So assuming the idealized but useful image of language-genesis as tree-branching, abstracting away from communities, grammars, etc. for the sake of a clean story, we can characterize WGmc in terms of structural innovations defining a new branch:

(i) West Germanic gemination. In general, any consonant except /r/ lengthened or doubled (see §3.3 for discussion on this concept) when preceded by a short accented vowel and followed by a liquid or nasal: OE *settan* 'set', OS *settian* vs. Go *satjan*, OIc *satja* < */sɑt-jɑ-n/ (recall that /j/ is treated here as a liquid). Important as this is from a WGmc perspective, I will postpone discussion until the next chapter, as it had profound effects on OE phonology and morphology, and interacts with other changes in a complex and interesting way.

(ii) Loss of final *[z]. This simple phonological change has major grammatical effects, chiefly the loss of the nom sg ending in many noun classes. (The commonest IE nom sg suffix was */-s/, which > *[z] by Verner's Law, later /r/ by Rhotacism in NWGmc.) So Go *dag-s* 'day', OIc *dag-r* vs. OE *dæg*, OHG *tag*, etc. After this change the nom/acc distinction is lost in nouns of this type: OIc nom sg *dag-r* vs. acc sg *dag*, but OE *dæg* for both. (For morphological details, see §6.1.)

(iii) The split of */eu/. A new diphthong */iu/ arose in WGmc in a number of environments, e.g. when some final */-o:/ raised to */u:/ after */-e:/, as in early OE *hīo* 'she' < earlier */xi-u:/ < */xe:-u/ (where /-u:/ is a feminine ending added to certain stems (see Campbell 1959: §§120, 331.5 for discussion).

By the time WGmc is established as a distinct dialect type, its phonological system is:

(2.13) i: i   u u: p p: t t: k k:
        e: e   o o: f f: θ θ: s s: x x:
                ɑ ɑ: β β: ð ð: γ γ:
                        m m: n n:
        ɑi ɑu iu eu   w w: r r: l l: j

This was the basis for the later evolution of Ingvaeonic and Anglo-Frisian, and thus the foundation for OE phonology. The following general points are worth noting:

(a) The vowel system:
    (i) No low front vowels.[9]
    (ii) Rounding is nondistinctive. Front and low back vowels are unround, and only nonlow back vowels are rounded.
    (iii) All diphthongs end in /-i/ or /-u/.

[9] At least phonemically. It is of course possible that the low back vowels already had front allophones before following */i, j/ (as was later clearly the case after *i*-umlaut: §3.8). But there are problems in dating this change so early (Lass 1992b).

(b) The consonant system:
  (i) No voiced stops (phonemically), but only fricatives: though with stop allophones after nasals.
  (ii) No palato-alveolar consonants like /ʃ/ or /tʃ/.
  (iii) No phonemic velar nasal /ŋ/.
  (iv) No phonemic glottal fricative /h/.

Most of this changes during the run-up to Old English proper, or by the earliest attested OE. Only the lack of a phonemic velar nasal and /h/ remain firm as properties of English until much later (seventeenth century). We will explore most of the changes in the following chapter.

Part II:

Old English phonology

I have taken the liberty that historians have taken from the time of Herodotus to put into the mouths of the persons of my narrative speeches that I did not myself hear and could not possibly have heard. I have done this for the same reasons as historians have, to give liveliness and verisimilitude to scenes that would have been ineffective if they had been merely recounted . . . The intelligent reader will see for himself where I have used this artifice, and he is at perfect liberty to reject it.

W. Somerset Maugham, *The razor's edge*

3 Evolution of Old English phonology: the major early sound changes[1]

3.1 Sound change and linguistic structure

A number of important changes leading to attested OE cluster in the Ingvaeonic/Anglo-Frisian periods, and the rather misty area the handbooks call 'Primitive OE', i.e. roughly from the fifth to the seventh centuries. Many of these have profound effects both on the shape of particular OE words or morphemes, and on the grammatical systems involving them. A knowledge of these changes and their interactions will help to explain why many OE forms look the way they do, and why the phonological material is deployed as it is in the morphology. This historical background provides answers to questions like:

(i) Why do certain verbs have double consonants in some parts of the paradigm, and singles elsewhere? E.g. *trymann* 'strengthen', pres 1 sg *trymme*, but pres 3 sg *trymeð*, pret 1 sg *trymede*.

(ii) Why do verbs like *sellan* 'sell', *tellan* 'tell' have preterites *sealde*, *tealde* rather than **sellede*, **tellede*?

(iii) Why do certain strong verbs which historically ought to have the same vocalism not do so? E.g. cl III *singan* 'sing', pret sg *sang*, but in the same class *helpan* 'help', pret sg *healp*, and *weorpan* 'throw', pret sg *wearp*?

(iv) Why do some nouns have an /æ/ ~ /ɑ/ alternation, like nom/acc sg *dæg*, gen sg *dæges* but nom/acc pl *dagas*, dat pl *dagum*?

(v) Why do certain inflectional processes sometimes appear to involve vowel change? E.g. nom sg *fōt* 'foot', gen sg *fōtes*, gen pl *fōta*, dat pl *fōtum*, but dat sg, nom/acc pl *fēt*; also the formation of certain comparatives: *eald* 'old', *ieldra* 'older'. And note the same kind of thing in word-formation processes: *beald* 'bold', *bieldan* 'make bold'.

---

[1] For an overview of the material covered in this chapter see Hogg (1992b); more detailed accounts will be found in Campbell (1959: chs. 5, 6, 9), Steponavičius (1987: ch. 4), and Lass & Anderson (1975: chs. 2–5). Lass & Anderson purports to be primarily a synchronic phonology of Old English, but much of the discussion is explicitly historical, and some that pretends not to be actually is. (We in fact note this in a long discussion, ch. 6, §3.)

3.2   West Germanic Gemination[2]

A notable feature of the morphology of many OE verbs is the alternation of root-final single and double consonants, as in the paradigm of *hyllan* 'hide':

		PRESENT	PRETERITE
(3.1)		1 hyll-e	hyl-e-de
		2 hyl-(e)-st	hyl-e-dest
	Sg	3 hyl-(e)-ð	hyl-e-de
		Pl hyll-að	hyl-e-don

INF hyll-an   PRES PART hyll-ande   PAST PART hyl-ed

The source of this alternation is suggested by a typical Gothic paradigm of the same class (weak I), in this case the cognate *huljan*:[3]

		PRESENT	PRETERITE
(3.2)		1 hul-ja	hul-i-da
	Sg	2 hul-ji-s	hul-i-dest
		3 hul-ji-þ	hul-i-da
		3 pl hul-j-and	hul-i-dēdun

INF hul-j-an   PRES PART hul-j-ands   PAST PART hul-i-þa

Leaving aside for the moment the pres 2,3 sg, we note that generally wherever OE has a double consonant, Gothic has a /j/ following the root; wherever OE has a single consonant, Gothic has /i/. So *hul-ja* = *hyll-e*, but *hul-i-da* = *hyl-e-de*. (We can assume that the early WGmc paradigm was very like the Gothic.) Geminate consonants like these are characterized in the literature as either 'long' or 'double'; as we will see below this is really not a distinction, as length will always be analysed as a form of clustering. The change producing the long consonants is called **West Germanic Gemination** (*Konsonantendehnung* or *Konsonantenverdoppelung* in the German handbooks). This change (henceforth **WGG**) in its most extensive form is characteristic only of WGmc (though there are sporadic similar developments in NGmc); it therefore can be taken as dating back to the split of NWGmc into the later N and W branches (probably early in the Christian era).

Now PGmc as we saw already had some geminates from assimilation and other sources (*full* < */pl̥n-/*, etc., cf. §2.61). But WGG not only

[2] See Lass & Anderson (1975: Appendix II) for the ancestor of my treatment here, and some useful references.
[3] Not all of these particular forms actually survive in Gothic; but enough verbs of this type are attested in part to allow us to recover a full paradigm.

greatly expands the incidence of geminates in simplex roots (e.g. OE *cynn* 'kin' < */kun-jo:/); it also integrates the single/geminate contrast into the morphology.

In order to understand the effects of WGG, we must note one other early change: that of the sequence */-ji-/ to /-i:-/, later /-i-/ in unaccented positions. At the time of WGG, this had already affected the */-ji-/ in the pres 2, 3 sg, so that these forms alone in the present system did not have /j/ following the root. Thus the pres 1 sg was */xul-j-ɑ/, whereas 2, 3 sg were respectively */xul-i-s/, */xul-i-θ/. (For details of the verb endings, especially the final /t/ in the OE 2 sg and the lack of it in Gothic, see §7.5). For this reason as well there is no gemination at all in the pres 2, 3 sg and the whole past system.

Stated rather baldly, WGG works this way:

(3.3)   -VCjV- > -VCCjV-
          CONDITION: C is not /r/

That is: any single consonant except /r/ geminates (doubles, has a copy of itself inserted) if preceded by a short vowel (/V/) and followed by /j/. If the preceding nucleus is long or diphthongal (i.e. /VV/), gemination does not occur. So WGG in OE *settan* 'set' (Go *satjan*), but not *sēcan* 'seek' (Go *sōkjan*) or *dǣlan* 'divide' (Go *dailjan*); and no gemination either in *nerian* 'save' (Go *nasjan*: /r/ here from rhotacism). Gemination also fails if the consonant in question is the last member of a cluster: OE *wendan* 'turn' (Go *wandjan*), not **wenddan*.

Except for the strange exclusion of /r/, the motivation for WGG is not phonetic but structural. It is a matter of syllable structure and syllable-constituents in particular positions, not of specific phonetic quality (e.g. voicing, place of articulation, nasality, etc.).[4] To clarify this (and a number of other important changes discussed here and in the next chapter), we will require a short digression on syllable-structure, at least on the model I use here.

A syllable (σ) may be conceived of as a hierarchical structure, consisting of the following major constituents:[5] (i) **onset** (O): all material preceding the syllabic element (e.g. /k/ in *cat* /kæt/); (ii) **rhyme** (R): the syllabic

---

[4] We made a rather desperate attempt to deal with the exclusion of /r/ on phonetic grounds in Lass & Anderson (1975: 258). A more satisfactory account, 'structural' in the sense that it's based on relative 'strength' of consonants and PGmc syllable-structure, is given in Murray & Vennemann (1983), but I am still not convinced.

[5] For an account of syllable structure in this general framework, with arguments for the various constituents, see Lass (1984: §10.3). A somewhat 'flatter' view of the syllable, without a distinct rhyme constituent, is given in Katamba (1989: ch. 9). Katamba's chapter (though I do not accept all of it) is an excellent introductory account.

element and all material to its right (e.g. /æt/ in *cat*). The rhyme is in turn divided into: (iii) **nucleus** (N): the syllabic element (e.g. /æ/ in *cat*); and (iv) **coda** (Co): any material to the right of the nucleus (e.g. /t/ in *cat*). Thus *cat* would have the following structure:

(3.4)

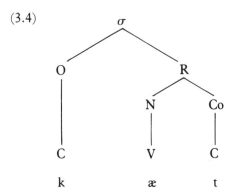

Syllables may be characterized as having **quantity** or **weight**, as defined by their rhyme structure:

(i) **Light** (σ̆): the rhyme consists of no more than two constituents, i.e. neither the nucleus nor the coda is complex (branches): so the rhymes of *a*, *cat*, /-V/, /-VC/.[6]

(ii) **Heavy** (σ̄): one constituent of the rhyme is complex (branches): either the nucleus is a long vowel or diphthong /VV/, or the coda is geminate or a cluster /CC/; so the rhymes of *beet*, *bite* /-VVC/ *bee*, *buy* /-VV/ and *band* /-VCC/.

(iii) **Superheavy (hypercharacterized)** (σ̿): both the nucleus and coda are complex, as in *bind* /-VVCC/.

Many handbooks confusingly refer to light syllables as 'short' and heavy ones as 'long'. I reserve these latter terms for duration or complexity of nuclei or codas, i.e. only vowels and consonants can be long or short; syllables are light or heavy.

Given a style of representation like (3.4), both length (of nuclei and codas) and quantity/weight (of syllables) have a natural interpretation in terms of 'branching' or complexity. If a long vowel or diphthong is /VV/ and a long consonant or cluster is /CC/, then the rhymes of light, heavy and superheavy syllables will look like this:

---

[6] Some languages (e.g. Latin) treat /-VC/ rhymes as heavy; Germanic groups them with /-V/ as light. See Lass (1986), Katamba (1989: §9.5). This view has been challenged in Dresher & Lahiri (1991), who treat /-VC/ as heavy; it is supported in Hogg (1992c). The arguments are complex (having to do mainly with metrics), and are too technical to go into here. Despite some problems, however, I will assume this (traditional) view throughout.

(3.5)

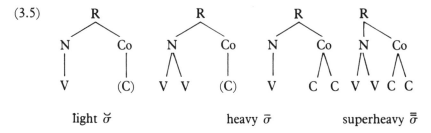

light ŏ̄   heavy σ̄   superheavy σ̄̄

(Bracketed Cs are optional: a rhyme in -V only or in -VC is light, one in
-VV only or -VVC is heavy.)

With this background we can speak more generally about WGG and
what it does. The environment is a light syllable followed by /j/; no heavy
syllable allows gemination. The restrictions (except that on /r/) have the
following effect: WGG does not occur if it would produce a superheavy
syllable; it must occur if the syllable before /j/ is light. Taking */sɑt-j-ɑn/ 'set'
and */sook-j-ɑn/ 'seek', we can see what would happen if WGG applied in
both cases:

(3.6)   Input   sɑt-j-ɑn   sook-j-ɑn

           σ-structure   ŏ̄-j-   σ̄-j-

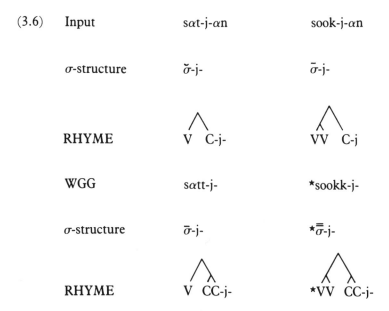

           RHYME   V C-j-   VV C-j

           WGG   sɑtt-j-   *sookk-j-

           σ-structure   σ̄-j-   *σ̄̄-j-

           RHYME   V CC-j-   *VV CC-j-

The outcome then is that (a) light syllables are disallowed before /j/, and
(b) so are superheavy ones. Gemination converts an 'overlight' syllable in
this environment to a heavy one, and fails if superheaviness would result.

We will see later that the light/heavy distinction plays a central role in the phonology of the early WGmc dialects, particularly of OE; change after change involves adjustment of syllable weight, or is dependent on the weight of a particular syllable in some environment (chapter 4). We might also note that an apparent 'dislike' of superheavy syllables is fairly general in OE; where such syllables do occur in historical times, normally either the heavy coda after a long vowel is split by a boundary (*grēt-te* 'he greeted'), or the cluster involved is /sC-/ (*prēost* 'priest'). Cases like *hlūttor* 'shining' are in the minority; and in all such configurations the vowels normally shorten in late OE or early ME.

One further remark on WGG. It is sometimes claimed in the handbooks that it took place before nasals and /r, l, w/ as well as /j/. Indeed it did; but much less regularly, and normally without any clear morphophonemic effects. Thus before /r/ OHG *snottar* 'wise', OE normally *snotor* < */snotr-/; only /p, t, k, x/ geminate in OE with any frequency in non-/j/ environments, and that not without exceptions: examples are *æppel* 'apple', *wæccer* 'awake', *hweohhol* 'wheel' (*-ol* < */-wol/).

3.3   Pre-nasal vowels in Ingvaeonic and Anglo-Frisian

The following forms suggest some interesting developments involving nasals:

(3.7)

Go	OIc	OHG	OE	OFr	
mēna	máni	māno	mōna	mōna	'moon'
mēnoþs	mánaðr	mānod	mōnaþ	mōnath	'month'

The original vowel here is IE */e:/: cf. Gr *mḗn* 'moon', L *mēnsis* 'month', etc. OIc and OHG show the typical NWGmc */ɑ:/ for IE */e:/ (cf. §2.7). The same thing shows up in the pret pl of verbs like 'come': Go *nēmum*, OHG *nēmun*, OE *nōmon*. (Given other correspondences, we would expect OE /æ:/ here, for reasons that will become clear later: Go *bārum*, OE *bǣron* 'they bore'.)

Clearly the following nasal is the key. The usual assumption is that */ɑ:/ (and as we will see later, short */ɑ/) nasalized here, and the nasalized vowel was subject to rounding and raising. The presumed evolution of 'moon' would be:

(3.8)

PGmc:	me:nɑ > mæ:nɑ
NWGmc:	mæ:nɑ > mɑ:nɑ
WGmc:	mɑ:nɑ > mɑ̃:nɑ > mõ:nɑ > mo:nɑ

The denasalized [o:] merges with /o:/ < IE */ɑ:/ (*brōþor* 'brother') and */o:/ (*fōt* 'foot').

A related, specifically Ingvaeonic development is compensatory lengthening following loss of nasals before fricatives. Compare OE *fīf* 'five', *gōs* 'goose', *tōþ* 'tooth' with OHG *finf*, *gans*, *zand*. The latter two cases show the same development as in *mōna*, etc.[7] The original nasals are visible in Skr *páñca-* 'five', L *anser* 'duck', *dent-* 'tooth'. This change is a pointer to the 'mixed' or 'hybrid' origins of Dutch (cf. §1.4): the number 'five' has an Ingvaeonic form *vijf* /fɛif/, whereas 'goose' and 'tooth' are non-Ingvaeonic: *gans* /xɑns/, *tand* /tɑnt/.

At about the same time, or perhaps a bit later (but certainly before the fifth century), short */ɑ/ before nasals (other than those with fricatives following) seems to have nasalized as well; at any rate, in pre-nasal positions it is not subject to one major Anglo-Frisian sound change, and in addition is often spelled in OE with <o> as well as <a>: thus *mann*, *monn* 'man' from earliest times (I will return to this in §3.5).

3.4   West Germanic */ɑ:/ and */ɑi/ in Ingvaeonic

These two categories participate in changes that do much to establish the uniquely OE vowel system, and illustrate a tendency still operative in Modern English: the least stable points in the vowel systems are typically at the low corners.

In Ingvaeonic, WGmc */ɑ:/ fronted to /æ:/; connected with this, or following it (see below), */ɑi/ monophthongized to /ɑ:/. Thus for */ɑ:/ OE *lǣtan* 'let' (= OHG *lāzzan*), for */ɑi/ OE *stān* 'stone' (OHG *stein*). The usual view is that the two changes must have occurred in the order (1) Fronting, (2) Monophthongization. If monophthongization had occured first, the argument goes, then the monophthongized */ɑi/ would have fallen together with */ɑ:/. The merged categories would then have fronted together to /æ:/, giving OE *lǣtan* as expected, but also incorrect *stǣn*, not *stān*. Consider the results if the order were Monophthongization, Fronting:

(3.9)

	WGmc input	stɑin	lɑ:tɑn
	Monophth.	stɑ:n	–
	Fronting	stæ:n	læ:tɑn
	OE	*stǣn*	*lǣtan*

---

[7] The nonlow vowels appear to show no qualitative change when nasalized.

But with the reverse order:

(3.10) WGmc input   stɑin   lɑ:tɑn
        Fronting   –   læ:tɑn
        Monophth.   stɑ:n   —
        OE   *stān*   *lǣtan*

Obviously then only the order (3.10) gives the correct OE forms. But looking at the changes in terms of the shape of the whole vowel system suggests a different analysis. The relation might not be sequential, but implicational: a **chain shift**, in which two or more categories move 'in tandem'. That is, as */ɑ:/ fronts, it can 'drag' */ɑi/ into its vacated position in the system; or as */ɑi/ begins to monophthongize, it can 'push' */ɑ:/ out of its place.[8] Diagrammatically:

(3.11)   i: u: i: u: i: u:

         e: o: e: o: e: o:

            ɑ: æ:◄–ɑ: æ: ɑ:

                         ɑi:

        Before   During   After

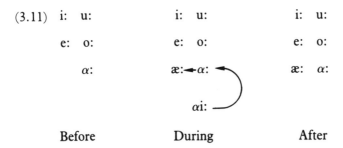

The result is a vowel system of this shape:

(3.12)   i   u   i: u:
         e   o   e: o:
              ɑ   æ: ɑ
                       iu eu ɑu

This story (like many other sequences in the history of English) shows a good deal of 'see-saw' movement, alternating splits and mergers, appearance, disappearance and reappearance of category-types. The basic developments of IE */ɑ:, o:, e:, ɑi/ up to Ingvaeonic give this pattern:

[8] For discussion of chain-shifts in general, and some Germanic illustrations, see Lass (1976: ch. 2).

(3.13)

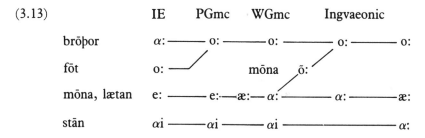

We will see in §3.5 how the short low front /æ/ slot gets filled, creating the fully symmetrical OE system; the diphthongs will be dealt with in §§3.6, 3.8

3.5 Anglo-Frisian Brightening, Restoration of [α] and the OE /æ/:/α/ opposition[9]

There are no fewer than six reflexes of WGmc */α/ in OE:

(i) <æ> /æ/ before single non-nasal consonants, either final or followed by a front vowel: *dæg* 'day' (nom/acc sg), *dæge* (dat sg), *dæges* (gen sg), *æðele* 'noble'.
(ii) <a> /α/ before (most) geminates: *catt* 'cat', *bratt* 'cloak'; and before a back vowel: *dagas* 'day' (nom/acc pl), *daga* (gen pl), *dagum* (dat pl), *lagu* 'water'.
(iii) <a ~ o> before nasals: *mann, monn* 'man', *wanian, wonian* 'wane'.
(iv) <ea> /æα/ before /rC, lC, x/: *wearp* 'he threw', *healp* 'he helped', *seah* 'he saw'.
(v) <e> /e/ before nasals and liquids in certain cases: *sendan* 'send', *cennan* 'conceive', *sellan* 'sell', *tellan* 'tell'.
(vi) <ie> /iy/[10] in certain cases, often alternating with <ea>: *bieldan* 'make bold', *ieldra* 'older' (cf. *beald* 'bold', *eald* 'old').

For the original */α/ in all these cases: (i) OIc *dagr* 'day'; (ii) Late Latin *cattus* 'cat'; (iii) OHG *mann* 'man'; (iv) Go *warp*; (v) Go *sandjan*; (vi) OHG *bald*.

The diverse OE outcomes result from a number of changes, most of which have repercussions in the morphophonology: both inflectional as in *dæg/dagas*, and derivational as in *beald/bieldan* (as well as for the shapes of

---

[9] For general discussion and references, see Lass & Anderson (1975: ch. 2); on the /α/:/æ/ contrast, see Colman (1983).
[10] The characterization of <ie> as /iy/ is controversial; for the arguments see §3.8.2 below.

simplex words). These developments involve (a) allophonic proliferation due to context-sensitive changes, and (b) phonologization of some of the new allophones through loss of contexts. In this section we will consider only the changes leading to reflexes (i–iii); (iv) will be taken up in §3.7, along with the further adventures of the diphthongs, and (v–vi) in §3.8.

The new short vowel, most probably [æ], arises through a process called **Anglo-Frisian Brightening** or **First Fronting** (henceforth AFB).[11] The effects can be seen in comparing say OE *dæg*, OFr *deg* with Go *dags*, OIc *dagr*, OHG *tag*. (The original [æ] was later raised in Frisian.)

In outline, AFB turns low back */ɑ/ to [æ], except before nasals (hence OE, OHG *mann* but *dæg* vs. *tag*. It is usually accepted that at some point before AFB (which probably dates from around the early fifth century), */ɑ/ > [ɑ̃] before nasals, and the nasalized vowel blocked AFB. This vowel later denasalized, and the allophone showed – both in OE and OFr – what is usually interpreted as a rounded variant, as in the spellings *mann*, *monn* cited above. The variation even appears in single texts, from quite early on: the famous Northumbrian version of Cædmon's Hymn (Moore, MS, AD 737) has *-gidanc* 'thought' (usual later form *gebanc*), as well as *moncynnæs* 'mankind's' (usual later *manncynnes*).

If this vowel was indeed rounded, it seems to have been distinct from OE /o/ (perhaps lower?), since it behaves differently, and in most dialects eventually merges with /ɑ/, not /o/. This is not however a necessary interpretation. It is well known that low back *un*rounded nasalized vowels may be perceived as rounded. Many English speakers for instance typically hear (and produce!) French /ɑ̃/ in say *dent* as [ɔ̃] or [õ]. (Though in some dialects, judging from later developments, the vowel was rounded; certainly in parts of the West Midlands, and perhaps in the Far North.)

If AFB had done only what is described above, its systemic effect would be nil; there would still be only one (phonemic) low vowel, with the allophones [ɑ] and [æ]. Because [ɑ] appears in the more restricted set of contexts, we might want to call the vowel /æ/; on this interpretation, all that AFB does, systemically, is:

(3.14) i u   i u
    e o   e o
      ɑ   æ
  Before AFB   After AFB

---

[11] 'Brightening' is an over-literal translation of G *Aufhellung*; in older German phonetic terminology front vowels are *hell* 'clear, bright'.

The systems (as collections of distinctive units) are 'the same', except for the location of the low vowel; there are no new phonemic oppositions, and only one low vowel (nondistinctive as to place), which is unround. (Though it does of course have both back and front allophones.)

But later developments, including occasional failures of AFB, and most of all analogical remodelling of certain paradigms, produced at least a marginal contrast. For instance, the past participles of class VI strong verbs like *bacan* 'bake', *faran* 'go' should be *bæcen, *færen (cf. *dagas* vs. *dæges*). But they are in fact *bacen, faren*. The vowel of the present system has been analogically transferred to the past participle, so that instead of predicted [æ] before /e/ we get the [ɑ] that 'ought to' appear only before a back vowel. (For discussion of the strong verbs see §7.2.)

The traditional story behind this is as follows. At some time considerably after AFB (later, probably, than the changes to be discussed in the next few sections, but still 'prehistoric' – i.e. before the earliest texts), there was a 'harmonic' change, generally called **Restoration of [ɑ]**. This is (though it's not usually so described) a kind of umlaut (cf. §§2.6–7, 3.8): assimilation of a vowel to one to its right. Stressed [æ] followed by a back vowel /u, o, ɑ/ retracts to [ɑ], as in *dagum, dagas, faran, lagu*, etc.[12]

The history leading to the root-vowel alternation in nouns of the *dæg* type then reconstructs as follows (I use the neuter *fæt* 'vessel' to avoid some complications in the root-final consonants of *dæg, dagas*, which will not come up till §3.7):

(3.15)

	NOM SG	GEN SG	NOM PL	GEN PL
WGmc input	fɑt	fɑt-es	fɑt-u	fɑt-ɑ
AFB	fæt	fæt-es	fæt-u	fæt-ɑ
Restoration	–	–	fɑt-u	fɑt-ɑ
OE form	*fæt*	*fætes*	*fatu*	*fata*

If Restoration of [ɑ] had worked out completely, it would, as suggested above, produce only paradigms of the *fæt/fatu, bacan/*bæcen* kind; but it

---

[12] The history would of course be much simpler if rather than fronting and then retraction there had simply been one AFB rule that blocked before back vowels as it did before nasals. The argument for a separate and later retraction (cf. Campbell 1959: §§157–63, Lass & Anderson 1975: 66ff) depends on the vocalism of verbs like *slēan* 'slay' as opposed to *dragan* 'draw'. Both have the same historical nucleus (respectively */slɑxɑn, drɑɣɑn/). But the <ēa> /æɑ/ in *slēan* presupposes 'breaking' (§3.6) of */æ/ before */x/, with later deletion of /x/ and lengthening. If */ɑ/ had not gone first to [æ] in this environment, there would be no way of getting the diphthong /æɑ/, since */ɑ/ did not diphthongize before /x/; instead of *slēan* we should get *slān (/x/-deletion plus lengthening). So despite the extra step it seems that we do need 'restoration'.

was interfered with in a number of ways (as was AFB itself). Restoration is actually quite a bit later than AFB, and some other major developments (notably Breaking, §3.6) intervene; I will return to this in the appropriate place.

A historiographical note: it's not always possible – though one ought to try – to tell stories in strict chronological sequence. Sometimes quite distantly separated changes make up 'thematic' blocks, which have to have their parts put together earlier than they perhaps should be to make the block coherent. Restoration comes here rather than later, because of its explanatory importance for the OE <a ~ æ> alternation, the morpho-phonological difference between strong verbs with root WGmc */α/ like *faran* and nouns like *dæg*; and because it illustrates nicely the way analogical change can distort expected outcomes, and contribute to phonemic restructuring.

So far we considered AFB only in its effect on short */α/ before consonants. But the vowel [α] occurred in two other places: (a) as the first element of the long vowel */α:/ = /αα/; and (b) as the first element of the diphthong */αu/. Was it subject to AFB in these positions as well? The answer seems to be no for */αα/ < */αi/ (otherwise *stān* would be **stæn*); but yes for */αu/. This diphthong appears in OE normally spelled <ea>, which we have good reason to believe means /æα/; it is also spelled <æu, æo> in some early texts, and is the 'long *ēa*' of the handbooks (see the next section). It appears to have become [æu] initially, and then by a process called Diphthong Height Harmony (§3.6) to have become [æα].

The phonemicization of the /α:/:/æ/ contrast results in quite a new kind of short vowel system, symmetrical at all heights in front and back. Recall (cf. (3.11)) that monophthongization of */αi/ and fronting of */α:/ had already produced symmetry in the long vowels. The whole story of AFB and retraction, as far as the monophthongs go, can be summed up this way:

(3.16)	i	u		i	u		i	u
	e	o		e	o		e	o
		α		æ			æ	α
	WGmc			Anglo-Frisian			Old English	

Typologically, we might then view WGmc as a period of relative 'stability', Anglo-Frisian as the time when low-vowel allophones prolif-erated, and early OE as a period when the phonemic split between front and low short back vowels was stabilized.

3.6   Diphthongs old and new: Breaking and related processes[13]

3.6.1   'Long' and 'short' diphthongs

There were two early diphthongizations of front vowels in certain environments; curiously, when these affected short vowels, the new diphthong outputs merged neither with diphthongized long vowels, nor with the historical Germanic diphthongs. The upshot of these developments is, in the standard view, a new type of vowel system with four distinct types of accented nuclei:

(3.17)   (i)   Short vowels: *eft* 'again', *ræt* 'rat'
           (ii) Long vowels: *fēt* 'feet', *glæm* 'gleam'
           (iii) Short diphthongs: *eolh* 'elk', *fleax* 'flax'
           (iv) Long diphthongs: *fēond* 'fiend', *sēam* 'seam'

There are structural and etymological reasons for the length marking (which like virtually all indications of vowel length in OE is editorial, not from the texts); the first two will be discussed here, the third in §3.6.2.

   First, note that 'long <e>' and 'long <eo>' both come down as modern long vowels, as do 'long <æ>' and 'long <ea>'; 'short <e, eo>' and 'short <æ, ea>' on the other hand emerge as short vowels. Using orthographic representations for the OE categories, and disregarding special developments (e.g. 'short <ea>' in *sealt, eald* gives long vowels in *salt, old*), the outcomes are:

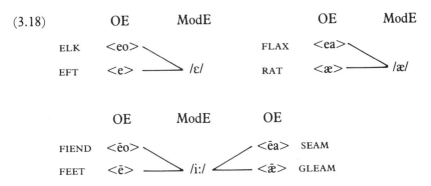

(3.18)

---

[13] Breaking and the resultant change in the OE diphthong system has precipitated one of the more complex and acrimonious debates in the history of OE scholarship. This 'digraph controversy' is discussed, with citation of the literature, in Lass & Anderson (1975: 75ff). The major documents are Daunt (1939), Stockwell & Barritt (1951), Kuhn & Quirk (1953), Stockwell & Barritt (1955), Hockett (1959), and Kuhn (1961). The sequence of arguments is still worth reading, as an enormous amount of interesting information on Old English is adduced, and important methodological points are made in most contributions. For the traditional account, Campbell (1959: §§139–56).

Similar relations show up within OE itself: nouns of the neuter *a*-stem declension, for instance (§§4.3.2, 6.1) have a final -*u* in nom/acc pl if the root syllable is light (*scip-u* 'ships' *hof-u* 'dwellings'), but lose it after a heavy syllable (*bān* 'bone(s)', *word* 'word(s)'). Here the assumed short diphthongs behave like short vowels (*gebeod-u* 'prayers'), and the long diphthongs like long vowels or /-VCC/ rhymes (*dēor* 'animal(s)'). I.e. a long diphthong creates a heavy syllable, a short one with one following consonant a light syllable.

The system type in (3.17) has been considered odd enough for some scholars to reinterpret it as something else; usually the revisionist view is that the 'short diphthongs' were in fact really monophthongs, with the second letter of the digraph indicating retracted or centralized quality, or velarization of the following consonant(s): for the literature see notes to this section. The reinterpretation is not necessary: languages with four-category systems like (3.17) are well known, even within Germanic: Icelandic, Afrikaans, some varieties of modern English (Lass 1981, 1988).

But what exactly are 'short' and 'long' diphthongs? The usual notations like <ēo> or /e:o/ or /eo:/ as against <eo>, /eo/ suggest that a long diphthong is an ordinary diphthong 'plus'. There is however nothing to suggest that say <ēo> was longer than <ē>; and generally in languages with phonemic vowel length and one set of diphthongs, the diphthongs pattern phonologically and durationally with the long vowels. The 'marked' or 'odd' category is the short diphthong: a complex nucleus that behaves like and is durationally the same as a short vowel. Under our previous definition (§3.2), a long vowel is phonologically /VV/, as is a diphthong; a short vowel is /V/. If */VVV/ is ruled out for a long diphthong, and /VV/ for a short one, what can the latter be?

The answer lies in distinguishing between syllable positions or 'timing slots' and the material that fills them. For example: an affricate, like English /tʃ/, normally has the duration of a single consonant, but within that duration ('one segment long', as it were) there is a rapid transition from one quality to another. So /tʃ/ in the coda of *batch* could be represented as a single C dominating two segments (each of 'half-length'), whereas the coda of a heavy syllable like *hand* would have two separate C-positions. The rhymes of the two syllable types:

(3.19)

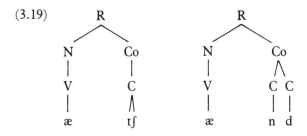

Similarly, a short vowel occupies a single V-slot in the nucleus, and a long vowel or 'long' = normal diphthong two V-slots, and a short diphthong, like a short vowel, one V-slot. Using OE categories as examples:[14]

(3.20)

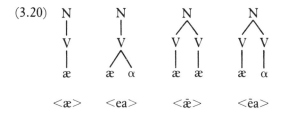

So there is a timing/quality 'mismatch' in the case of the short diphthong: one unit, two qualities. In terms of comparative duration:

(3.21)

	V	V
Long vowel	æ	æ
Diphthong	æ	ɑ
Short vowel	æ	
Short diphthong	æ ɑ	

On this interpretation, the short diphthongs are the relatively rare or 'special' category. I will therefore follow the notational practice I have used elsewhere (e.g. Lass 1988, 1992b), and represent the long diphthongs simply as vowel clusters like /æɑ/, /eo/; the short ones will carry a diacritic

[14] In terms of contemporary autosegmental theory (cf. Goldsmith 1989), a more proper representation of the long vowels would be

i.e. one quality associated with two timing slots. For technical reasons the representations of long vowels in (3.20) may be ill-formed, as they violate what's known as the 'obligatory contour principle', whereby two adjacent skeletal positions may not each be associated with the same segmental content. The representations here are merely illustrative of a general point.

indicating shortness, /ǣɑ/, /ĕo/. This means of course that opposite categories will be 'marked' in orthographic and phonological/phonetic representations; the slight confusion this may produce at first is (I think) worth it from the point of view of historical and structural clarity.

3.6.2   Breaking, Retraction, and Diphthong Height Harmony[15]

At last we can return to the history of Old English. Beginning in prehistoric times, but probably taking until about the ninth century for full implementation, there was a major change called **Breaking** (also **Fracture**, G *Brechung*). Here front vowels (long or short) tended to diphthongize in certain environments: (a) before /r/ or /l/ + following consonant (this includes geminate /rr/, ll/); and (b) before the velar fricative /x/. To illustrate these environments for /æ/ < WGmc */ɑ/:

(a.i) /-rC/: *bearn* 'child' (Go, OHG *barn*), *earm* 'arm' (Go *arms*, OIc *armr*).
(a.ii) /-lC/: *eald* 'old' (Go *alþeis*, OHG *alt*); *eall* 'all' (Go *alls*, OIc *allr*).
(b)   /-x/: *seah* 'he saw' (OHG *sah*); *eahta* 'eight' (Go *ahtau*, OHG *ahto*).

Breaking of a short vowel gives a short diphthong, as above; the only exception is when there is secondary lengthening (see below under breaking of */e/). Breaking of a long vowel gives a long diphthong, and these generally fall in with the Germanic diphthongs.

Breaking is a complex and not always 'regular' change; in some contexts particular vowels are only 'likely' or 'unlikely' to undergo it. Judgements of this kind of course depend on interpretation of spelling evidence: does the occurrence side by side of <self> and <seolf> for 'self' mean that breaking is optional and/or variable, or merely that the orthography is not noting it in some cases, or even that the texts may be dialectally 'mixed'? This is a moot question; but my general impulse is to assume that spelling variation in such cases is quite likely to represent phonological variation as well (see also §3.8.1).[16] We will be concerned here mainly with the most regular outcomes, which can be characterized for the individual vowels (except */æ/, which was treated above, and will be considered again below) as follows:

*/i/: Here as in the case of */e/ (see below), another environment is added: /w/. The initial result of breaking of */i/ in all cases is /īu/, spelled

---

[15] The literature and problems concerning these processes are canvassed in Lass & Anderson (1975: ch. 3). For a recent argument against our account (and therefore in essence the one here, which largely follows Lass & Anderson), see Howell (1991).

[16] For discussion of the general question of whether orthographical variation is likely to represent phonological variation, see the positive view in Lass (1992a), and the *caveats* in King (1992).

<io> in early texts, later mainly but not exclusively <eo>, and presumed to merge with /ēo/ from other sources, e.g. breaking of */e/. Breaking of */i/ is commonest before /w/ (*niowul* 'prostrate'), and before /xC/ (*Peohtas* 'Picts'); before /r/ there is little evidence, and there appears to be no breaking before /l/.

*/i:/: Here breaking is initially to /iu/ <io>, later usually merging with /eo/ from other sources: *lēoht* 'light' (in weight) < */li:xt/. In many cases the environment is later destroyed: so *wrēon* 'wrap' < */wriuxɑn/ < */wri:xɑn/, with loss of medial /x/ and contraction of the sequence */-iuɑ-/ (see §3.9.2).

*/e/: Breaking is regular before /rC/ (*eorþe* 'earth'), and /x/ (*feoh* 'cattle'). Before /lC/ it occurs mainly where C = /x/ (*eolh* 'elk' but *helpan* 'help'). Otherwise, it occurs before /lC/ most often when there is a preceding /s/ (nobody seems to know why): *seolf* 'self' (also *self*) vs. *melcan* 'milk', *helpan* as above. Some broken */e/, under conditions similar to those described under */i:/, produce long /eo/: *sēon* 'see' < */seoɑn/ < */sĕoxɑn/ < */sexɑn/. Breaking before /w/ occurs in *eowu* 'ewes' and others.

*/e:/: This does not appear in West Saxon in the relevant environments (here it is replaced by long */æ:/). All long /eo/ from Breaking in fact derive from lengthened breakings of */i, e/ or from */i:/ (see above).

*/æ:/: Breaking is regular only before /x/ as in *nēah* 'near' < */næ:x/ < */nɑ:x/; with loss of /x/ we have e.g. *nēalǣcan* 'approach' with the same root.

Breaking appears originally to be the insertion of [u] between a front vowel and the environments specified above: /r, l/ if followed by another consonant, /x/ alone, and sometimes /w/. But what do these have in common that might provoke this response? The usual answer is that they are all 'back' environments, which would naturally prompt insertion of a 'transition' vowel of back quality as an assimilatory response to the front-to-back movement.

Backness is self-evident for /x, w/; but not immediately for /r, l/. Yet we would certainly not want to relegate these to some other category, since they trigger the same response. It is surely better to have one kind of breaking than two or three unrelated ones. There are some interesting arguments that converge on this, and show the essential 'backness' involved even more strongly than the mere argument from simplicity. This material provides a nice example of what is often needed to make sense of complex developments, and illustrates an interesting 'theme' in the development of the English vowel system.

(i) Pairing of Breaking and Retraction. In Anglian dialects of OE (not the WS 'literary language') /æ/ does not break in some of the classic environments. But instead of remaining unaffected, it retracts to /ɑ/: *all, half* 'half', *haldan* 'hold' vs. WS *eall, healf, healdan*. Both [u]-insertion and retraction are reasonable responses to backness. In Northumbrian, retraction is also common before /rC/: early Nth *uarp* 'he threw', *barnum* 'children' (dat pl), WS *wearp, bearnum*. Even in WS, however, there is evidence for a close connection between breaking and retraction: /e/ breaks before /w/ as in *cnēowes* 'knee' (gen sg), but /æ/ retracts as in *awel* 'hook', *gesawen* 'seen'. It rather looks as if two related processes are 'apportioned' among the different back environments, with different dialects illustrating the same principle in different ways.

(ii) Back umlaut. In this later change (§3.6.3), short front vowels diphthongize, just as they do in breaking, before a following back vowel. In WS this is especially the case with /e/, as in *beofor* 'beaver', *heofon* 'heaven', etc. Here (as with /w, x/) there is no possible doubt that backness is involved, and the same kind of change is triggered.

(iii) Inhibition in palatalized environments. If a potential breaking context was followed by */i, j/, breaking did not occur. Hence breaking in *eall* < */æll/ < */ɑll/, but not in *sellan* 'give' < */sælljan/ < */sɑljan/, breaking in *eowu* 'ewes' but not in the sg *ewe* < */æwi/ < */ɑwi/ (on the changes in the accented vowels here, see §3.8). The fact that the change occurs only in environments without a following palatal again implicates backness.

If retraction and [u]-insertion are both triggered by backness, then /r, l, x, w/ and the back vowels ought to form a natural class. There is no problem with /l/: since more varieties of Modern English than not (as well as related languages like Afrikaans and Dutch) have a 'dark' (velarized or uvularized) [ɫ] in syllable codas, we can project this back to OE as well. This leaves us with /r/. Various suggestions have been made, e.g. that it was retroflex (Wright & Wright 1925, Lehnert 1965), or uvular (Lass & Anderson 1975), or that it was velarized like modern US /r/ (Lass 1983). The latter view seems to be the simplest: all the breaking and retraction environments then share some approximation or contact between the tongue back and the velum.

So breaking proper is the insertion of [u] after front vowels in certain back (continuant – not stop or nasal) environments. But the term 'breaking' in the handbooks conflates two developments: the actual [u]-insertion, and the later change to the special type of diphthongs spelled <ea, eo>, etc. This second process is not usually isolated as a distinct development, and was not given its own name until Lass & Anderson (1975), where we christened it **Diphthong Height Harmony** (DHH). The term is not yet in the tradition as a 'sound-change name' on a par with breaking, etc., but the process is now recognized, and the name is familiar enough to be used.

The nature of DHH can be illustrated by the sequences leading to OE *eald* /æɑld/ and *weorpan* /wĕorpɑn/: */ɑld/ [ɑɫd]> [æɫd] (AFB) > [æuɫd] (Breaking) > [æ̆ɑɫd] (DHH); */werpɑn/ > [wĕurpɑn] > [wĕorpɑn]. DHH then is a condition on complex nuclei that both elements must be of the same height, and that the second assimilates to the first. The condition of course holds by default of long vowels, but changes diphthongs in /-u/ with nonhigh first elements. The import of this will be clearer if we turn for a moment to the fates of the original Gmc diphthongs.

Recall that after monophthongization of */ɑi/ (§3.4), the diphthong system was */iu, eu, ɑu/. Of these, only */iu/ was already height-harmonic. Historical */ɑu/ > [æu] by AFB (§3.5), so that by the time of breaking the system was */iu, eu, æu/. Since */iu, eu/ generally fell together in OE in /eo/, our main concern is with the evolution of */æu/ and */eu/, which of course surfaced as 'long' diphthongs.

Consider the histories of *eald* 'old', *eolh* 'elk', *bēam* 'tree', *nēah* 'near', *bēodan* 'offer', and *lēoht* 'light':

(3.22)	WGmc	*ɑld	*elx	*bɑum	*nɑɑx	*biudɑn	*liixt
1	α: > æ:	—	—	—	nææx	—	—
2	AFB	æld	—	bæum	—	—	—
3	Breaking	æ̆uld	ĕulx	—	nææux	—	liiuxt
4	VVV > VV	—	—	—	næux	—	liuxt
5	iu > eu	—	—	—	—	beudɑn	leuxt
6	DHH	æ̆ɑld	ĕolx	bæɑm	næɑx	beodɑn	leoxt
7	OE form	eald	eolh	bēam	nēah	bēodan	lēoht

The change called 'VVV > VV' may be considered the implementation of a general constraint on nucleus weight: no more than two V-slots may occur, so that shortening (i.e. deletion of one of two identical Vs) is automatic.[17] Observe that the result of all these processes is to set up a new group of short diphthongs, and to cause the long diphthongs from breaking to merge with the orginal Germanic ones. (Further developments of the diphthongs will be taken up in §§3.8–9.)

3.6.3   Back umlaut[18]

Back Umlaut (also **Velar Umlaut**, **Back Mutation**) might just as well be called 'breaking before back vowels'. The main differences from breaking

---

[17] See Lass & Anderson (1975: 95–6) on 'trimoric nucleus simplification'.
[18] For details see Campbell (1959: §§205–21) and Lass & Anderson (1975: 102ff).

proper are that it is considerably later, affects only short vowels, and is much more sporadic. It is also less evenly distributed across the dialects: most regular in Mercian and Kentish, much less so in West Saxon.

Disregarding restrictions for the moment, /i, e/ and /æ/ appear respectively as <io, eo> and <ea> before back vowels in the following syllable. In one WS text, the Tanner MS of the Alfredian translation of Bede's story of Cædmon, we find:

> /i/: *heora* 'their', *wreoton* 'they wrote', *leomu* 'limbs', but *gifu* 'gift'.
> /e/: *meotudes* 'God's', *heofon* 'heaven', but *regol* 'rule', *sprecan* 'speak'.

The form *wreoton* (more usually *writon*) is an excellent example of the neutralization of the potential /iu/:/eo/ contrast (§3.6.2); this suggests that both DHH and the /eu/ > /iu/ rule or some relic of it persist for some time.

In WS there is generally no back umlaut of /æ/, since (cf. §3.5) [ɑ] had been restored in stressed syllables before a back vowel. If it hadn't, we'd expect for instance **fearan* 'to go', **deagum* 'day' (dat pl) instead of *faran*, *dagum*. In Mercian, however, where by a later change called **second fronting** /ɑ/ > [æ] again, we do in fact find *fearan* and the like < /færɑn/ < /fɑrɑn/ < /færɑn/. In WS back umlaut is rare before /ɑ/, but it is common here in Mercian: WS *sprecan* 'speak', Merc *spreocan*, etc.

The general WS picture: back umlaut of /e, i/ is fairly common before /u, o/, rare before /ɑ/; it is commoner before liquids and labial consonants than elsewhere, and normally blocked by velars. Hence typically *heorot* 'hart', *weorod* 'troop', but *medu* 'mead', *regol* 'rule', *helan* 'conceal'.

3.6.4   Morphophonemic effects of diphthongization

Any sound change can have a morphological effect if its environments happen to appear in morphologically sensitive places. And since certain changes feed others (e.g. AFB produces the [æ] that breaking acts on), there may be long chains of 'cooperating' mutations that can distort the original structure of paradigms. I will give one example here of this kind of interaction and its effects; others will turn up later.

Consider the strong verbs of class III (for details §7.1.2). Here the basic historical pattern is /e/ in the present and /æ/ in the preterite sg, but it only shows up in a few atypical verbs, like *bregdan* 'move', pret sg *brægd*. The original alternation is usually obscured, since verbs of this class typically contain a nasal or liquid in the root, thus providing the environments for failure of AFB which produces /æ/, or for breaking. More characteristic of class III are *helpan* 'help', pret sg *healp*, *weorpan* 'throw', pret sg *wearp*, and *bindan* 'bind', pret sg *band*. An outline of the historical developments (PNR = Pre-nasal Raising, §2.6, Brk = Breaking):

(3.23)

Input	breɣdɑn	brɑɣd	bendɑn	bɑnd	xelpɑn	xɑlp	werpɑn	wɑrp
PNR	–	–	bindɑn	–	–	–	–	–
AFB	–	bræɣd	–	–	–	xælp	–	wærp
Brk	–	–	–	–	–	xæulp	wĕurpɑn	wæurp
DHH	–	–	–	–	–	xæɑlp	wĕorpɑn	wæɑrp
OE	bregdan	*brægd*	bindan	band	helpan	*healp*	weorpan	*wearp*

This is rather simplified; the /ɣ/ in *bregdan, brægd* for instance comes out as /j/ in OE by processes to be discussed in the next section. But the mini-histories in (3.23) do show how apparently irregular or irrational synchronic structures often make considerable sense if one knows their origins.

3.7   Palatalization[19]

Pre-OE Germanic had three contrastive places of articulation for obstruents (stops and fricatives): labial, dental/alveolar, and velar. There was nothing at all (phonemically) in the palato-alveolar or palatal area except the approximant */j/ (cf. displays 2.10, 2.13). In the transition to Old English a new series was created, occupying this previously empty region (which I will call 'palatal' as a general cover-term): the affricates /tʃ, dʒ/ and the fricative /ʃ/.

The developments leading to this new series are complex, and it will be necessary once again to get ahead of our chronology to make sense of them, and to approach the problem a bit indirectly. Perhaps the best place to start is with one intricate aspect of OE spelling practice: the use of the symbols <c, g>. Confusingly for beginning students (though not for native speakers), OE tended to use <c> indifferently for voiceless velars and palatals, and <g> for voiced velars and palatals. To a certain extent there is structural method in this madness:

(i) A <c> or <g> before a back vowel represents a velar: *catt* 'cat', *cōlian* 'cool', *cuman* 'come'; *gāt* 'goat', *gōd* 'good', *gutt* 'gut'.

---

[19] For historical bacground and theoretical discussion, see Lass & Anderson (1975: ch. 4, §§1, 5–8).

(ii) A <c> or <g> before a consonant represents a velar: *clǣne* 'clean', *cradol* 'cradle'; *glæs* 'glass', *grǣg* 'grey'.

(iii) A <c> or <g> before /i(:)/ or long or short <ea, eo> represents a palatal: *cinn* 'chin', *cīdan* 'chide', *ceaff* 'chaff', *ceorl* 'churl', *cēosan* 'choose'; *gieldan* 'yield', *geard* 'yard', *geolca* 'yolk'.

Leaving aside (ii), the fact that the vowels in (i) are back and those in (ii) front suggests some kind of palatalization: fronting of velars in front environments. Alternations of this kind are common: think of German velar [x] after nonfront vowels (*Bach*, *Buch*) and [ç] after front vowels (*ich*, *sprechen*), or the English palatal initials of *keel*, *geese* vs. the velars of *cool*, *goose*.

At least this is how it looks at first, and will again shortly. But there is a class of complications: note the expected palatal in *cinn* 'chin' but a velar in *cynn* 'kin'; a palatal in *gieldan* 'yield' as expected, but a velar in *gyldan* 'gild'. Does this mean that palatalization occurs before front /i/ but not before front /y/? In fact there is something very odd here: in general velars never appear before /i/, and palatals never appear before /y/. A fronting process under front-vowel influence should not give results like this. Either the interpretation is wrong, or something else is involved. And /y/ isn't the only front vowel that appears not to palatalize. There also seem to be 'two kinds of' /e(:)/, one that causes palatalization as in the examples above, and one that doesn't, as in *cemban* 'to comb' (cf. *(un)kempt*), *cēne* 'keen', *Cent* 'Kent'. Does /e/ cause palatalization then only if it stands before /o/ (*cēosan*, *ceorl*)? One would not like to accept this sort of irrationality.

Such hiccoughs in what otherwise look like phonetically conditioned alternations should make us suspect that the processes involved were indeed once phonetically natural. The problems are historical residues, where something as it were has changed behind our backs. Suspicions like this are always good stimuli for historical investigation, and often – as here – there is a payoff. Consider some comparative data on two groups of forms with voiceless velar or palatal initials: (a) those that show 'proper' palatalization, and (b) those that don't:

(3.24)   (a) Palatalization:
          cinn 'chin': Go *kinnus*, OHG *kinni*
          cild 'child': Go *kilþei* 'womb'
          cēosan 'choose': Go *kiusan*, OHG *kiosan*
          (b) No palatalization:
          Cent 'Kent': < L *Cantia*
          cēne 'keen': OHG *kuoni*
          cylen 'kiln': < L *culīna*
          cyssan 'kiss': OS *kussian*

In general, wherever we find an OE front vowel that fails to cause palatalization, we are likely to find (a) evidence for a historical back vowel in the root (whether the word is native Germanic or a loan from Latin or elsewhere); and (b) an /i/ or /j/ in the following syllable of an ancestral or ancestor-like form. Further, non-palatalizing front-vowel items often have related back-vowel forms: for *Cent* there is *Cantwarabyrig* 'Canterbury' ('city of the Kent-burghers'), for *cyssan* the noun *coss* 'kiss', for *cemban* the noun *camb* 'comb', for *gyldan* the noun *gold* 'gold'. There seems to have been some change that fronted back vowels (and raised low front */æ/ as we will see) before a following */i, j/. This process, to be discussed in detail in §3.8, is called *i*-**Umlaut**. In short, the front vowels that do not cause palatalization are secondary, not original; they arise only after palatalization and certain other processes affecting velars before original front vowels.

To get ahead of ourselves again, and simplify to establish the principle: suppose palatalization is older than *i*-umlaut, and the apparent messiness of the OE velar/palatal distribution is due to this ordering in time. If palatalization takes */k, γ/ directly to [tʃ, j] (but see below), the histories of some exemplary forms would be:

(3.25)

	'chin'	'kin'	'yield'	'gild'	'good'
WGmc input	kinni	kunnj-	γeldɑn	γuldjɑn	γo:d
1 Palatalize	tʃinni	–	jeldɑn	–	–
2 Umlaut	–	kynnj-	–	γγldjɑn	–
3 i/j-delete	tʃinn	kynn	–	γγldɑn	–
4 γ > g	–	–	–	gyldɑn	go:d
OE form	*cinn*	*cynn*	*gieldan*	*gyldan*	*gōd*

The deletions under (3) will be discussed in chapter 4 and under the relevant morphological headings in chapter 6–7; the /γ/ > /g/ change will come up a bit later in this section, and §3.9.[20]

[20] Note that stage 3 phonemicizes the palatal/velar contrast, in that both palatals and velars can now stand before front vowels.

A few problems arise in this story. First, how likely is a direct transition from [k] to [tʃ]? Given what we know about the phonetics of palatalization in living languages, this is a bit too radical, at least for a primary change. More likely there was an intermediate stage, probably a voiceless palatal stop [c] (like the initial of *keel*). Another problem is a bit more difficult: had */ɣ/ become a stop /g/ (as it surely had by historical OE times) before palatalization, or did this happen later?

Recall that IE */gh/ did not become a stop in early Germanic except after nasals and perhaps liquids (cf. §2.3); indeed, it still hasn't in Netherlandic, which is fairly close to Anglo-Frisian. If the change /ɣ/ > /g/ took place before palatalization, the voiced and voiceless velars developed in parallel, as suggested in Lass & Anderson (1975: ch. 4). We proposed two processes, (i) **Backness Accommodation** (palatalization proper), and (ii) **Palatal Softening**, both after the **Hardening** (turning into a stop) of */ɣ/. Thus for the sequence velar + /i/, voiceless and voiced:

(3.26)	WGmc input	*ki-	*ɣi-	*ɣo-
	Hardening	–	gi-	go-
	Backness Accomm.	ci-	ɟi-	–
	Palatal Softening	tʃi-	ji-	–

([ɟ] is a voiced palatal stop, as in the initial of *geese*.)

If on the other hand hardening is later, the inputs to palatalization are */k, ɣ/, and hence palatal softening affects only the descendants of */k/; */ɣ/ was already a fricative. (On the fricative output of palatal softening becoming an approximant or 'glide', see below.) On this interpretation hardening occurs initially only before back vowels, and the histories are:

(3.27)	WGmc input	*ki-	*ɣi-	*ɣo-
	Backness Accomm.	ci-	ji-	–
	Palatal softening	tʃi-	–	–
	Hardening	–	–	go-

(Actually the hardening of */ɣ/ is not an independent issue; it is part of a larger process affecting, in one way or another, all voiced fricatives, e.g. those from IE */bh, dh, gh/ and Verner's Law acting on Gmc */f, θ, x/: see §3.9.3.)

It is difficult to argue conclusively for one story or the other; what is clear is that the voiced velar has a weaker (less occluded) output, which could be due either to the inherent weakness of voiced as opposed to voiceless consonants (cf. Lass 1984: ch. 8), or to the fact that the velar was a fricative at the relevant point. The version with late hardening is simpler, and I will tentatively adopt it here.

Before tying these developments together, we must look at palatalization in another environment: after front vowels. As modern developments suggest, */ɣ/ was palatalized after front vowels (e.g. *day* < *dæg* /dæj/), and */k/ after front vowels except */æ(:)/, i.e. nonlow ones (*pic* 'pitch' but *bæc* 'back'). Medial */ɣ/ between back vowels remained [ɣ] in OE, and weakened to [w] in Middle English: hence the alternation now in *day* < *dæg* vs. *dawn* < *dagung* (and OE *dagas* 'days' comes down in some ME dialects as *dawes*).

Consider as a review the histories of some further items (and compare with (3.23)):

(3.28)

	'good'	'day'	'dawn'	'back'	'pitch'
WGmc input	ɣoːð	ðaɣ	ðaɣung	βak	pik
AFB	–	ðæɣ	ðæɣung	βæk	–
Restoration of [α]	–	–	ðaɣung	–	–
Backness Accom.	–	ðæj	–	–	pic
Palatal Soft.	–	–	–	–	pitʃ
Hardening	goːd	dæj	daɣung	bæk	–
OE form	gōd	dæg	dagung	bæc	pic

The palatalization of */ɣ/ > [j] creates a merger between the new [j] and the original Gmc */j/ < IE */j/ as in *geoc* 'yoke' (cf. L *jugum*, Go *juk*). And overall, since both [j] and [tʃ] can now appear before both front and back vowels, the velar/palatal contrast is phonemicized: even if there is not a huge number of contrasting items, and few minimal pairs, there is enough contrast so we can claim that the system has been restructured. E.g. [k] in *cemban*, *cynn*, *camb* vs. [tʃ] in *cinn*, *ceorl*, *ceaff*, [j] in *geoc* (where <ge> = [j]) vs. [g] in *gyldan*, etc.

One more new phone-type (and eventually phoneme) is added by this complex of processes: the affricate [dʒ]. This arises in two distinct environments: first, from palatalization of */ɣ/ [g] after nasals as in *sengean* 'singe' < */saŋjan/; second from palatalized geminate */ɣɣ/ as in *mycg* 'midge' < */muɣɣj-/. This new [dʒ] becomes phonemic, even giving rise to near minimal pairs like *weg* [wej] 'way' vs. *wecg* [wedʒː] 'wedge'; at least there is a contrast between short /j/ and long /dʒː/.[21] In outline:

---

[21] One could just as well write /dːʒ/, since with long affricates it is typically the hold rather than the release that is long. I put the [ː] after the second element to indicate that significant length belongs to the affricate as a 'unit', not to its first element.

(3.29)

	'singe'	'midge'
eWGmc input	sɑngjɑn	muɣjɑ
WGG	–	muɣɣjɑ
AFB	sængjɑn	–
Backness Accomm.	sæn̞jɑn	muɟɟjɑ
Palatal Softening	sænd͡ʒɑn	mudd͡ʒjɑ
i-umlaut	send͡ʒɑn	mydd͡ʒjɑ
Weak-σ deletions	send͡ʒɑn	mydd͡ʒ
OE form	*sengean*	*mycg*

To sum up these developments diagrammatically:

(3.30) catt, cinn

geoc

gōd, gieldan, mycg

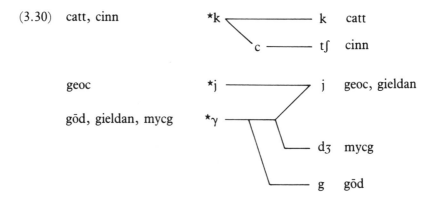

A different sort of palatalization contributes further to the new series: a change of */sk/ > /ʃ/. The mechanics are not clear, but one reasonable suggestion would be something like [sk] > [sc] > [sç], with a later 'compromise' articulation [ʃ] emerging from the back-to-back alveolar and palatal. Or, the [k] may have weakened first to [x], as in modern Dutch, without palatalizing; in this case we could see at least three of the stages mirrored in modern Germanic, in the verbs meaning 'to write': Swedish *skriva* /skri:va/ representing the original, Dutch *schrijven* /sxrɛivə(n)/ a further development, and German *schreiben* /ʃraebən/ the final stage (cf. English *shrive*).

The reason for this palatalization is obscure; it occurs in both front and back environments, and before consonants, so it is not obviously assimilatory like the ones discussed above. The OE spelling <sc> for instance appears to represent /ʃ/ not only in *scīnan* 'shine' (cf. OIc *skína*), *sc(i)eran* 'shear' (OIc *skera*), but also in *scofl* 'shovel' (OSw *skofl*), *scanca* 'shank' (Du *skank*), *scūr* 'shower' (Go *skūra*).

There is however occasional failure in back environments, as shown by the spelling <x> = /ks/, which is due to metathesis (/sk/ > /ks/), in places where <sc> would be expected. This must have occurred while the cluster was still /sk/. Palatalized and nonpalatalized variants of one lexeme may even occur in the same text: the poem *Andreas* has for 'fish' (Go *fisks*) both gen sg *fisces* and dat pl *fixum*. Failures of palatalization (or dialectal variants: see below) also lead to doublets in later periods, even including ModE: hence *ask* (OE *āscian*, *ācsian*), now frequently with the nonstandard doublet *ax* (which was the norm in many pre-modern standard varieties). Another example is *tusk* (OE *tūsc*, pl *tūscas*, *tūxas*), where the nonpalatalized form has come down in most standard varieties, but there are many dialects with *tush*.

But the form of a word containing Gmc */k, ɣ, sk/ in WS Old English (or any written variety) is not necessarily a key to its modern pronunciation. For instance, the normal form for 'give' in WS is *giefan* or *gifan*, which must have a palatal; and indeed the usual London form as late as Chaucer is *yeve(n)*. ModE *give* then reflects a nonpalatalized northern variant; palatalization was restricted in Northumbrian, and still is: Scots *kirk* vs. southern *church* and the like. On the other hand, we may have what the handbooks tend to call 'Scandinavian influence'. This might mean borrowing of a cognate form (cf. OIc *gefa*), or an inhibition of palatalization due to extensive contact with North Germanic dialects, which at that point did not palatalize. (In that case of course 'northern provenance' and 'Scandinavian influence' may, sociolinguistically speaking, amount to the same thing.) It is certain in any case that many words come down into the modern standard dialects in forms that could not possibly derive from southern (e.g. WS) OE. Other examples are *skirt* (OE *scyrte* gives the doublet *shirt*), *guest* (OE *giest* should give **yest*), *gift* (OE *gift* should give **yift*). (On spellings like <giefan>, with an apparent diphthong, see the discussion of 'palatal diphthongization' in the appendix to this chapter.)

3.8   *I*-umlaut[22]

3.8.1   *From allophonic rule to phonemic contrast*

The period from Proto-Germanic to historical OE might be called 'The Age of Harmony'. During this time harmonic processes (in particular regressive vowel harmony, or umlaut) are a dominant theme in phonolo-

---

[22] For data and a traditional account (if with a few eccentricities) see Campbell (1959: §§190–204). For theoretical discussion Lass & Anderson (1975: ch. 4, §§3–4).

gical evolution. After about the tenth or eleventh century they are at best marginal. We have already seen examples of harmonization to high segments (§2.4), to low segments (*a*-umlaut, §2.7), to back segments (restoration of [α], §3.5, back umlaut, §3.6.3), and general harmonization of height in abutting vowels within a nucleus (DHH, §3.6.2).

But perhaps the most far-reaching and important of these harmonic processes is ***I*-umlaut** (also *i*-mutation): because of the number of vowels affected, the creation of entirely new vowel types, and its profound morphological effects. This change was triggered by suffixal */i, j/; and these occurred in a large number of inflections and derivational suffixes (cf. §3.8.3 and chapters 6–8). In essence, *i*-umlaut (IU) is the 'attraction' of vowels towards the upper front corner of the vowel space. In terms of the qualities involved (for exceptions and other problems see §3.8.2), the 'ideal' shape of IU is:

(3.31)

	[−back]			[+back]
[+high]	i	y	←	u
	↑			
	e	ø	←	o
	↑			
[+low]	æ		←	α

Before syllabic /i/ or nonsyllabic /j/, the affected vowel moves 'one step' along the relevant parameter: backness ([+back] > [−back]) as first choice, then if this is not available, highness ([+low] > [−low], [−high] > [+high]), i.e. for vowels already front. (The [e] > [i] arrow represents not the later process discussed here but the early 'precursor' raising discussed in §2.6.) Hence fronting of /u, o, α/ and raising of /æ/ are not distinct processes, but differential responses to features of the trigger, which is of course [−back, +high].

Given (3.31), we can note two immediate effects of IU: (a) increased incidence of the qualities [æ, e]; and (b) the creation of two new vowels of a type previously unknown in Germanic: front rounded [y, ø]. (The only such vowel in earlier IE was /y(:)/ in Attic and Ionic Greek, from earlier */u(:)/, spelled upsilon <*v*>, and normally confusingly transliterated <u>: so *lúō* 'I loose', phonemically /lyɔ:/.) The new [æ, e] have no systemic import; these qualities are already distinctive within the system, and new instances simply merge with the existing ones. But [y, ø] are novel; and when they are finally phonemicized (a story we will get to shortly), they produce a transition of this kind:

(3.32) i u   i y   u
        e o   e ø   o
        æ ɑ   æ   ɑ
        pre-IU   post-IU

In the pre-IU system, rounding is nondistinctive; front and low back vowels are predictably unround, and nonlow back vowels are round. In the restructured post-IU system, roundness is distinctive for nonlow front vowels. But this is a late development, contingent on loss of the umlaut triggers /i, j/ in weak positions; the very definition of IU given above identifies it (at least initially) as allophonic. Immediately following IU proper there is of course a new phonetic system with [y, ø]; but the phonologization story is complex and not entirely clear. I will look at this first, and then turn to IU in detail, and its morphological implications.

The evolution from allophonic process to phonemic contrast can be illustrated with the ancestors of ModE *mouse, mice* (OE *mūs, mȳs*). In pre-IU times, the nom sg and nom pl forms were respectively */mu:s/ and */mu:s-iz/ (these two will exemplify the whole process; the story is the same in principle for all the vowels). The sequence is:

(3.33) 1 Input   mu:s   mu:s-i-
        2 IU   mu:s   my:s-i-
        3 i-deletion   –   my:s
        4 OE output   mu:s   my:s

That is, at stage 1 the sg/pl contrast is coded by the ending containing /i/, and nothing else; at stage 2, IU fronts /u:/ to [y:], but effects only a phonetic, not a phonological change; at stage 3 the loss of /i/ produces a minimal /u:/:/y:/ contrast, creating a new phoneme, and at the same time shifts the burden of signalling plural to the new contrast:

(3.34)   *Stage 2*   *Stage 3*
       Phonemic   /mu:s/, /mu:s-i/   /mu:s/, /my:s/
       Phonetic   [mu:s], [my:s-i]   [mu:s], [my:s]

Now representations like these, and labels like 'stage 1', etc., can suggest that the processes both of change and restructuring are somehow 'catastrophic'; but of course linguistic change does not proceed this way (even if its outputs may let us pretend that it does). In fact the restructuring, with phonologization of the new vowels, took a considerable time, measured probably in centuries rather than decades. Though the first evidence for IU as a phonetic change is as early as the sixth to seventh centuries, it was probably not completely phonologized until the late eighth or early ninth.

We can see how this came about (and incidentally get some insight into why OE spelling is sometimes inconsistent in certain ways), by looking at some very early texts, such as runic inscriptions or eighth-century glossaries. In these texts we find three types of spellings for potential IU forms, which give us a capsule history of the process, and suggest that we are seeing the end of a long period of variation and slow codification.

Some examples from the eighth-century *Corpus Glossary* (a Latin/OE dictionary of 'hard words') will illustrate. Forms with potential IU (here illustrated with Gmc */o:/ and /u:/ before */i/) display three types of spellings:

A: No front-rounded vowel symbols, IU environment intact:
   unsmoþi 'rough' (later *-smēþe*: on the source of /e:/ see the next section)
   hurnitu 'hornet' (late OE *hyrnet*)
B: Front-rounded vowel symbols, IU environment intact:
   groeni 'green' (later *grēne*)
   cyri 'choice' (later *cyre*)
C: Front-rounded vowel symbol, IU environment destroyed:
   suoetnis 'sweetness' (later *swēt-*)
   mygg 'midge, gnat'

There is also variation within the text: 'rough' appears as both *unsmoþi* and *unsmoeði*, for example. Within Corpus itself, the spellings are distributed roughly this way: type A 2 per cent, type B 20 per cent, type C 78 per cent. I.e. on one interpretation we have reached a point where two processes – the spread of IU itself, and its phonologization – may be proceeding at different rates within one dialect, and neither is complete. In other words, a classic instance of the kind of phonological variable we are familiar with from 'variationist' studies of living languages.[23]

I stress this, because it may be a useful corrective to a view that seems to be enshrined in the handbooks (and the general way historians tend to talk about such things): that a sound change is a 'point mutation', with no extension in time, and that changes follow each other in simple linear sequence. What the early data on IU seems rather to indicate is that in the dialect of the Corpus glossator, the following apparently contradictory propositions could all be true at the same time:

[23] For detailed discussion of this data, see Lass (1992a).

(i) IU had not occurred: 'smooth' is [smoːði];
(ii) IU had occurred, but /i/ is intact: 'smooth' is [smøːði];
(iii) IU had occurred, and /i/ was lowered or deleted: 'choice' is /kyre/, 'midge'/ is /mydʒːː/.

(The variant *[smøːðe] could of course have existed too, but no one word seems to appear in all three types.)

The three propositions are not in fact contradictory, provided that each holds for a form in a particular utterance. Given the ratios above we could suggest for instance that the odds on a given occurrence of a particular word showing no umlaut are 49:1 against, the odds on it showing umlaut and retained /i/ are 4:1 against, and the odds on it showing both umlaut and lost or lowered /i/ are 39:11 in favour. Such calculations of odds would of course hold only over a large number of utterances; but since such distributions are typical of sound change in progress in modern speech communities, we have a warrant for assuming that the same was true in ancient times. Without fully codified spelling systems, writing may have been more like 'transcription' than the automated behaviour of modern literates; it can at least be argued that written texts may mirror spoken variation. There are also cases where we know that texts were written from dictation; these of course cannot be anything but transcription.[24]

If we believe this, we can argue (contrary to the handbooks) that IU was still (marginally) 'in progress' as late as the eighth century, and was categorically established and phonemicized only around 800 or so. Early ninth-century texts show the classic umlaut picture familiar from the literary corpus.

A look back however at the characteristics of type A and B spellings may raise doubts at first even for late OE. What about *cyning* for instance, which looks like type B, or worse, *hunig* 'honey', *bodig* 'body', which appear to be type A? These are not quite what they seem; once IU had been phonologized, it was to some extent morphologized as well. That is, it came to be associated with certain morphological, syntactic or semantic properties, and not with others – whatever the history may have been. Thus in the end certain suffixes containing /i/ may be umlaut-causing, others may not, and still others may be variable. But at this stage there is nothing phonological involved, any more than there is in the fact that the modern plural of *house* is *houses*, not *hice*. When umlaut was no longer a phonetic or phonological process, a suffix of the type that caused IU in the seventh century could be added to any root without affecting it; and even

[24] See Bierbaumer (1988) on scribal 'slips of the ear'.

in the early days /i/ in the second elements of compounds, for instance, especially names, did not cause it (e.g. *Osric*, never **Oesric* or **Esric*).

3.8.2   I-umlaut in detail

The schematic (3.31) above captures the principle of IU, but does not do justice to the somewhat less orderly fine detail. For instance, IU is less potent for front than for back vowels; */æ:/ is unaffected, and */æ/ only partially. And due to other changes and restrictions, certain vowels simply do not occur in the right places: */e:/ never does, and short */o/ is extremely rare (see below). And of course there is the question of the diphthong umlauts, not touched on in the diagram; this, unsurprisingly, is extremely complicated. I will look here at the affected vowels individually, in articulatory sets.

A. The low vowels

(i) */ɑ/. Because of AFB (§3.5) this mainly occurs before nasals; in Anglian it also occurs as a result of retraction (rather than breaking) of */æ/ before /l/ (§3.6). Before nasals, the oldest sources show /æ/ as expected: *ænid* 'duck' (OHG *enit*, Lith *ántis*), *ænd* 'and' (OHG *anti, enti*) and so on. Later the normal result is /e/ (*ened* 'duck', *sendan* 'send' < */sɑnd-jɑn/), presumably through a recurrence of pre-nasal raising (cf. §2.6). The word 'and' however normally occurs in its unmutated form *and, ond* in later texts; probably from a variant with a different final vowel (cf. OFri *and(a)*, OHG *unta*).

Before /l/, Anglian as expected shows umlaut of retracted */ɑ/: *fællan* 'fell', *cwælman* 'kill' < */fɑlljɑn, kwɑlmjɑn/*; WS here has umlaut of /æu/ < */æ/ (*/fæulljɑn/*, etc.): hence *fiellan, cwielman* (see D below for the nucleus spelled <ie>).

(ii) */æ/. As expected, when IU occurs the result is /e/: *herian* 'praise' (Go *harjan*), *tellan* 'tell' (OIc *telja*). But there is considerable variability: IU is most regular if */æ/ is followed by a single consonant or geminate, as above; it is less likely if a cluster follows, as in *hrefn, hræfn* 'raven', *efnan, æfnan* 'perform'. Some words that ought to show IU apparently never do: e.g. *fæstan* 'fasten', which must be < */fɑstjɑn/ (cf. *fæst* 'fast').

(iii) */ɑ:/, */ɑi/ and '*ǣ₁*' and '*ǣ₂*'. Recall that OE /ɑ:/ comes from Gmc */ɑi/ (§3.4). Thus non-OE cognates of OE /ɑ:/ words will normally show a diphthong (spelled <ai> in Gothic, <ei> in OHG). The result of IU of this vowel is typically /æ:/, as expected: *hǣlan* 'heal' (cf. *hāl* 'whole', Go *hails, hailjan*), *clǣne* 'clean' < */klɑin-i-/ (cf. OHG *kleini*).

This particular WS /æ:/ is often called '*ǣ₂*' in the handbooks, to distinguish it from another /æ:/ of different origin, this time from WGmc

*/ɑ:/, which is called 'ǣ₁', as in *hǣr* 'hair' (OS, OHG *hār*), *dǣd* 'deed' (OHG *tāt*). This distinction is important both for OE studies and for later history; it is only in West Saxon that IU of /ɑ:/ < WGmc */ɑi/ and WGmc */ɑ:/ unmutated collapse in /æ:/. In Anglian they are distinct, with /æ:/ in 'heal', 'clean' but /e:/ < WGmc */ɑ:/ in 'hair', 'deed'. So WS *hǣlan, hǣr*, Anglian *hǣlan, hēr*.

The fact that there are 'two *ǣs*' is of course relevant mainly in a cross-dialectal perspective for OE itself; but it has historical repercussions, since /æ:/ and /e:/ develop differently in Middle English. So *ǣ₁* and *ǣ₂* would be expected to rhyme in ME dialects of WS provenance, but not in Anglian ones. (They would rhyme in Kentish as well, but on /e:/, due to other changes.) So 'seed' (WS *sǣd*, Angl *sēd* < */sɑ:d/) with *ǣ₁* should not rhyme in Anglian-derived dialects with *ǣ₂* 'to lead' (WS, Angl *lǣdan* < */lɑidjɑn/). That they do rhyme in ModE is due to later developments.

To untangle this rather involuted story, the reflexes of WGmc */ɑ:, ɑi/ and umlauted */ɑi/ are as follows in WS and Anglian:

(3.35)

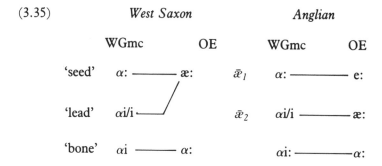

B. The nonlow back vowels

(i) */u(:)/. IU straightforwardly gives /y(:)/: *trymman* 'strengthen' < */trumjɑn/ (cf. *trum* 'strong'), *drȳ* 'magician' < OIr */dru:i/, *cylen* 'kiln' < L *culina*. The last two show that loanwords of the appropriate shape at a given time usually behave like native items with respect to general sound changes.

In the earliest sources the spelling <ui> appears alongside <y>; thus *buiris* 'chisel', later *byres*. The <ui> writing is probably based on continental (German or Franconian) practice, and most likely involves a diacritic technique based on a simple 'feature' analysis. That is, <u> stands as it were for lip-attitude, and <i> for frontness (two simultaneous features written in sequence). This principle can also be seen in the (earlier) rune for /y/, which is <ᛦ>: the /u/-rune <ᚢ>, with a small copy of the /i/-rune < ᛁ > inside. The same idea lies behind the spellings

<oi, oe> for the umlaut of */o(:)/ (see below). For a modern version, compare the alternatives <ue, oe> for German <ü, ö>; in fact the umlaut symbol <¨> derives from a small copy of <e> written above the relevant letter in earlier German.

(ii) */o(:)/. Again the initial development is straightforward: in all dialects the result is /ø(:)/, written <oe> as a rule in earlier texts, though with some <oi> spellings, especially in personal names: so *smoeði*, *groeni* as mentioned in the last section, *doeman* 'judge' (cf. *dōm* 'judgement'). Native */o/ is almost unknown before */i/, since it had earlier rasied to */u/ (§2.6); but it was analogically reintroduced in a few forms, like *doehter* 'daughters' (cf. sg *dohtor*); it occurs in loans as well, e.g. *oele* 'oil' < L *oleum*, presumably in the late Latin form */olju/.

Unlike /y(:)/ however, these /ø(:)/ are not stable; while they remain in early Northumbrian, and in Mercian well into the ninth century, they begin to unround quite early in West Saxon; by the Alfredian period they have generally merged with /e(:)/. From the late ninth century only two WS items normally appear with <oe>: *oele* as above, and *oeþel* 'homeland'; and both also have /e(:)/: *ele*, *ēþel*.[25] Unrounding also took place in Kentish, but this involved /y(:)/ as well, and is part of another story, not relevant here (see Anderson 1988a).

By WS times then, /ø(:)/ had unrounded to merge with /(e(:)/, so that *foet* 'feet' was now *fēt*, *doehter* 'daughters' now *dehter*. This produced a smaller system with only one front-rounded vowel quality, long and short /y/. The development of the quality systems is:

(3.36)
i		u		i	y	u		i	y	u
e		o		e	ø	o		e		o
æ		ɑ		æ		ɑ		æ		ɑ
1 pre-IU				2 post-IU				3 Later WS		

Curiously, at the end of the OE period /ø(:)/ revives in the dialects of the SW and SWML (the descendants of West Saxon), from a quite different source: monophthongization of /ĕo, eo/. So *beon, bon* 'to be' < *bēon*, *heorte, horte* 'heart' < *heorte*. In these dialects /y(:)/ also remained (elsewhere they unrounded to /i(:)/; by around 1100 dialects of WS origin have gone from a type 3 system to a type 2, while others either keep /ø(:)/ only for a short time, or revert very quickly to something like type 1. We have already seen an example of this kind of see-saw pattern with AFB and restoration of [ɑ] (§3.5).

---

[25] As a matter of interest, ModE *oil* cannot descend from the OE form, but must be a later borrowing from French: OE *ele* would give **eal*.

I noted above (under A) the occasional failures of IU of */æ/. There is another group of forms that on the surface also look like 'failures' but in historical perspective can be seen not to be. These are weak verbs of class II (see §7.3.2), which apparently show (a) failure of IU of */u, o, α/, (b) failure of West Germanic Gemination (§3.2), and (c) retention of the */j/ that should have caused both. Examples are *lufian* 'love', *bodian* 'announce', *macian* 'make': why not **lyffan*, **boeddan* > **beddan*, **mæccan*?

This behaviour is due to ancestral structures clearly visible only in a comparative perspective: the /j/ in these verbs was once preceded by an */o:/, which blocked IU of the root vowel. The originals were of the type */luβ-o:j-αn/, etc. Something of this can be seen in verbs of this class in Old Saxon and OHG: the cognates to OE *macian* are OS *makōn*, OHG *mahhōn*. Despite appearances, then, these are not like class I weak verbs in -*ian*, which have umlaut of the root vowel, but no gemination of medial /r/, like *herian* 'praise', *nerian* 'save' (= Go *harjan*, *nasjan*). They do not show 'failed' IU; at the relevant time the root vowels were not in an IU context (cf. §7.3.2).

C. The diphthongs

Another violation of chronology becomes necessary here; we must return to a point in the evolution of the diphthong system before the operation of DHH (§3.6.2), and certain other changes. DHH, you will recall, produces, from the breaking and other diphthongs, the new OE type with both elements of the same height. Recall also that the first breaking diphthongs had [-u] as their second elements: *eald* 'old' /æald/ < */æuld/, *heorte* 'heart' /xĕorte/ < */xĕurte/. (On the representation /x/ for <h> see §3.9.) While we are back-tracking, recall finally that the original */ĭu/ from breaking of /i/ and */ĕu/ from breaking of /e/ fell together in late WS, but were still largely distinct (as were long /iu, eu/ or their descendants) in early WS: *niowol* 'prostrate', *heorte*.

The 'long' diphthongs, whether original or from breaking, also initially had [-u] as second element: *nēah* 'near' with /æα/ < */æu/ < */æ:/, *bēam* 'tree' with /æα/ < */æu/ < Gmc */αu/, *līoht* 'light' with /iu/ < */i:/, *bēodan* 'offer' with /eo/ < */eu/. Here also /iu, eu/ eventually fell together in /eo/. (We presume that the nuclei spelled <io> in early West Saxon and other dialects should be interpreted as /ĩu, iu/: see below.)

So at the time of IU, the OE diphthong system is:

(3.37)   Short: ǽu, ĕu, ĭu
        Long: æu, eu, iu

Long /eu/ never occurred in IU environments, but the rest did. We will see shortly why it is necessary to start before the /iu/: /eu/ merger and before DHH; and, incidentally, why the usual handbook statements that deal with 'the *i*-umlaut of *ea*' and the like cannot be taken at face value.

In early WS, strangely, the IU of all diphthongs appears to be (qualitatively) the same: a nucleus spelled <ie>. It is <ie> forms that are usually given in dictionaries and cited in historical discussions, so they require close attention. Let us begin with what might be seen as the umlauts of /æɑ, æɑ/, since these will illustrate the story nicely; we will take up the others later on.

The historical relations between the nuclei spelled <ie> (long and short) and the other diphthongs are transparent: thus *hīeran* 'hear' < */xæɑr-jɑn/ < */xæurjɑn/ < */xɑurjɑn/ (cf. Go *hausjan*), *ieldra* 'older' < */æɑldirɑ/ < */æuldirɑ/ < */ældirɑ/ (cf. Go *alþiza*). They are however difficult to interpret, and they have been the subject of considerable controversy. The problems with the <ie> diphthongs are: (a) they occur in this context only in early WS; (b) there are no certain later survivors of eWS that help to pinpoint the quality; (c) by the ninth century they had generally monophthongized, either to /i(:)/ (*nieht* 'night' > *niht*), or /y(:)/ (*ieldra* > *yldra*); and (d) the obvious phonetic interpretation, /ie/, is probably untenable. The last two points however contain the germs of a solution.

We begin with (d), which leads to (c). An interpretation /ie/ (or as some authorities prefer, /iə/) would first of all violate DHH, which otherwise seems to be a general condition on OE diphthongs. (This is a weak argument, of course; but it's generally better to assume symmetry unless there are good reasons not to.) Second, and equally or perhaps more important, such a value would make it hard to see why the typical later result should be /y(:)/. On these (and other) grounds Lass & Anderson (1975: ch. 4) argue against the traditional views, and suggest that: (a) the two elements must be the same height, and (b) at least one of them must be rounded (so that both rounded and unrounded nuclei would be natural outputs of monophthongization). If <i> represents /i/, as the later developments (all high and front) suggest, then the <e> must be either /u/ or /y/. (There is no insuperable problem with <e>, in this context, representing either: see the appendix to this chapter.) Since all the other OE diphthongs have a back vowel as second element, /iu/ is the more plausible value (so Lass & Anderson).

But we failed to consider some important data, and a subsequent argument by Fran Colman (1985) makes it clear that /iu/ is wrong. In the same eWS texts that show <ie> for the umlauted breaking of */æ/ (*ieldra*) and of */æu/ (*hīeran*), the spelling <io> occurs for unumlauted breaking of */i/ (*niowol*) and for Gmc */iu/ (*ge-þīode* 'speech': cf. Go *þiuda* 'nations'). There is no doubt that this must be /iu/; is it then conceivable that <ie> should represent phonetically, when it stands for an umlaut-output, the same thing as unumlauted */iu/, but nonetheless be distinguished in spelling?

Another problem with our analysis is that an output /iu/ would suggest that only the first element of the diphthong was umlauted, whereas the rule for complex nuclei (e.g. in long vowels considered as vowel clusters) is that both elements were: *mȳs* /myys/ < */muus-i/, etc. If we take it that IU affected both elements as it ought to have, and further that it preceded DHH, we have, according to Colman's neat argument, a simple and phonetically natural story:

(3.38) 1 Input   æu . . . i
        2 IU   ey . . . i
        3 Raising   iy . . . i

That is: /æ/ umlauts as expected to /e/, and /u/ to /y/; stage 3 is a quite reasonable assimilation within the nucleus itself, where the following /y/ acts rather like /i/ and causes a kind of mini-umlaut. This is both consistent with the historical facts, and phonetically plausible. Note also that DHH does not have to apply here, since the nucleus is already height-harmonic.

Now for the IU of the other diphthongs. Consider input */eu/ and */iu/. Since IU can raise nonhigh front vowels, and fronts back ones, the expected output for */eu/ would be /iy/.[26] Since /i/ in */iu/ is already high and front, only the second element is vulnerable, and it fronts, giving of course /iy/. On this interpretation it is virtually inconceivable that, given the phonetic substance present in the first place, the result should be anything but a merger, regardless of the heights of the input nuclei.

Perhaps a few exemplary cases will clarify matters: consider the likely histories of *ieldra*, *hīeran*, *hierde* 'shepherd', *līehtan* 'lighten':

(3.39) 1 Input   ɑldirɑ   xɑurjɑn   xirdi   liuxtjɑn
        2 AFB   ældirɑ   xæurjɑn   –   –
        3 Breaking   æ̆uldirɑ   –   xĭurdi   –
        4 IU   ĕyldirɑ   xeyrjɑn   xĭyrdi   liyxtjɑn
        5 Raising   īyldirɑ   xiyrjɑn   –   –
        6 i/j-loss   īyldra   xiyrɑn   –   liyxtɑn
        7 i-lowering –   –   xĭyrde   –
        OE form   *ieldra*   *hīeran* *hierde* *līehtan*

(On the processes loosely grouped under 6 and 7, see the discussion of changes in weak syllables in chapter 4.)

[26] Actually IU seems to be problematic for both long and short */eu/, for various reasons (see Campbell 1959: §202); but we should expect <ie> if it did occur.

3.8.3   I-umlaut and Old English morphology

Many OE inflexional and derivational suffixes historically contained */i,
j/; IU therefore produced an important set of morphophonemic alternations. In ModE (as in Dutch, but unlike German) these have been largely
wiped out by analogical changes. E.g. only *man, tooth, foot, goose, mouse,
louse* have umlaut plurals now (whereas not only these but the ancestors of
book, oak, nut, cow, stud, goat, turf, furrow, friend, once did). These have
all of course passed over into the {-s} plural declension. A few other
alternations remain as well, e.g. those in *food* vs. *feed, blood* vs. *bleed*; but
these too are marginal.

To see the more important structural role that IU played in OE, we
must distinguish those cases where it is visible as the principle underwrit-
ing an alternation (as in *eald, ieldra*) from those where it is merely the
historical cause of an invariant vowel quality (e.g. *hierde* 'shepherd' <
*/xiurd-i/, where /-i/ is simply a noun-class marker). Only the former are
of interest here.

The following list gives some of the more important and typical
instances (more details in discussions of morphology in chapters 6–8).

A. Inflection

(i) Certain noun-classes had */i/-containing formatives in nom/acc pl and
dat sg: so *fōt* 'foot', gen sg *fōtes* but dat sg, nom/acc pl *fēt*. Similarly *tōþ*
'tooth', *bōc* 'book', *mann* 'man'.

(ii) /e/ > /i/ (the IU 'precursor', which can structurally be taken as part
of the umlaut system: cf. §2.6): this distinguishes pres 2, 3 sg of certain
classes of strong verbs from other parts of the present system: *beran* 'bear',
pres 2, 3 sg *bir(e)st, bir(e)ð*, similarly *weorpan* 'throw', pres 2 sg *wierpst*,
etc.

(iii) Some class I weak verbs show IU in the present but not the
preterite: *sellan* 'sell', pret 1, 3 *sealde* < */sal-jan, sal-ðα/: so IU of
*/æ/ < */α/ in the present, breaking of unmutated */æ/ in the past.
Similarly *þencan* 'think', pret *þōhte* < */θαnk-jan, θαnx-tα/, and the like.
Such verbs generally have heavy root syllables; with light-syllable roots a
connecting element */-i-/ is usual in the preterite: *nerian* 'save', pret
nerede < */nαr-jan, nαr-i-ðα/, with IU throughout the paradigm, and
hence vocalism indistinguishable from inherited */e/.

(iv) Comparatives and superlatives. These often show IU, due to the
suffixes */-ir-, -ist-/: *brād* 'broad', comp *brǣdra, eald/ieldra/ieldesta, grēat*
'great'/*grietra, strang* 'strong'/*strengra*, etc. Other adjectives did not have
these suffixes, and some are variable (see §6.3).

B. Derivation

(i) Deadjectival weak verbs (formed by */-jɑn/ suffixation from adjectives): *trymman* 'strengthen' (cf. *trum* 'strong') < */trum-jɑn/; likewise *cūþ* 'known'/*cỹþan* 'make known', *feorr* 'far'/*afierran* 'make distant'.

(ii) Denominal weak verbs (from noun roots): *blēdan* 'bleed' (cf. *blōd* 'blood'), < */βlo:ð-jɑn/, *ofost* 'haste'/*efstan* 'hasten', *fōd* 'food'/*fēdan* 'feed'.

(iii) Causative verbs formed from the pret sg root of strong verbs: e.g. *drǣfan* 'herd' < */ðrɑ:β-jɑn/ (cf. *drīfan* 'drive', pret 1, 3 sg *drāf*), *rǣran* 'rear' < */rɑ:s-jɑn/ (cf. *rīsan* 'rise', pret 1, 3 sg *rās*).

(iv) Denominal adjectives like *gylden* 'golden' < */ɣulð-in/ (cf. *gold* 'gold' < */ɣulθ-ɑ-/), *mennisc* 'human' < */mɑnn-isk-/ (cf. *mann*).

Some suffixes cause variable IU; thus *-ing* < */-inɣɑ/ in *earming*/*yrming* (< *ierming*) 'wretch' (*earm* 'poor, wretched'); for discussion of this and related matters see chapter 8.

3.9   The fricatives: voicing, devoicing, hardening and deletion[27]

3.9.1   OE /f, θ, s/

The symbols <f, þ/ð, s> in OE seem to have represented:

(i) Voiceless [f, θ, s]:
(a) Initially: *faran* 'fare'; *þencan* 'think'; *singan* 'sing'.
(b) Contiguous to another obstruent (including geminates): *æfter* 'after', *pyffan* 'puff'; *moþþe* 'moth'; *brēost* 'breast', *cyssan* 'kiss'.
(c) Finally: *wulf* 'wolf', *þēof* 'thief'; *āþ* 'oath', *fylþ* 'filth'; *ears* 'arse', *hūs* 'house'.
(ii) Voiced [v, ð, z]:
   Only intervocalically, under specific conditions: (a) a stressed vowel precedes, optionally followed by a liquid; (b) an unaccented vowel follows: *ofer* 'over', *wulfas* 'wolves'; *ōþer* 'other'; *hūsas* 'houses'. (This is of course the origin of the modern voice alternation in *wolf*/*wolves*, *house*/*houses*, etc.)

---

[27] The developments of the Germanic fricatives are treated at length in Lass & Anderson (1975: ch. 5): though we would now both withdraw some of the wilder suggestions there. For some problems in the analysis of the voice opposition as discussed below see Bammesberger (1988), and on the whole matter of the fricatives and their realizations Anderson (1988b).

So voiced and voiceless fricatives are in complementary distribution; this suggests three 'underlyingly' voiceless fricatives /f, θ, s/ (or perhaps three fricatives unspecified for voice), and a simple voicing rule of this general kind:

(3.40)
$$
\begin{bmatrix} f \\ \theta \\ s \end{bmatrix} \longrightarrow \begin{bmatrix} v \\ ð \\ z \end{bmatrix} \ / \ V \ (L) \ \_\_V
$$

Given the phonetic naturalness of voicing in such a context, it would be tempting to suppose that (3.40) simply mirrors the history: these fricatives were originally all voiceless, and at some point they voiced. But in fact many of the voiced medials reflect original voiced fricatives, and many of the voiceless finals derive from devoicing of voiced ones. Things are not as simple as they look, and some etymological investigation is in order.

Let us begin with OE /f/. Initially, it derives from IE */p/ via Grimm's Law (§2.3): for *faran* cf. OCS *perǫ* 'I fly', Gr *póros* 'ford'. Other familiar examples are *fæder* 'father' (L *pater*), *fisc* (L *piscis*). OE /f/ in clusters with another obstruent normally has the same source: *hæft* 'captive' = L *captus*; though it may also reflect later borrowing of L /ff/ (*offrian* 'offer' < L *offere*).

Medial [v] however has three quite different sources. One is PGmc */f/ < IE */p/ by Grimm's Law as above, but voiced by Verner's Law (§2.4). So *ofer* 'over', cognate to Gr *hupér*, Skr *upári* (= Go *ufar*, OHG *obar*). The OHG /b/ is due to hardening of *[β], which we assume the original output of Verner's Law must have been; this later becomes labiodental [v].

The second source is also IE */p/, but this time by a later, independent voicing younger than Verner's Law, and hardening to /b/. Examples are *hæfer* 'goat' (= L *caper* as in *Capricorn*), *hēafod* 'head' (cf. L *caput*). The motivation for positing a second voicing will be discussed below, after consideration of the other fricatives.

The third source of medial [v] is IE */bh/, which by Grimm's Law became *[β]. This hardened to a stop as well in certain positions, but remained a fricative in others: thus both *brecan* 'break' (cf. L *frēgī* 'I have broken', Skr *bhráj-* 'breaking through' < */bhre:g-/) and *lufian* 'love' (L *lubet* 'it pleases', Skr *lúbhyati* 'he desires' < */lubh-/) show reflexes of IE */bh/: a stop /b/ in the first case, and a voiced fricative [v] = OE /f/ in the second.

Final /f/ also represents both IE */p/ and */bh/. For */p/, *lāf* 'remnant' (cf. Toch *lip* 'remain over'), *hrif* 'belly' (as in *(mid)riff*: the same root in L *corpus* 'body', Skr *kṛp-* 'shape'). This is less common than */bh/, which in final position is devoiced and appears as /f/ in e.g. *lēof* 'dear' (same root as in *lufian*: OCS *ljubū* 'beloved', OHG *liob*), *turf* 'turf' (OHG *zurba*, Skr *dárbha* 'tuft of grass'). Many words in final /f/ seem to have no cognates outside Germanic, but OHG and other forms with final /b/ suggest ancestral *[β] from some source: OE *þēof* 'thief' (OHG *diob*), *drāf* 'he drove' (OHG *treib*).

To sum up this complex story: medial [v] in *ofer* is the result of an early voicing (Verner's Law); in *hæfer* it is from a later one; in *lufu* it is retention of an original voiced fricative. The initial [f] in *fisc* and the final one in *lāf* represent a Gmc voiceless fricative; the final [f] in *lēof* is from devoicing of an original voiced one.

The story of IE */t, dh/ is similar. For initial IE */t/ > /θ/ by Grimm's Law we have e.g. *þynn* 'thin' (cf. L *tenuis*). For non-initials, with Grimm's Law in all cases, Verner's Law in some, and the later voicing, we have the various forms of the verb *weorþan* 'become' (cf. discussion in §2.4). First the infinitive and e.g. pres 1, 3 sg *weorþe*, with [ð], and then pret pl *wurdon* with [d]. The [ð] in *weorþe* is from late voicing of *[θ], the [d] in *wurdon* from early voicing of [θ] > [ð] (Verner's Law), and then hardening. In final position we have [θ] < */t/ unchanged in pret 1, 3 sg *wearþ*. Initial */dh/ can be seen in *duru* 'door' (Gr *thúrā*), medial */dh/ in *medu* 'mead' (Skr *mádhu* 'sweet', Gr *méthus* 'wine'). In final position as well, the result is /d/: *lēod* 'people, nation' (OCS *ljudū* 'people', Gr *eleútheros* 'free').

We now have an indication of why there have to be two separate fricative voicings at different dates. In *wurdon* and the like original *[ð] from Verner's Law has gone to a stop; in fact all earlier *[ð], from whatever source, have hardened in all positions (unlike *[β], which did so only initially). Therefore the only possible source for an OE [ð] = /θ/ is voicing at some later point, after hardening is no longer productive. More on this below.

The story of */s/ is not so complex (since there is no hardening to stop or ancestral voiced fricative involved); though of course Verner's Law and rhotacism are complicating factors. For initial position, *seofon* 'seven' (L *septem*); for final *mūs* (L *mūs*). Medially, when the accent followed, we have VL and rhotacism: *curon* 'they chose' < *[kuzún] < *[kusún]. This new /r/ merges with original IE */r/ as in *herian* = Go *harjan*. With root accent and no VL or rhotacism, but only the later voicing, *cēosan* 'choose' (Go *kiusan*, OIc *kjósa*); intervocalic */s/ here goes to [z] after rhotacism.

This ties up the evidence for a second voicing, later than VL, rhotacism and hardening. The labials furnish no useful evidence, since hardening occurs only initially; but the dentals and */s/ require the later voicing. Consider what would happen if all voicing took place at the same time as

VL, and was complete before rhotacism and hardening, as in the ancestors of what have come down as *weorþan/wurdon*, *cēosan/curon*. In the display below, 'Misc' covers breaking, palatalization, etc. – all changes not relevant to this particular matter:

(3.41)	Input	wérθαn	wurθún	kíusαn	kusún
	Voicing	wérðαn	wurðún	kíuzαn	kuzún
	Accent-shift	–	wúrðun	–	kúzun
	Rhotacism	–	–	kíurαn	kúrun
	Hardening	wérdαn	wúrdun	–	–
	Misc.	wéordαn	wúrdon	tʃéorαn	kúron
	OE result	*weordan*	*wurdon*	*cēoran*	*curon*

Obviously then there was a second voicing, operative only after an accented syllable (precisely the opposite of Verner's Law). It must have been historically later than all the processes producing voiced fricatives originally. This seems to be the only way to prevent *weorþan* from having medial /d/ while ensuring that *wurdon* has it, and preventing *cēosan* from having medial /r/ while making sure that *curon* does. A simple rewriting of (3.41) with VL replacing 'voicing' and a voicing rule of the type (3.40) ordered after Hardening will give the proper results.

3.9.2   The velars

In all but the earliest texts, IE */k/ (> *PGmc /x/ by Grimm's Law) shows up written <h>: *heorte* 'heart' (L *cord-*), *eahta* 'eight' (L *octō*), *sulh* 'furrow' (L *sulc-us*). The Verner's Law results of course are different; I will come to them later. The handbooks agree that initial and non-initial <h> have different phonetic import: the consensus is that initial <h> means [h], and postvocalic <h> means velar [x] after back vowels and palatal [ç] after front vowels. OE then had the same kind of distribution of [h, x, ç] as German: cf. *hoch* 'high' [ho:x], *höchst* 'highest' [hø:çst]. Is this just an extrapolation from German by (German speaking) older OE scholars, or is there evidence?

There is, if not a great deal in OE itself. The earliest texts show some spelling asymmetry, suggesting different values in pre- and postvocalic positions. Thus 'night' in the eighth-century glossaries is not only *neht*, *naeht*, but also *nect*, *naecht*; similarly for 'through' (*þorh*, *þorch*), 'willow' (*salh*, *salch* = L *salix*). The <c, ch> spellings come only after vowels, and vary with <h>; initially there is only <h>. This suggests that while different values were predictable in different positions, the stronger or more occluded ones occurred only after vowels (<c> of course is the typical writing for a stop /k/). Later developments bear this out: in the sixteenth century initial [h] and postvocalic [x] are well described for London English (cf. Lass 1987: 30ff); and modern dialects that retain /x/ have what we posit for OE, e.g. Scots [h] in *hert*, but [x] in *nicht* [nɛxt ~ nɛçt].

The evidence for palatals after front vowels and velars after back is not conclusive for OE. Many WGmc dialects now do not have this kind of alternation, but only a velar [x] or uvular [χ] in all positions (Yiddish, varieties of Dutch and Afrikaans). But such a difference must have developed in English no later than say the thirteenth century; from then on we get original /x/ either deleting or becoming /f/ (as in *night* < *niht*, *rough* < *rūh* respectively); only the ones with preceding back vowels ever become /f/ (for more examples *high, sigh, fight* vs. *tough, trough*). Though ones with preceding back vowels may also delete (*bough, through*). Initial [h] and postvocalic [x] are well enough established for OE; [ç] is uncertain, but possible.

Synchronically then OE had a single fricative phoneme in the velar-to-glottal area, probably realized as [h] initially in the foot (before a stressed vowel: see chapter 4), and [x] or [x, ç] elsewhere. There was no independent /h/ phoneme; this did not develop until the loss of postvocalic /x/ sometime after 1600.

One way in which /x/ differs from /f, θ, s/ is in not having medial voiced allophones; OE had [ɣ] (see §3.7 and below), but not from this source. The reason for this is clear from the OE materials: single <h> does not occur between vowels, in the position where /f, θ, s/ are subject to voicing. We find <h> = /x/ initially and postvocalically; but in the latter case, only in the coda of a final syllable. Medially we get only <hh> (*hlæhhan* 'laugh' < */xlɑx-jɑn/). The simplest explanation is that medial single /x/ must have deleted at some point prior to voicing.

Indeed, there is both comparative and internal evidence for this. Compare for example OE *slēan* 'strike, slay' with OHG *slahan*, or *sēon* 'see' with OHG *sehan*. Medial /x/ has dropped in OE, leaving behind a heavy nucleus instead of the expected short vowel; but it's also clear that the diphthongs are the kind one would expect from breaking (which means that this deletion must come after breaking). The histories would be:

(3.42) | Input | slɑxɑn | sexɑn |
AFB	slæxɑn	–
Breaking	slæ̆uxɑn	sĕuxɑn
DHH	slæ̆ɑxɑn	sĕoxɑn
/x/-deletion	slæ̆ɑɑn	sĕoɑn
'Contraction'	slæɑn	seon
OE form	*slēan*	*sēon*

('Contraction' is a loose cover-term for processes including the loss of the infinitive vowel /ɑ/ and lengthening of the nucleus.)

The environment for /x/ deletion, interestingly, is precisely the same as that for voicing of /f, θ, s/: even to the extent of allowing an optional preceding liquid (*seolh* 'seal', gen sg *sēoles*, *mearh* 'horse', gen sg *mēares*). This suggests that the two processes are really one: both are weakenings, but that of /x/ (the weakest obstruent category) has gone a step further, to complete loss.[28]

Looking again at *slēan*, we note that its pret pl is *slōgon*, and its pp *slǣgen/slagen*; similarly *flēan* 'flay' (*flōgon*), *gefēon* 'rejoice' (*gefǣgon*). That is (cf. *weorþan/wurdon*), these verbs show Verner's Law as expected, with original */x/ producing */ɣ/, which remains as [ɣ] (*slōgon*) or palatalizes to [j] (*gefǣgon*: cf. §3.7).

Now [ɣ] is of course also the Grimm's Law output of IE */gh/: *gōs* 'goose' (Gr *khḗn*, Skr *haṁsa-* < */ghɑns-/); *hagol* 'hail' (Gr *kákhlēks* 'pebble' < */kɑgh-/), *beorg* 'hill' (Skr *bṛhánt* 'high', MIr *brig* < */bṛgh-/). (As an etymological aid, IE */bh, dh, gh/ devoice in Greek to voiceless aspirates; */bh, dh/ generally remain in Sanskrit, but */gh/ most often goes to /h/.)

This [ɣ] apparently remains into early OE, and hardens in some positions only to [g] (e.g. initially). Finally however it seems never to become a stop, but remains a fricative, whether plain or palatalized to /j/. In later WS it is subject to variable final devoicing: *beorg/beorh*, etc. This devoicing is apparently later than that of *[β] < */bh/ as in *lēof* (§3.9.1); the <h> spellings are never exclusive, and appear much later than <f> spellings for older *[β] (see §3.9.3). The claim that *[ɣ] never hardened to [g] in final position may seem to be contradicted by ModE words like *frog*, *egg*, *jig*; but these are either from OE geminates (OE *frogga*), Scandinavian loans (OSc *egg*), or from Romance (OF *gigue*).

3.9.3 Fricative hardening and its consequences

The hardening of */β, ð, ɣ/ in certain positions resulted in (among other things) the restoration of a voiced stop system, which was lacking in PGmc and WGmc (see displays (2.10), (2.14)). But there were some striking distributional asymmetries, due to the non-uniform implementation of hardening, which resulted in some new types of alternation. These developments were largely laid out in the last two sections; but the

---

[28] It is not unusual for one positional class in a system to be weaker than others: e.g. in Finnish 'gradation' (consonant-weakening) /p/ > /v/ (*tupa* 'living room', gen sg *tuvan*), /t/ > /d/ (*mato* 'worm', gen sg *madon*) but /k/ generally goes to zero (*joki* 'river', *joen*) or the approximant /j/ (*jalka* 'leg', *jaljen*). For further discussion, see Lass & Anderson (1975: 183ff).

patterns were buried in a mass of detail, and at least one aspect – the treatment of geminates and nasal clusters – was not discussed. I will sum up here and add this new material.

(i) */β/ > /b/ initially (*brecan*); medially and finally it remained a fricative, voiced in the first instance (*lufu*), voiceless in the second (*leof*). Medially it falls in with the output of Verner's Law voicing of */f/. Geminate */ββ/ uniformly hardened to /bb/ (*hebban* 'raise' < */xaβ-jɑn/). After nasals the result was /b/ as well: *cemban* 'comb' < */kamβ-jɑn/. (It is at least possible that IE */bh/ after nasals never went through a fricative stage, but was [b] from the beginning; though it would still have been phonemically */β/. The same may be true of */dh, gh/.) Thus by OE, /b/ occurred only initially, after nasals, and in gemination.

(ii) */ð/ > /d/ in all positions: initially (*dæg*), medially (*medu*), finally (*hrēod* 'reed'), in gemination (*hreddan* 'rescue' < */xrɑð-jɑn/), and after nasals (*findan* 'find'). So OE /d/ had a full distribution.

(iii) */γ/ > [g] initially (*gōs*); medially and finally it remained a fricative well into OE times, though subject of course to palatalization. So velar [γ] in *dagas, dagum, beorg* 'hill' (in the latter case variably devoiced, leading to merger with /x/), palatal [j] in *dæg, dæges*. In gemination it became a stop, either velar (*frogga*) or palatal (*secgan* 'say' < */sɑγ-jɑn/).[29] After nasals it also became a stop, again either velar (*singan* 'sing') or palatal (*sengean* 'singe').

These developments led to a wide-ranging restructuring, at least of the labial series. By OE times, the situation was as follows: [v] < */β/ (of whatever source) occurred only medially; it was therefore in alternation with initial and final [f]. On the other hand, [b] occurred only initially, after nasals, and geminate. This led to an obvious phonemic reassignment: [v] was interpreted as an allophone of /f/, and /b/ became an independent phoneme. This seems to have been rather late; there is still some hesitation in the early texts about how to spell [v]. The glossaries for example often use <b> to represent what is later uniformly spelled <f>: the Epinal Glossary has *hræbn* 'raven', *uuibil* 'weevil', *salb* 'salve', later *hræfn, wifol, sealf*. On the other hand, Epinal also has <f>: *sifunsterri* 'Pleiades' (i.e. 'seven-stars'), *ifge* 'ivy' (normal later spellings *seofon, ifig*). There is also a possibly interesting spelling *nabfogar* 'auger' (later *nafo-*), which may illustrate a hesitation between the older and newer modes of spelling (or may be a scribal error, though I don't think so).

The result of this restructuring is, aside from the [f, v] allophony of /f/, a morphophonemic alternation between /bb/ and /f/ in medial and final

---

[29] Velar geminates of course are never from WGG, since the following */j/ would give palatals, not velars.

position. So *hebban* 'raise', pret 1, 3 sg *hōf* < */xαβ-jαn, xo:β/*; likewise *habban* 'have', pres 3 sg *hafað*, pret 1, 3 sg *hæfde*.

With the dentals the picture is much simpler, since hardening of */ð/ occurred everywhere. Morphophonemically, there are alternations with /θ/ via Verner's Law, as expected (*weorþan/wurdon*, etc.). Early texts show some <d> spellings for /θ/ as well: e.g. *modgidanc* 'thought' from an early version of Cædmon's Hymn, rather than the other possibilities at this time, <-*þanc, -ðanc, -thanc*> The problem in this case is an unsettled orthography, not (as with the labials) an uncertain phonemic interpretation; there was never any doubt about the /θ/:/d/ distinction. There may also be some Continental influence here, since */θ/ had gone to /d/ in Old Low Franconian and Old High German. I mention this just to suggest (if there's any need at this stage) that nothing historical is very simple, and that what are apparently two instances of the same thing may not be.

The velars show a pattern like that of the labials: *[γ] from Verner's Law remains a fricative, spelled <g> (*slōgon*, cf. §3.9.2), as does *[γ] < */gh/ medially and finally (*dagas, dæg*). Initially, after nasals, and in gemination, the result is a stop [g] (*gōs, singan, frogga*), or a palato-alveolar affricate [dʒ(:)] (*mycg, sengean*). In historical OE then, [g, γ, j] can generally be interpreted as allophones of one phoneme, perhaps best characterized as /g/; though there is of course an independent phonemic /j/ (before back vowels) as in *geong* 'young' /jung/.

We have now dealt with all the OE fricatives except /ʃ/, which arose later than the developments considered here, and was not subject to any further change, e.g. voicing. The voiced palato-alveolar fricative /ʒ/ does not in fact appear in English until the seventeenth century, from palatalization of /zj/, as in *vision*. The histories discussed above finally led (along with other changes like palatalization) to the formation of an OE obstruent system of this kind:

(3.43)   p   t   tʃ   k
          b   d   dʒ   g
          f θ s   ʃ   x

(Most could appear geminate as well, but not /ʃ/.)

By historical times the /j/ from Gmc */j/ and palatalization of */γ/ had probably lost its friction, and could be considered a member of the liquid system, along with /r, l, w/.

3.9.4   Appendix: 'Palatal Diphthongization'

The scare-quotes in the heading indicate a controversy. According to the general scholarly tradition, the <ie> spellings in *scieran* 'shear', *giefan* 'give', and the <ea> spellings in *sceaft* 'shaft', *scēap* 'sheep' indicate just what they seem to: diphthongs, long or short according to the etymological length of their ancestors. These result from a sound change called **Palatal Diphthongization** (sometimes 'Diphthongization by Initial Palatals').

The controversy is whether there was indeed such a sound change, or whether these digraph spellings are a purely orthographic matter, with no phonological import. The majority view is that Palatal Diphthongization (PD) was a genuine change; but a vociferous minority (mainly Stockwell & Barritt 1951, 1955, Lass & Anderson 1975: Appendix III, Colman 1985) take the view that it is spurious. In the past decade and a half I have found no reason to change my mind.

In West Saxon (especially) there are numerous instances of digraph spellings, supposedly indicating diphthongs, where single-letter representations would be expected, as in:

(i) <ie> for <e>: *scieran, giefan, gielpan* 'boast';
(ii) <īe> for <ē>: *gīet* 'yet', *gīe* 'ye' (poetical);
(iii) <ea> for <æ>: *sceaft, sceal* 'shall', *geat* 'gate';
(iv) <ēa> for <ǣ>: *scēap, cēace* 'jaw', *gēar* 'year'.

(Length-marking here is an etymological indicator: OIc *skera* 'shear', OHG *scāf* 'sheep', etc.)

The standard view is that palatals – whether original Gmc */j/ or the new /tʃ, j, ʃ/ – caused diphthongization of following nonhigh front vowels. There are a number of problems with this.

First, lack of phonetic motivation. If indeed the outputs of PD are what they seem to be, we have a very peculiar situation with <ea>. Here the same diphthong is produced from the same vowel in palatal environments as is produced by totally different changes in back environments. Thus the <ea> in *sceaft* < */ʃæft/ is due to the palatal acting on /æ/, whereas the <ea> in *seah* 'he saw' < */sæx/ is due to the influence of back /x/ (breaking), and that in *ealu* 'ale' < */ælu/ is due to the back vowel /u/ (back umlaut). The same process is initiated by preceding palatals and following velars. It seems difficult to have it both ways; and anyhow, why should palatals diphthongize front vowels? We might expect, if anything, that they would do it to back ones. Breaking and back umlaut appear to be assimilations; it's not easy to decide what PD might be.

More (or as) significantly, similar spellings occur in other environments, where diphthongization is never suggested. 'Odd' <e> or <i>, when a back vowel graph follows, are normally treated as diacritics indicating the palatality of the consonant preceding. Nobody supposes that there is a diphthong in *geong* 'young', or in the second syllables of *fisceas* 'fish' (nom/acc pl) or *lufigean* 'love' (common variants of *fiscas, lufian*). Here <e> is always taken as a palatal diacritic.

Now such a treatment makes considerable sense in a case like *geong*; if it were written **gong* the temptation would be to read it as /gong/. Therefore <geo-> says: 'read <ge-> as /j/', or <ge-> is simply a complex graph that means /j/, just as <æ> means a low front vowel and not a diphthong /ɑe/. But if this is accepted practice, why should <e> appear in the other cases, and why should we get the particular digraphs we do? Stockwell & Barritt proposed an elegant and ingenious totally orthographic argument, which I find convincing. Let us assume that the 'ideal' spelling for palatals involves <e> as a class-marker, i.e. that /j/ should be spelled <ge>, /ʃ/ should be spelled <sce>, and /tʃ/ should be spelled <ce>. This is the fundamental principle of WS palatal/velar writing.

But like all orthographies, WS had its own special conventions; one of them, borne out by all the data, is a prohibition against trigraphs. Now take *geat*: this should in principle be written **<geæt>, since <ge> is the ideal writing for /j/, and the stressed nucleus is /æ/ (cf. OIc *gat* 'hole'). This however would fall foul of the trigraph prohibition as <æ> is transparently <a + e> (many early scribes in fact write <ae>). Now since the /æ/:/ɑ/ contrast is only partial (§3.5), and in many places the two are in complementary distribution, one way out of the bind is to write <ea>, with the provision that here <a> represents /æ/. (In the diphthongs, remember, it means /ɑ/; and in fact the writing <ea> for /æɑ/ can be explained on the same grounds: **<æa> violates the trigraph constraint.) So in words of the relevant type, <ea> stands for /æ/ preceded by a palatal.

Similarly, to indicate palatality before /e/, the natural or ideal choice would again be <e>; but this would lead to **<geefan> for 'give', violating another easily deducible constraint: no digraphs consisting of two identical elements are allowed either.[30] Here the graph of choice was (quite naturally) <i>, giving <ie>, which is the norm for /e/ after palatals (*giefan, scieran*). And later results (ME *yeve(n)* 'give', ModE *yelp* < *gielpan*) suggest that nothing phonetic actually happened to the nuclear vowels.

In other words, so-called 'Palatal Diphthongization' is really 'Post-Palatal Digraphy'. A summary of the conditions producing the attested spellings:

---

[30] Some scribal traditions do permit occasional double-vowel spellings, e.g. <oo> in *good* 'good'; but (a) rarely, and (b) only for long monophthongs.

(i) <ge>, <ce>, <sce> are writings of choice for palatals.

(ii) No trigraph spellings are allowed, and <æ> is a digraph.

(iii) <gea>, <cea->, <scea->, then, because *<geæ->, *<ceæ->, *<sceæ-> are not allowed.

(iv) No digraph spelling <V$_i$V$_i$> is allowed.

(v) <gie->, <cie->, <scie->, then, because *<gee->, *<cee->, *<scee-> are not allowed.

A similar interpretation applies to the spelling of historical /ju/ as <geo>: the sequence <eu> was also not allowed by the orthographical rules. <gu>, which was allowed, would indicate a velar; hence <ge> to show a palatal before a back vowel, and <o> because <eu> is illegal.

I find this a delicious argument, since everything follows from two premises which are necessary in any case: there are no trigraphs or double-vowel graphs in WS (simple empirical fact), and <e> is often used to show that a preceding consonant-graph is palatal (low-level inference). Of such things is history often made.

Lest it be thought that this is just a clever ploy to get rid of an undesirable sound change, and nothing else, it's worth pointing out that this kind of arbitrariness is not uncommon. Spelling systems are notoriously prone to outlaw things for no apparent reason. Modern English for instance has an irrational prohibition of <v> in final position: hence the 'meaningless' <e> at the end of *love*, which looks as if it ought to rhyme with *prove* or *grove*. (And hence the 'eye-dialect' device of writing *luv* – which couldn't indicate anything else than one's normal pronunciation of *love* – to show that a speaker is non-standard.) Or consider the refusal of Swedish to write <kk> for geminate /k:/, whereas all other consonants can be written double: *hemma* 'at home', *tvätta* 'to wash', but *vacker* 'beautiful', not **vakker*. The actual positive argument for PD as a sound change is a very intricate one, based entirely on one word: late WS *cȳse* 'cheese'. The claim is that this form presupposes the existence of a genuine phonetic diphthong; the chain of argument is worth looking at, as it too has its merits, and the problem it raises is an important one for historians.

The origin of this word is apparently Latin *cāseus*. If this is so, then lWS /y:/ is difficult. There are two sources for /y:/: one is *i*-umlaut of **/u:/, and the other is late monophthongization of <ie> /iy/, as in *hȳran* 'hear' < *hīeran*. *Cȳse* must therefore go back to an unattested eWS **cīese*, since there is no reasonable way to get a **/u:/ into the etymological sequence. And the only way this could arise is by a sequence that begins with **/kɑ:si/*, and includes fronting to **/kæ:si/*, palatalization to **/tʃæ:si/*, PD to **/tʃæusi/*, DHH to **/tʃæɑsi/*, *i*-umlaut to **/tʃiysi/*, with later lowering of final /i/, giving */tʃiyse/, which would of course be spelled *<ciese> – if it happened to survive. And of course eWS */tʃiyse/ would give late WS /tʃy:se/, which would be spelled <cyse>; and this is what does appear.

Now if *cȳse* really meant /tʃy:se/ and had survived, it would have given *chyse or *chise /tʃaɪz/; and no such form is attested anywhere. But aside from this, how good really is the above argument, as the only solid support for PD as a sound change? It would seem to be utterly convincing for this one word; but it is not needed anywhere else. As Stockwell & Barritt (1955: 382f) say, 'if *cȳse* is a test case, it is a curiously circular one, since no matter how often it appears in the MSS, it is an isolated item which has no etymological parallels throughout every stage of its reconstruction'. They add a crucial methodological point:

Unique etymologies are not ordinarily used to establish sound laws if the sound laws thus established contradict laws which are needed to describe a set of nonunique items.

They further note that L *cāseus* and WS *cȳse* are the only attested relevant forms; by and large the other Gmc dialects either show straight *i*-umlaut of */ɑ:/ as in G *Käse* < OHG *kāsi*, or no significant change, as in Dutch *kaas* /ka:s/; and that we often do get divergent developments from a single ancestor, sometimes unique ones. We summed it up this way in Lass & Anderson (1975: 222):

There are . . . clearly such things as exceptional items in languages, and it is fallacious to assume that every word has an 'etymology' in the usual sense . . . It is even more fallacious to set up . . . a phonological process . . . which is actually needed for one item only, and then extrapolate this to the entire history of the language.

This is rather a simplification; it would be instructive to read the monuments in the debate, as laid out in Lass & Anderson (1975: 279ff), going back to the original texts.

The important thing is that *cȳse* is a problem, and we all recognize it as one; but there is often nothing to do but leave problems hanging about until someone comes up with a good solution, i.e. to recognize them as 'anomalies', and wait until (maybe) a general explanation comes up that can subsume them as special cases.

4   Suprasegmentals

4.1   Suprasegmentals

In contemporary usage the term 'suprasegmental' refers among other things to syllable-structure, quantity, tone, and stress. The conceptual theme uniting these is structural: they seem to be best represented in terms of independent structures larger than (though incorporating) segments, and relations other than simple linear sequence. To illustrate: we could (as is often done) think of stress in a purely segmental way: as a property of vowels. So we might say that *suspicion* is 'a word stressed on its penultimate vowel'. But it makes better sense to call it 'a three-syllable word with penultimate stress', because this is the case regardless of the number of vowels a given version of the word happens to have. Consider three increasingly casual and rapid pronunciations: in the first, all segments are given 'full' value; in the second the vowel in the last syllable is deleted, leaving a syllabic /n/; in the third the vowel in the first syllable is deleted, leaving a syllabic /s/ (stress marked with an acute):

(4.1)   səspíʃən → səspíʃn̩ → s̩spíʃn̩
       1   2   3

The vowel count decreases from three to two to one; but both the number of syllables and the location of the main stress remain constant. If the stress was indeed on the penultimate vowel, version (2) would be *[sə́spɪʃn̩] – which it isn't. Thus the syllable is an autonomous unit, independent to some extent of the segments it happens to be made of.

Similarly, quantity or syllable-weight is best thought of as involving higher-level constructs: in the model of syllable structure outlined in §3.2, the configuration of the rhyme – not the segments making it up – defines heavy vs. light syllables. The higher-level constructions that the syllable-parts enter into are what count, and the syllable itself, as a 'layered' or hierarchical construct.

So there is phonological structure beyond or 'above' simple sequences of consonants and vowels; the representations of choice are, to use the current term, **nonlinear**.[1] Talking about syllables or stress involves more than one level or **tier** of representations:

(4.2)

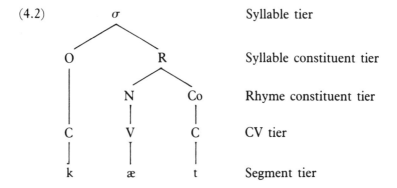

There is (see §4.2) even more structure than this. But (4.2) illustrates the basic construal here of 'suprasegmental': a general name for phenomena in whose description we need recourse to levels of structure 'above' the segment.

4.2   Germanic stress and Old English stress

4.2.1   *Stress rules and 'degrees of stress'*[2]

In many (most?) languages with stress systems these are (largely) rule-governed; some general principle assigns major prominence to a particular syllable in some domain – most often the word. What 'prominence' is may vary from language to language; a stressed or accented syllable may be louder, longer, different in pitch from an unaccented one, may show pitch-movement where unaccented syllables are static, or any combination. In standard Finnish, for instance, the first stressed syllable of a word is louder than any other(s) and shows a slight pitch-rise; in many varieties of English it is higher, louder, and longer; in Danish it is lower, louder, and longer. What counts is that the accented syllable is perceptually distinct from the others, in a way that can be interpreted as 'salient'.

[1] For an excellent textbook introduction to the basic concepts of nonlinear phonology, see Katamba (1989: chs. 9–11).
[2] There is a good introductory account of the concept of stress and its representation involved here in Katamba (1989: ch. 11); for more advanced treatments see Giegerich (1985: ch. 1), Hogg & McCully (1987).

Where prominence is not associated primarily with pitch-movement or level, but with loudness and/or length, we generally talk of a 'stress-accent' (or simply stress), as opposed to a 'pitch-accent'. I will use 'stress' to refer to prominence in languages built like English, and 'accent', as a general term, especially but not exclusively in reference to languages where pitch plays a major role (as in Greek or Sanskrit: see below).

Languages with stress systems tend to organize their rhythmic structure in terms of units now customarily called **feet**; a **foot** is a phrase-like construction whose head is a stressed syllable, which may be accompanied by some number of unstressed 'satellite' syllables. In Germanic, feet are left-strong; they consist of a strong or stressed syllable (s), followed by zero to two (or in exceptional cases perhaps three) unstressed or weak syllables (w).

A stress rule may be seen as a device which takes as input a string of phonological elements (with or without morphosyntactic specification – this depends on the language), and assigns the labels s, w to syllables. In other words, it constructs feet according to some predefined recipe.

I will assume for this chapter a rather oversimplified reductionist 'metrical' model, where the sole basic elements are the prominence-labels s, w. Here 'stressedness' is a purely relational and binary notion; s, w are relations holding between adjacent syllables (or as we'll see, feet and larger elements as well). Thus a foot will be minimally of the form s w, as in ModE:

(4.3)

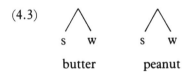

If the relation must hold between adjacent elements, then trisyllabic feet would have an extra layer of prominence relations; compare

(4.4)

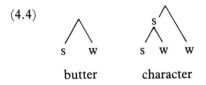

The claim is that *char-* is stronger than *-ac-*, and that in turn the group *charac-* is stronger than *-ter*. (The difference in complexity between di- and trisyllabic feet is historically relevant, as we will see in §4.3.)

But what about monosyllables? If s, w are purely relational terms (a syllable is only stressed in relation to another one), then what could a stressed monosyllable be? One answer is to claim that the minimal foot is always s w, and that if there is only a strong syllable, this is so by contrast to an 'unrealized' or 'empty' zero-syllable.[3] So:

(4.5)

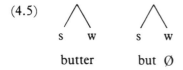

        s   w   s   w

    butter   but Ø

One motivation for this derives from the durational properties of these or similar pairs like *wood/wooden*, *would/wouldn't*, *have/hafta*, etc. The disyllable is roughly the same length as the monosyllable, but its stressed vowel is shorter than that of the monosyllable. In a **stress-timed** language like English or German (and we assume Old English), the basic timing-unit, the foot, has a certain 'ideal' duration. The 'zero' then is a piece of unused material in the monosyllable, but is filled in the disyllable, and may be filled by certain processes when two monosyllables come together, as in negative cliticization in ModE:

(4.6)

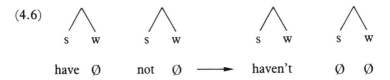

    s   w   s   w   s   w   s   w

    have Ø   not Ø ⟶ haven't   Ø   Ø

(A foot with no material under either s or w has no phonetic interpretation, i.e. 'deletes'.)

This s, w notation is fine for describing cases where there is only one stressed syllable; but what about 'secondary stress', as in a compound like *peanut-butter*, where both members are s w, but the first as a whole is more prominent than the second as a whole? A conventional notation might be *péanut-bùtter*; but this implies that primary (´) and secondary (`) stress are somehow different categories. Yet they are intuitively 'degrees of' the same one. A useful approach is to take secondary stress as 'subordinated' stress. Say for instance that in addition to a rule assigning stress at the level of the simplex word, there is a rule operating at a higher level: crudely,

---

[3] For the zero-syllable see Giegerich (1985). This notion grows out of a long tradition of taking rhythmic structure to contain significant but 'silent' elements (see e.g. Abercrombie 1964). This notion is far from standardly accepted in current theory; I am using it here mainly as an expository device, and little hinges on any 'serious' theoretical import.

this rule, applying 'after' word-stress, says that a compound (whatever its
constituent elements and their stress patterns) is itself s w. So:

(4.7)

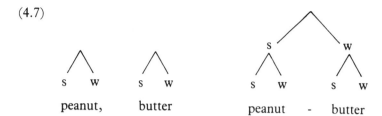

peanut,   butter   peanut - butter

This notation also enables us to distinguish between the overall compound
stress pattern s w and the phrasal stress pattern w s, as in *rancid butter*:

(4.8)

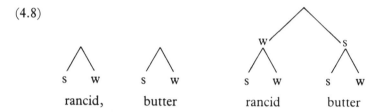

rancid,   butter   rancid   butter

We can now turn to the origin and nature of the OE stress system.

4.2.2   The Germanic Stress Rule[4]

It is not entirely clear what kind of accentual system PIE had; but the
evidence from Sanskrit and Greek suggests that the main correlate of
prominence in the earlier stages may have been pitch-salience. The
primary word accent in Sanskrit is described by the ancient grammarians
as *udātta svara* 'raised tone'; Greek grammarians used the term *tónos* 'tone',
and described the main accent as *oksús* 'sharp, acute'. The Greek tradition
also recognized *barús* 'heavy, grave' and *perispomenon* 'circumflex'. Latin
on the other hand appears to have had an accent defined primarily by
amplitude rather than pitch (cf. Allen 1965: 84, quoting one grammarian
who describes the accented syllable as that *quae plus sonat* 'which sounds
louder').

PIE accent seems to have been determined mainly by lexical and
morphosyntactic categories (cf. §2.4). Such systems, where phonology
proper plays a minimal role, are still visible in some of the ancient dialects,

---

[4] For detailed discussion of Proto-Germanic accent, see Bennett (1972); On the IE accent see
Szemerényi (1989: §V.2), which also has an exhaustive bibliography.

e.g. Sanskrit. Greek also retains an accent roughly of this kind, but – as in later Latin – there is a new type of constraint defined by word-edges. In both Latin and Greek the position of the accent is ultimately controlled by the 'three-syllable rule'; the accent may be no further to the left (from the end of the word) than the antepenult.

The Classical Latin system is a late development (the original IE accentuation first became initial-stress in Old Latin); but it is worth looking at briefly for typological comparison with the Germanic one. In Latin the three-syllable rule applied, as in Greek; but in addition syllable weight was an important determinant of accent placement. A simplified version, but adequate for our purposes:[5]

(i) Final syllables in Latin, unless they are the only syllable in the word (in which case they are accented by default), are **extrametrical**. That is, they are outside the domain of accent-assignment, 'invisible' to the accentuation rule.[6] Therefore any disyllabic word, regardless of the weight of the first syllable, will be initial-accented: *régō* (ŏσ̄) 'I rule', *rēxī* (σ̄σ̄) 'I have ruled'.

(ii) In polysyllables, accent the penult if it is heavy: *amícus* 'friend', *magíster* 'master' (σ̄σ̄σ̄). Otherwise accent the antepenult, regardless of weight: *ténebrae* (σ̄σ̄σ̄) 'darkness', *príncipis* (σ̄σ̄σ̄) 'prince' (gen sg).[7]

This rule has three typological features that are diametrically opposed to the new Germanic system, and the later and more complex OE one:

(i) The Latin rule is 'right-handed'; the position of accent is calculated from the right-hand edge of the word.
(ii) It is quantity-sensitive; accent is attracted to heavy syllables.
(iii) It is insensitive to morphology: the labelling of the accented syllable (root or suffix, etc.) is generally irrelevant.

The **Germanic Stress Rule** (GSR) on the contrary was:

(i) left-handed: the first syllable of the word was generally accented.
(ii) insensitive to quantity: either light or heavy syllables could be accented, with no preference (but see below).

---

[5] The now classic source on Greek and Latin accentuation is Allen (1973); simpler treatments can be found in any reliable Greek or Latin grammar.
[6] For discussion of extrametricality see Hogg & McCully (1987: §3.6).
[7] Latin syllabification is assumed to be 'onset-maximal', i.e. /VCV/ is syllabified as /V.CV/, and in general /VCCV/ as /VC.CV/. Unlike Germanic, Latin counts /-VC/ rhymes as heavy (but see discussion below).

(iii) ultimately sensitive to morphology: initial syllables were generally (but see below for special cases) not stressed if they were prefixes. (A late development, as we will see in the next section, but probably relevant as early as NWGmc.)

(On the role of syllable weight in suprasegmental phenomena other than stress see §4.6.) The ModE system is actually based on something closer to the Latin than the GSR pattern; this is due to the huge influx of Latin and Greek loans into English that began during late OE and reached enormous proportions in ME.[8]

The GSR, whose implementation constitutes the Accent-Shift discussed in §2.4, can be informally stated as follows:

(4.9)   *Germanic Stress Rule*
          (a) Starting at the left-hand edge of the word, construct a binary s w foot.
          (b) Add at most one additional w.

Examples of one-, two- and three-syllable words:

(4.10)

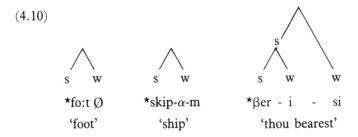

s w	s w	s w w
*fo:t Ø	*skip-α-m	*βer - i - si
'foot'	'ship'	'thou bearest'

The provisions of (4.9) cover virtually all PGmc stress in non-compound words; roots of more than one syllable were rare, as were suffixes of more than two syllables, or non-compound words of more than three.[9] For compounds and complex dervied forms of more than three syllables, we assume that stress was handled by (4.9) and a **Compound Stress Rule** (CSR), which was in effect a reiteration of the GSR at a higher level, after

---

[8] Alternatively, we could probably say (more accurately, perhaps) that ModE has 'a dual system for native + nativized vocabulary vs. Latinate vocabulary' (Dieter Kastovsky, personal communication).

[9] As far as I know, all suffixes of more than one syllable in Germanic are morphologically complex in one way or another. E.g. the */-i-si/ in */βer-i-si/ has a thematic vowel (see §6.1) plus an ending, the */-o:jα-n/ (OE -ian) in the infinitive of class II weak verbs (§7.3.2) consists of two derivational markers and a neuter nom sg inflection.

determination of word-stress. In other words, a sequence of s w feet was itself marked s w, provided it met certain morphosyntactic conditions:

(4.11)   *Compound Stress Rule*
For any sequence [ₓ A, B], where X is a lexical category (Noun, Verb, Adjective, Adverb), A is strong and B is weak.

Compound stress assignment then is two-layered:

(4.12)
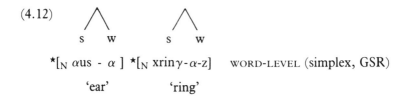

*[N αus - α] *[N xrinγ-α-z]   WORD-LEVEL (simplex, GSR)

'ear'   'ring'

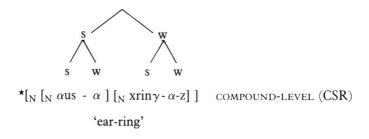

*[N [N αus - α] [N xrinγ - α-z]]   COMPOUND-LEVEL (CSR)

'ear-ring'

It may be doubtful whether there was in fact such a PGmc compound; Go *ausa-hriggs*, OE *ēar-hring* do not by themselves prove it, as the compound might well have been reinvented time and again (see chapter 8). But there undoubtedly were PGmc compounds of this type, and if this one did exist, it would have been stressed more or less in this way.

This account, while in essence (if not notation) traditional, is not the only possible one. A quite different view of Old English and early Germanic stress is argued by Dresher & Lahiri (1991), and following them, Stockwell & Minkova (Forthcoming). They posit an innovative and characteristic 'Germanic foot', in which the strong syllable is always heavy. (In their theoretical framework, only heavy syllables are stressable, and therefore /-VC/ is heavy: see below.) One primary piece of evidence for this is the behaviour of word-internal /-VC/ rhymes in verse, where they appear – contrary to the model suggested here – to attract secondary stress. E.g. *Hengestes* 'Hengest's' scans *Héngèstes*, not *Héngestes* as the stress-rule given here would imply.[10] In this analysis, it is only at the end of the OE period that the 'Germanic foot' decays, and the type of structure I suggest here first appears.

Such a view, though supported by metrical evidence, raises a number of problems. From a methodological point of view, it is synchronically over-complex, in that all final /-VC/ syllables are stressed in the first instance by the stress rule, and then have to be 'defooted' so that they surface unstressed.[11] Stockwell & Minkova further claim that /-VC/ is heavy 'on universal moraic-theoretic grounds'; but this is untrue. In North Germanic languages (except Danish), /-VC/ patterns with /-V/, not with /-VV, -VCC/; in these languages /-V, -VC/ cannot be the strong syllable of a foot. And in the course of the 'Scandinavian Quantity Shift' (Árnason 1980), /-VC/ rhymes in stressed positions became either /-V:C/ or /-VC:/ (cf. Lass 1984a: §10.3.2). So it is at least arguable that Germanic has a tendency to treat /-VC/ as light; despite the strong arguments to the contrary I will retain this analysis here.[12]

4.2.3 Old English stress

Given the mass of information available (metrical, comparative, historical), the OE stress system appears somewhat more complex than the original Gmc one, as far as we can recover that. In particular, a number of historical developments introduced an element of morphological conditioning.

Old English generally has initial stress; but not simply word-initial, as was probably the case in at least early PGmc. Rather the operative version of the GSR might best be described as 'root-accent': stress falls on the first syllable of a simplex word, but on the first syllable of the lexical root in morphologically complex words whose first element is a prefix. The OE version of the GSR appears to 'skip' certain kinds of prefixes.

[10] Important as metrical evidence is, it must be used with caution (cf. Lucas 1987). Verse practice may reflect extremely archaic features that are not part of 'the structure of the language' at a given time, or may be idiosyncratic and in some cases based on scholarly theories that in fact run counter to actual linguistic structure, as in the attempts by Elizabethan poets like Campion to write Latin-style 'quantitative' verse in English. If indeed there was a 'Germanic foot', and if the analysis of verse suggesting accentuation like *Héngèstes* are correct, then it may be that the quantity-insensitive stress-rule I suggest here is in fact not 'Germanic' but a later development. But I do not see it as operative in post-NWGmc times.
[11] Any synchronic analysis that 'overgenerates' (produces material that is ill-formed at the 'surface') in such a way that the effects of a rule have to be 'undone' in order to get the correct final output is to my mind unacceptable.
[12] That /-VC/ is light is assumed as well in Hogg (1992b). For further counterarguments, and a well-motivated attack on at least some of my positions, see McCully (1992).

As a first illustration, OE has a good number of prefix doublets, where the same Gmc prefix appears in two forms, one stressed and the other unstressed (and often phonologically reduced as well). A partial list, with typical examples and stress indicated:

(4.13)

Original	Stressed	Unstressed
*/ɑf-/	ǽf-þànca 'offence'	of-þýncan 'displease'
*/ɑnɑ-/	án-gìnn 'beginning'	on-gínnan 'begin'
*/ɑnð-/	ánd-sàca 'apostate'	on-sácan 'deny'
*/inn-/	ín-stæ̀þe 'entrance'	in-stǽppan 'enter'
*/unθ-/	úþ-gènge 'evanescent'	oþ-gā́n 'escape'
*/βi:-/	bí-gènga 'inhabitant'	be-gā́n 'occupy'
*/wiθɑr-/	wíþer-sàca 'adversary'	wiþ-sácan 'refuse'

It looks at first as if noun and adjective prefixes are stressed, and verb prefixes unstressed. But not always: note ínn-gàngan 'enter', ǽfter-spỳrian 'inquire after', ánd-swàrian 'answer', which are verbs with stressed prefixes; and be-bód 'command', for-gífness 'forgiveness', which are nouns with unstressed prefixes. Is there in fact a generalization?

It seems that there are at least three morphologically based ones, which make the situation a bit clearer. If we retain the original noun/verb distinction, the 'exceptions' come under the following main headings:

(i) If the first element (apparent 'prefix') is an independent adverb (inn, æfter) it is stressed.[13]

(ii) If a prefixed verb derives from an initial-stressed noun, the stress-pattern of the noun remains intact: ánd-swàrian < ánd-swàru.

(iii) If a noun is derived from a verb with an unstressed prefix, the stress-pattern of the verb remains: be-bód < be-bóden, past participle of be-bḗodan 'command' (i.e. 'that which is commanded'), for-gífness < for-gífan.

There seem to be two distinct explanatory principles here: types (i, ii) are not genuine prefixation, but a sort of compounding: the first elements of these complex verbs are lexical items that get their own stress by the GSR (4.9), and the verb as a whole is stressed by the Compound rule (4.11).[14]

---

[13] These stressed verbal prefixes still appear in the 'separable-prefix' verbs of Modern Continental WGmc languages like German and Dutch: e.g. über-setzen 'pass over', er setzt über 'he passes over' vs. über-sétzen 'translate', er übersetzt 'he translates'. The independent status is often still transparent, as in the preposition über 'over'.

[14] Or at least the first constituents of the nouns in (ii) are treated by the stress rules as if they were lexical items: they have a kind of 'quasi-word' status. Usually of course the first member of a compound is a word, not an affix (this is virtually a definition of 'compound': see chapter 8 below). There are however cases of this type even in ModE: compounds with bound first

Type (iii) on the other hand involves genuine prefixes, and has an interesting historical origin; this accounts for the general opposition stressed-prefix noun vs. unstressed-prefix verb. It seems that prefixed verbs like *be-gān, on-ginnan*, etc. as well as past participles prefixed by *ge-* (which is always unstressed) are not a PGmc inheritance. The items that later became these weak prefixes were once separate words: unstressed clitics to verb phrases, which often occurred in positions other than immediately to the left of the verb stem. A Gothic example will illustrate: the particle *us-* (roughly 'out') in the verb *us-giban* 'give out, restore'. The present 2 pl of this verb does occur in the prefixed form *us-gibiþ*; but it also occurs with the particle *nū* 'therefore', in the construction *us-nū-gibiþ*. Such a state of affairs is unthinkable with a genuine prefix, which would be bound to its stem. It looks as if these proto-prefixes were (before NWGmc times anyhow) not lexically attached to (or 'univerbated' with) verbal roots, but were autonomous and positionally free, and hence escaped the implementation of the GSR.

At a later period they were joined to the root, and no material could intervene; at this point, if the original stress pattern was to remain (as it did), a morphological specification had to be added to the GSR. This would perhaps say something like: the foot-building instruction must not only proceed from the left-hand edge of the word; it must proceed from the left-hand edge of the root. That is, it must apply only to a syllable bracketed as belonging to a major lexical category – Noun, Verb, Adjective, Adverb. Any initial syllable not so bracketed is 'invisible' to the stress rule, or extrametrical, outside the domain for foot-construction (cf. §4.2.2).

So the basic OE Stress Rule is more complex than the original GSR, since it must take account of the post-PGmc verbal prefixes.[15] We could state it as:

(4.14)   *Old English Stress Rule*[16]
(a) Starting at the left-hand edge of the word, look for a syllable bounded on the left by a major category label.
(b) Construct a binary foot s w.
(c) Add at most one additional w.

---

elements like the notorious *cran-* in *cranberry*, and so-called 'neoclassical' compounds like *gastr-o-scope, spermat-o-phore*.

[15] An alternative (and not unattractive) solution might ignore the details of morphology completely and assign stress to these complex items on a lexical and semantic basis. The separable vs. inseparable prefixes would then be sorted out on the basis of the meaning of the verb, and this would enable us to bypass the somewhat suspect procedure of assigning class-labels in order to get the rules to work. (Suggested to me by Dieter Kastovsky.)

[16] For a very different formulation of the OE stress rule, taking it as quantity-sensitive, see McCully (1992).

I assume that the stressable prefixes would have been more 'word-like' than the unstressable ones, and would carry major class labels (presumably 'Adv' in most cases). Stress-assignment at word-level for *ánd-sàca* and *on-sácan* might be visualized this way:

(4.15) 1 Input   [Adv and-] [N saca]   on- [V sacan]

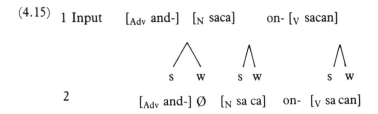

2   [Adv and-] Ø   [N sa ca]   on- [V sa can]

Since *and-saca* as a whole belongs to a major lexical category (N), the Compound Rule (essentially the same as the PGmc one) applies:

(4.16)

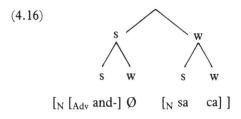

[N [Adv and-] Ø   [N sa   ca]]

Unstressable prefixes then are simply unmarked for category, and invisible to the stress rule. Virtually all other forms have their stress assigned by (4.14) or this plus the compound rule.

One further class of unstressed prefixes or prefix-like items is worth mentioning: prepositions that become clitic to nouns or directional adverbs, as in *tō-dǽg* 'today', *be-fóran* 'before', *be-híndan* 'behind'. If in such constructions the root following and the preposition are in hiatus (two vowels meeting back-to-back across the boundary) the preposition may be further reduced: hence *būfan* 'above' < *be-úfan*, *būtan* 'outside' < *be-útan*, *binnan* 'inside' < *be-innan*. This occurs elsewhere in WGmc as well: cf. Dutch and German *binnen* 'inside, within', Dutch *buiten* 'outside'. OE *būtan* of course survives in ModE *but* (original sense 'without'); both *būtan* and *binnan* remain in Scots *but and ben* 'in and out' (especially of a two-roomed cottage).

We now have the basis for understanding another aspect of OE stress that the simple GSR would not have led us to expect: apparent stressed suffixes. Unlike the (pseudo-)prefixes,[17] these get not primary but second-

---

[17] Problematic items whose status is somewhere between that of affixes and full words are often referred to as **affixoids** (so prefixoids, suffixoids, etc.).

ary stress, which suggests how we might interpret them even before we look at the data. Examples are, *drēam-lèas* 'joyless', *wúldor-fùll* 'glorious', *mǽgð-hàd* 'maidenhood'. Many of these suffixes, like the prefixes *ūp-*, *and-*, etc., are also bound, do not occur as independent words. But some – and this provides the key to their stressedness – are also independent words: *full* 'full', *hād* 'estate, condition' (cf. Go *full-s*, *haid-u-s* 'kind'). These forms then do not have 'suffixes' in the usual sense, but are compounds; the compound rule therefore applies to *drēam-lēas* the same way it does to *and-saca*, or to a compound with two free elements like *ēar-hring* or *wuldor-fæder* 'glory-father' (= God).

In some cases, the second elements of these and other compounds eventually reduce to genuine suffixes, or even lose their identity completely: so alongside *hlāf-weard* 'steward' (lit. 'loaf-warden') we have *hlāford* 'lord, master'; alongside *ful-wiht* 'baptism' (lit. 'cup/beaker sanctification') we have the reduced and opaque *fulluht*.[18]

4.3 Major developments in weak syllables[19]

4.3.1 Final reduction and loss

Many of the changes discussed earlier were independent of position in the foot: e.g. Grimm's Law, AFB. Others were restricted to foot-initial (strong) positions: breaking, restoration of [α], DHH. Some, like West Germanic Gemination, were sensitive to syllable weight (gemination only after light syllables). Most however had little or nothing to do with suprasegmental environments. The developments treated here could have been put in their chronological places in chapters 2–3; but I've preferred to group them together because they all have something in common: weakening or obscuration of contrast in weak syllables, and in some case a sensitivity to the weight of preceding (strong) syllables.

The historical phonology of weak syllables in Germanic is quite different from that of strong ones; weak position in the foot is a prime site for shortening of long vowels, deletion of short ones, cluster-simplifications, and loss of final segments. There is a widespread belief in

---

[18] There is some controversy about secondary stress in non-compound words. Campbell for instance (1959: §§88ff) argues for secondary accent in all sorts of places on what seem to me to be very shaky metrical grounds. So he claims that 'heavy' derivational suffixes like *-els*, *-en*, *-ung* have secondary stress after a heavy syllable or two light ones; he also says that the pseudo-suffixes like *-hād*, *-lēas* are completely unstressed except when followed by an inflectional syllable. There is no support in the behaviour of Germanic stress in general for such claims. In the Dresher & Lahiri (1991) model (cf. §4.2.2), such syllables are in fact stressed at a 'pre-surface' level, but lose their stress by a later rule of defooting.

[19] For standard philological discussion of the developments treated here, see Campbell (1959: ch. 7 on vowels, chs. 7, 9, *passim*).

some kind of 'causal' relation between initial stress and post-stress loss. A representative view is that of Krahe (1963: §123), who says that the 'cause' of these developments is 'the strong dynamic initial accent'; this 'caused the originally fuller word-endings to become ever more "eroded"' (my translation). There is however no necessary relation between initial stress and the erosion of post-stress material. Many languages have initial stress at least as 'strong' (whatever that means) as is typical of Germanic, and no such weakening or erosion at all. Finnish for example has long vowels and long consonants; these remain unchanged in unstressed syllables (*taloon* [tálɔ:n] 'into the house', *talossa* (tálɔ s:α] 'in the house'. Non-reduction in weak syllables is common in other Uralic languages, and Bantu languages of the Nguni group (Zulu, Xhosa). Reduction under low prominence is a language-specific choice – one that Germanic happens to have made; there is no 'causal' relation to stress.

The most important early changes in weak syllables are:

(i) *Simplification in codas.* Most final consonants except */r, s/ dropped: e.g. OE *nefa* 'nephew' < */nefo:ð-/ < */nepo:t-/ (L *nepos, nepot-is,* Skr *nápat*); NWGmc *horna* 'horn' (acc sg) < */xorn-α-n/ < */kr̥n-o-m/ (= L *corn-u-m*), etc. IE final */s/ appears first as *[z]: NWGmc *gast-i-z* 'guest', later OIc *gest-r* (rhotacism), Go *gast-s* (final devoicing), OE *giest* (loss of *[z]). This loss, plus later vowel-reduction, led at times to enormous inflectional change: OE *ber-e* 'bear' (pres subj 3 sg) goes back ultimately to IE */bher-oi-t/ (Skr *bar-e-t*, Go *bar̃-ai*), which merged with pres ind 1 sg *ber-e* < */bher-o:/.

(ii) *Vowels in weak syllables.* There are several main tendencies: simplification of complex nuclei (shortening of long vowels, monophthongization of diphthongs to short vowels); loss of short vowels; and articulatory change, with non-deleted final weak vowels tending first to end up at the extreme corners of the vowel space, i.e. as /i, u/ or /α/. At a later stage, beginning about the sixth century but not completing until the eighth, remaining */i, α/ tended to merge in /e/: *ber-e* (pres ind 1 sg) (cf. Go *bar̃-a* with final /-α/ < /-o:/: see below), *win-e* 'friend' < */win-i-z/ (cf. OS *win-i*).[20] The upshot is a massive reduction in the structural variety of post-stress syllables. What follows is a rather sketchy outline of a very complex set of developments.

(a) IE tonal accent (?) and post-tonic complex nuclei

Early IE final heavy syllables, if accented, have been claimed by some scholars to have had two possible tone contours: either a 'normal' high

---

[20] This merger in /e/ is often taken to be a 'reduction'/ to schwa [ə]. I am not convinced of the reality of [ə] as a category before late Middle English, if even then. See the discussion reduction in Middle English and Early Modern English in Lass (1992b, Forthcoming).

tone, or an 'abnormal' (as many of the handbooks put it) compound accent, normally referred to as 'circumflex'. If this existed,[21] it was probably a rise-fall distributed over the two morae of the nucleus; whatever its nature, it seems to have had the effect of protecting long vowels and diphthongs in (Germanic, post-Accent-Shift) weak syllables from reductions they would otherwise have undergone. At least this was so until the E/NW split. This must mean that even after the establishment of the GSR, syllables with an original 'circumflex' accent retained some distinguishing tonal or other property.

The effect is clearest in Gothic, where non-initial long vowels with reconstructed 'acute' accent often shorten and change quality, but 'circumflex' long vowels remain. So in ō-stem nouns (§6.1.3) Gothic nom sg in -a < */-o:/ < IE */-ɑ:/, but gen sg in -os < IE */-a-/ (= Gr -as). We will not be concerned with this accentual problem any further, as by and large its effects were ironed out in NWGmc, and both types of final vowels fell together; but the accentual distinction does play some part in certain inflectional endings, and is sometimes mentioned in the handbooks; it is useful at least to be aware of it.

(b) Long vowels and diphthongs in weak syllables

1 PGmc */i:/ < IE */i:, ei/ shortened to /i/, as in pres subj 3 sg wil-e 'will' < */wil-i/ (cf. L uel-i-t). Final /-i/ which were not lost by High Vowel Deletion (§4.3.2) lowered to /e/.

2 PGmc */o:/ < IE */o:, ɑ:/ shows up as /u/: early OE ber-u 'I bear' < */βer-o:/ (cf. L fer-ō), but as /ɑ/ in Gothic (baír-a). Final /u/ seems later to have split in OE, ending up as /e/ in pres 1 sg of verbs (ber-u > ber-e), and in certain weak feminine nouns, when a nasal had followed: tung-e 'tongue' nom sg < */tunɣ-o:n/ (cf. Go tugg-ōn). Otherwise, when not deleted, as in the nom sg of ō-stem nouns with light root syllables, it remains /u/ (gief-u 'gift' < */ɣeβ-o:/).

3 PGmc */ɑi/ < IE */ɑi, oi/ first follows the same course as in accented syllables, i.e. */ɑi/ > /ɑ:/ > /æ:/ (cf. §3.4). Then it shortens and falls in with the reflex of PIE */e:/, which shortens in weak position. So dæg-e 'day' (dat sg) < */ðɑɣ-ɑi/ < */-oi/ (cf. Gr -oi).

4 PGmc */ɑu/ < IE */ɑu, ou/ follows the development of PGmc */o:/ before nasals, i.e. it becomes /ɑ/: eahta 'eight' = Go ahtau < */okt-o:n/, sun-a 'son' (gen sg) = Go sun-aus.

---

[21] There are conflicting traditions in IE scholarship as to whether there was indeed such an accentual distinction; see Szemerényi (1985: 16ff), and the 'new' versions of the IE accent in Kiparsky (1973), Kiparsky & Halle (1977). Whatever the status of the 'circumflex' accent, there are two types of final heavy syllables that behaved differently in certain situations, and that's all one has to believe.

(c) Short nonhigh vowels

The high vowels */i, u/ have special developments which will be treated in the next section; here we consider only */e, ɑ/.

1 PGmc */e/ < IE */e/ deletes in absolute final position: Go *wait*, OE *wāt* 'he knows' < */woid-e/ (cf. Gr *oîd-e*). If protected by a retained /r/, it remains, as in *fæder* (cf. Gr *patér-a*, acc sg). If protected by any other following consonant, it raised in the first instance to /i/: *fēt* 'feet'/ < */fo:t-iz/ < */fo:t-es/ (cf. Gr *pód-es*). These /i/ were later lowered when not deleted; but it is worth noting that there are, as in this case, instances of *i*-umlaut where the triggering /i/ is not of IE date, but represents a special low-stress Gmc reflex of */e/.

2 PGmc */ɑ/ < IE */ɑ, o/ deletes finally: thus *wait, wāt* as above are also pres 1 sg (= Gr *oîd-a*). Otherwise it becomes /e/, as in gen sg *dæg-es* < */ðɑɣ-ɑ-sɑ/. WGmc loss of final *[z] left many */ɑ/ in final position, which later dropped: so nom sg *dæg* < */ðɑɣ-ɑ-z/. Weak */ɑ/ protected by a nasal either remain, as in the infinitive ending *-an*, or become /e/ as in the strong past participle suffix *-en*.

4.3.2   High vowel deletion and medial syncope[22]

We now come to a group of changes that seem to depend not merely on a vowel being in a weak syllable, but on the total weight of the foot. The fates of short high */i, u/ in weak positions are largely determined by the weight of the preceding strong syllable. In outline, they deleted after a heavy syllable, but remained after a light one, in the case of */i/ usually lowering to /e/ at a later stage. Some typical examples:

---

[22] High Vowel Deletion is discussed from a quite different point of view in Keyser & O'Neill (1985), and cf. McCully (1992).

(4.17)   *Foot-configuration*   *pre-OE*   *OE*

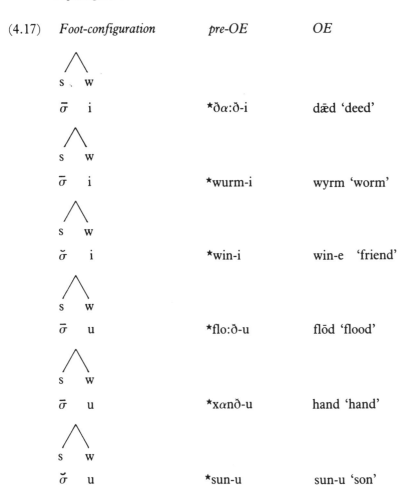

		pre-OE	OE
σ̄	i	*ða:ð-i	dǣd 'deed'
σ̄	i	*wurm-i	wyrm 'worm'
σ̆	i	*win-i	win-e 'friend'
σ̄	u	*flo:ð-u	flōd 'flood'
σ̄	u	*xanð-u	hand 'hand'
σ̆	u	*sun-u	sun-u 'son'

(the 'pre-OE' forms represent the stage after WGmc deletion of final *[z]: §2.8.)

The same pattern occurs medially in trisyllabic feet, e.g. in thematic preterites of weak verbs (§7.2). The old *\/-i-/ that came before the preterite suffix dropped after a heavy root syllable, but remained and later lowered to /e/ after a light one:

(4.18)   *Foot-configuration*   *pre-OE*   *OE*

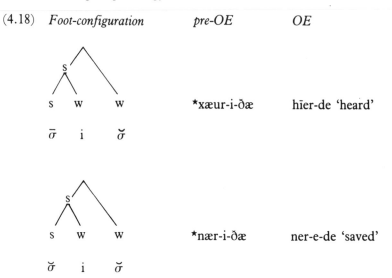

	pre-OE	*OE*
	*xæur-i-ðæ	hīer-de 'heard'
	*nær-i-ðæ	ner-e-de 'saved'

Obviously both deletion and lowering must postdate *i*-umlaut, which gives us a firm relative chronology, and sets these changes fairly late in the pre-OE period.

High Vowel Deletion (HVD) has considerable morphophonemic significance in OE, because of the large number of grammatical categories realized by short high post-tonic vowels. Its results show up in the following places (among others):

(i) *a*-stem neuter nom/acc sg: light *scip-u* 'ships' vs. heavy *word* 'word(s)', *bān* 'bone(s)'.
(ii) *ō*-stem feminine nom sg: light *gief-u* 'gift' vs. heavy *lār* 'learning'.
(iii) *i*-stem nom sg: light *win-e* 'friend' vs. heavy *cwēn* 'queen'.
(iv) *u*-stem nom sg: light *sun-u* 'son' vs. heavy *hand* 'hand'.
(v) Neuter/feminine strong adjective declension: light *sum* 'a certain', fem nom sg, neut nom/acc sg *sum-u* vs. heavy *gōd* 'good', fem nom sg *gōd*.
(vi) Thematic weak verb preterites (examples in (4.18)).

The HVD pattern appears to reflect a weight-based constraint on foot structure that says in effect: a heavy syllable + /i, u/ is 'overheavy'; a light syllable + /i, u/ is legal. A visual representation suggests an interesting equivalence:

(4.19)   Overheavy   Legal

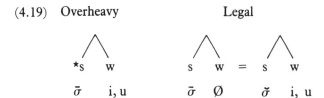

That is: in certain contexts (mainly phonological, but partly morphological as well), one heavy syllable and two light syllables count as equivalent in weight. This suggests a possible prediction: in historical trisyllables, high vowels ought to delete after two light syllables just as they do after one heavy one. And indeed this is borne out, though not as neatly as for disyllables. So *byden* 'tub' < L *butina*, *we(o)rod* 'troops' < */wered-u/ in eWS, but later both expected *wered* and analogically reformed *wered-u*.

The principle here (σ̄ = σ̆σ̆) is often referred to in discussions of IE metrics as **resolution**: a sequence of two light syllables 'resolves to' or is metrically/quantitatively equivalent to, one heavy one. This plays a role in OE, Greek and Latin metrics, and in a number of historical processes in IE and Germanic (see McCully 1992 for detailed discussion).

But some trisyllabic forms appear to misbehave. In a trisyllable with a heavy penultima, the final high vowel drops, as expected: so *leornung* 'learning' < */lirn-unɣ-u/, i.e. σ̄σ̄-u. But in trisyllabic feet of the shape σ̄σ̆-u, the high vowel normally does not delete: *hēafod* 'head', nom/acc pl *hēafod-u* (usually), not **hēafod* as expected. Aside from possible morphological conditioning here, this non-deletion may be explicable under the assumption that the first heavy syllable constitutes a foot by itself, and the second is σ̆-u, which of course does not condition deletion.

It remains to ask what the various instances of HVD have in common, from an overall quantitative point of view. In terms of general foot-configurations, we can see a motivation:

(4.20)

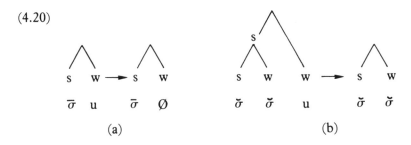

(a)   (b)

In (a) the foot is 'lightened' by the removal of phonetic material from the weak position, leaving a minimal heavy foot. In (b), a layer of prominence contouring is removed, leaving ŏŏ, the equivalent as we saw above of ō. Thus both instances of HVD seem to 'conspire' (in a limited context anyhow) at producing some kind of 'optimal' foot-shape.

This general type of simplification is reflected elsewhere in OE, in deletion of weak (but not necessarily high) vowels. Such medial syncope goes back to earliest Germanic: compare Skr *duhitar* 'daughter', representing the old shape of the word, with Go *dauhtar*, OE *dohtor*. Within OE itself, this is a rich (if irregular) source of alternative root-shapes in certain noun declensions. Masculine and neuter *a*-stem disyllables often show deletion in inflected forms that would otherwise be trisyllabic: e.g. *fugol* 'bird', *wæter* 'water', *hēafod* 'head':

(4.20)	NOM/ACC	fugol	wæter	hēafod
	GEN	fugl-es	wætr-es	hēafd-es
	DAT	fugl-e	wætr-e	hēafd-e

The picture in the texts is however somewhat messy, with frequent restoration of the dropped vowels, especially (and this is significant in the light of the above discussion) if the root syllable is light: so *wæter-es*, etc. (See Campbell 1959, §574 for discussion.)

We are not dealing here with a (strict) 'sound-law' of the familiar kind, like Grimm's Law; rather something more like a very strong tendency to maximize certain apparently 'preferred' foot-configurations, and get rid of others. Such tendencies toward the stabilisation of preferred foot-types continue for quite some time in the history of English. Toward the end of the OE period and running into early ME there are a number of developments of this type. One shortens long vowels before consonant clusters (thus getting rid of superheavy strong syllables): so OE *cēpan* 'keep', pret *cēpte* > *cĕpte*, hence the ModE short/long alternation in *keep* vs. *kept*. A similar development shortened long vowels in the first syllables of trisyllabic feet, as in *sūþ* 'south' *sūþerne* 'southern' > *sŭþerne*, hence ModE *south* vs. *southern*.[23]

---

[23] For discussion of these shortening processes, and the general problem of 'quantity adjustment', see Lass (1992: §2.5), Ritt (Forthcoming), and chapter 10 below.

Part III:

Morphophonemic intermezzo

Hypothesen sind Wiegenlieder, womit der Lehrer seine Schüler einlullt;
der denkende treue Beobachter lernt immer mehr seine Beschränkungen
kennen, er sieht: je weiter sich das Wissen ausbreitet, desto mehr
Probleme kommen zum Vorschein.

Goethe, Nachlass

5   Ablaut, the laryngeal(s) and the IE root

5.1   The basic alternations

This chapter is a kind of bridge: its subject is phonology and morphology
intertwined, with segmental and suprasegmental connections. It also
introduces some of the more complicated aspects of IE historical linguistics; some knowledge of these areas is needed for understanding
what would otherwise be highly puzzling features of morpheme- and
word-shape in IE languages, including Old English.

As an introduction, consider the following IE cognates:

(5.1)   L *teg-ō*, Gr *tég-ō*, 'I cover', Gr *(s)tég-os* 'roof', OCS *o-steg-nǫti*
         'cover', OIr *teg* 'house', Lith *stóg-as*, OPr *stog-is* 'roof', L *tog-a*
         'toga' (a garment as 'covering'), OIc *þak* 'roof, thatch, bed-cover',
         OHG *dah* 'roof', OE *þæc* 'roof, thatch', L *tēc-tum* 'covered' (pp of
         teg-ō), *tēg-ula* 'tile'.

(On the forms in initial /s-/ see §5.6.)

These obviously contain 'the same' IE root, with a basic sense like
'cover'; and the consonantal 'skeleton' easily reconstructs as */tVg-/. This
gives L, Lith, OIr /tVg-/, and by Grimm's Law (§2.3) Gmc */θVk-/, which
by regular changes gives all the Germanic shapes listed.

So much then for the consonants. But it seems impossible to reconstruct
a unique ancestral vowel. IE */e/ would account for *teg-ō*, *o-steg-nǫti*, *teg*;
but *tog-a*, *stóg-as*, *þak*, *dah*, *þæc* require */o/, and *tēg-ula*, *tēc-tum* require
*/e:/. If no single IE vowel could give all these reflexes, what is the shape
of the ancestral root? Or is this the right question to ask? If we think not
segmentally, in terms of the inheritance of consonants and vowels in the
daughter languages, but morphologically, in terms of roots-as-wholes, the
problem becomes tractable.

That is, vowel-alternations within a root are familiar; we have already
seen them as products of various Germanic and OE sound changes such as
i-umlaut (*mūs/mȳs*, *eald/ieldra*) and AFB (*dæg/dagas*). These have their

ModE relics as well, as in *mouse/mice*, *old/elder*, *day* and the old /α/-vocalism indirectly reflected in *dawn* < OE *dagung*. But there is a much older stratum of alternations, reflecting processes of IE date: a typical OE example is the vowel-gradation in the strong verb (e.g. *rīdan/rād/ridon*), which also survives in ModE (*ride/rode*). The array of vowels in (5.1) could easily derive from some such ancestral alternation: especially when we find a number of vocalisms in the same root in one of the more ancient languages, as in Latin *teg-ō*, *tog-a*, *tēg-ula*. As a first approximation, whatever form of the */tVg-/ root lies behind *teg-ō* also lies behind *o-steg-nati*, *teg*; the form behind *tog-a* lies behind *stog-is*, *pak*, *dah*, etc. What kind of thing this form might be is the interesting question.

This all derives from a complex of IE alternations known collectively as **Ablaut** (also **Gradation, Apophony**). The subject is enormously complex; I will give only a brief outline here.[1] The basic point is this: for perhaps the majority of IE roots there is no 'fixed' or 'inherent' vowel. A typical (major category) root had what is called a 'basic' or 'normal' */e/ vocalism; under certain conditions this could be replaced by */o/, could lengthen, reduce, or delete. Each such possible vocalism for a root is called a **grade**. Hence we speak of the *e*-grade, *o*-grade, reduced or zero-grade form of a root.

The examples in (5.1) happen to reflect only three grades:

(5.2)   a. *e*-grade */teg-/: L *teg-ō*, Gr *(s)tég-os*, OCS *-steg-nati* . . .
       b. *o*-grade */tog-/: L *tog-a*, Lith *stóg-as*, OHG *dah*, OE *pæc* . . .
       c. Lengthened *e*-grade */te:g-/: L *tēg-ula*, *tēc-tum* . . .

The zero and lengthened *o*-grades are transparent in the forms of another root, */pet-/ 'fly':

(5.3)   a. *e*-grade */pet-/: Gr *pét-omai* 'I fly', L *penna* 'feather' < */pet-nα:/, OE *feber*, OHG *fedara* 'feather', OWelsh *eterinn* 'bird' < */pet-/
       b. *o*-grade */pot-/: Gr *pot-ế* 'flight'
       c. zero-grade: Gr *pt-éruks* 'wing', *e-pt-ómen* 'flew', L *pro-(p)t-eruus* 'vehement'
       d. lengthened *o*-grade: Gr *pôt-atai* 'he flutters'

---

[1] Perhaps the best account of ablaut available in English is still Prokosch (1938: §§44–7), even if this is a bit dated. It is also not easy, but well worth the trouble. For those who read German, the most up-to-date and well-referenced treatment is Szemerényi (1989: §VI.3). There is a useful if elementary discussion in Palmer (1972: 216ff), with some good exemplification; I have taken some examples (but not the mode of presentation) from Palmer. Most introductions to historical linguistics treat these phenomena somewhere, but rarely in a coherent way.

There are two kinds of alternation grouped under the heading of ablaut, called **qualitative** and **quantitative**. Qualitative ablaut (G *Abtönung*) is essentially the /e/ ~ /o/ (occasionally /a/ ~ /o/, see below) alternation; quantitative ablaut (*Abstufung*) is 'normal' /e/, /o/ grade alternating with lengthened and zero grades.[2]

Even though */e/ is assumed as the basic or 'normal' full grade for most IE roots, a good number do not at first glance reconstruct this way (e.g. there is no *e*-grade attested). In particular there is a class of roots in */a/, and some with long */a:/ or */o:/. An important */a/ root is */ag-/ 'drive': normal grade in Gr *ág-ō* 'I drive', *o*-grade in *óg-mos* 'swath', lengthened *a*-grade in L *amb-āg-es* 'a going about, circumlocution'. A typical long-vowel root is */sta:-/ 'stand': normal grade in L *stā-re* 'to stand', zero grade in pp *stā-tus* ('zero' of long vowels shows up as loss of a mora: see §5.5 below), *o*-grade in Lith *stuo-mas* 'growth, shape'. There is an alternative and more interesting interpretation of these apparent */a, a:, o:/ roots, which I will return to in §5.3.[3]

5.2   The conditioning of ablaut

Whatever the possible effect of tone in the very early stages of the parent language, the attested dialects, insofar as they exhibit systematic ablaut, typically show a complex of morphological and accentual conditioning. So for instance the suffixal or root-extending element */-ter/ occurs in three grades in the Greek paradigm for 'father', and in two other degrees in derivatives:[4]

---

[2] Perhaps this borrowed terminology should be unpacked for non-German-speaking readers. *Ablaut* is from G *ab* 'away from' + *Laut* 'sound'; *Abtönung* is from *ab* + *Ton* 'tone', and *Abstufung* from *ab* + *Stufe* 'degree, step'. (Some scholars believe that qualitative ablaut is connected with an IE tonal accent, but this is at best not proven.) The alternative term *apophony* is (with splendid philological pedantry) an anglicization of a deliberate translation of *Ablaut* into Greek! (< Gr *apó* 'off, away from' + *phonē* 'sound').

[3] The fundamentals of ablaut had already been worked out for Sanskrit by the pre-Christian Indian grammarians. Their analysis was however somewhat different. They took (what we now see historically as) the zero-grade as 'fundamental', and derived *e*- and *o*-grades (called *guṇa* 'excellence, high degree') from this, and then further the lengthened grade (*vṛddhi* 'increase, growth'). Thus fundamental *bhṛ-ta-* 'borne', guṇa *bhar-a-ti* 'he bears', vṛddhi *bhār-a-* 'burden'. (Skr /a/ is often the reflex of IE */e/: see §5.5). For discussion see Mayrhofer (1972: §§35–7), and the rather old-fashioned but very detailed account in Whitney (1889: §§235ff).

[4] *Eupátōr* is an adjective 'of a noble father', an epithet of Mithridates Eupator, king of Pontus: *eupatoría* 'agrimony' is a herb supposedly named after Mithridates, who is reputed to have discovered its efficacy against poison.

(5.4) 1 acc sg *pa-tér-a*   *e*-grade
       2 nom sg *pa-tḗr*   lengthened *e*-grade
       3 gen sg *pa-tr-ós*   zero-grade
       4 *eu-pa-tor-ía*   *o*-grade
       5 *eu-pá-tōr*   lengthened *o*-grade

The conditioning here shows one of the basic accentual factors: normal and lengthened *e*-grades characteristically occur under accent, and zero-grade in unaccented syllables with a following accent. There are more examples in (5.3) above (*pt-éruks*, etc.). But morphology is involved as well: note the *o*-grade in example (5.4) with following accent (and see below).

This historical conditioning is often obscured by later accentual changes, and there are clear cases where suffix accent does not trigger zero, as above and Gr *hom-ós* 'same'; or where zero-grade coexists with a preceding accent (L *pá-tr-is* 'father', gen sg). In some ancient dialects, gradation is tied into morphological subsystems, as in a certain verb type where *e*-grade is associated with present, *o*-grade with perfect, and zero with aorist. So Gr *leíp-ō* 'leave' < */leik^w-/:

(5.5)   *e*-PRESENT   *o*-PERFECT   ZERO-AORIST
         leíp-ō   lé-loip-a   é-lip-on

It may seem odd at first to call the aorist root a 'zero' grade, since the sequence /lip-/ contains a vowel; but on reflection it does make sense. In a diphthongal root (or one with a liquid or nasal following the vowel: see below), the postvocalic sonorant counts for ablaut as part of the root. Hence the root skeleton above is /lVip/, with /ei/ as *e*-grade, and /oi/ as *o*-grade; /-i-/ represents deletion or non-realization of the vowel-slot otherwise filled by /e/ or /o/. When the vowel is deleted, the remaining element becomes the syllabic if it is not an obstruent (see further §5.5). Comparing this with 'fly', (cf. (5.3)): /leip-/ = /pet-/, /loip-/ = /pot-/, and /lip-/ = /pt-/. There are also roots in */Vu/, as in Gr *pheúgō* 'flee', aorist *éphugon*, and so on.

If the root skeleton contains a resonant */r, l, m, n/ after the vowel, the result of zero is parallel to that in /leip-/: deletion of the vowel leaves a resonant that becomes the syllabic of the root, i.e. syllabicity is transferred to the nasal or liquid as it was to the second vowel. So in Skr *vart-* 'turn' < */wert-/:

(5.6)   PRES 1 SG   PERF 1 SG
         várt-a-mi   va-vr̥t-i-má

The lengthened grade is controlled by a complex of factors, mostly morphological. One common trigger is the type of aorist called 'sigmatic' (i.e. containing /s/), which is the source among other things of certain Latin perfects, as in *reg-ō* 'rule':

(5.7)   PRES 1 SG (*e*-grade)   PERF 1 SG (lengthened *e*-grade)
         reg-ō   rēx-ī = {reg:-s-i:}

We will return to the zero/lengthened grade aorist in §7.1.1, as it explains certain peculiarities in the shape of the strong verb preterite plural.

Other typical loci for lengthened grade are nominative sg of some consonant-final stems (Gr *patēr* 'father', *poimēn* 'shepherd', *kēr* 'heart'); and comparatives, e.g. L *maiōr* 'greater' < */meg-jo:-s/.[5]

The *o*-grade is at least partly conditioned by phonological environment (segmental or accentual). Note in /leip-/ in (5.5) that the *o*-grade perfect does not have root accent (*lé-loip-a*); there is also an adjective from the same root, *loip-ós*. (Though of course *o*-grades do occur under accent as well, as in Gr *gón-u* 'knee', and Doric *pôs*.) A following nasal or liquid may also have predisposed to *o*-grade, as in the change of the acc sg of certain noun-types from */-e-m/ to */-o-m/ (= L -*um*, Gr -*on*).

5.3   The laryngeals: 'irregular' ablaut regularized and a new look for IE root-structure

A crucial source of detailed knowledge of the linguistic past is what I like to call 'Verner's Principle': every exception to an otherwise regular process ought (ideally) to be explained in terms of some as yet undiscovered regularity. So the /d/ in OE *wurdon, worden* (cf. §2.4) is at first sight an 'irregular' reflex of IE */t/; but it is quite regular if we take account of the position of the IE accent.

This approach to some of the more puzzling ablaut phenomena has yielded an unexpected result: an apparent glimpse into a more remote IE past than would have been thought possible, and suggestions of a radically different structure for early PIE than we have been assuming so far for the input to Germanic. In this section I will have to go into the history of linguistic scholarship in more detail than elsewhere, as the issues will simply not make sense otherwise.

By the 1870s it had become apparent to some scholars that the traditional five-quality IE short vowel system (cf. §2.2) was insufficient,

---

[5] Some apparent lengthened grades in consonant-final roots may not be due directly to ablaut, but to assimilation and compensatory lengthening after loss of a nom sg ending (Szemerényi 1989: §VI.2.7): so Doric Greek *pôs* 'foot' (cf. Attic *pod-*) could arise by the sequence */pod-s/ > */pos-s/ > */po:s/.

at least to account for all the correspondences in the more ancient languages. This led to the positing of an additional short vowel, a schwa */ə/. The primary motivation was a set of 'irregular' correspondences: e.g. Skr *pitár* 'father' = L *pater*, OE *fæder*, Skr *sthitás* 'standing' (verbal adjective of *sthā-* 'stand') = L *stă-tus*. Here a Sanskrit /i/ apparently corresponds to /α/ elsewhere in IE, while the normal correspondence is /i/ = /i/ (Skr *vidhavā* 'widow' = L *uidua*, Go *widuwō*, etc.). This suggests an extra protovowel, which merges with */α/ except in Indic:

(5.8)   *Indic*   *Non-Indic*

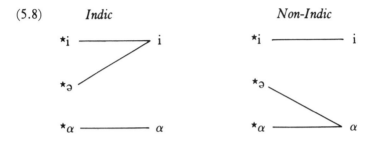

This new */ə/ (as is so often the case) had unexpected spinoffs: for one thing, it provided a unitary interpretation for other 'anomalous'[6] ablaut relations, without compromising the basic pattern */e ~ o ~ e:/o: ~ ∅/. Consider for instance the apparent */α:/-roots with zero-grade in /α/ discussed above (L *stā-re ~ stă-tus*). Comparison with Skr *sthā- ~ sthi-* suggest an original paradigm */stα:- ~ stə-/ (on the aspirated consonants see below). And this in turn suggests a parallel to the zero-grade formation in dipthongal roots like Gr *leip- ~ loip- ~ lip-*, where the nuclear vowel of the zero-grade alternant is the residue left by deletion of the first vowel. The /α/ in *stă-tus* (and the /i/ in *sthi-tás*) then reflect a */ə/ left behind by zeroing: we can posit a set of */-Və-/ roots, parallel to those in */-Vi-, -Vu-/. On this interpretation the /α:/ in *stā-re, sthā-* is the reflex of a diphthong */αə/, presumably with the second mora assimilated to the first. So:

(5.9)   *Full grade*   *Zero-grade*
         IE *-αə-   *-ə-
         Skr -α:-   -i-
         L   -α:-   -α-

This extends easily to the other 'unusual' root type, that in apparent original */o:/: L *dō-num* 'gift' ~ *dă-tus* 'given': now /o: ~ α/ can be seen as

---

[6]'Anomalous' of course is a loaded term here: it implies that there's something 'wrong' with roots that don't have basic */e/. The consequences of this view will be spelled out below.

parallel to /α: ~ α/. Here then we have original */o/ > /o:/, and zero-grade */ə/ > /α/.[7]

With this equipment we can now account for yet another alternation involving short /α/: that in the perfect and supine participle of some Latin verbs: *fēc-ī* 'I did' ~ *fāc-tus* 'done'. Once again, the long vowel can be derived from a */Və /-diphthong (*/eə/ > /e:/) and /α/ is the */-ə/ residue of the original zero-grade.

The patterns of monophthongization then are:

(5.10) *eə > ee = e:
        *oə > oo = o:
        *αə > αα = α:

But while this explains both length and the quality of the zero-grade vowel in some roots, it still leaves the whole ablaut system somewhat unsystematic, or at least not as unified as we might like it to be. Given the preponderance of /e/-vocalism as the 'normal' basic grade of an IE root, is there a way to get even /α:, o:/ as reflexes (in some sense) of */e/? (They could of course not be: but there is reason for trying, given the apparent regularity of so much of the system.)

This solution was in fact achieved in an extraordinary study by Ferdinand de Saussure (1879), which led to a revolutionary reconsideration of the structure of PIE. Saussure argued that */e/ was in fact the nuclear vowel of ALL IE roots.[8] The root could have */e/ alone, or */e/ plus what he called a 'coéfficient sonantique', a resonant or sonorant that could apparently have both consonantal and vocalic allophones. Saussure posited two of these 'sonant coefficients', *A* and *O*, which had the following effects:

(5.11) eA > α:
        eO > o:

They thus replace the original */ə/ with two phonetically unspecified but formally satisfying segments, which either 'colour' and lengthen original preceding */e/, or if */e/ is deleted, can stand alone as nuclear vowels.

---

[7] The treatment of IE schwa is vastly oversimplified, as the concept is now primarily of historical importance (see below). At one time scholars proposed two schwas, our */ə/ ('schwa primum') and */ʙ/('schwa secundum'), which was supposed to be a 'reduced' but 'zeroed' form of certain unaccented short vowels (see Prokosch 1938: §34 for some discussion).

[8] Excerpts from Saussure's monograph are translated in Lehmann (1967). For an excellent account of this work and a *précis* of the main arguments and their influence, see Koerner (1985).

In 1880 Hermann Møller added a third one: an E which had no colouring effect but could lengthen a preceding vowel. This completed the set, so that:

(5.12)   eE > e: (*fēc-* < */feEk-/)
          eA > α: (*stā-* < */steA-/)
          eO > o: (*dō-* < */deO-/)

During the late nineteenth century a number of scholars had been toying with the idea of a genetic relation between Indo-European and Semitic.[9] One feature of Semitic, rather 'exotic' from a general IE viewpoint, is the presence in many consonant inventories of a large number of what were called as a catchall 'laryngeal' segments: i.e. glottal stop, /h/, and various pharyngeal articulations. Since one of the 'coéfficients' had the effect of aspirating an immediately preceding stop (as in *sthi-* < */stA-/), one might suspect that it could have been a 'laryngeal' too: not surprising if there is indeed a kinship between IE and Semitic.

But 'laryngeal theory' was a rather marginal aspect of IE scholarship until the decipherment of Hittite in the early twentieth century. About a decade after the first major Hittite publications, Kuryłowicz (1927) pointed out a striking and important fact: in many of the places where Saussure had posited a 'coéfficient sonantique' and Møller a 'laryngeal', there appeared a segment normally transliterated as <ḫ>, which evidence suggested was a glottal /h/ or something similar. In particular, long vowels in other IE dialects appeared to correspond to /-Vh-/ sequences in Hittite: so Hitt *paḫš-* 'protect' (L *pāscō* 'protect, feed'), *paḫḫur* 'fire' (Gr *pūr*), *šeḫḫur* 'urine' (OE *sūr* 'sour', OIc *saur* 'semen'), *waḫ-* 'turn' (Skr *vāya* 'weaving'), etc. The three IE laryngeals (as they are now called) had apparently collapsed into one in Hittite; but the presence of /h/ in so many places where some laryngeal was posited seemed to be beyond coincidence.

---

[9] This has been revived in a vastly extended form as the 'Nostratic' hypothesis: the claim that IE, Semitic, Uralic, and a large number of other families are all descended from a common ancestor, and form a Nostratic Superfamily. There is no doubt some kind of relation among these groups, since there are shared features that would be outlandish if there were no genetic connection (e.g. an /-m-/ formative in the first person and a /-t-/ in the second person throughout the group). Extremely inflated claims for a reconstructable protolanguage however have been made; but the methodology is to my mind suspect, and so-called 'Nostratic etymologies' do not meet the usual criteria for genuine reconstructions. For discussion of Nostratic and similar proposals see Ruhlen (1987), and the review and literature citations in Fleming (1987). To get some idea of the complexity of the issues involved in deciding on matters of this kind, see Lyle Campbell's fascinating study of Uralic and Indo-European tree-names (1990), and Dolgopolsky (1989) on Semitic/IE relations.

Kuryłowicz noted something else, which rather than merely supporting the laryngeal idea eventually transformed our notions of what IE syllable structure might have been like: in many cases where all the other IE dialects have vowel-initial words, Hittite has an initial /h/: ḫanti 'front' (L ante 'before', OHG enti 'front'), ḫaštai 'bone' (Skr ásthi, L os, Gr os-téon), and many others.

So we have three **laryngeals**, now conventionally $*/H_1, H_2, H_3/$,[10] corresponding to the old $*/E, A, O/$. Saussure's original arguments, plus the presence of these segments in initial position in Hittite, led to a fundamental recasting of previous ideas of PIE structure. One claim that was made early (and is accepted by many today) was that all IE roots (even those that show up nowhere but in Hittite with an initial consonant, or even have no initial consonant in Hittite) had the structure $*/CVC/$. Assume that only postvocalic laryngeals can lengthen vowels, but that prevocalic ones can 'colour' a following /e/. If $*/H_1/$ is the 'neutral' laryngeal, $*/H_2/$ the a-colouring one, and $*/H_3/$ the o-colouring one, we can extend Saussure's claim that $*/e/$ is the basic IE vocalism even to short-vowel roots in (later) /a, o/. This leads to reconstructions of this kind:

(5.13) $*H_1$ed- 'eat': L edō, OE *etan*
         $*H_2$eg- 'drive': L agō, Skr ájāmi
         $*H_3$ed- 'smell': L odor, Gr odmḗ 'smell'

And if long vowels can result from fusion of short vowels with a following larygneal, we have:

(5.14) $*reH_1$g- 'king': L rēx, Skr rāja
         $*meH_2$- 'mother': L māter, OE mōdor
         $*deH_3$- 'give': L dō-num, Lith dúoti

These moves have startling consequences: (a) all IE roots have initial consonants; (b) vowel-length is not original, but a late development following loss of laryngeals; and (c) the original protolanguage could have had only ONE vowel, $*/e/$. Points (a, b) are acceptable, if problematic; point (c) cannot be accepted, because there are no clear (non-reconstructed) examples of one-vowel languages (the minimum appears to be three: see

---

[10] Also $*/X_1, \ldots /$ or $*/ə_1, \ldots /$. Where the particular laryngeal involved is not at issue, but only the presence of one, unsubscripted representations like $*/X/$, $*/H/$ are sometimes used.

Szemerényi 1985: 4).[11] Laryngeal theory has transformed our view of IE structure in many ways, and certainly made sense of many irregularities in ablaut; but in its extreme form it is untenable, if a testament to the cleverness of some linguists. Perhaps the safest view is that reconstruction at least of an initial laryngeal requires special justification for any item that does not show it in a Hittite cognate; this leaves the way open for an original five-vowel system, with '*/ə/' replaced by a laryngeal which vocalizes when it becomes a syllabic, and perhaps vowel-length as a late development.[12]

One issue remains to be discussed briefly (largely because at present it is not at all well resolved): what kind of segments were these mysterious laryngeals? There is no consensus: but if there were indeed three, judging from the colouring effects on neighbouring vowels, it is at least possible that */H₁/ was glottal (either [ʔ] or [h]), */H₂/ was pharyngeal, perhaps a voiceless fricative [ħ] or a voiced fricative or approximant [ʕ], and */H₃/ was velar, and probably rounded, e.g. [ɣʷ].

It is clear that except in Hittite, and in the /h/-release of the voiceless aspirates in Indic, the laryngeals had vanished by the historical IE period. They are of profound importance for the early history and comparative phonology and morphology of all Indo-European languages, given a wide enough perspective, but have little direct relevance to local problems of Germanic.

5.4   Roots and extensions[13]

Further developments based in part on laryngeal theory have led to a rather different view of what the basis for IE word-formation might have

[11] The primary constraint on historical reconstruction is the 'uniformitarian' assumption (for discussion Lass 1980: ch. 2, Appendix): nothing that is impossible in the present could have been the case in the past in any domain of rational inquiry. (Operating without some such constraint makes rational history impossible, because anything goes, and there is no sure way to know when you're talking rubbish.) That is, it is part of the definition of 'natural language' that such an object has at least three vowels in its system. Similar constraints make the formerly popular reconstruction of PIE as having the three vowels */e, o, α/ nearly impossible, since with either no exceptions or only some dubious ones, a language has to have at least one high vowel. (There was a view that IE */i, u/ existed only as the zero-grades of diphthongs, not independent vowels.)

[12] The number of laryngeals at one point got up to around ten, which need not concern us here. Since the heyday of 'laryngealism' in the 1950s, soberer views have tended to prevail. Now Szemerényi (1989: §V.4) has demonstrated a number of cases of irreducible original */i, u, α/ vocalism, restoring a permissible vowel system to the parent language; and Collinge (1970: ch. 5) argues elegantly for one laryngeal only. The episode is still not closed, and I've deliberately presented a fairly extreme version, which is useful for anybody venturing into the technical literature. The best overall account of the development of laryngeal theory up to the 1960s is probably Polomé (1965); this is immensely technical and difficult, but worth trying.

[13] On the structure of the IE root, the best discussion is that in Szemerényi (1989: chs. 5–6, passim).

looked like, and to some new and satisfying etymological connections, bringing together more of the lexicon than one might have thought possible. If the current view of IE root-structure is tenable, the morphology of the protolanguage was much more tightly-knit and productive than that of virtually any of its daughters. The old view of the IE lexical root was relatively unconstrained: it was taken as an indivisible unit, normally monosyllabic (though occasionally disyllabic), with possible rhyme-shapes like -VC (*/ɑg-/ 'drive'), or -VV (*/dhe:/ 'put'), or -VCC (*/wert-/ 'turn'). But some scholars have proposed a much more reductionist theory,[14] in which the basic form of the root itself, as a minimal or 'nuclear' lexical element, is always CVC (in the extreme version, */CeC/); all 'roots' that apparently end in more than one consonant actually consist of a 'triliteral' (as they're called) root plus one or more suffixes, often called 'determinatives' or 'extensions'.[15] Under this interpretation, each IE root + determinative complex could appear in three ablaut forms: (I) full-grade root and zero-grade suffix; (II) zero-grade root and full-grade suffix; or (III) zero-grade in both root and suffix.

This allows clearer and more satisfactory etymologies in many cases. Take for instance the root */der-/ 'tree, wood', with a determinative */-w-/. The three forms (and some of their descendants) are as follows:

(5.15)   I. */der-w-/: W *derwen* 'oak', Lith *dervà* 'pinewood', OE *teoru* 'tar'
         II. */dr-ew-/: Go *triu*, OE *trēow* 'tree'
         III. */dr-w-/: Skr *dru-* 'wood', Gr *drūs* 'oak', Irish *druadh* (gen pl), Scots Gaelic *druidh* 'Druid'[16]

The motivation for positing such a complex structure is clearer in certain cases where on semantic and (partly) on formal grounds there is no doubt that the same root is involved, but where there are as it were too many phonological forms for a unique reconstruction. A good case is the IE root meaning 'pour', and its developments:

(5.16)   A. Gr *khé-ō* < */khew-o:/ 'pour', Skr *hu-* (pres 3 sg *ju-hō-ti*), L (perf 1 sg) *fūdī*
         B. Go *giutan* 'pour', OE *gēotan*
         C. L *fu-n-d-ō* 'I pour'

---

[14] See especially Benveniste (1935), and the brief discussion in Polomé (1965: 15f).
[15] Prokosch (1938: §51) has a very lucid and well-exemplified discussion of determinatives and root-structure.
[16] 'Druid' is presumably connected via association with oak worship; but there may be a further connection with another derived sense of this root, 'firm, healthy, true', as in OE *trum* 'firm', OE *trēowe*, OS *triuwi*, Go *triggws* 'true', i.e. that which is 'true' is firm or tree-like.

Group A suggests an IE */gheu-/, and group B */gheud-/. L *fundō* in C suggests the zero-grade of longer */gheud-/, with a nasal infix, i.e. */ghu-n-d-/.[17] Do we want two unsegmentable proto-roots, */gheu-, gheud-/, both with the same meaning? To avoid this, we can separate out the /d/, and then the identical root is manifested in all the forms: either simple */gheu-/ or extended */gheu-d-/.

An even more extreme case is illustrated by L *trem-ō* 'tremble', *trep-idus* 'anxious', *ter-re-ō* 'frighten', OCS *tre-petŭ* 'tremble', Skr *tra-s-ati* 'tremble', *tar-ala-* 'trembling'. Surely the shared meaning suggests a residue of the shape */ter-/, with zero-grade */tr-/, plus extensions of the shapes */-m-, -r-, -p-, -s-/, rather than five separate indivisible and synonymous roots that all happen to have the first consonants in common!

One further example will illustrate the fruitfulness of combining laryngeal theory and the particular view of the IE root discussed here. Consider a putative root */H₂ew-g-/, with the sense 'increase'. In this form, since */H₂/ normally becomes /α/ in many of the dialects, it gives L *aug-eō* 'increase', Go *auk-an*, OE *ēac-ian*, *ēac-en* 'pregnant' (< */æuk-/ < */αuk-/). (We assume that a final */w/ becomes [u] by default.)

Now consider a form with zero-grade of the root and *e*-grade of the first determinative, plus another suffix */-s-/, i.e. */H₂w-eg-s-/. This will yield L *aux-* /αuks-/, as in *auxilium* 'help, aid'. And, considering the fact that initial laryngeals drop in Germanic, and that a sequence */αuV-/ is abnormal, the *o*-grade */H₂w-og-s-/ gives Go *wahsjan* 'grow, increase', OE *weaxan* /wæαxs-αn/ < */wαx-s-/ (and hence ModE *wax*). Since OE /æα/ as in *ēac-* becomes ModE /i:/ (*ēacian* > *eke* (*out*), as well as *nickname* < *eke-name*), with the help of laryngeals and the idea of root-extensions we can now show that *eke, aug-ment, aux-iliary, auc-tion* (< L *auc-tiō, -ōnis* 'increase'), and *wax* share a common IE basis, not only semantically but phonologically.

5.5   Zero-grade revisited

We have a pretty good idea now of the mechanism of zeroing, but the phonetic exponents of zero-grade may still pose some problems. One major puzzle for the etymological beginner is the kind of statement in which a perfectly 'normal' vowel in an IE word is said to go back to a zero-grade of the root. We have already seen an example in Gr /leip-/, where the fact that /-i-/ is 'zero' is explicable in terms of the whole shape of the ablaut system: it is a 'default syllabic', what is left behind after

---

[17] Such infixation is common in Latin presents, e.g. *rumpō* 'break', pp *ruptus*, the root clearly being *rup-*, hence *ru-m-p-*, etc.

zeroing. Other cases are similar, but less obvious on the surface, e.g. Go *tunþ-us* 'tooth', where /tunθ-/ is said to represent a zero grade */dn̥t-/ of the root */dent-/, or OE *wulf* 'wolf' < */wl̥kʷ-ó-s/, or Lith *širdìs* 'heart' < */kr̥d-/.

The key is that Germanic and Baltic do not have syllabic liquids and nasals in accented position; it therefore stands to reason that */-n̥-/, etc. in these languages would have to become something else. In Germanic, the typical result of zero-grade in a root with a coda -RT (the conventional notation for resonant + obstruent) is the transfer of syllabicity to an epenthetic /u/ inserted before the resonant:

(5.17)		*e*-grade	*o*-grade	zero-grade
	IE	-eRT	-oRT	-R̥T
	Gmc	-eRT	-αRT	-uRT

Similarly, /i/ is the usual Baltic reflex of a syllabic resonant: OE *wulf* = Lith *vil̃kas* (note the retained /R̥/ in Skr *vr̥k-áh*), and so on.

So the actual results of zeroing may be rather unexpected in some languages. Let us consider one more complex case in Sanskrit, since this language so often figures (rather opaquely) in the cognate lists in dictionaries, from which one is supposed to be able to see historical relations. In Sanskrit, to begin with, there is a major innovation which disrupts the inherited ablaut system: IE */e/ merges with */α/, which means that no ancestral e-grade will be transparent: *bhar-* 'bear' reflects IE */bher-/, and corresponds to L *fer-*, Gr *phér-*.

So one limitation on the transparency of historical origins is the actual phoneme inventory of the daughter language: Sanskrit has no short /e/. A further one, suggested by Lith *šird-* above, is the constraints (phonemic and phonetic) a language imposes on sequences of segments. Sanskrit permits the syllabic liquids /r̥, l̥/, but not syllabic nasals; therefore the typical zero-grade reflex with a following nasal involves a default vowel (confusingly, usually /α/). So from the root */men-/ 'think', *e*-grade gives *man-as* 'sense', but zero */mn̥-t-/ gives *ma-ti* 'understanding'. 'Zero' here correlates not only with /α/, but with loss of the nasal.

In a TVT (obstruent-V-obstruent) root, to take another problem, the results of zeroing may depend on whether the language allows obstruent clusters in a particular position, and also on morphological criteria. So IE */pt-/ can remain in Greek (*ptér-*) in a syllable onset, but this would not be possible in Germanic; if such a sequence were to arise, there would be substitution of another grade, and the results would be historically indecipherable. Gothic for instance shows zero-grade in *tunþ-us* (see above); we might therefore expect that other nouns of the same historical class like 'foot' might show it as well. But if it had come down in this form, the result would be *ft-us; therefore in the course of its selection of grades for roots, Gothic could not have chosen zero, and what appears is lengthened o-grade, fōt-us.

Another example, illustrating morphological constraints as well, occurs in the past participles of strong verbs. These derive from an IE verbal adjective in /-o-nó-/, and hence should have the reflex of zero-grade. And indeed with some roots they do: so in pp bunden 'bound' < */bhņdh-o-nó-/, IE */-ŖT/ > Gmc /-uRT/ as expected. But consider class V brecan 'break', root */bhreg-/. The participle ought to reflect an IE zero-grade */bhŗg-o-nó-/, and we should have *burcen. But OE and other Germanic languages apparently do not like allomorph pairs like /brek-/, /burk-/ for the same verb; there is an analogical transfer of the present-stem vowel /e/, giving brecen. (Just to make things worse, this is later replaced by a completely 'unhistorical' transfer to the participle vowel of the born type (cl IV), so broken instead of expected *breaken.)

5.6   Appendix: consonantal alternations

There is something like a consonantal parallel to ablaut, if much more sporadic and less systematic. In particular, a number of roots appear to exist in two forms, with varying consonantism. One of the most important of these alternations is the so-called 's-mobile'.

As we saw in teg-ō vs. stég-os, etc. (§5.1), certain roots appear to have an 'optional' initial /s/; or perhaps better, to occur in two forms, one with and one without */s/, hence the conventional description of this phenomenon as 'mobile s'. The root 'cover' then might be represented as */(s)teg-/, or */steg-, teg-/. In addition to the /s/-forms listed in (5.1) above, the same root also gives OIc stak-a 'hide', and OCS o-steg-u 'clothing, coat'. Another root of this kind has the sense 'see':

(5.18)   (a) */spek-/: Skr spas- 'spy', Avestan spas-yeiti 'he sees', L spec-iō 'I look at' (cf. spec-ulum 'mirror', spec-tātor 'looker-on', etc.), OHG speh-ōn 'watch'.
         (b) */pek-/: Skr pas-yati 'he sees', Avestan pas-ne 'in view of'.

A similar root is */(s)leim-/ 'slime, mucus': OE slīm 'mucus', līm 'lime, mortar', G Schleim 'slime', Leim 'glue'. We can also add L līm-us 'mud, slime', līm-ax 'slug, snail', and Gr lím-nē 'marsh'. It is worth noting (again the importance of native phonological structure in elucidating – or not elucidating – history) that even though OE līm/slīm show that this is a 'mobile *s*' root, there is no way of telling which version is ancestral to the Greek or Latin forms: neither of these languages tolerates initial /sl-/.

Another such root is involved in *melt/smelt* (< OE *meltan*, MLG *smelten*): cf. also OE *smolt*, G *Schmalz* 'fat'. The /s/-less root-alternant appears in L *moll-is* 'soft, tender' and OCS *mladŭ* 'young, tender'.

Awareness of *s*-mobile suggests an interesting perambulation through the lexicon of a language like English, given its enormous propensity for borrowing. The root */(s)teg-/ (in its various ablaut grades) appears in English in at least nine lexemes, both native and borrowed. *Thatch* of course we have already seen, and *tile* < OE *tīgele* < L *tēg-ula*. We also have borrowed L *toga*, and from this via French *togs*, a clipping of *tog(e)mans* 'cloak'. Still on the *s*-less alternant, there are various derivatives of L *teg-ō* and its forms, like *in-teg-ument*, *pro-tec-t* '(pro(vide) shelter for', *de-tec-t* 'un-cover'. The *s*-root is not well represented in English, but from (neo-)Greek we have the dinosaur *steg-o-saurus* 'roofed or covered lizard', and the rare sixteenth-century coinage *steg-ano-graphy* 'secret or cryptic writing'.

Another alternation involves roots in */Cw-, C-/. There seem to be a number of cases of a '*w*-mobile' (though it's not called this). Among these are two important pronominal roots, (a) the accusative 2 sg and (b) one form of the reflexive; and (c) the number 'six':

(5.19) (a) */t(w)e-/: Skr *tva-(m)* vs. L *te*, OE *þē*;
  (b) */s(w)e-/: Skr *sva-yam* 'self' vs. L *se*, Go *si-k*;
  (c) */s(w)ek-/: Welsh *chwech*, Avestan *xšvaš* vs. Gr *hek-s*, L *sex*, Go *saíh-s*, OE *siex*.

For more on these and other alternations see Szemerényi (1989: ch. 5.)

At least one scholar (Hodge 1986) has suggested that here were more systematic consonantal alternations, involving not just /C ~ CC/ as above, but rather a genuine (qualitative) consonantal ablaut. As an example Hodge suggests an alternation */m ~ b(h)/, in the (putatively) related roots */bhle:-/ 'bleat' (OE *blǣtan*, OCS *blěja*, Latv *bleju*), */bhel-/ 'resound' (OE *bellan* 'roar', *belle* 'bell', Lith *balsas* 'voice, tone'), */mel-w- ~mle-w-/ 'speak' (OE *mæðelian* 'speak', Lith *mluva*, Russian *molvá* 'speech'). Hodge's arguments and data are interesting; but even if the relationships he posits are genuine, the alternations of course do not play the same kind of fundamental role in IE morphophonology as ablaut 'proper'.

Part IV:

Morphology, lexis and syntax

Es war einmal ein Lattenzaun,
mit Zwichenraum, hindurchzuschaun.

Ein Architekt, der dieses sah,
stand eines Abends plötzlich da –

und nahm den Zwischenraum heraus
und baute draus ein großes Haus.

Der Zaun indessen stand ganz dumm,
mit Latten ohne was herum,

ein Anblick gräßlich und gemein.
Drum zog ihn der Senat auch ein.

Christian Morgenstern, 'Der Lattenzaun'

6 Inflectional morphology, I: Nouns, pronouns, determiners and adjectives

6.1 The Noun[1]

6.1.1 *Root vs. stem, thematic vs. athematic*

Traditional Germanistic discourse is often 'historical' in a rather opaque way (cf. the discussion of ablaut grades in chapter 5). Categories from older (even reconstructed) Indo-European are treated as 'still there', even if their traces are invisible to any but a well-trained eye. This is particularly true of the morphology sections of older handbooks, which refer to nouns for instance as *a*-stems, *i*-stems or *ō*-stems. It's not easy however for the student to see why OE *stān* 'stones', *lār* 'learning', *dǣd* 'deed' respectively should be said to belong to these classes. Such terms are not directly descriptive, but rather invoke characters of ancestral IE nouns or those in more ancient dialects, certainly not (generally) of attested Germanic ones. The same is true for descriptions of verbs: e.g. of *gān* 'go', *dōn* 'do' as 'athematic root-verbs', or 'to be', with its present forms *eam*, *eart*, *is* as a '-*mi*-present'. This chapter and the next aim to clarify such matters, and make the handbooks more usable (as well as making OE morphology more historically transparent).

The point of departure is IE word-structure, at least the structure of major-category words like nouns and verbs. We have already introduced (§5.4) the IE **root**: an element assumed to carry the lexical sense of a word-form, and in its oldest and perhaps commonest form a /CVC-/ structure with possible extensions of uncertain semantic function. So for instance the root */wer-/ 'turn, bend' appears in *e*-grade with a */-t-/ extension in the verb *weorþan* 'become' (with breaking before /rC/), in *o*-grade with the same extension in the preterite singular *wearþ* (IE */o/ > PGmc */ɑ/ > OE /æ/, plus breaking), and in zero-grade in the past plural *wurdon*, (with Verner's Law). The IE shape */wVr-t-/ lies behind all of these: the same root, with other extensions, gives OE *wyrm* 'worm',

---

[1] For an excellent introduction to the conceptual basis of morphology, and the kinds of theoretical categories invoked in this and the following two chapters, see Bauer (1988: chs. 1–3).

L *uermis* (*/wṛ-m-/), probably L *uergō* 'bend', and OE *wringan* 'twist'
(*/wr-en-g-/) *wrang* 'wrong' (*/wṛ-on-g-/ = twisted?), and perhaps (though
this is less clear) the root in OE *weorpan* 'throw'.

One root then can appear in words of different grammatical categories,
and in different forms, simple and extended, and in different ablaut
grades. The root in this sense is the basis for the construction of words in
the older IE languages.

A noun, verb or adjective is assumed to have had, in perhaps the
majority of instances, a basic structure consisting of the root, followed by a
thematic vowel (or consonant in certain cases), followed by the relevant
endings. In the case of a simple noun:

(6.1)   ROOT + Thematic Vowel + Endings (case, number, etc.)

This kind of structure is still relatively transparent in the older IE
dialects, like Greek or Latin. So for 'horse' (R = root, T = thematic
vowel):

(6.2)   L *equus* =   equ – u – s
                               R   T   nom sg
          Gr *hippos* =   hipp – o – s
                               R   T   nom sg

The root plus thematic vowel forms a **stem**: that morphological constituent to which the case/number endings are added. (The thematic element
is essentially an 'empty morph' which has no semantic content but is
needed for the morphological operation of stem-construction.)[2] We could
represent *equus* then as:

(6.3)

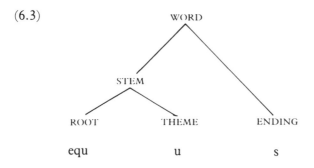

² 'Empty' at least in most instances in the attested IE dialects. It is likely that at an earlier
stage the themes may have been word-formation devices, which were later downgraded or
grammaticalized to stem-formatives, markers of inflectional classes. In addition, it may well
have been that in early IE many (or most) roots were not marked for grammatical category

Nouns like this are called **thematic**: in historical grammars noun classes are generally named according to the thematic vowel that followed the stem in IE, which as mentioned usually shows up fairly clearly in the older (non-Gmc) dialects, as in L *equ-u-s*, *can-i-s* 'dog', etc.

There are two partially different naming systems in use, one for IE and one for Germanic. When an IE vowel has a different Germanic reflex, the stem classes have different names. So, since IE */o/ = Gmc */ɑ/ (L *octō* 'eight' = Go *ahtau*), an IE *o*-stem is a Germanic *a*-stem; and since IE */ɑ:/ = Gmc */o:/ (L *māter* = OE *mōdor*), an IE *ā*-stem is a Germanic *ō*-stem. Other classes are unchanged (*i*-stems, *u*-stems).

Much of this morphology is opaque in Germanic, even in Gothic, due to centuries of erosive change; but the names are convenient as well as traditional, and do display historical relations. Further, at least within certain limits, which should be clear below, each identifies a declension type in a reasonably non-cumbersome way. That is, '*a*-stem' is more convenient than 'class whose masculine members in OE have *-as* in nom-acc pl and whose masculines and neuters have *-es* in genitive sg'; and historically more illuminating than arbitrary numbering (like the 'first declension', etc. of Latin grammars).

In Germanic grammars nouns with vocalic themes are generally called 'strong'; a small class with stems in */-Vn/ are called 'weak'. The weak type can be seen in Latin 'third declension' nouns like *homo* 'man', gen sg *hom-in-is*: cf. the OE cognate *guma* 'man', gen sg *gum-an*. In addition to thematic nouns there are **athematic** or 'root-nouns' (G *Wurzelnomina*), also called 'consonant stems'. Compare L *equ-u-s*, *can-i-s* above with *uōx* 'voice', *rēx* 'king', morphologically {wo:k-s}, {reg:-s}. Here the endings are added directly to the bare root.

The original details of the thematic types may no longer be visible as such in Germanic; but the IE structures have consequences even for relatively late and highly modified dialects like OE. For instance, in the Germanic *a*-stem and *ō*-stem declensions, there are complex subtypes where the theme vowel was preceded by a /w/ or /j/ (called *wa-*, *ja-*, *wō-*, *jō-* stems, as opposed to 'pure' *a*-stems, etc.). These prethematic segments (which functioned in part as derivational markers) have morphophonemic effects: in the *ja*-stems for instance, the /j/ causes umlaut of the preceding vowel (cf. §3.8), so that no noun of this class can have a back root vowel. More interestingly, the type with preceding /w/ has as relics a final /-u/ in some paradigm members and a /w/ preceding the ending in others:

(as is generally true in Semitic and Balto-Finnic for instance); in this case the themes may have originally served as part-of-speech markers, e.g. nominalizers, verbalizers, aspect markers, etc. until the attested suffixes developed (suggested to me by Dieter Kastovsky.)

(6.4)   *bearu* 'grove' (nom sg) < */βαr-wα-z/
         bearwes (gen sg) < */βαr-wα-sα/

Thus a noun in -*u* that is a historical *wa*-stem will have non-nom sg forms
with -*w*- after the stem; whereas other themes that also come down as -*u* do
not have this effect, e.g. in *ō*-stems and *u*-stems. Compare *bearu/bearwes*
with:

(6.5)   *ō*-stem: *caru* 'care' (nom sg) < */kαr-o:/
         care   (gen sg) < */kαr-o:-z/
         u-stem: *sunu* 'son' (nom sg) < */sun-u-z/
         suna   (gen sg) < */sun-αu-z/

Different stem classes could select different endings for particular case/
number forms. So although */-s/ was the commonest nominative singular
ending in IE, *ā*-stems typically had nominative in zero: compare L *port-a*
'door' (*ā*-stem) and *port-u-s* 'harbour' (*u*-stem). In the *o*-stem (Gmc *a*-stem)
class, masculines typically had nom sg in */-s/, neuters */-m/: L *hort-u-s*
'garden' vs. *jug-u-m* 'yoke' (OE *geard, geoc*).

6.1.2   IE noun-inflection: gender, number, case[3]

The main inflectional categories of the IE noun were gender, number and
case. The earliest forms of the parent language probably had only two
genders, 'animate' vs. 'inanimate'.[4] At a later stage, but before the
emergence of the attested dialects, the animate class seems to have split
into what are now feminines and masculines in those IE dialects with a
three-gender system. Germanic descends from a late variety of PIE that
already had the three-way system we find in Latin, Greek, Sanskrit and
Old Germanic.[5]

---

[3] There is a very detailed discussion of all the IE inflectional categories in Kuryłowicz
(1964). For the noun see chs. 8–9.
[4] 'Gender' as a grammatical term does not refer to 'sex'; any parameter that nouns can be
classified on (animacy, rationality, shape, concreteness, etc.) can form the basis for a gender
system. Many of the most familiar ones (whatever their original 'natural' or semantic basis)
are essentially arbitrary (so-called 'grammatical' rather than 'natural' gender). There is
nothing 'male' about a stone (OE *stān*, G *Stein*, m.), and definitely something non-neuter
about a woman (OE *wīf*, G *Weib*, n.). For an excellent cross-linguistic introduction to the
topic, see Corbett (1991).
[5] On the development of IE gender see Prokosch (1938: §78), Szemerényi (1989: ch. 6, §1.2
and references). Three-gender systems of the old type remain in Icelandic, Faroese, German,
and Yiddish; Danish, Swedish, most varieties of Norwegian, Dutch and Frisian have a
two-way 'common' vs. neuter split; Afrikaans and English have lost grammatical gender.

The original number system was also trifurcated: singular vs. dual (two and two only) vs. plural. The noun dual generally vanished early, except in a few cases such as Slavic, where names of paired body-parts like eyes, ears have dual forms; otherwise it remains only as a pronoun category in most Old Germanic dialects (see §6.2.1).

PIE appears to have had a case system with at least eight distinct categories. These, with their typical functions and reconstructed endings, are:

(i) NOMINATIVE. Subject, predicate nominal. Endings sg */-s, -Ø/, du */-e, -i(:)/, pl */-es/.

(ii) VOCATIVE. Direct address. Sg */-Ø/, du */-e, -i(:)/, pl as nominative.

(iii) ACCUSATIVE. Direct object, motion-into, across, extent. Sg */-m, -m̥/, du as nom, voc, pl */-ns, -n̥s/.

(iv) GENITIVE. Possession, partitivity.[6] Sg */-es, -os, -s/, du ?*/-ous, -o:s/, pl */-o(:)m/.

(v) DATIVE. Motion-towards, indirect object, subject of verbs of feeling, experience. Sg */-ei/, du */-bhjo:, -mo/, pl */-bh(j)os, -mos/.[7]

(vi) ABLATIVE. Motion-from. Sg */-es, -os, -s, -ed, -od/, du, pl as dative.

(vii) LOCATIVE. Location-in. Sg */-i/, du */-ou/, pl */-su/.

(viii) INSTRUMENTAL. Means-by-which. Sg */-e, -bhi, -mi/, du as dat, abl, pl */-bhis, -mis, -o:is/.

The standard view is that in earliest IE there was a single set of case-endings (those given above) for all nouns, regardless of stem-class. Later, as the individual dialects developed, particular endings or ablaut grades of endings came to be associated with certain stem-classes (not always the same in different languages) and ultimately with specific combinations of gender and stem-class. Thus the general IE endings for nom sg were */-s/ or zero; but in some dialects a formative in */-m/ came to mark neuter nom sg in certain classes (L -um, Gr -on < */-om/).

Case systems of the original size rarely survive, and never in all declensions in one language. A comparative survey of one declension, the o-stem (Gmc a-stem) masculine, will give some idea of what Germanic looks like in general compared to the rest of IE, and how 'advanced'

---

[6] I.e. extraction out of a set of possible referents, part of a whole, 'some'. Note the 'genitive' prepositions in a cup of coffee, F une tasse de café, partitive case in Finnish kuppi kahvi-a (nom kahvi). For further discussion of the semantics of the cases in historical perspective see §9.3.

[7] Dative (and instrumental) endings in both */bh-, m-/ are reconstructed because /m/ types occur in Germanic, Baltic and Slavic only, and /b(h)/ elsewhere. It is not clear whether the former really belong to the protolanguage, or are a NWIE innovation. My /j/ = the /y/ in the literature; in this book the latter symbol only = a front-rounded vowel.

dialects like OE compare to conservative ones like Gothic. I set out the cases in two groups below: first the essentially 'grammatical' ones (nominative, vocative, accusative, genitive); then the 'local' cases, those involving movement in space or what from a ModE perspective might be thought of as 'prepositional' relations (dative, ablative, locative, instrumental).

In (6.6) below, a '−' for a category means that the language in question does not have it as a distinct case anywhere; repeated endings (e.g. L dat/abl) mean that in some declensions (but not here) the two are distinct; -Ø means that a category is unmarked in this declension, but has an ending in others.

(6.6)			Skr	Lith	Lat	Gr	Go	OE
		nom	-a-s	-a-s	-u-s	-o-s	-s	-Ø
		voc	-a	-e	-e	−	-Ø	−
		acc	-a-m	-a	-u-m	-o-n	-Ø	-Ø
	sg	gen	-a-sya	-o	-ī	-o-io	-is	-es
		dat	-ā-ya	-ui	-ō	-ō-i	-a	-e
		abl	-a-d	−	-ō	−	−	−
		loc	-e	-e	−	−	−	−
		ins	-a	-u	−	−	−	−
		nom	-ā-s	-a-i	-ī	-o-i	-ōs	-as
		acc	-ā-s	-i-s	-ō-s	-o-i	-ōs	-as
		gen	-a-m	-u	-ō-rum	-ō-n	-ē	-a
	pl	dat	-e-bhyas	-a-ms	-īs	-o-isi	-a-ms	-um
		loc	-e-su	-uose	−	−	−	−
		ins	-a-is	-a-is	−	−	−	−

None of these languages distinguishes vocative or ablative plural. Not all the endings in (6.6) of course are cognate; nor do they all reflect the pattern reconstructed for PIE, since there has already been considerable restructuring. But relationships are clearer in some categories in other declensions, e.g. Skr dat pl -*bhyas* = L dat/abl pl -*bus* in nouns of the type of *homo* 'man', dat/abl pl *hom-in-i-bus*.

The transition from late IE to PGmc involved a collapse and reformation of the case system; nominative, genitive and accusative remained more or less intact, but all the locational/movement cases merged into a single 'fourth case', which is conventionally called 'dative', but in fact often represents an IE locative or instrumental.[8] This codes pretty much

---

[8] The Germanic dative and its origins are discussed, with reference to early OE forms, in Lass (1991).

all the functions of the original dative, locative, ablative and instrumental. A few WGmc dialects do still have a distinct instrumental sg for some noun classes, e.g. OS *dag-u*, OHG *tag-u* for 'day' vs. dat sg *dag-e*, *tag-e*; OE has collapsed both into dative (along with locative, instrumental and ablative), though some traces of an instrumental remain in the pronouns (§6.2).

The new system had only four basic categories, so there was just too much material around, as it were, to underwrite the much smaller set of contrasts that Germanic selected. The different declensions more or less chose one IE form to represent the conflation of at least four original cases (some specific examples are discussed below).

6.1.3   The major noun classes[9]

In this section we look at paradigms for typical members of the most important stem-classes, with Gothic and Old Icelandic examples to illustrate different treatments of inherited materials, and different patterns of innovation.

(i) *a*-stems (IE *o*-stems). These are masculine or neuter only, with a stem-formative $*/-\alpha-/$ (= L *-us/-um* 'second declension', Gr *-os/-on*). Example: $*/\eth\alpha\gamma-\alpha-z/$ 'day' (m).

(6.7)

		Go	OE	OIc
	nom	dag-s	dæg	dag-r
	gen	dag-is	dæg-es	dag-s
sg	dat	dag-a	dæg-e	deg-e
	acc	dag	dæg	dag
	nom	dag-ō-s	dag-as	dag-ar
	gen	dag-ē	dag-a	dag-a
pl	dat	dag-am	dag-um	dǫg-um
	acc	dag-ans	dag-as	dag-a

This is the commonest declension in Germanic, the source of the ModE and Dutch {-s} plurals, and many Scandinavian {-r} plurals (Swedish *dag-ar*). Scandinavian /r/ here is from rhotacized $*[z] < */s/$, and both OIc *-a* and OE *-as* in acc pl reflect original $*/-\alpha-n-s/$, as shown still in Gothic.[10]

The Gothic dat sg in *-a* is not a historical dative; it is from a zero-instrumental with lengthening of the theme vowel, as in the Sanskrit

---

[9] For good overall surveys of Germanic noun morphology and its IE origins, see Prokosch (1938: §76–88), Campbell (1959: ch. 11), and the full-length treatment in Bammesberger (1990).

[10] The Gothic ending *-ans* is not segmented; it seems unlikely that the theme vowel could have been synchronically separable from the /-ns/.

example in (6.6), with later shortening in weak position, i.e. $*$/-α-α/ > /-α:/. The OIc vowel alternations have various sources: dat sg *deg-e* has *i*-umlaut, and reflects a locative in $*$/-i/ (possibly the zero-grade of IE $*$/-ei/: cf. §5.2); *dǫg-um*, where <ǫ> = /ɔ/, shows a NGmc *u*-umlaut.

There are also *ja*- and *wa*-stems: *here* 'army' < /xɑr-jɑ-z/ (Go *har-j-is*), *cnēo* 'knee' < $*$/kniu-wɑ-z/ (Go *kniu*, gen sg *kni-w-is*, OE *cnēo-w-es*). The paradigms show how many distinctions have already been lost; only Gothic retains (for this class) a separate morph for each case/number category. And this is by far the morphologically richest declension.

The *a*-stem neuters lack the *-s* ending in nom/acc plural. Here the marker is *-u*; but its presence or absence is determined by the weight of the root syllable. So light roots with *-u*, heavy roots endingless (*scip-u* 'ships' vs. *bān* 'bone(s)', *word* 'word(s)'). This is a reflex of the old high vowel deletion (HVD) process discussed in §4.3; we will see more cases later. In one group of disyllabic nouns with either a heavy first syllable or a root-final liquid preceded by a stop, there is syncope (medial deletion: again see §4.3): *engel* 'angle', *hleahtor* 'laughter', *hēafod* 'head', gen sg *engl-es*, *hleahtr-es*, *hēafd-es*.

The gen sg in *-es* belongs historically to the masculine and neuter *a*-stems alone. When this occurs in other classes (as in the *i*-stem and consonant-stem masculines and neuters – see below), it is an analogical transfer from the *a*-stems. As one might gather from the fact that all ModE nouns have gen sg in {-s}, the *a*-stems have been a kind of analogical 'target' throughout the history of the language; and the great preponderance of {-s} plurals (the only normal type now) reflects this too.[11]

(ii) **ō-stems (IE ā-stems)**. Feminine only; stem formative $*$/-o:/, zero nom sg (= L 'first declension' in *-a*, Gr *-a/-e*). Example: $*$/γeβ-o:/ 'gift'.[12]

---

[11] The *a*-stems have another character in common with ModE nouns, which makes them an expectable target for later developments: no distinction between nom and acc in the singular (no OE nouns make this distinction in the plural). The unmarked nom sg creates a situation where (unlike the case in some other declensions) stem = word; hence this type foreshadows the later development of English, where 'stem' in the older sense virtually disappears as a distinct morphological category. The particular choice of the *a*-stems may also reflect the status of the zero nom sg; while other declensions also show these (e.g. the *ō*-stems, *i*-stems, *u*-stems: see below), in these cases they alternate with vocalic endings after heavy syllables, so they are not declension 'markers' *per se.*

[12] Note that the old theme vowel $*$/-o:/ has been reinterpreted as a nom sg marker; in later times, when inflections were beginning to collapse (chapter 10), and *giefu* > *giefe*, this ending became part of the stem again, which then = the word.

(6.8)

		Go	OE	OIc
	nom	gib-a	gief-u	gjǫf
sg	gen	gib-ōs	gief-e	gjaf-ar
	dɛt	gib-ai	"	gjǫf
	acc	gib-a	"	
	nom	gib-ōs	gief-a/-e	gjaf-ar
pl	gen	gib-ō	gief-a/-ena	gjaf-a
	dat	gib-ōm	gief-um	gjǫf-um
	acc	gib-ōs	gief-a/-e	gjaf-ar

HVD after heavy syllables shows up here too: light roots *gief-u*, *luf-u* 'love', heavy *beorc* 'birch', *lāf* 'remnant'. Similarly, there is no nom sg ending in disyllables (recall the 'resolution' principle, §4.3.2, that allows ŏŏ to count as ō): *feter* 'fetter', *sāwol* 'soul' (the latter with syncope in oblique cases: *sāwl-e*, *sāwl-um*, etc.).

This pattern holds only for simplex (non-derived) nouns. In some derivationally complex ō-stems, a final -*u* appears even after a heavy root, e.g. in abstract nouns in */-iθ-o:/ like *strengþu* 'strength' < */strɑnɣ-iθ-o:/ (cf. *strang* 'strong'), *cȳþþu* 'native land' (*cūþ* 'known'), *þīefþu* 'theft'. Endingless forms like *cȳþþ*, *þīefþ*, also occur. (This derivation is the origin of the modern {-t} in {*thef-t*}, etc., which is a dissimilation of the original {-þ}; the fricative remains in {streng-th}, {warm-th} and the like.)

Some retained -*u* also occur in *jō*-stem derivatives, like *streng-u* 'strength' < */strɑnɣ-i:n-jo:/, *brǣdu* 'breadth' (*brād* 'broad'). In most of these the original */-n-/ formative has vanished, though it remains in *byrþen(n)* 'burden', *fyxen* 'vixen', *byrgen* 'tomb' (cf. *fox*, *byrigean* 'bury'). Other important derived *jō*-stems include those in -*ness* < */-nɑs-jo:/, e.g. *þrī-ness* 'trinity'. (For more details see §8.3.3 below.)

The *wō*-stems are much like the ordinary or 'pure' ō-stems, except that they have /-w-/ in oblique cases: either alternating with /-u/ in nom sg of light roots (*bead-u* 'battle', dat sg *bead-w-e*) or with zero in heavy roots (*mǣd* 'meadow', *mǣd-w-e*).

(iii) *i-stems*. M, f, n with formative */-i-/ (= L 'third declension' in -*is*, Gr -*is*). Example: */ɣɑst-i-z/ 'guest' (m).

(6.9)

		Go	OE	OIc
	nom	gast-s	giest	gest-r
sg	gen	gast-is	giest-es	gest-s
	dat	gast-a	giest-e	gest
	acc	gast	giest	"
	nom	gast-eis	giest-as	gest-er
pl	gen	gast-ē	giest-a	gest-a
	dat	gast-im	giest-um	gest-um
	acc	gast-ins	giest-as	gest-e

The OE paradigm shows why the conventional listing of nouns by (historical) stem-classes can be misleading – though it makes sense given a wide enough perspective. OE *giest* is morphologically an *a*-stem (cf. (6.7)), and it is only comparison with Go *gast-s* and a cognate like L *host-i-s* that shows why it is classified as an *i*-stem.[13] The *i*-umlaut of the root vowel is the only evidence left for its original declension; and even this is opaque except by comparison with Gothic or Latin, which show the old back vowel. This opacity however does not hold for derived forms like certain deverbal nouns: *cyme* 'coming' < *$/$kum-i-z/ (cf. *cuman*), *cyre* 'choice' < *$/$kur-i-z/ (cf. pret pl *curon*). The Gothic singular is also *a*-stem in form; in Germanic, the Gothic plural alone retains a clear *i*-stem identity. So even before the E/NW split, it seems, the *a*-stems were an analogical template for the reformation of other noun paradigms.

At least this was the case for masculines and neuters. The *i*-stem feminines have also been largely remodelled, but this time on the *ō*-stem pattern. This is quite general in older Germanic: when there is analogical restructuring, masculines and neuters go to *a*-stem, feminines to *ō*-stem. These seem to have been interpreted as the 'prototypes' for their gender-classes. So *i*-stem feminines have -*e* in gen/dat/acc sg, and -*e*/-*a* in nom/acc pl just like the *ō*-stems (cf. (6.8)): *cwēn* 'queen', gen/dat/acc sg *cwēn-e*, etc. We would actually expect zero in the dat sg here, through deletion of the original ending *$/$-i/ (an IE locative) after a heavy root; but the *ō*-stem -*e* has replaced it. There seem to be no light-stem feminines in this declension in OE; they went over to *ō*-stems in prehistoric times.

The original thematic *$/$-i-/ leaves two relics: *i*-umlaut throughout the paradigm (no *i*-stem may have a back root vowel), and nom sg in -*e* after light roots vs. zero after heavy ones: *win-e* 'friend', *hyg-e* 'mind' vs. *giest*, *mǣw* 'seagull'.

---

[13] It would be best of course to call it a 'former *i*-stem', but once you understand the tradition the problem disappears.

This class contains an important group of deverbal nouns, formed from the past participle roots of strong verbs: *bite* 'bite' < */βit-i/ (*-biten*), *cym-e* 'coming' < */kum-i/ (*-cumen*).

(iv) *u*-**stems.** M, f, n with formative */-u-/ (= L *-us* 'fourth declension', gen sg in *-ūs*, Gr *-us*). Example: */sun-u-z/ 'son' (m).

(6.10)

		Go	OE	OIc
	nom	sun-us	sun-u	sun-r
sg	gen	sun-aus	sun-a	son-ar
	dat	sun-au	"	syn-e
	acc	sun-u	sun-u	sun
	nom	sun-jus	sun-a	syn-er
pl	gen	sun-i-wē	"	son-a
	dat	sun-um	sun-um	sun-um
	acc	sun-uns	sun-a	sun-o

OE has extensively remodelled the plural, losing the original umlaut-causing */-i, -j/ formatives (Go *sun-jus* = OIc *syn-er*, and cf. G *Sohn/ Söhne*).[14]

This example has a light root; as expected, final *-u* is lost after a heavy one (*hād* 'condition', *feld* 'field'). Feminines are declined like masculines. Neuter *u*-stems did occur in Germanic (Go *faíh-u* 'cattle' = L *pec-u-s*), but are virtually unknown in OE; these appear as *a*-stem masculines (OE *feoh*).

A number of other nouns which may once have been *u*-stems are *a*-stems in OE: *ār* 'messenger', *dēaþ* 'death', *flōd* 'flood' (Go *air-us*, *dauþ-us*, *flōd-us*). These however may not actually be 'transfers' to a new class; it is quite possible that from early times there existed doublets for many nouns, one of which might be selected by one dialect, another by another. (For a modern English parallel, cf. *index*, *formula*, which may belong to different declensions in different varieties; plurals *indexes* or *indices*, *formulas* or *formulae*, etc.) Certainly Gothic *u*-stems include other

---

[14] Note how mere possession of a 'rich' inflectional morphology doesn't imply lack of ambiguity for any particular morphological class. The common argument connecting later loss of freedom in word order with erosion of noun inflection (order was stabilized to 'prevent confusion') collapses here: except for some declensions in Gothic and OIc, all Gmc noun plurals merge nom/acc, and they are rarely distinct in the singular. Yet the older dialects have a quite 'free' word order. Clearly lack of morphological distinction even between such basic cases as those coding subject and direct object is not a 'problem' for these languages, so the fixation of word order can't be a 'solution'. One could of course say that the richer morphology of determiners and pronouns was a disambiguating factor: but not for indefinite subjects and objects. (See further §6.1.4 below, and Lass 1980: chs. 3–4, where I argue that no property of a language's structure can possibly be a 'problem' for its speakers.)

nouns that belong to different classes elsewhere, especially consonant-stems: *fōt-us* 'foot' and *tunþ-us* 'tooth' are *u*-stems nowhere except in Gothic.[15]

(iv) ***n*-stems (IE *-en*/*-on* stems).** M, f, n; theme */-Vn-/, with varying vowel grades (= L 'third declension' nouns in *-ō*, with oblique forms in *-in-*, Gr *-en*). Example: */xαn-en-, -αn-/ 'hen'. The oblique stem is given here, since only the nom sg lacks the /-n-/ formative. This also dropped in Latin: OE *gum-a* 'man', gen sg *gum-an* = L *hom-ō*, *hom-in-is*. So Go, OE *han-a* < */xαn-o:/, oblique stem */xαn-o:-n-/.

(6.11)

		Go	OE	OIc
	nom	han-a	han-a	han-e
	gen	han-in-s	han-an	han-a
sg	dat	han-in	"	"
	acc	han-an	"	"
	nom	han-an-s	han-an	han-ar
	gen	han-an-ē	han-ena	han-a
pl	dat	han-am	han-um	hǫn-um
	acc	han-an-s	han-an	han-a

OIc shows some remodelling (presumably an *a*-stem source for nom pl); other final *-a* are due to Scandinavian dropping of /n/ in weak syllables (cf. NGmc infinitives in *-a* vs. E, WGmc in *-an*).

Old English also shows some restructuring: the dat sg should (cf. Gothic and the Latin type *hom-in-ī*) have /-i/, from an IE *e*-grade locative */-ei/. If this had been retained it would give umlaut in dat sg, hence OE *hæn-e. This restructuring is therefore at least older than IU.

Some *n*-stems had */j/ before the */-Vn-/ theme; these have umlaut in the root syllable, and (in light roots) gemination (cf. §3.2): *brytt-a* 'distributor' < */βrut-jo:-/. The masculine *n*-stems contain an important class of deverbal agent nouns, where the suffix {-a} has much the same function as ModE {-er}: *hunt-a* 'hunter', *gesac-a* 'adversary', *gefēr-a* 'companion' (cf. verbs *huntigan* 'hunt', *sacan* 'struggle', *fēran* 'travel').[16]

The feminine *n*-stems are very like the masculines, except for having *-e* in nom sg: *tung-e* 'tongue', *fold-e* 'earth', *ūl-e* 'owl'. (Since this *-e* does not derive from a historical high vowel, it does not drop after a heavy root syllable.) Some feminines however developed a new nom sg in *-u* on the

---

[15] The historical problem of nouns with variable declension-membership is discussed in Lass (1986).

[16] 'Much the same' does not mean 'the same', and this is crucial: the *-a* (whatever its precise 'meaning') is not a derivational affix but a nom sg marker, i.e. an inflection. This ending, like the */-j-/ themes mentioned below, probably started life as a deverbal suffix, but was reanalysed as an inflection. It does however, as is often the case, retain something of the semantics of its original.

ō-stem model, so *spad-u* ~ *spad-e* 'spade', *wic-u* ~ *wic-e* 'week'. This class also contains feminine agentives in *-estre*, like *lǣr-estre* 'teacher' (cf. *lǣran* 'teach', *lār* 'lore'), *hlēap-estre* 'dancer' (*hlēapan* 'leap'). This suffix remains in a somewhat obscured form in (originally occupational) names like *Baxter* < *bæcestre* 'baker', *Webster* < *webbestre* 'weaver'.

The neuters are a tiny class, with nom sg on the feminine model: *ēag-e* 'eye', *ēar-e* 'ear', and *wang-e* 'cheek'.

The *n*-stems were widely extended in later times in some of the Germanic dialects (e.g. the very common German and Dutch plurals in {-n}), but they receded in English. The only 'pure' relic now is *oxen* (OE *ox-a*, *ox-an*), though a few others have added a weak ending to another plural, like *child-r-en* (on *r*-stems like this see below), and the archaic *kine* (OE *cū* 'cow', pl *cȳ* + *-n*). Some varieties of English still retain other weak plurals (Scots *een* 'eyes'), or new *n*-stem types extended to other declensions (Scots *shoon* 'shoes', originally an *a*-stem).

(v) **Athematic consonant stems** (root-nouns, G *Wurzelnomina*). Endings added directly to the root (e.g. L *rēx* 'king' /re:k-s/ < */re:g-s/, gen sg *rēg-is*; Gr *núk-s* 'night' < */nukt-s/, gen sg *núkt-os*). Addition of the nom sg */-s/ to the consonant-final stems (as in the examples above) can alter the root and produce an alternation where only the oblique cases show the full form. In Germanic, which allowed much freer coda-clustering than Latin or Greek, this did not usually happen (Go nom sg *naht-s* 'night'). But even where modification might be expected, as in dialects like OE that did not generally allow syllable-final /ts/, etc., the expected type does not appear: for 'foot' the development should have been */fo:t-z/ > */fo:t-s/ * > /fo:s-s/, but the attested form is *fōt*, not **fōss*.

This class had a very chequered history in Germanic, and not much of the original morphology survives. Many nouns went over either partly or totally to other declensions; this went further in Gothic than elsewhere, and we will consider only NWGmc for comparative purposes. A fairly typical example is 'foot' (m):

(6.12)

		OE	OIc
	nom	fōt	fót-r
	gen	fōt-es	fót-ar
sg	dat	fēt	fœt-i
	acc	fōt	fót
	nom	fēt	fœt-r
	gen	fōt-a	fót-a
pl	dat	fōt-um	fót-um
	acc	fēt	fœt-r

(OIc <œ> = /ø:/; OE /e:/ here is from /ø:/: cf. §3.8.2.)

The nom/acc pl show IE */-es/ > PGmc */-iz/; the dat sg is an old locative in */-i/ (clear in OIc), lost in OE through HVD after a heavy root (§4.3.2). Feminines are similar: *bōc* 'book', dat sg, nom/acc pl *bēc*. Feminines however may have an alternative gen sg ending with umlaut and zero ending, e.g. *bēc* < */bo:k-iz/ (cf. L gen sg -*is*). This is in fact the expected gen sg; the masculines have adopted the *a*-stem form, and the feminines most often have an *ō*-stem gen in -*e* (so *bēc* ~ *bōc-e*). In late OE the umlauted dat sg usually goes over to the majority type in -*e*: *fōt-e*, *bōc-e*.

In post-OE times, only *foot, goose, man, louse, mouse* have not gone over to the *a*-stem pattern; but the class once include *āc* 'oak', *brōc* 'trousers', *burg* 'city' (also *ō*-stem), *cū* 'cow', *gāt* 'goat', *turf* 'turf', *furh* 'furrow', *hnutu* 'nut'. The plural of *brōc*, i.e. *brēc*, does remain in the double-plural form *breeches*, though the singular (which would be **brook*) has been lost. Dutch and Afrikaans however have *broek* '(pair of) trousers', Afrikaans plural *broek-e*. As an example of how language-contact can complicate history, South African English has reborrowed this singular from Afrikaans, and added the native pl {-s}, so that *broeks* /bruks/ is now a common SA English word for 'underpants'.

(vi) **Minor noun declensions.** A number of small classes with inflectional peculiarities of historical interest deserve some comment:

(a) Kinship nouns in /-r/ (Type: L *pater*, gen sg *patr-is*, dat sg *patr-ī*). This group contains *fæder* 'father', *mōdor* 'mother', *brōþor* 'brother', *sweostor* 'sister', *dohtor* 'daughter'. The IE stems had a formative */-tVr/, which appeared in various ablaut grades (see chapter 5). So Gr *patér* (nom sg), *patér-a* (dat sg), and cf. L *pater*, *patr-* above. The suffix accent illustrated in Greek is the source of the Verner's Law consonantism (OE *fæder* instead of **fæþer*).

These are similar in some ways to the athematic consonant-stems, e.g. umlauted dat sg (*mōdor*, dat sg *mēder*, cf. Gr. *mētr-ī*) is common. They also frequently have zero gen sg, though analogical types like *a*-stem *fæder-es* occur as well. Except for *doehter/dehter*, they do not generally show umlaut in nom/acc plural.

(b) Masculine /-nd-/ stems. These are often called *Substantivierte Partizipia* 'nominalized participles' in the handbooks, since their stem-formative is the same as the present-participle suffix (-*end* < */-anð-ja-/: cf. §7.2.4). Examples are *frēond* 'friend', *hettend* 'enemy', *hǣlend* 'saviour', *āgend* 'owner' (cf. the verbs *frēogan* 'love, embrace', *hettan* 'chase, persecute', *hǣlan* 'heal', *āgan* 'own'). The type is widespread in Germanic: OE *frēond* = OHG *friunt*, OIc *frǣndi*, Go *frijōnds*.

Declension is of a mixed type, showing athematic and thematic properties; *a*-stem genitives and nom/acc pl occur (*frēond-es*, -*as*) alongside zero genitives, and one noun, *frēond*, shows umlauted forms (*frīend*, *frȳnd*). Athematic datives (*frīend*) and *a*-stem types (*frēond-e*) are attested. One peculiarity of this group (probably reflecting its origin in a participle form) is the presence of a gen pl in *-ra* in disyllabic nouns like *hettend*; this seems to be an old adjectival ending.

(c) *r*-stems (IE *-es/-os* stems). (Type: L *genus* 'kind', gen sg *gen-er-is* < */gen-es-os/*). These have /r/ as a plural marker in Germanic (derived from */s/* by Verner's Law and rhotacism; the latter occurs in oblique cases in Latin as well). Singulars are usually *a*-stem, but with nom/acc pl *-ru*, gen pl *-ra*, dat pl *-rum*. Common examples are *cealf* 'calf' (*cealf-ru*, etc.), *lamb* 'lamb', *ǣg* 'egg' (cf. G *Ei*, pl *Ei-er*).

This class has now vanished, but a trace remains in *children* (< OE *cild-er-u* + *n*-stem suffix). Survivors in other Germanic dialects often show reinterpretation of the /r/ as part of the root, or at least as a kind of plural 'extension' requiring another ending; *children* on this view might be interpreted as [[child]r]+en]]. Dutch *ei* 'egg', pl *ei-er-en* exhibits the same kind of reinterpretation as *children*; Afrikaans has gone one step further and incorporated the /r/-extension into the root: sg *eier*, pl *eier-s*. The same development can be seen in Dutch *kind* 'child', pl *kind-er-en*, Afr *kinder*, *kinder-s* (cf. G *Kind*, *Kind-er*). In German however this class was extended, and is the basis for the common plural type with umlaut of the root vowel and suffix *-er*: *Buch/Bücher* 'book(s)', an original consonant-stem, etc. In Yiddish the *r*-stem + umlaut pattern was even extended to loanwords, as in Hebrew *toxes* 'arse', pl *texes-er*, or English *švits-šop* 'sweatshop', pl *švits-šep-er*.

A few OE nouns already show attachment of /r/ to the root: *sigor* 'victory' (also *sige*, cf. Go *sig-is*, OIc *sig-r*), *ēar* 'ear of grain', older Northumbrian *æhher*; the /r/ has coalesced with the root in this word in OS, OHG *ahar* as well, but the unincorporated form can be seen in OIc *ax*, Go *ahs*, and the original declension type in L *acus* 'awn, bristle', gen sg *ac-er-is*.[17]

(d) 'Heteroclitic' nouns. A small group of consonant-stems (the so-called **heteroclites** or **heteroclitic** nouns) are mentioned in the handbooks but rarely explained. Heteroclisis is the simultaneous membership of an item in two declension classes; this phenomenon helps to explain some complex correspondences between Germanic and other dialect-groups. Heteroclites in IE have *r*-stem nom/acc sg, but are otherwise generally *n*-stem, or occasionally *r*-stem + *n*-stem. Two well-known examples are L

---

[17] One of the most striking trends in the development of English (and some other Germanic languages) is a move from 'stem-based' to 'word-based' morphology, i.e. from the older IE type to the modern one, where words tend to have an invariable shape, with all morphological information concentrated on affixes. For comment see Kastovsky (1990, 1992).

fem-ur 'thigh', gen sg *fem-in-is*, *iec-ur* 'liver', gen sg *ioc-in-er-is* (cf. Skr *yak-ṛt*, gen *yak-n-as*, Gr *hépa-r*, gen *hépa-t-os* </-ṇ-to-s/).

The most important heteroclite from a Germanic point of view is probably 'water', IE */wed-, wod-, ud-/;[18] the various reflexes of this root present a fascinating picture of what happens when an old declension-type decays, and its remnants are scattered through the descendant dialects. This root appears in Gr *húdo-r* 'water', gen sg *húda-t-os*, Umbrian *utur*, loc sg *une* < */ud-n-i/*, Hittite *wadar*, gen *wed-en-as*. In Germanic, we see signs of heteroclitic declension in Gothic *watō* (nom sg) < /wɑt-o:-r/, gen sg *wat-in-s* < */wod-en-os/*. The *r*-stem type has been generalized in OE (*wæt-er*, gen sg *wæt-er-es*), and elsewhere in WGmc; NGmc however generalises the *n*-stem (OIc *vat-n*). The /-n-/ formative also shows up (indirectly) in OE *ȳþ* 'wave' < */u-n-d-i/* (Ingvaeonic deletion of /n/ accounts for the long vowel): cf. OHG *undea*, OIc *unnr*, and L *unda* 'wave'. The *r*-stem appears in E *otter* < OE *ot(t)or*, which = Gr *húd-r-os* 'water-snake', *húd-r-a* 'hydra'.

6.1.4   A note in retrospect

The apparent complexity of OE noun-declension is a bit misleading: there's actually very little there, even if its distribution is rather elaborate. The total inventory of the devices for indicating case/number categories is:

(i) Vocalic endings: {-e, -u, -a}
(ii) -VC(V) endings: {-es, -as, -um, -an, -ena}
(iii) Zero
(iv) *i*-umlaut[19]

So at the stage in the evolution of West Germanic represented by Old English, there are only ten inflectional devices for the noun system. Mathematically this would seem not to be a 'problem', since no noun actually requires more than eight distinctions (four cases, two numbers). Yet the richest declension, the masculine *a*-stems, has only five distinct categories (62.5 per cent of the potential maximum). Historical changes have determined that this relatively poor collection of machinery gets a bit under two-thirds of the mileage that it potentially could – and that in the most differentiated class (compare the *n*-stems!). In many cases (e.g. all neuters, all plurals, consonant-stem sg, heavy-base *i*-stems), even the

---

[18] */ud-/ is the zero-grade of this root, characteristically for the sequence */wVC-/.
[19] More properly, the morphologized results of IU, i.e. the alternations as markers, not the phonological process itself.

apparently crucial nominative and accusative are nondistinct. The moral is that there is a great difference between what a language has and what it does with it; this should make one suspicious of any kind of facile argument suggesting that changes are 'caused' by the growth of morphological ambiguity.

6.2   Pronouns and determiners

6.2.1   Personal pronouns

Proto-Germanic did not inherit a fully coherent pronoun or determiner system; nothing quite like this reconstructs even for Proto-IE. Rather the collections labelled 'pronouns' or 'articles' or 'demonstratives' in the handbooks represent dialect-specific selections out of a mass of inherited forms and systems. There are clear IE first-, second-person pronoun systems:[20] we can easily identify a first-person nom sg root $*/H_1egh-/$ (L *eg-o*, Go *ik*, OE *ic* 'I') and a second-person root in $*/t-/$ (L *tu*, OCS *ty*, OE *þū*). There is an interrogative in $*/k^w-/$ (L *qu-is*, OE *hw-ā* 'who?') and a deictic in $*/to-/$ (Gr *to* 'def art, masc nom sg', OE *þæ-s* 'def art m/n gen sg). There is no reconstructable third-person pronoun, however. The personal pronouns may be heterogeneous even across Germanic: Go *is*, OE *hē* 'he' are not cognate. But overall the main systems are related, at least in outline.

We will look at the personal pronoun systems one person at a time.

(6.13)   *First person*

		Go	OE	OIc
	nom	ik	ic	ek
	gen	meina	mīn	mín
sg	dat	mis	mē	mér
	acc	mik	mē, mēc	mik
	nom	wit	wit	vit
dual	gen	–	uncer	okkar
	dat/acc	ugkis	unc	okr
	nom	weis	wē	vér
	gen	unsara	ūre, ūser	vár
pl	dat	uns(is)	ūs	oss
	acc	"	ūs, ūsic	"

[20] Though the term 'system' may have to be used loosely: there are at least, if not reconstructable protoforms, collections of roots that associate with particular persons and cases (see Szemerényi 1989: ch. 8, §4.3).

Note that here (as in the second person, below), there are three rather than two numbers; singular, dual and plural. The dual is an old IE category, which in some languages, like Greek and Sanskrit, also controls verb concord, and in Germanic still does in Gothic, but nowhere else.

The singular continues familiar IE roots: nom */H₁eg(h)-/ (see above), oblique */me-/ (L *me*, OE *mē*) and so on. The acc sg /-k/ is probably by analogy to the nom sg; i.e. 'false separation' or 'metanalysis' as it's called, say construal of *ik* as {i-k}, so then {mi-k}, etc. The dual nominative may reflect a compound, obscured by phonological change: cf. Lithuanian *vè-du* 'we two'. The same root in */w-/ appears in the nominative plural as well (attested elsewhere in IE only in Indic, Hittite and Tocharian).

The rest of the plural shows forms of an IE root */nVs-/, here the zero-grade */n̥s-/, which gives Gmc */uns-/ (see §5.5). The same root appears in lengthened o-grade in L *nōs* 'we'. OE *ūs*, OIc *oss* < */uns/ show expected developments: Ingvaeonic nasal-loss and compensatory lengthening in OE (cf. §3.3), NGmc assimilation in nasal clusters (also in *okkar*, *okr*).

(6.14) *Second person*

		Go	OE	OIc
sg	nom	þu	þū	þú
	gen	þeina	þīn	þín
	dat	þus	þē	þér
	acc	þuk	þē, þēc	þik
dual	nom	–	git	it
	gen	igqis	incer	ykkar
	dat/acc	igqis	inc	ykr
pl	nom	jus	gē	er
	gen	izwara	ēower	yþrar
	dat	izwis	ēow	yþr
	acc	"	"	"

The acc sg shows the same /-k/ formative as in first person. The IE basis is generally transparent: for the sg, L *tu*, acc *te* = *þū*, *þē*, etc. The pl continues an IE second-person root in */j-/ (Skr nom pl *yu-yam*), as well as one in */w-/ (Skr 2 acc pl *vaḥ*). The etymology of the oblique plurals is complicated, and the standard account not very satisfactory, but still worth considering. The suggestion is that OE *ēow* and Go *izwis* have the same source, a reduplicated */iz-wiz/, which by rhotacism gives */ir-wir/, followed by dissimilatory loss of the first /r/, which produces */iwir/, which can if you think about it give OE *ēow* (just).[21] OIc *it* is cognate to OE *git*; NGmc tends to lose */j/ before front vowels.

---

[21] After Krahe (1965: §33). For further discussion see Szemerényi (1989: ch. 8, §4.3).

The third person is more complex historically. First, it does not continue any single IE pronoun system; second, in addition to number and case it is marked (in the singular) for gender. I will look first at the singulars by gender, and then at the plural.

(6.15)   *Masculine singular*

	Go	OE	OIc
nom	is	hē	hann
gen	"	his	hans
dat	imma	him	honom
acc	ina	hine	hann

(6.16)   *Neuter singular*

	Go	OE	OIc
nom	ita	hit	þat
gen	is	his	þess
dat	imma	him	því
acc	ita	hit	þat

The OIc neuters are in fact not really 'personal pronouns', but demonstratives, cognate with the OE neuter 'articles' (see below); the same root occurs in L (*is-)tud* 'that'.

Note that the Go and OE masculines and neuters, and the OIc masculines, can largely be segmented into a pronominal stem and a case/gender morph: for OE {h-ē}, {h-i-s}, {h-i-m}, {h-i-ne}, for Gothic ({i-ta}, {i-s}, {i-mma}, etc. It looks as if /s/ is a genitive marker (m or n: cf. the *a*-stem noun declension), /t/ is a neuter nom/acc marker,[22] /m/ is dative, and /n/ masc acc sg. We will see these same morphs in other pronominal and adjectival forms, suggesting a kind of coherence in the core of nominal morphology alien to Modern English (though still just visible in German: masc 3 sg dat *ih-m*, acc *ih-n*).

There are two main IE roots here: the vowel-initials show an old pronominal base */ei ~ i/ (L *ei-us* 'his', *i-d* 'it'); the <h>-forms (/x-/ < IE */k-/) reflect a deictic root in */k-/ (L *c-is* 'this side').

(6.17)   *Feminine singular*

	Go	OE	OIc
nom	si	hēo	hon
gen	izōs	hiere	hennar
dat	izai	"	henne
acc	ija	"	hana

[22] This neuter /t/ also appears in the NGmc neuter definite article and adjective: cf. Swedish *barn-et* 'the child', *det* 'it', *varm* 'warm', neuter *varm-t*.

These mostly go back to the */ei ~ i/ root; the /x/ <h> appears to be analogical, on the basis of masculine and neuter. Go *si* has a different source, yet another demonstrative in */s-/, which we will meet later when we look at the article.

The 3 pl does not normally distinguish gender; Scandinavian is an exception, and in fact its 3 pl pronoun is rather article-like, and built on the */t-/ base. We look at Gothic and OE first:

(6.18)   *Third-person plural pronoun; Gothic and OE*

	Go	OE
nom	eis	hīe
gen	izē	hiera
dat	im	him, heom
acc	ins	hīe

The Gothic forms suggest the basic origin; the initial <h> in OE is secondary. Gothic gen in /z/ gives the source for OE /r/: rhotacism again.

(6.19)   *Third-person plural; Old Icelandic*

	m	n	f
nom	þeir	þau	þær
gen	þeirra	þeirra	þeirra
dat	þeim	þeim	þeim
acc	þá	þau	þær

Observe that the ModE 3 pl does not continue the OE system; it was borrowed from a Scandinavian type like this one in very late OE or early ME times, and appears first in northern texts, only spreading to London as a complete system in the fifteenth century. As late as the end of the fourteenth-century Chaucer for instance has only nom *thei*, but still gen *hir(e)*, dat/acc *hem*. Apparently the NGmc masculine was borrowed as the nom pl for all genders, which is in keeping with the lack of gender distinction in the OE plural system.

6.2.2   *'Definite article'/demonstrative*

Scandinavian, unlike E, WGmc, uses the same forms for demonstrative pl as for 3 pl personal pronouns. It also has the definite article normally postposed to the noun: OE *se wulf* 'the wolf' vs. OIc *úlfr-inn* (nom sg). We will be concerned here only with the free preposed forms, which syntactically resemble either articles of the ModE kind, or demonstrative adjectives like *this, that*. The paradigms for the three genders are as follows:

(6.20) *Masculine*

		Go	OE	OIc
	nom	sa	sę	sa
	gen	þis	þæs	þess
sg	dat	þamma	þæm/þām	þeim
	acc	þe	þone	þann
	nom	þai	þā	
	gen	þizē	þāra	
pl	dat	þaim	þæm/þām	see 3 pl pronoun
	acc	þans	þā	

(6.21) *Neuter*

		Go	OE	OIc
	nom	þata	þæt	þat
	gen	þis	þæs	þess
sg	dat	þamma	þæm/þām	þeim
	acc	þata	þæt	þat
	nom	þo		
	gen	þizē		
pl	dat	þaim	as m	see 3 pl pronoun
	acc	þo		

(6.22) *Feminine*

		Go	OE	OIc
	nom	so	sēo	sú
	gen	þizōs	þære	þeirrar
sg	dat	þaim	"	þeirri
	acc	þo	þā	þá
	nom	þos		
	gen	þizō		
pl	dat	þaim	as m	see 3 pl pronoun
	acc	þos		

Taken as a whole, this reflects a well-attested type of IE demonstrative system, even down to the idiosyncratic detail of having an */s-/ stem for masculine and feminine nom sg, and a */t-/ stem (Gmc /θ-/) for neuter nom sg and all other forms.[23] A clear analogue can be seen in Sanskrit: the proximal deictic 'this' has the stems *sa-* (m), *sa-* (f), and *tad* (n), with

[23] This may reflect the old IE animate/inanimate gender system (cf. §6.1.2): masculine and feminine continue a root associated with animacy (since these result from the split of an old single category); the neuter has the inanimate */t-/ throughout. See further Szemerényi (1989: ch. 8, §§1–2).

t-forms elsewhere in the paradigm. The Greek definite article shows the same pattern: masculine nom sg *ho* < */so/, feminine *hē* < */sɑ:/, neuter *to* < */tod/.

To illustrate the likenesses in detail, let us consider just the masculine singular:

(6.23)   nom: OE *se*, Skr *sa-ḥ*, Gr *ho*
          gen: OE *þæ-s*, Skr *ta-sy-a*, Gr *tou-s*
          dat: OE *þǽm*, Skr *ta-sm-ai*
          acc: OE *þo-ne*, Skr *ta-m*, Gr *tó-n*

The OE dat sg comes from deletion of */s/ in */-sm-/ and compensatory lengthening; the /n/ in *þone* is due to a common change of final */m/ > /n/ in early Germanic (the *-e* is a later addition). In weak syllables /m/ remains only if followed by a vowel in pre-PGmc: hence the Germanic dat pl *-um* = OCS instrumental *-mi*, Lithuanian *-mis*.

There are remains of what is usually called an 'instrumental' in the masculine and neuter sg; this term as Campbell remarks 'is traditional, but reflects neither their origin nor their prevailing use' (1959: §708n). The two forms are *þon*, *þȳ*, neither of which is historically transparent. In use they are most frequent in comparatives, e.g. *þȳ mā* 'the more' (cf. ModE *the more, the merrier*), and as alternatives to the dative in expressions like *þȳ gēare* '(in) this year'. There is probably some relation to the 'instrumental' interrogative *hwȳ* 'why?', which in sense is a real one (= 'through/by what?'), but the /y:/ is a problem; *hwȳ* has an alternative form *hwī*, which is 'legitimate' in that it can be traced back to the interrogative base */kʷ-/ + deictic */ei/. (For discussion and other suggestions, see Krahe 1965: §42.)

This inconclusive discussion suggests that not every form in a language necessarily 'has an etymology' in the usual sense, i.e. can be reconstructed as the end-point of a chain of regular developments of some ancestral material. Forms can simply be – to one degree or another – 'invented' (see further comments on lexical invention in chapter 7).

NWGmc has another demonstrative (a new development, not attested in Gothic), which gives ModE *this*, G *dieser*, and the like. This has the same deictic bases as the article, IE */s-/, */t-/, with a new suffix */-s(s)-/. Most of the paradigm is in */t-/, with */s-/ only in NGmc m/f nom sg.

(6.24)   *'This', masculine and neuter*

			OIc		OE		
			m	n	m	n
		nom	sjá, þessi	þetta	þēs	þis
		gen	þessa	þessa	þis(s)es	þis(s)es
		dat	þessum	þetta	þi(s)sum	þis
sg		acc	þenna	þetta	þisne	þis
		ins	–	–	þȳs	þȳs, þis
		nom	þessir	þessi	þās	
		gen	þessa	þessa	þissa	
pl		dat	þessum	þessum	þis(s)um	as masc
		acc	þessa	þessi	þās	

The OE plural is the same in all genders; OIc has a distinct nom/acc feminine *þessar*. The OE nom/acc *þās* is the source of modern *those*; ModE *that* of course is from the article (neuter nom/acc sg) *þæt*. The *this/that* opposition is a later development.

Note again the recurrence of certain morphs marking particular categories: masculine acc sg *-ne* (cf. *þo-ne*), and *-um* in dat sg as well as plural (cf. dat sg article *þǣ-m*). We will see these again in the interrogative pronoun, as well as in the adjective declension (§5.3).

(6.25)   *'This', feminine*

	OIc	OE
nom	sjá	þēos
gen	þessar	þisse
dat	þesse	"
acc	þessa	þās

The OE feminine oblique forms in *-sse* derive from older ones in /-sr-/, e.g. */θis-re/, etc. The /r/ is sometimes restored (probably by analogy to the feminine article type *þǣre*) in late OE (*þissere, þisre*, etc.).

6.2.3   *Interrogative pronouns*

Some interrogative pronouns, like OE *hwǣþer* 'which (of two)?', *hwelc/ hwilc* 'what (kind of)?' were declined like adjectives (see §6.3); but one, 'who?', had an independent paradigm. This pronoun appears in all the Gmc dialects only in the singular, and only in masculine and neuter; there is no separate feminine. The masculines (with neuters in brackets):

(6.26)   Go   OE   OIc
        nom   hvas (hvat)   hwā (hwæt)   hverr (hvat)
        gen   hvis   hwæs   hvess
        dat   hvamma   hwǣm/hwām   hveim (hví)
        acc   hvana (hvat)   hwone (hwæt)   hvern (hvat)

The now familiar inflectional markers for genitive, dative and accusative are clearly visible. The source is an IE interrogative base */kʷ-/; this was normally formed into an *i*-stem (L *qu-i-s*) or an *o*-stem (Skr *ka-ḥ* < */kʷ-o-s/). In Germanic the *o*-stem (> *a*-stem) predominates; certainly some of the parallels hold morph for morph, e.g. OE {hw-æ-t} = OIc {hv-a-t} = L {qu-o-d}. Other forms have been partly remodelled after the definite article.

6.3   The adjective

6.3.1   The basic inflections

The IE adjective was not a distinct 'part of speech'; it had no case/number and gender inflections of its own, but was simply a nominal root, formed into a stem by the appropriate thematic elements, and taking its endings by concord to its head noun. Most adjectives had two base forms: an *o*-stem for masculine and neuter (L *nou-u-s, nou-u-m* 'new' < */now-o-/), and an *ā*-stem for feminine (L *nou-a* < */now-α:-/). These were declined like nouns of the equivalent class, e.g. masculine nom sg *nou-us hort-us* 'new garden', gen sg *nou-ī hort-ī*, dat sg *nou-ō hort-ō*, etc.; feminine *nou-a sell-a* 'new saddle', gen sg *nou-ae sell-ae*, etc. Some adjectives were treated as *i*-stems; these had the same forms for masculine and feminine, but a separate neuter: *grau-is* 'heavy' (m/f nom sg), *grau-e* (n).

In Germanic the adjective became an autonomous category, and grew a complex new inflectional pattern. Eventually two separate declensions developed, called **strong** (or **definite**) and **weak** (or **indefinite**). Their syntax is complicated, and varies from language to language; for details see any standard OE grammar.[24] The strong declension is a mixture of forms from the strong noun and the demonstrative/pronoun declensions; the weak is built mainly on the weak (*n*-stem) noun. There were already some adjectives in IE with this kind of mixed morphology, notably the Sanskrit demonstratives; but the systematic establishment of an independent adjective of this kind is a Germanic innovation.

---

[24] There is a particularly good brief account in Quirk & Wrenn (1955: 68).

There were some differences in declension according to adjective origin (e.g. *a*-stem vs. *ō*-stem). These however are minor; the example here is the commonest type, the *a*-stems. In the displays below, I indicate the composite origins of the strong declension by italicizing those endings whose origin is pronominal (compare the endings of the definite article), while those of nominal original are left in roman.

(6.27)   *Strong adjective endings, masculine*

		Go	OE	OIc
	nom	-s	-Ø	-r
	gen	-is	-es	-s
sg	dat	*-amma*	*-um*	-um
	acc	*-ana*	*-ne*	-an
	nom	*-ai*	*-e*	-er
	gen	*-aizē*	*-ra*	-ra
pl	dat	-aim	-um	-um
	acc	-ans	*-e*	-a

We now see a complete pattern of recurrence: the pronouns {hi-ne}, {þo-ne}, {hwo-ne} and say the masc acc sg of *gōd* 'good', {gōd-ne}; the pronouns {hi-m}, {þǣ-m}, {hwǣ-m} and the masc dat sg {gōd-um}, etc.

(6.28)   *Strong adjective endings, neuter*

		Go	OE	OIc
	nom	-Ø	-Ø	*-t*
	gen	-is	-es	-s
sg	dat	*-amma*	*-um*	-u
	acc	*-ata*	-Ø	-an
	nom	-a	-u/-Ø	-Ø
	gen	*-aizē*	*-ra*	-ra
pl	dat	-aim	-um	-um
	acc	-a	-u/-Ø	-Ø

The -*u*/-Ø alternation in nom/acc pl is controlled by the weight of the root syllable: see *a*-stem neuter nouns, §6.1.3. The same is true for feminine nom sg, below. The Scandinavian neuter nom sg {-t} is the same ending as in *þa-t* (and OE *þæ-t*), the IE neuter marker */-d/ as in L (*is-*)*tu-d*, Skr *ta-d*; in NGmc it is generalized as a neuter suffix, and still remains (cf. note 22 above).

(6.29)   *Strong adjective endings, feminine*

		Go	OE	OIc
	nom	-a	-u/-ø	-ø
	gen	-aizōs	-re	-rar
sg	dat	-ai	-re	-re
	acc	-a	-e	-a
	nom	-ōs	-a/-e	-ar
	gen	-aizō	-ra	-ra
pl	dat	-aim	-um	-um
	acc	-ōs	-a/-e	-ar

The weak adjective has more or less the endings of an *n*-stem noun, with a few minor deviations. Old English has an alternative pronominal form, *-ra*, for the genitive plural.

(6.30)   *Weak adjective endings, masculine*

		Go	OE	OIc
	nom	-a	-a	-i
	gen	-ins	-an	"
sg	dat	-in	"	-a
	acc	-an	"	"
	nom	-ans	-an	-u
	gen	-anē	-ena	"
pl	dat	-am	-um	-um
	acc	-ans	-an	-u

(6.31)   *Weak adjective endings, neuter*

		Go	OE	OIc
	nom	-o	-e	-a
	gen	-ins	"	"
sg	dat	-in	-an	-u
	acc	-o	"	"
	nom	-ona		
	gen	-anē	as masc	as masc
pl	dat	-am		
	acc	-ona		

(6.32)   *Weak adjective endings, feminine*

		Go	OE	OIc
	nom	-ō	-e	-a
	gen	-ōns	"	"
sg	dat	-ōn	-an	-u
	acc	-ōn	"	"
	nom	-ōns		
	gen	-ōnō	as masc	as masc
pl	dat	-ōm		
	acc	-ons		

Comparison with the strong declension makes it clear that the weak carries very little information about the categories of a modified noun; in some cases little more than nominative vs. oblique. Though in this respect it is still more informative than the noun-declension itself.

6.3.2   Comparison

There were two regular comparative/superlative formations in Germanic, which can be illustrated by Gothic and Old English forms:

(6.33)   A. */-iz-, -ist-/

	Positive	*Comparative*	*Superlative*
Go	alþ-eis 'old'	alþ-iz-a	alþ-ist-s
OE	eald	ield-ra	ield-est

B. */-o:z-, -o:st-/

	Positive	*Comparative*	*Superlative*
Go	arm-s 'poor'	arm-ōz-a	arm-ōst-s
OE	earm	earm-ra	earm-ost/-ast

Type A reflects an IE suffix found in Latin comparatives of the type *mai-ōr-em* 'greater' (acc ag) < */mag-jo:s-m̥/; the zero-grade is /-is-/, and this remnant gives (by Verner's Law) Gothic -*iz*-, and later with rhotacism OE -*r*-. The -*a* ending is probably from the weak *n*-stem noun declension. This suffix of course causes umlaut of the root vowel, and leaves behind a front /e/ in the superlative.

The B suffix is a Germanic development of unclear antecedents; it may reflect an original *a*-stem (IE *o*-stem) ablative ending */-o:-d/, which was used to form adverbs (type: L *subit-ō* 'suddenly', Go *ga-leik-ō* 'similarly': see §8.4.2). One possible scenario (Krahe 1965: §56) is a development in these adverbs of a comparative in */-oːis-/, later */-oː-s/; this served as an analogical target for the creation of a new suffix, and its extension to the adjective. Be that as it may, both A and B suffixes appear in all the Germanic dialects, but distributed differently; the A type is commoner in Gothic, the B type in NGmc and OE, while OHG shows a pretty even mixture.

In OE, the choice of one or the other seems to be largely lexically determined; the adjectives that most often have type A are *eald* (*ieldra, ieldest*), *geong* 'young' (*gi(e)ngra*), *hēah* 'high' (*hīer(r)a*), *lang* 'long' (*lengra*), *sceort* 'short' (*scyrtra*); others that occasionally show it are *brād* 'broad' (*brǣdra* ~ *brādra*), *strang* 'strong' (*strengra* ~ *strangra*). Some basic A adjectives sometimes have B forms as well, e.g. *geong* with mainly *gi(e)ngra* but occasionally *geongra*.

7 Inflectional morphology, II: The verb

7.1 Historical preliminaries[1]

Statistics by themselves don't mean very much; but here are some numbers that cast an interesting light on the development of the Germanic languages, in particular English. A typical Sanskrit verb paradigm may have as many as 126 distinct finite forms (that is, marked for tense/person/number, excluding infinitives, participles, verbal nouns, etc.); the most complex Germanic system, Gothic, has twenty-two; Old English, somewhat more typically for Old Germanic, has a maximum of eight; ModE at its richest has three. While not all the Sanskrit forms represent original categories (at least eighteen, and possibly thirty-six, may be innovations), the general trend is clear: most of the ancient IE dialects have enormously complex verb systems compared to Germanic. Assuming these older types are closer to the IE original, the evolution of the Germanic verb involved a radical simplification (and as we will see, restructuring as well).[2]

Just what the original IE verb system was like is a matter of considerable controversy, but we can safely reconstruct at least the following major inflectional categories:

(7.1)   Voice: active vs. middle
Mood: indicative vs. subjunctive vs. optative vs. imperative
Aspect/tense: present vs. aorist vs. perfect

(There is some debate about aspect/tense: it is at least possible that IE had an imperfect and pluperfect as well, and perhaps a future, though there is

[1] On the IE verb in general, see Szemerényi (1989: ch. 9), Kuryłowicz (1964: chs. 2–6); on the Germanic verb see Prokosch (1938: §§52–75), Bammesberger (1986).
[2] The striking exception is Hittite, attested as early as 1700 BC (the first Sanskrit remains are at least three centuries later). Hittite has two moods and two tenses, as compared to Vedic Sanskrit with four or five moods, and seven tense/aspect categories. But consistent evidence for significant categories (like aorist and perfect, both missing in Hittite) in the most geographically widespread IE languages supports the usual assumption. The 'minimal' Hittite system is in fact innovatory, not archaic, and this means that Germanic is too. (See discussion in Szemerényi 1989: ch. 9, §1.)

no agreement about this.) Each of these categories had further inflections marking concord with the subject; these were

(7.2)   Number: singular vs. dual vs. plural
          Person: 1 vs. 2 vs. 3

As far as the coding of temporal categories is concerned, the PIE system was probably mainly aspectual, rather than tense-based; insofar as tense proper was marked, it was subsidiary. In the IE schema, present = habitual or progressive, aorist = punctual past, and perfect = completed action (very roughly). The primary Germanic innovation was a complete scrapping of this system (but not of all its morphology: see §7.2), and the substitution of a simple two-way tense opposition, **present** vs. **preterite**.[3] Aspectual distinctions such as simple present vs. progressive (*I see* vs. *I am seeing*) or quasi-aspectual ones like simple past (aorist) vs. perfect (*I saw* vs. *I have seen*) are late developments, not fully built into the grammar until the 'Middle' periods of the Germanic languages, or later.[4]

The active voice was more or less like the active in modern Germanic dialects; the middle (as far as we can reconstruct its semantics from the languages that preserved it fairly intact, like Greek and Sanskrit) was a kind of semantic cross between a passive and a reflexive, characteristically reflecting notions like 'relevance of the action to the agent', or 'to do X for oneself'.[5]

The subjunctive may have had a dual function: grammatical, as a marker of certain kinds of subordinate clauses (hence L *sub-junctivum* 'that which is adjoined below'), and semantic, marking unfulfilled or unreal states; the optative was a mood of wishes and the like. The imperative was the mood of commands and orders, but was also marked for person and number, in which case it must have been rather what in Latin would be

---

[3] Or perhaps better 'non-past' vs. 'past'. Many of the functions of the IE 'present' (which henceforth will not have inverted commas) are not strictly temporal, but aspectual ('I write books' is habitual aspect, not 'present tense' in the usual construal); others express notions like 'generic' truth ('Lions are carnivores'). For excellent cross-linguistic studies of tense and aspect see Comrie (1985, 1976).

[4] If at all. E.g. progressive aspect is obligatorily marked in English (*I read* is not synonymous with *I am reading*, and if the latter is meant the *be V-ing* form must be used); whereas in Afrikaans *ek lees* can mean either of the two. If however (optionally, under pragmatic conditioning) it is desirable for progressive to be expressed, there is a form for it: *ek is besig om te lees* 'I am busy at to read'. Progressive aspect is obligatory only in English among the Germanic languages; the new post-PGmc aorist/perfect distinction has been lost in Yiddish, Afrikaans, and many varieties of South German, and is on its way out in some English dialects (see Lass 1987: ch. 6).

[5] For a sophisticated cross-linguistic study of the middle voice, see Klaiman (1991). Indo-European (especially Sanskrit and Greek) are treated in detail in §2.2.

called a 'hortatory' subjunctive: a 1 pl imperative would have a sense like 'let us X', and so on.

The mood and voice systems were also restructured in North and West Germanic; Gothic, the most archaic dialect, retains indicative vs. a highly inflected subjunctive and a rather full imperative (2, 3 sg vs. pl, 2 dual, 1–3 pl), as well as a middle voice (usually called 'mediopassive'), with both indicative and subjunctive. Old English retains the indicative vs. subjunctive opposition, but with loss of person marking in the indicative plural, and only a sg/pl contrast (no person-marking) in the subjunctive. The middle has been lost in OE, and a new syntactic passive (auxiliary + participle) is used instead. Gothic is also unique in retaining dual inflection for the verb (though the dual of course remains elsewhere as a pronominal category); all the others merge it with plural.

7.2   The strong verb

7.2.1   Ablaut in the strong verb, classes I–V

The Germanic verb system then is partly defined by the loss of the old IE aspects, and the creation of a quite new and much simpler conjugation. In broad outline, the old present stayed on as a present, and the aorist and perfect merged in the new preterite. But the original morphology, i.e. the ablaut grades associated with the aspect categories, remained; this was, to put it simply and perhaps controversially, redeployed, and used to construct the strong verb system.[6] This new construction still reflects, if indirectly and at times obscurely, the primary IE verbal ablaut: *e*-grade present, *o*-grade perfect, and zero- or lengthened-grade aorist (cf. §5.2).

A strong verb may be conceived as having four so-called **principal parts**, basic grades from which the rest of the paradigms can be constructed. These are: PRES (infinitive, present sg); PRET₁ (preterite 1,3 sg); PRET₂ (preterite 2 sg and pl); and PART (past participle).[7] The strong verbs are conventionally divided into classes (sometimes called 'ablaut series', *Ablautreihen*), pretty much according to these vowel grades; as we will see below, they reflect with fair precision the ablaut alternations plus original root structure. As a reminder, the pattern we are assuming behind

---

[6] For more details see Lass (1990). The view presented there (and here) is in essentials that given in Prokosch (1938: §§56–7). Prokosch discusses the older (and among some scholars still current) view that the whole strong verb past system continues the IE perfect; the evidence and argument there are worth looking at. The quite different history of the weak preterite will be taken up in §7.3.

[7] These terms are not traditional; they were first used as a mnemonic convenience in Lass & Anderson (1975), and are still useful.

the entire strong verb structure is the one that shows quite transparently in a Greek verb like *leíp-ō* 'leave', root /lVip/:

(7.3)

PRESENT	PERFECT	AORIST
(*e*-grade)	(*o*-grade)	(zero-grade)
leíp-ō	lé-loip-a	é-lip-on

The first five classes look like this in Gothic and Old English:[8]

(7.4)

CLASS		PRES	PRET$_1$	PRET$_2$	PART
I 'bite'	Go	beit-an	bait	bit-um	bit-ans
	OE	bīt-an	bāt	bit-on	bit-en
II 'offer'	Go	biud-an	bauþ	bud-um	bud-ans
	OE	bēod-an	bēad	bud-on	bod-en
III 'bind'	Go	bind-an	band	bund-um	bund-ans
	OE	bind-an	band	bund-on	bund-en
IV 'bear'	Go	baír-an	bar	bēr-um	baúr-ans
	OE	ber-an	bær	bǣr-on	bor-en
V 'eat'	Go	it-an	at	ēt-um	it-ans
	OE	et-an	æt	ǣt-on	et-en

The fourth 'principal part', the past participle PART, is given here primarily to show its relationship to the other three, but it will be discussed later (§7.2.3); its development lies outside this historical ablaut pattern, and it has its particular vocalism for rather different reasons.

A bit of etymological commentary may help to show how these apparently heterogeneous collections actually reflect the simple IE verbal ablaut pattern shown in (7.3).

(i) IE */e/ > Go /i/ everywhere except before /r, x/, and <ei> = /i:/ = /ii/. Hence cl I PRES is no problem (IE */ei/ > Gmc /i:/). Similarly, Gmc */eu/ > Go /iu/, OE /eo/ (by DHH: §3.6.2). Therefore *itan* = *etan* (L *ed-*), *biud-* = *bēod-*. Gmc */ɑi/ > OE /ɑ:/ (§3.4), so *bait* = *bāt*. Go <aí> [ɛ] is a special development of */e/ before /r/; /i/ in *bindan* is from PGmc pre-nasal raising (§2.6).

(ii) Recall that IE */o/ > Gmc */ɑ/ (§2.2), and that */ɑ/ > /æ/ in OE by AFB except before nasals (§3.5): hence *band* but *bær*.

(iii) Classes I, II obviously have roots in /-i/, /-u/. Since Gmc */ɑi/ > OE /ɑ:/, and Gmc */ɑi, ɑu/ can reflect IE */oi, ou/, and Gmc */ɑu/ > /æu/ (AFB) > /æɑ/ (DHH), we then have all of PRES and PRET$_1$ accounted for.

---

[8] Classes VI–VII pose special problems, and will be treated in the next section.

PRES and PRET₁ of classes I–V then contain IE */e/ and */o/ respectively; they faithfully reflect the ancestral present /e/, perfect /o/ pattern. So *bītan*, *bāt* < */bheid-, bhoid-/, *beran*, *bær* < */bher-, bhor-/.

(iv) Now to PRET₂. Observe that there is a short vowel in cl I–III and a long vowel in IV–V; this correlates with the weight of the root syllable. Classes I–III are heavy (/-VVC/ or /-VCC/), and IV–V are light (/-VC/). Recall that IE syllabic nasals and liquids (/R̥/) give a sequence (-uR/ in Germanic (§5.5); so *bund* /bund-/ derives naturally from */bhn̥dh-/, i.e. a zero-grade aorist.

(v) Keeping on this track, and looking back at the Greek forms in (6.3), we can see that class I–II PRET₂ are also zero-grades: they show the /-i, -u/ left behind by deletion of the root vowel.

(vi) We also saw (§5.2) that there are lengthened-grade aorists in IE as well; in this case, classes IV–V, with light roots and 'basic' /e/-vocalism in PRES, display IE */e:/ in PRET₂, which comes out as Gothic /e:/, OE /æ:/ in the regular way. We can now refer all PRET₁ to original perfects, and all PRET₂ to aorists.

So behind these five verb-classes, for all their surface heterogeneity, lie quite simple IE and Germanic archetypes. Using VV for long vowels as well as diphthongs, N for nasals, R for nasals/liquids, and C for other consonants, we can set out two archetype-groups: one for the heavy bases (classes I–III) and one for the light bases (classes IV–V) as follows:

(7.5)   *Archetypes for heavy-root classes*

		PRES	PRET₁	PRET₂
I	IE	-eiC-	-oiC-	-iC-
	Gmc	-iiC-	-αiC-	-iC-
	OE	-iiC-	-ααC-	-iC-
II	IE	-euC-	-ouC-	-uC-
	Gmc	-euC-	-αuC-	-uC-
	OE	-eoC-	-æαC-	-uC-
III	IE	-eNC-	-oNC-	-N̥C-
	Gmc	-iNC-	-αNC-	-uNC-
	OE	-iNC-	-αNC-	-uNC-

(7.6)   *Archetypes for light-root classes*

		PRES	PRET$_1$	PRET$_2$
IV	IE	-eR-	-oR-	-eeR-
	Gmc	-eR-	-αR-	-ææR-
	OE	-eR-	-æR-	-ææR-
V	IE	-eC-	-oC-	-eeC-
	Gmc	-eC-	-αC-	-ææC-
	OE	-eC-	-æC-	-ææC-

These displays do not of course imply that the grade-organization was of IE date: simply that the forms lying behind the Germanic ones were of this type (whatever their source), and were later coopted into a new system.[9]

The actual OE forms of course often reflect later sound changes; the example for cl III (*bindan*) was a nasal stem, but there are different paradigm-types with liquid-final stems in this class, e.g. *weorpan* 'throw' (*wearp, wurpon*), *helpan* 'help' (*healp, hulpon*), showing breaking of /æ/ in PRET$_1$ rather than /α/ from failure of AFB, *weorpan* showing breaking of /e/ before /rC/ in PRES but *helpan* not showing it before /lC/, etc. (§3.6.2). There are however some rather more radically 'deviant' strong verbs that belong – for mainly historical but also partly synchronic reasons – in particular classes, but show marked differences from the more 'regular' members. The following are the more important (and interesting) types:

(a) Aorist presents. PRES reflects not an ancestral (present) *e*-grade, but a zero-grade: most likely, though the motivations are obscure, an aorist, hence the name. Typical paradigms:

(7.7)	CLASS	PRES (expected)	PRES (actual)	PRET$_1$	PRET$_2$
	I 'reap'	*rīpan	ripan	rāp	ripon
	III 'mourn'	*meornan	murnan	mearn	murnon
	IV 'come'	*c(w)eman	cuman	c(w)ōm	c(w)ōmon

Cl I *ripan* descends from a root */reib-/ > */ri:p-/ (cf. MLG *reipen*); for *murnan* the *e*-grade is apparent in Gr *mér-meros* 'sorrowful'; 'come' is from */g^{w}m̥-/, *e*-grade in Skr *gám-ati* 'he goes', perhaps L *uen-iō* (though

---

[9] The question of the synchronic status of ablaut (is it, as a process, still active in Old Germanic?) could be raised here: but it's really beyond my remit. It has been claimed (Lass & Anderson 1975: ch. 1) that the whole IE ablaut apparatus, pretty much, was still alive and well in the OE verb system: but this requires a very abstract analysis that I no longer feel happy with.

zero-grade /R̥/ can give L /e/ as well). The PRET₂ /o:/-vocalism of *cuman* instead of expected /æ:/ reflects Ingvaeonic developments before nasals (as in *mōna* 'moon' rather than expected *mǣna*: cf. §3.4). The long vowel in PRET₁ is apparently extended from the plural; there is an alternative (expected) sg type *cam*.[10]

(b) Weak presents. These had a thematic */-j-/ in the present system, but were not otherwise conjugated as weak, as one might expect (*/-j-/ is the marker of weak class I: see §7.3). Hence these verbs, if they have light roots, show gemination in the present (not normally the case for strong verbs), and /i/ if the root vocalism was /e/. Most of them appear to belong to class V or VI: typical cl V examples are *biddan* 'ask' (Go *bidjan*), *sittan* 'sit' (Go *sitan*): PRET₁ *bæd*, *sæt*, PRET₂ *bǣdon*, *sǣton*. On cl VI weak presents see the next section.

(c) Cl II /u:/-presents. There are a number of verbs with /u:/ rather than /eo/ in PRES, which nonetheless behave otherwise like cl II: *brūcan* 'enjoy', *lūcan* 'lock' are typical, PRET₁ *brēac*, *lēac*, PRET₂ *brucon*, *lucon*. These are difficult to explain; they are usually taken to represent a kind of analogy to cl I, where the original root */ei/ > */i:/ = /ii/ in Germanic by a regular change. This is obviously parallel in principle: original */eu/ > /u:/ = /uu/. Though why it should be restricted to just this small group of verbs, and not be found anywhere else, is a mystery (one of many, as should be clear by now).

(d) 'Contract verbs'. Quite a large number of verbs in classes I, II, V show a monosyllabic PRES containing a long diphthong followed directly by the infinitive marker {-n}, rather than the usual disyllabic structure of {ROOT-an}. The rest of the paradigms are more or less what is expected for the particular class. Some typical examples:

(7.8)

CLASS	PRES	PRET₁	PRET₂
I 'cover'	wrēon	wrāh	wrigon
II 'flee'	flēon	flēah	flugon
V 'see'	sēon	seah	sāwon/sǣgon

The key is the velar in the root; since */-x-/ was deleted in foot-medial position in prehistoric OE (see §3.9.2), the infinitives can be identified as deriving respectively from ancestral */wri:xɑn/, */fliuxɑn/, */sex(w)ɑn/.

---

[10] Or perhaps analogy to class VI (itself a problem: see the next section), which has both PRET₁/PRET₂ in /o:/. There is only one nasal-stem in this class (*spanan* 'entice, allure'), but this may not be an obstacle to this explanation. It is however hard to see how to distinguish between this and the account given above, except that the PRES /u/-vocalism might militate against analogy to cl VI, where PRES is in /ɑ/.

For support, cf. OHG *(int)-rîhan* '(un)-cover', L *rîca* < */wri:k-α/ 'head-scarf'; Go *pliuhan*, OHG *fliohan*; Go *saíhwan*, OHG *sehan*. Assuming loss of /-x-/ in PRES, the immediate results would be three-vowel sequences of a type that OE prohibited: */fleoαn/, etc. The result of these (potential) sequences is loss of the suffix vowel; in *sēon* there is lengthening first. The PRET$_2$ consonantism is due to Verner's Law: since the ending is */-ún/, the medial /x/ voices to [γ], and is later lost. The only difficulty is the /w/ in the common PRET$_2$ variant *sāwon* (the /α:/ is due to retraction of /æ:/ before /w/, §3.6.2); this may be due to retention of the /w/-element already in the root, suggested by Gothic, and L *sequ-or* 'follow', which is cognate (IE root */sek^w-/).

7.2.2   The strong verb, classes VI–VII

Class VI is often referred to in the handbooks as simply 'the sixth ablaut series', or something of the sort. But a typical cl VI verb like *faran* 'go' shows a very different pattern from what we have seen so far in classes I–V:

(7.9)

		PRES	PRET$_1$	PRET$_2$
VI 'go'	Go	far-an	fōr	fōr-um
	OE	far-an	fōr	fōr-on

Surely a series /α ∼ o: ∼ o:/ looks nothing like a reasonable descendant of the IE verbal ablaut described in the previous section. There is /α/ instead of /e/ in PRES, a long vowel with no apparent diphthongal source in PRET$_1$ (unlike cl I /α:/ < */αi/), and the same long vowel in PRET$_2$. (The /α/-vocalism of PRES also appears in PART, which is again 'deviant', but see below). The only character that looks mildly 'normal' is the long PRET$_2$, which we would expect in a light root with a rhyme in /-VC/. According to root-structure, cl VI seems to consist largely of a mixture of cl IV (*faran* = *beran*) and cl V (*bacan* 'bake' = *brecan*) types.

Class VI has been a perennial problem: is it in fact 'really' an ablaut series in the strict sense, or something rather different? There is no generally accepted solution; one problem is that many cl VI verbs seem to have uniquely Germanic roots, and no secure IE etymologies. But there have been a number of (partial) stories devised for them, and I will try to tell what looks like a reasonable one.

One clue comes from the undoubted existence of aorist presents in other classes (cf. the previous section). Recall that alternations involving /α/ and /α:/ occur in verbs in non-Germanic IE languages, which could in fact be ancestral, by regular sound-correspondences, to Germanic /α ∼ o:/: L *stă-tus*, *stā-re* (cf. §5.3). In addition, there are even more suggestive alternations involving /α/-roots, e.g. Latin verbs with short /α/ in the present and a long vowel in the perfect: *căp-iō* 'seize', perf 1 sg *cēp-ī* (perhaps analogically for *cōp-ī). Latin perfects of this kind go back to old aorists; the aorist and perfect merged in Latin as well as in Germanic, but were not systematically redeployed in the same way.

On this basis,[11] we might suggest that cl VI does not represent a 'normal' ablaut series at all, but a new, restructured paradigm type, after an IE aorist-present model. This would account for the /α/-vocalism in PRES, and the /o:/ in PRET₂, since the former comes from a zero-aorist (/α/ as zero-grade of */α:/) with original suffix-accent, and the latter from an aorist plural with full grade and root-accent. Since PART (see §7.2.3) typically had suffix-accent (as evidenced by zero-grades like *bunden*), the /α/ here is reasonable as well.

Some verbs of this group may not be aorist presents, but either original *o*-grade roots (*faran*, cf. Gr *póros* 'ford'), or *e*-grades with a preceding laryngeal, e.g. *alan* 'nourish' < */H₂el-/ (cf. L. *alere*, OIr *alim*, and §5.3). The only thing that remains really problematic on this interpretation is PRET₁: there is no regular source for the long vowel or its quality (unless this has a laryngeal too, e.g. *faran* < */pH₂er-/, *fōr* < */pH₂or-/: but in this case it is difficult to see why there should be lengthening in PRET₁ but not in PRES). The PRET₁ vocalism however is usually taken as an analogical extension from PRET₂, as perhaps also happens in cl IV nasal stems (see the previous section). Under any interpretations, then, class VI is not an 'ablaut series' in the strict sense, but a Germanic innovation, if with elements of original ablaut.

Class VII is rather a mixed bag, historically less transparent and less homogeneous then I–VI. Most of these verbs however share the cl VI property of having the same (long) vocalism in PRET₁/PRET₂.

In the handbooks cl VII is often called 'reduplicating' (G *reduplizierende Präterita*); the appropriateness of this term is not immediately apparent from OE paradigms like:

(7.10)		PRES	PRET₁	PRET₂
	'let'	læt-an	lēt	lēt-on
	'fall'	feall-an	fēoll	fēoll-on
	'beat'	bēat-an	bēot	bēot-on
	'mix'	bland-an	blēnd	blēnd-on
	'seize'	fōn	fēng	fēng-on

(*Fōn* is a contract verb like *wrēon*, etc.; see below for discussion.)
But consider the verbs 'let', 'seize' in Gothic:

---

[11] The arguments are spelled out in detail in Prokosch (1938: §§54, 60).

(7.11)

	PRES	$PRET_1$	$PRET_2$
	lēt-an	laí-lōt	laí-lōt-um
	fah-an	faí-fah	–

Cf. Gr *leíp-ō*, perf *lé-loip-a*; the characteristic reduplication of the IE perfect surfaces transparently in this class only in Gothic. Reduplication is widespread in Sanskrit and Greek, much less so in Latin; but even here there are some survivals, like *can-ō* 'sing', perf 1 sg *ce-cin-ī*, *teg-ō* 'cover', perf *te-tig-ī*, etc.

So historically many verbs of this class reduplicated in Germanic, though the remains are clear only in Gothic.[12] But there is still a rather degenerate reflex in the $PRET_1$ forms of some OE cl VII verbs; here they are compared with their Gothic counterparts:

(7.12)

		PRES	$PRET_1$
'counsel'	OE	rǣd-an	reord
	Go	rād-an	raí-rōþ
'be called'	OE	hāt-an	heht ~ hēt
	Go	hait-an	haí-hait

The historical reduplication shows up simply as the presence of two consonants in the (synchronic) root, where only one is expected: /r . . . r/, /x . . . x/. The vowel in $PRET_1$ seems to represent the reduplicated syllable (etymologically with */e/), and the actual root is expounded by a consonant cluster. These forms are mostly restricted to Anglian dialects, and especially to verse (an archaizing register); but *heht* does occur in WS prose as well. Other verbs with this pattern are *lacan* 'leap, play', reduplicated *leolc*, *ondrǣdan* 'dread' (*ondreord*), and *lǣtan* 'let' (*leort*). The latter is apparently due to a rather rare (for English) dissimilation: one of two identical liquids in a root takes on the opposite value for laterality. (This is very common in Romance: L *arbor* 'tree' > Spanish *arbol*, *peregrinus* 'pilgrim' > F *pèlerin*, etc.)[13]

Classes VI–VII also contain some of the 'deviant' verb-types given in the previous section for I-V.

[12] Perhaps more accurately, there were two preterite types available in PGmc: note the alternant perfects of L *pangō* 'fasten': *pēgī* (an old aorist) and *pe-pigī* (a reduplicated perfect). The aorist type was the majority selection in NWGmc, the perfect type in Gothic: but see below. (For full discussion, see Prokosch 1938: §62.)

[13] Not all scholars accept this interpretation of *heht*, etc. For a contrary view, see Prokosch (1938: §62).

(a) Weak presents. Cl VI *hebban* 'raise', (*hōf, hōfon*: cf. Go *hafjan*, OS *hebbian*), *hliehhan/hlæhhan* (Angl) 'laugh' (*hlōg, hlōgon*). Note also *swerian* 'swear' (*swōr*, etc.), with lack of gemination of /r/ and retention of /-j-/, like weak I *herian* 'praise' (see §3.2), and cl VII *wēpan* 'weep' (*wōp*) with no gemination in a heavy root (cf. Go *wōpjan*, OS *wōpian*).

(b) Contract verbs. Cl VI *flēan* 'flay' (*flōg, flōgon*), *slēan* 'slay', cl VII *fōn* 'sieze' (*fēng*), *hōn* 'hang' (*hēng*). Unlike cl V contracts, these have generally extended the Verner's-Law consonantism of PRET$_2$ into PRET$_1$ (cf. cl V *sēon, seah* not *sæg); but there are variants in <-h> (*slōg ~ slōh*), which either reflect the original or are due to devoicing. For the original */-x-/ cf. OFri *of-flecht* 'splintering', Go *slahan, fahan* < */fɑnx-ɑn/, *hahan* < */xɑnx-ɑn/.

A final group of some interest is a small class with nasal infixes in some parts of the paradigm, e.g. cl VI *wæc-n-an* 'wake' (*wōc, wōc-on*), *sta-n-d-an* 'stand' (*stōd, stōd-on*). The roots without infixes are clearly visible also in cognates like Go *wak-an* (as well as the synonymous OE verb *wac-ian*), L *stā-re* 'stand'. Such infixation is a well-known feature of the present systems (especially) of certain verbs in older IE: cf. L *li-n-qu-ō* 'leave', pp *lic-tu-s, ru-m-p-ō* 'break', pp *rup-tu-s*, and the related pair *pug-n-ō* 'fight, strike' and *pu-n-g-ō* 'sting'.[14]

7.2.3   The strong past participle

The PART grade was not discussed in detail in the last two sections; its descent is not always very neat. To begin with, it is historically not really 'part of' the verb paradigm; it is originally an independent thematic adjective (IE *o*-stem, Gmc *a*-stem) formed off the verbal root. The basic development would be:

(7.13)   IE   PGmc
       *ROOT - o - nó- > *ROOT - ɑ - nɑ-

The original structure is transparent in Sanskrit, and still for the most part in Gothic; some Sanskrit verbal adjectives and Gothic strong past participles are morph-for-morph equivalents, and both reflect the original IE type (here nom sg):

(7.14) IE   *wr̥t - o - nó - s   PGmc *wurð - ɑ - nɑ - z
        Skr vr̥t - a - ná - ḥ   Go   waúrd - a - n - s

[14] Class VII especially poses a number of problems that still have no generally accepted solutions, especially with relation to the origin of the long vowels in certain ones. This is too complex to go into here; for a survey of the problems see Prokosch (1938: §62).

The Gmc accent-shift of course sets the accent on the root syllable (§4.2.1); the acute in Go *waúrd-* does not represent the accent but a convention for writing this vowel. Accent is marked only for IE and Sanskrit, to indicate that Verner's Law is generally to be expected in past participles of this historical origin.

We can now look at PART as an integrated component of the OE strong verb system:

(7.15)	CLASS	PRES	PRET$_1$	PRET$_2$	PART
	I 'bite'	bīt-an	bāt	bit-on	bit-en
	II 'offer'	bēod-an	bēad	bud-on	bod-en
	III 'help'	help-an	healp	hulp-on	holp-en
	IV 'bear'	ber-an	bær	bǣr-on	bor-en
	V 'eat'	et-an	æt	ǣt-on	et-en
	VI 'bake'	bac-an	bōc	bōc-on	bac-en
	VII 'fall'	feall-an	fēoll	fēoll-on	feall-en

Even though PRET$_2$ in the light-root classes (IV–V) is lengthened grade, PART reflects a zero-grade, because of the original accented suffix: *boren* < */βur-α-nα-z/ < */bhr̥-o-nó-s/. The expected form would be **buren*, but the root vowel has lowered before the following historical low vowel (§2.6). The expected /u/ surfaces where lowering has been blocked, e.g. before a nasal as in *bunden* < */bhn̥dh-o-nó-s/.

Note however PART in classes V–VII. Here we do not find the expected zero-grade reflex, but an analogical formation based on PRES. The reason for this was suggested in §5.3: either (a) a 'true' zero would be impossible in obstruent-final roots (*bacan* would have **bc-en*); or (b) the result would be an allomorph apparently diverging too much from the norm for a particular class-type (*blandan* would have **blunden*, a type associated with cl III). The original pattern *e*-PRES, *o*-PRET$_1$, zero-lengthened-PRET$_2$, zero-PART then is intact only in I–IV; various factors have diverted development in V–VII.

7.2.4   Infinitive and present participle (strong and weak)

The infinitives and present participle have the same sources for both the strong and weak conjugations, and can be treated together. The Germanic infinitive, like the past participle, is based on an *o*-stem nominal formation. The IE type can be seen in a Sanskrit verbal noun like *bháraṇam* 'the carrying':

(7.16)   IE   *bhér - o - no - m
           Skr bhár - a - ṇa - m[15]

Here (unaccented) */-no-/ forms a verbal noun from the root, defined as an *o*-stem by the theme vowel, and as a neuter by the nom sg ending /-m/. The Germanic descendant of such a structure would then be an *a*-stem neuter, with full root grade because of the unaccented suffix (recall what essentially the same suffix does in PART of strong verbs when it carries accent: §7.2.3). For 'bear' then the Gmc infinitive would descend from IE as follows:

(7.17)   IE   *bhér - o - no - m
              PGmc   *βér - α - nα - m
         Late PGmc *βér - α - nα - n

The most however that has survived in any Germanic dialect is the theme + /n/: East, Northwest and West Germanic generally have -*an*, NGmc and Northumbrian OE have lost the nasal and have only -*a*. For this root typical attested infinitives are Go *baíran*, OE *beran*, OIc *bera*. The assumption that the original of the infinitive is a neuter noun, then, is just that: unlike the reconstructed nom sg */-s/ in PART, which does surface in Gothic.

The infinitive retains vestiges of its original nominal character in being inflectable: marginally in OE, more so in OHG, OS. OE has a dative form (originally a neuter *ja*-stem) in -*nne*, normally after the preposition *tō* 'to'; this occurs in purpose and similar constructions, e.g. *tō beranne* '(in order) to bear'. OS and OHG have genitives (OS *berannias*, OHG *berannes*), and OHG also has an instrumental (*berannu*), all (judging from the geminate /n/) from the *ja*-stem base */βer-αn-jα-/ plus inflections.

The present participle is morphologically the same in both strong and weak verbs in OE: present stem (if different from the preterite) + -*ende* (*ber-ende*, *luf-i-ende*, etc.). All Gmc dialects have related forms: Go -*and-s*, OIc -*andi*, OHG -*anti*. The source is an IE *o*-stem verbal adjective, of the type seen in Gr *phér-o-nt-* 'bearing', with a following accented */-í/, probably an original feminine ending. This provides the environment for Verner's Law, hence the sequence */-o-nt-í/ > */-α-nθ-í/ > */-α-nð-í/, with accent shift and later hardening */-α-nd-í/, then IU to /-æ-nd-i/, and finally /-e-nd-e/ with lowering. The /-i/ remains in the earliest OE forms, which are -*ændi*, -*endi*.

---

[15] The retroflex /ṇ/ in *bháraṇam* is due to the influence of the preceding /r/: Sanskrit dentals tend to retroflex in the vicinity of /r, u, k, i/ (the so-called 'ruki' class: for a description see Allen (1951).

7.3   The weak verb

7.3.1   The weak preterite suffix and past participle[16]

The origin of the weak preterite is a perennial source of controversy. The main problem is that it is a uniquely Germanic invention, which is difficult to connect firmly with any single IE antecedent. Observing the old dictum *ex nihilo nihil fit* (nothing is made out of nothing), scholars have proposed numerous sources, none of which is without its difficulties. The main problem is that there are at least three consonantisms: /d/ (Go *nasida* 'I saved', inf *nasjan*), /t/ (Go *baúhta* 'I bought', inf *bugjan*), and /s/ (Go *wissa* 'I knew', inf **witan*).

But even given this complexity, the most likely primary source seems to be compounding of an original verbal noun of some sort with the verb **/dhe:-/* 'put, place, do' (OHG *tuon*, OE *dōn*, OCS *dějati* 'do', Skr *dádhati* 'he places', L *fēcī* 'I made, did').

This leads to a useful analysis of a Gothic pret 3 ppl like *nasidēdun* 'they saved':

(7.18)   nas - i - dē - d - un
          SAVE-theme-reduplication-DO-3 pl

I.e. a verbal root followed by a thematic connective followed by the reduplicated perfect plural of 'do'. This gives a periphrastic construction with a sense like 'did V-ing'; with, significantly, Object-Verb order (see chapter 9), i.e. (7.18) has the form of an OV clause 'NP-pl sav(ing) did'.[17] An extended form also existed, in which a nominalizing suffix **/-ti/* or **/-tu/* was intercalated between the root and the 'do' form, e.g. in Go *faúrhtidēdun* 'they feared', which can be analysed as {faúrh-ti-dē-d-un}. This suffix was in many cases later weakened; first the vowel dropped, so that **/-ti-d-/* > **/-td-/*; this led to assimilation **/-tt-/*, and then eventual reinterpretation of the /t/-initial portion as a suffix itself, and loss of the 'do' part from verbs of this type (so Tops 1978: §§4.2–3). The problematic /s(s)/ forms may go back to a different (earlier) development also involving **/-ti/*, in which the sequence **/tt/* > /s(s)/ (Wright 1899: §120), but this is not clear.

---

[16] For a detailed discussion of the controversy surrounding the weak preterite (or 'dental suffix' as it is often called), see Tops (1978). The literature is also canvassed in Prokosch (1938: §§66–7), especially the arguments against the view proposed here (which essentially follows Tops).

[17] The emergence of the weak verb, with no ablaut machinery, suggests a close connection with the emergence of the new Gmc tense system. If ablaut remains as a 'relic' of the old aspect system (even if now recruited for tense-marking), the weak verb is the prototypical (hence productive) new Germanic formation. (Suggested to me by Dieter Kastovsky.)

This portion of this account involving 'do' is actually somewhat oversimplified. Gothic, which has the most complex attested weak preterite system, is usually taken as representing something close to the original type. Here, apparent reduplications like *-dēd-un*, etc. occur only in the dual and plural; the singular has something rather simpler, with only one /d/. So for class I weak verbs (on the classes see §7.3.2), Gothic has:

(7.19)	Sg	Du	Pl
1	-i-d-a	-i-dēd-u	-i-dēd-um
2	-i-d-ēs	-i-dēd-uts	-i-dēd-uþ
3	-i-d-a	–	-i-dēd-un

This probably reflects two distinct pre-Germanic formations: the plural and dual from a reduplicated lengthened *e*-grade perfect stem */dhe:-/, the 1, 3 singular from an *o*-grade perfect */dho:/ without reduplication, and the 2 person from an unreduplicated */dhe:-/. Later there was shortening of */o:/ in weak position, then change as expected to */α/ in 1, 3 sg. (For further discussion and details of the personal endings see §7.5.3.) Gothic alone shows systematic traces of reduplication; even the earliest NWGmc inscriptions have only the single /d/ plus a personal ending: e.g. Nøvling Clasp (Denmark, c. AD 200) *talg-i-d-ai* 'he carved', Einang Stone (Norway, c. 350–400) *faih-i-d-o* 'I painted'. (There are however traces of reduplication in OHG, interestingly enough in the verb 'do' itself: infinitive *tuo-n*, pret 1 pl *tāt-um*.)

The Gothic system, then, and most other forms, suggest a familiar kind of evolution: over time, if this story is correct, 'do' was obscured and grammaticalized (semantically 'bleached' and reduced) from a lexical verb in composition with another root to an opaque inflection, with no semantic content except 'past'.[18]

In Gothic, all weak pasts are thematic, as in (7.19), though the vowels may differ from class to class. In NGmc it is mainly the athematic type that survives, after both light and heavy roots: light Go *nas-i-da* 'he saved', OIc *tal-þa* 'he told', heavy Go *haus-i-da* 'he heard', OIc *heyr-þa*. In OE, of course, the thematic/athematic distinction was largely controlled by the weight of the root syllable (at least in class I the theme vowel was */-i-/, and high vowels drop after heavy syllables: see §4.3.2, and the discussion in the following section). So Go thematic *nas-i-da*, *haus-i-da*, but OE thematic *ner-e-de*, athematic *hīer-de*.

---

[18] Not that 'do' has all that much semantic content anyway; this may in fact be one of the reasons it was selected for this purpose, as it was later in English to be a dummy auxiliary in questions and negations: *do you think? I don't think*, etc.

The weak past participle, like the strong (§7.2.4) is a nominal or adjectival formation. Here the original suffix is not */-nó-/, but */-tó-/, as found in e.g. Gr *do-tó-s* 'given', L *da-tu-s*. The historical relations are especially clear in Gothic and Old High German: Go *nas-i-þ-s* 'saved' is the same type as L *mon-i-tu-s* 'warned', *salb-ō-þ-s* 'anointed' is equivalent to the Latin *am-ā-tu-s* type, and OHG *gi-hab-ē-t* 'had' to L *obsol-ē-tu-s* 'worn out'. (These examples represent weak classes I, II, III respectively; see the next section for further discussion.) IE */-tó-/ became PGmc */-ða-/ (Verner's Law and the change of */o/ > /ɑ/); as usual, final */ɑ/ in weak syllables was lost (§4.3.1), giving simply */-ð/, later /-d/. The weak pp in Old English is normally represented by a theme vowel + dental stop as in *her-e-d* 'praised', *dēm-e-d* 'judged'.

Both weak and strong past participles in OE (and other WGmc languages) are very frequently, even characteristically (but not always) marked with a prefix: OE *ge-*, OHG, OS *gi-*. This appears to be an old collective/perfective marker, related in a complex way to L *con-* 'with' (see the discussion in §8.3.3 below).

7.3.2   The weak verb classes

The weak verbs in general continue IE derived or 'secondary' verb types – at least their present systems do. The specialized new past system (see note 16 above) may be a function of this origin. Weak verbs are traditionally divided into four classes (though only two are of major importance for OE); the division is superficially based on the morphology, but represents, at least in part, an IE distinction of semantic or derivational type.[19] I will give the IE/Gmc background to all four classes, even where it is not strictly relevant to OE, as the general picture is of considerable historical interest.

Class I. These have a stem-formative */-i-, -j-/, causing umlaut of the root vowel; no class I weak verb (just as no *i*-stem, *ja*-stem, *jō*-stem noun) can have a back root vowel in Old English in the present system (though of course they can in Gothic). These are usually called '*jan*-verbs', because of the infinitive formative, historical */-jɑ-n/, still unchanged in Gothic (*sat-jan* 'set' = OS *sett-ian*, OE *sett-an*). In OE the whole formative is clearly visible only in a small class of light roots in /-r/, like *herian* 'praise', *nerian* 'save' (Go *harjan*, *nasjan*). Most of these verbs are originally deverbal or deadjectival, i.e. formed from verb or adjective bases.

One important and regular group is the causatives, normally formed off the PRET₁ stem of a strong verb, with the sense 'cause (X) to V'. So the

---

[19] That is, the stem-formatives (see below) are originally derivational suffixes; these later lose their meaning and become simply (inflectional) class-markers.

example above, Go *satjan*, is formed by *jan*-suffixation of the PRET$_1$ root of the cl V strong verb *sitan* (pret *sat*); and one obvious gloss of 'set' is 'cause (X) to sit'.[20] The IE type is clear: Skr *dr̥s*- 'see', *dars-á-ya-ti* 'he shows' ('causes X to see'), where -*ya*- = the -*ja*- in Go -*jan*. The deadjectival verbs are sometimes called 'factitives'; their sense is 'cause to become Adj': so Go *hail-s* 'whole', *hail-jan* 'heal' ('cause to become whole'), OE *hāl*, *hǣl-an*, etc.

The allomorphy of the class I preterite suffix is complex. This is due in the first instance to the fact that the original was thematic, and the theme vowel was */-i-/, which was subject to High Vowel Deletion after heavy roots (§4.3.2). It looks at first as if this should simply produce the distinction mentioned in the previous section, thematic *ner-e-de* vs. athematic *hīer-de* with /-e-/ as remnant of the theme.

But deletion leads to special complications. The suffix as we have seen was voiced */-ð-/, later /-d-/; if the root ended in a voiceless obstruent, this would produce a voiceless + voiced cluster, which was generally illegal in OE. In such cases the suffix devoiced, giving /-t-/ rather than /-d-/: *mēt-an* 'meet', pret 3 sg *mēt-te*, *līx-an* 'shine', pret *līx-te*. (In this section I will use 3 sg as a general model for the preterite; for the person/number endings see §7.5.3.) Some early <d>-spellings for expected <t> (Corpus Glossary *ræfsde* 'reproved', *hyspdun* 'they mocked') are probably morphophonemic rather than phonetic, representing as it were 'underlying /d/'. This is suggested by the fact that the earliest attested forms of this kind (in NWGmc inscriptions) already show devoicing: *wurte* 'he wrought' < */wurx-ð-/ on the Tjurkö Bracteate (Sweden, c. AD 500), and pret 1 sg *wortaa* (Etelhem Clasp, Sweden, c. AD 500). In some cases manner assimilation could also occur, e.g. /-θd-/ > /-dd-/, as in *cȳþ-an* 'show', pret *cȳd-de* ~ *cȳþ-de*.

A small but important group of heavy roots seem to have lost the theme vowel early – certainly before the time of *i*-umlaut. These show unmutated vocalism in the preterite, as well as various other changes. The two main groups are:

(a) /l/-finals: *sellan* 'sell', *tellan* 'tell', pret *seal-de*, *teal-de*. The present shows IU of */æ/ < */ɑ/ (< */sɑl-j-/, etc.), the pret breaking of */æ/ and no IU (< */sɑl-ð-/). Later developments separate the two stems even further, as in ModE *sell/sold*.[21]

(b) Velar-finals. These may have a nasal cluster (*bring-an* 'bring', pret *brōh-te*, *þenc-an* 'think', pret *þōh-te*); a liquid cluster (*wyrc-an* 'work', pret

---

[20] More accurately, the stem formative */-j-/ is suffixed (and generalized to the whole paradigm). This produces a stem *{ROOT + j-}, to which the inflectional endings are added.

[21] There was however some variation in early OE: note the thematic form *astel-i-dæ* 'he created' from the Moore MS of Cædmon's Hymn (later versions have athematic *onstealde* (< *on-stell-an*). Thanks to Fran Colman for reminding me of this item.

worh-te); a heavy root with a plain velar (*sēc-an* 'seek', pret *sōh-te*); or a
light root with gemination (*bycg-an* 'buy', pret *boh-te*). The base vocalism
is */a/ in *pencan*, */u/ in *wyrcan*, *bycgan*, and */o:/ in *sēcan*. On the *pencan*
type see §2.6(iii); all of these reflect a change */k/ > [x] in clusters with /t/.

The same modifications, unsurprisingly, appear in the past participle: if
the preterite has /t/, the participle does too, e.g. *worh-te*, pp *worh-t*, *mēt-te*,
pp *mēt-t*, etc.

Class II. These have a thematic */-o:-/ < IE */-α:-/, in some dialects
with endings attached directly, in others with a post-theme */-j-/: OHG
salb-ōn 'anoint' < */salβ-o:-n/, OE *sealf-ian* < */salβ-o:j-αn/.[22] they may
be deverbal, with what is sometimes called an 'intensive' sense: OHG
sprangōn 'bubble, gush', cf. cl III strong *springan* 'spring', PRET₁ *spranc*.
But they are more often denominal, as in Go *fiskōn* 'to fish', cf. the noun
fisk-s.

In OE the infinitive is *-ian*, sometimes spelled *-ig(e)an*, and the endings
are different from those of class I, reflecting the back vowel theme (see
§§7.5.2–3). The theme blocks *i*-umlaut even if a */j/ follows, so verbs of
this class may have a back root vowel (*lufian* 'love' */luβ-o:j-/, etc.) The IE
type may be seen in Latin denominals in *-ā-re*: *planta* 'a plant', *plant-ā-re*
'to plant', *amor* 'love', *am-ā-re*, and so on.

The preterite and participle show none of the complexity of class I, but
are thematic throughout; this of course precludes the various assimilations, etc. induced by loss of the vowel. The normal WS theme is /-o-/,
e.g. *lufian*, pret *luf-o-de*, pp *luf-o-d*. The early form is *-u-*, which is attested
in the eighth-century glossaries and to some extent in eWS: so Epinal
gloss *aslac-ud-ae* 'he became slack'. This is expectable as a shortening of
*/o:/, as in the nom sg of *ō*-stem nouns (§6.1.3), e.g. *gief-u* < */γeβ-o:/.
While WS generally has *-o-*, other dialects show different vowels: *-a-* is
typical for Anglian and Kentish.

Class III. The theme is IE */-e:- ~ -ei-/, with very variable outcomes.
These are deverbal or deadjectival, and often express notions like continuation of an action (durative) or entry into an action or state (inchoative): OHG *werēn* 'continue' (cf. *wesan* 'be'), *fūlēn* 'rot' (*fūl* 'foul'). This
class is marginal in OE, only four verbs showing (very much obscured)
signs of original class III status: *habban* 'have', *libban* 'live', *secgan* 'say',
hycgan 'think' (see discussion in Campbell 1959, §§762–6). For the IE
type cf. Latin *-ē-re* verbs: *tac-ē-re* 'be silent', cognate to OHG *dag-ē-n*.

Class III is athematic in NWGmc except in OHG: so pret of 'have' is
OE *hæf-de*, OIc *haf-þa*, OS *hab-da*, but OHG *hab-ē-ta*, etc. Gothic is

---

[22] Clearly */-o:-, -o:j-/ are allomorphs of the same formative, originally; though their
conditioning is not clear.

thematic as well, i.e. *hab-ai-da*. It is not clear whether these forms go back to athematic doublets, or if this is an innovation.

Class IV. The marker is IE */-no-, -nα-/, and the semantics most often involve inchoativeness or causativity: the productive pattern is clear in Go *full-s* 'full', *full-n-an* 'fill'. Class IV retains distinctive morphology only in Gothic; elsewhere the /n/ may remain, but the verbs fall into other classes. So OIc *vakna*, OE *wæcnian* 'awake' are both class II.

7.4 Preterite presents and minor verb types

7.4.1 Preterite presents[23]

Some verbs combine features of both weak and strong conjugations. The **preterite presents** look at first more or less like strong verbs; but their PRET₁/PRET₂ – or what should be these forms – have present meaning, and their (actual) preterites are weak. Some typical examples:

(7.20)

	PRES SG	PRES PL	PRET SG
'can'	cann	cunnon	cūþe
'may'	mæg	magon	meahte
'shall'	sceal	sculon	sc(e)olde
'know'	wāt	witon	wiste
'must'	mōt	mōton	mōste

(There are many more verbs in this group: for a good overall treatment see Wright & Wright 1925: §§539ff.)

Just given this material, 'can' looks rather like cl III strong (cf. *band, bundon*), 'know' like cl I (cf. *bāt, biton*), 'must' like cl VI (cf. *bōc, bōcon*). The origin is a non-reduplicating IE perfect, which developed present sense: Skr *ved-a*, Gr *oîd-a* 'I know' < 'I have seen' (the same root in L *uid-eō* 'I see', OE *wāt*). The semantics are not however always (or often) this clear. The morphology is generally a bit aberrant: the infinitive, where it exists, is often zero-grade (*cunnan* 'can' < */gn̥-/, *witan* < */wid-/, zero-grade of */weid-, woid-/*). The preterite may reflect this grade (*wiste*), or perfect o-grade (*meahte* < */mog-/*).

Since the past sense was lost in these historical perfects, new pasts had to be constructed; and since the weak conjugation even in early times was the only productive one, this is the natural source. Some of these verbs are of course the ancestors of our modern modal auxiliaries; the fact that the present is 'really' (historically) a strong preterite accounts for one major

---

[23] For discussion of this class in OE, see Colman (1992b).

structural anomaly: the lack of 3 sg inflection (*he can*, not **can-s*). Since the strong PRET₁ has no ending here (§7.5.1), the descendants of these OE presents don't either. Therefore *he can* is really equivalent to *he sang*, not *he sing-s*.

7.4.2   Athematic root verbs and 'to be'[24]

The athematic verbs include a number of important and common ones, like *dōn* 'do', *gān* 'go' and parts of the paradigm of 'be' (see below). Here endings are added directly to the root, as in athematic nouns (§6.1). The distinction is an old one: Greek thematic *phér-e-te* 'he bears' vs. athematic *es-tí* 'he is'.

The usual present 1 sg marker in IE was **/-o:/* (L *fer-ō* 'I bear', etc.); this comes down in Germanic as Gothic *-a* (*baír-a*), OS, OHG *-u* (*bir-u*), and OE *-e* (*ber-e*). But there was another type of pres 1 sg ending, **/-mi/*, which was especially common with athematic verbs: Gr *ei-mí* 'I am', L *su-m*. This *mi*-present as it is called was extended to thematic verbs in some IE groups, especially Indic and Slavic: the Skr equivalent of Gr *phér-ō*, L *fer-ō*, OE *ber-e* is *bhár-a-mi*.

A number of these verbs also show *mi*-presents in Germanic: so Go *i-m*, OE *eo-m/ea-m* 'am', OHG *tuo-m* 'I do', *gā-m* 'I go'. These (except in 'am') are rare in OE, but are attested in some early texts, especially Mercian: Vespasian Psalter has pres 1 sg *dō-m* 'I do'. In some dialects, notably Mercian and early Northumbrian, this ending also appears on parts of the 'be' paradigm other than 'am': notably pres 1 sg of the *bēo-* root (see below), e.g. *bio-m*, *bēo-m* = *eo-m*.

'To be', or as the German handbooks sometimes call it, the *Verbum substantivum*, is not a single 'verb', but a collection of semantically related paradigm-fragments – in the rest of Germanic as well as OE. There are three IE roots represented in OE:

(a) an *s*-root (*eom, eart, is, sindon* = L *s-um, e-s, e-s-t, s-unt*);
(b) a *b*-root (*bēo, bist, biþ, bēoþ*, cognate to Skr *bhu-* 'remain', Latin perfect of 'be' *fū-ī*, OCS *byti* 'be', Gr *phú-* 'become');
(c) a *w*-root, in the infinitive *wesan*, pres part *wesende*, preterite *wæs*, *wæron*; this is cognate to OIr *feiss/foss* 'remain', Skr *vásati* 'he dwells'. *Wesan* is a defective cl V verb (as *wesan/wæs/wæron* suggest), whose PRET₁/PRET₂ serve as the only past for the other stems.

---

[24] These verbs are often called 'anomalous' in the handbooks. For a particularly good treatment of the Germanic background, see Prokosch (1938: §75).

The use of */wes-/ as the preterite of the 'be' verbs goes back to PGmc: Goth *im* 'am' vs. *was*, OIc *em* vs. *var*, OE *eom* vs. *wæs*. The incorporation of the *b*-root into this group seems to be a WGmc innovation.

The OE paradigms are as follows:

(7.21)   PRESENT

		Indicative		Subjunctive	
		s-root	*b*-root	*s*-root	*b*-root
	1	eom	bēo		
sg	2	eart	bist	} sīe	} bēo
	3	is	biþ		
pl		sindon, sint	bēoþ	sīen	bēon
		(e)aron			

PRETERITE

		Indicative	Subjunctive
	1	wæs	wǣre
sg	2	wǣre	"
	3	wæs	"
pl		wǣron	wǣren

For the indicative plural WS has only the *s*-forms; *(e)aron* is Anglian, and is of course the ancestor of ModE *are*. The usual infinitive is *bēon*, though *wesan* also occurs; until the eleventh century the only present participle is *wesende*, and there is no past participle. After this pres part *bēonde* and pp *ge-bēon* (> ModE *been*) appear. The imperative is usually in *b-* in earlier texts: sg *bēo*, pl *bēoþ*; later *wes*, *wesaþ* appear (*wes* remains buried in *wassail* < *wes hāl* 'be healthy'). There is some regional differentiation, with *b-* imperatives in WS and Merc, and *wes* Northumbrian, though *wes* also occurs in WS and Mercian.

The standard ModE system suggests more radical loss of the *b*-forms than was actually the case; as late as the 1950s some conservative rural varities in old West Mercian and West Saxon territory (e.g. the W Midlands and West Country) preserve paradigms like *I bin, thee bist, her is* (Cheshire and Shropshire), *I be, you be, her is, they be* (Warwickshire, Somerset), or *be* for all persons and numbers (Oxfordshire, Buckinghamshire, Somerset). For some discussion see Lass (1987: 232–3).

7.5   Person/number/mood inflection[25]

7.5.1   The strong verb

The IE verb as we have seen (§7.1) was (generally) inflected for two voices (active and middle), three persons, three numbers (sg/du/pl), and at least three moods (indicative, optative, imperative). In the three-mood systems of later IE (including Germanic), the irrealis/wish etc. modalities are usually grouped under the heading 'subjunctive', regardless of origin. Gothic and NGmc have mediopassives, but their sources are different, and neither concerns us here.

(i) **Present indicative.** The suffix pattern is historically clearest in the strong verb: pres ind in Latin, Go, OE, OIc for instance, of the verb 'bear':

(7.22)		L	Go	OE	OIc
		1 fer-ō	baír-a	ber-e	ber
sg		2 fer-i-s	baír-is	bir-es	ber-r
		3 fer-i-t	baír-iþ	bir-eþ	"
		1 fer-i-mus	baír-am	ber-aþ	ber-um
pl		2 fer-i-tis	baír-iþ	"	ber-eþ
		3 fer-u-nt	baír-and	"	ber-a

Old English, along with the rest of Ingvaeonic (Old Saxon, Old Frisian) has lost the person contrast in the plural; the 3 pl is generalized to all persons: -aþ < */-anθi/. The root /i/ in the OE 2, 3 sg is due to the original thematic */-i-/, which raises preceding */e/ (§2.6). This alternation is widespread, and still regular in some modern dialects, like German: geb-en 'give', pres 3 sg gib-t, etc.

(ii) **Preterite indicative.** The origins of the endings are less clear here, and do not seem to reflect an integrated IE paradigm; not surprising, considering the hybrid origins of the strong preterite itself (§7.1.2). Germanic comparisons, again for cl IV 'bear':

(7.23)		Go	OE	OIc
		1 bar	bær	bar
sg		2 bar-t	bær-e	bar-t
		3 bar	bær	bar
		1 bēr-um	bær-on	bór-um
pl		2 bēr-uþ	"	bór-uþ
		3 bēr-un	"	bór-u

---

[25] The IE background to the verb inflections is excellently covered in Szemerényi (1989: ch. 9, §2); see also Prokosch (1938: §§70–5).

The zero-ending forms reflect IE perfects in */-α, -e/, which dropped in Germanic (Gr *oîd-a* 'I know' = Go *wait*, OE *wāt*). The 2 sg -*t* is a joint E/NGmc innovation, and appears to be cognate with the Greek aorist ending -*tha*. The OE 2 sg -*e* is unclear; it may reflect an aorist ending, which would be in keeping with the fact that in OE the pret 2 sg of strong verbs has the PRET₂ vowel-grade, which derives from an aorist (cf. §7.2.1).

(iii) **Present subjunctive.** The Germanic subjunctive descends mainly from the old IE optative; typical paradigms:

(7.24)		Go	OE	OIc
	1	baír-a-i	ber-e	ber-a
sg	2	baír-ai-s	"	ber-er
	3	baír-ai	"	ber-e
	1	baír-ai-ma	ber-en	ber-em
pl	2	baír-ai-þ	"	ber-eþ
	3	baír-ai-na	"	ber-e

The basic IE thematic optative marker was */-oi-/, which > Gmc */-αi-/ as usual; this is still clearly visible in Gothic. The other dialects show the expected developments of this diphthong and following consonants in weak syllables (§4.3.1), except for the OE plural, where the -*n* is extended from the third person, as in the indicative. (The OIc forms without nasals here and in the indicative are due to the same deletion in weak syllables that gives NGmc -*a* for the infinitive.) Note how here, as in other parts of the verb paradigm, Gothic maintains the IE person-markers in a recognizable form: 1 */-m-/, 2 */-t-/, 3 */-n-/ in plural, 2 */-s-/ in sg (cf. the Latin forms in (7.22)).

The lack of person-marking in the OE subjunctive is still in a way reflected in the ModE present subjunctive 3 sg (in those varieties where it survives): optative *long live-Ø the king* vs. statement *the king live-s long*, *God save-Ø the Queen* vs. *God save-s the Queen*, etc.

(iv) **Preterite subjunctive.** Here the PRET₂ grade is extended to all numbers and persons; thus a form like OE *bǣr-e* is ambiguous between pret ind 2 sg and all persons subj sg. The thematic element is an IE optative marker */-i:-/, which was reduced to /e/ in OE and OIc before it could cause *i*-umlaut (but remains as short /i/ in OS, OHG).

(7.25)		Go	OE	OIc
	1	ber-j-au	bǣr-e	bær-a
sg	2	ber-ei-s	"	bær-er
	3	ber-i	"	bær-e
	1	ber-ei-ma	bǣr-en	bær-em
pl	2	ber-ei-þ	"	bær-eþ
	3	ber-ei-na	"	bær-e

The Gothic <ei> /i:/ ~ /j/ alternation depends on whether or not the suffix begins with a consonant.

(v) **Imperative.** The imperative normally has the vowel of PRES, and in OE is formally distinct only in the singular. Although Gothic has a quite full paradigm (2, 3 sg, 2 dual, 1–3 pl), none of the other dialect do; the OE 1 pl 'imperative' is identical in form to the present subjunctive plural, and may not be a true imperative all but a kind of optative ('let it be the case that we X'). Typical 2 sg and 2 pl imperatives for 'bear':

(7.26)		Go	OE	OIc
sg		baír	ber	ber
pl		baír-iþ	ber-aþ	ber-eþ

The sg forms go back to an IE type */bher-e/, i.e. root + theme with no personal endings: cf. Gr *phér-e*. The pl may have been distinct in IE, but in Germanic has fallen together with the present 2 pl indicative. This is not surprising; indeed, it is surprising that it didn't happen in the singular as well. That is, subject-deletion in imperatives is optional in Germanic, and the modality (indicative or imperative) of an utterance like *you leave (now)* is usually pragmatically recoverable.

7.5.2   *The weak verb: present system*

The weak subjunctive is marked like the strong by sg *-e*, pl *-en*; there are obviously no vowel grades to complicate matters as in the strong verb. The indicative endings are similar to those of the strong verb, most clearly in class I. Here endings alone (plus thematic elements in Gothic) are given:

(7.27)   Go   OE   OIc
              1 -j-a   -e   -Ø
       sg   2 -ei-s   -est   -r
              3 -ei-þ   -eþ   "
              1 -j-am   -aþ   -um
       pl   2 -ei-þ   "   -eþ
              3 -j-and   "   -a

The description of class II in §7.3.2 was slightly oversimplified. Recall that there was a thematic */-oː-/ after the root in all dialects, but that OE had a post-theme */-j-/ as well (possibly analogical to class I). This did not however occur in all paradigm members; it is restricted to the present system, and there to the nonfinites (infinitive, present participle), 1 sg, and the plural. The infinitive ended in */-oːj-ɑn/, and the 1 sg was */-oːj-oː/, the plural was */-oːj-ɑ-nθiː/; but the 2 sg was */-oː-siː/, and the 3 sg */-oθiː/. Thus a relic of the post-theme */j/ appears only in parts of the paradigm, and the theme proper affects the following vowel elsewhere:

(7.28)   Go   OE   OIc
              1 -ō   -i-e   -a
       sg   2 -ō-s   -ast   -ar
              3 -ō-þ   -aþ   "
              1 -ō-m   -i-aþ   -um
       pl   2 -ō-þ   "   -eþ
              3 -ō-nd   "   -a

The consequences of the post-radical thematic complex then are: (a) no umlaut (*lufian*, *lufie*, *lufaþ*, etc.); (b) back vowels in the endings of 2, 3 sg (*-aþ* vs. cl I *-eþ*); (c) *-i-* < */-j-/ in parts of the paradigm, e.g. *luf-i-e* vs. cl I *trymm-e*, etc., and (d), no gemination, since the */j/ did not immediately follow the coda of the root syllable (cf. §3.2). There are similar reflexes in the preterite (see the next section).

Class III in OE is rather a complex hybrid, and does not actually reflect a full paradigm. There seem to be three thematic elements involved: (a) */-eː-/; (b) a class II-like theme + post-theme */-eːj-/; and (c) a class I-like */-j-/. The most significant feature is a reflection of type (c) in the pres indicative 1 sg and subjunctive, and in the infinitive and present participle. This involves gemination and *i*-umlaut, as in the above-mentioned forms for *hycgan* 'think', i.e. *hycge*, *hycgan*, *hycgende*. Elsewhere, the (b) type seems to have been involved, with loss of the first element at some point later than gemination, but still early enough to cause umlaut: so pres 2 sg *hygst*, etc. The preterite system is remodelled after athematic class I or class II types. (For a thorough discussion of this complicated group, see Campbell 1959, §§762ff.)

7.5.3   The weak verb: preterite

(i) **Preterite indicative.** As we saw (§7.3.1), the weak preterite probably originates in compounding of a verb stem with the perfect of the verb 'do'; in the Gothic dual and plural this takes the form of a reduplicated perfect; elsewhere it is non-reduplicated. 'Do' was an athematic *mi*-verb (§7.4.2); the forms lying behind the attested singular paradigms consist of the 'do' root plus the endings */-m/ (1), */-s/ (2), */-t/ (3), the last of course becoming Germanic /-θ/. Apparently both *e*-grade and *o*-grade */dhe:-, dho:-/ were available as bases; in the first person Gothic -*d-a*, OIc -*þ-a*, OHG -*t-a* presuppose */dho:-m/ with normal developments in weak syllables, while Go 2 sg -*d-ē-s* suggests */dhe:-s/, but OHG -*t-ō-s* */dho:-s/. OE 1, 3 sg -*d-e* would be difficult except for surviving early forms in -*d-æ*, which show the origin to be the same as in the other dialects, that is */-α/ < */-o/. The plural, except in Gothic, is either formed after the singular (non-reduplicated 'do' + the normal IE personal endings), or has 3 pl generalized to all persons, as in the strong verb. Typical endings for class I:

(7.29)

		Go	OE	OIc
	1	-i-d-a	-(e)-d-e	-þ-a
sg	2	-i-d-ēs	-(e)-d-est	-þ-er
	3	-i-d-a	-(e)-d-e	-þ-e
	1	-i-dēd-um	-(e)-d-on	-þ-um
pl	2	-i-dēd-uþ	"	-þ-uþ
	3	-i-dēd-un	"	-þ-u

Note that Gothic is always thematic, OIc always athematic, and OE thematic after light roots (*trym-e-de*) and athematic after heavy roots (*dēm-de*) < */trum-i-ð-o:(m)/ and */ðo:m-i-ð-o:(m)/.

Class II is somewhat different; the theme vowel was nonhigh */-o:-/, and the conjugation is thematic across the dialects regardless of root weight. The endings are the same as class I, but preceded by Go -*ō*-, OE -*o*-, OIc -*a*-: Go 1 sg *salb-ō-da* 'I anointed', OE *sealf-o-de*, OIc *kall-a-þa* 'I called'. Class III again has the same endings, but is athematic except in Gothic: for 'I had', Go *hab-ai-da*, OE *hæf-de*, OIc *haf-þa*, etc.

(ii) **Preterite subjunctive.** As in the strong verb (§7.5.1), the subjunctive has a full paradigm only in Gothic and North Germanic; in OE it has been reduced to a two-way (sg vs. pl) opposition, marked by *-e* in the singular and *-en* in the plural. The sources of the endings are more or less the same as for the strong verbs, and will not be discussed further here.

(iii) **Imperative**. As with the strong verb, there are only two forms, 2 sg and pl. The 2 sg however is not merely the bare root; in class I light roots it is a thematic stem, e.g. *trym-e* 'strengthen!', *her-e* 'praise!'; after a heavy class I root the vowel drops, so *hīer* 'hear!'. This of course is another case of high vowel deletion after a heavy syllable (§4.3.2), since the historical class I theme is */-i-/. The plural is simply the present indicative form, e.g. *trymm-aþ, her-i-aþ, hīer-aþ*.

In class II the situation is slightly different; the imperative sg is the root plus the present theme, regardless of root-weight: *luf-a* 'love!', *lōc-a* 'look!'. The plural however is again the same as the indicative 2 sg, *luf-i-aþ, lōc-i-aþ*. Class III imperatives are all thematic in the sg: *haf-a* 'have!', *sæg-e* 'say', etc, and the same as the indicative in the plural.

8 Vocabulary and word-formation

8.1   The PGmc lexicon

The main focus of this book is the 'internal' history of Old English, the structural history of the language itself, rather than the sociopolitical or cultural history of the communities that spoke it. Indeed, the primary focus of linguistic history is always internal in this sense. But languages have 'external' histories too: speech-communities live social and political lives, come into contact with speakers of other languages and their cultures and institutions, are conquered by them or conquer them. Such contacts may also have their linguistic reflections. In the normal way of things, it is mainly vocabulary that reflects, if anything does, a language's external history. Contacts with other languages can easily lead to the transfer ('borrowing') of words: less easily (though not that uncommonly) of other structural materials like morphology, syntactic constructions, etc. Historically if not synchronically lexicons tend to be stratified,[1] with every major contact episode leaving some traces.

The OE lexicon is no exception; it consists of a large (majority) stock of items directly inherited from PGmc and its daughters NWGmc and WGmc; as well as items borrowed from other IE dialects (especially Latin), and many new formations. The first part of this chapter (§§8.1–2) will be concerned with the reflections of external history in the OE lexicon; the rest with word-formation processes of various degrees of productivity that reflect the IE and PGmc heritage.

---

[1] Purely historical stratification must be distinguished from the kind of synchronic stratification where the different layers are recognizable (in part) by their distinctive behaviour. In PGmc and Old Germanic generally, the layering of vocabulary is purely etymological: the strata lack distinct phonological or morphological properties. In Modern English on the other hand, the Latin, Greek and Romance elements often have their own special diagnostic features: e.g. adjective nominalization with -ity, with concomitant shortening of long vowels in antepenults (divine vs. divinity, serene vs. serenity), stop/fricative alternations of a certain type (critical vs. crisis, physics vs. physicist vs. physician, etc.).

The PGmc lexicon contained four major historical components:

(i) Direct inheritances from Proto-IE: by far the largest;
(ii) Borrowings from other (non-Gmc) IE dialects;
(iii) Items of unknown etymology, with no clear cognates in IE outside of Germanic, and not relatable to forms in other language-groups that PGmc was in contact with (e.g. Balto-Finnic). These may be loans from extinct and unattested languages, or PGmc inventions.
(iv) New coinages of early date, before the E/NWGmc split, based on inherited IE materials (e.g. compounds).

Aside from lack of synchronic stratification, it was of course shorter on loans because of the more restricted inter-cultural contacts within the relevant period. Some comments on the major components:

(i) *The PIE inheritance.* This includes the bulk of the 'core' vocabulary, e.g. body parts, kinship terms, animal and plant names,[2] numerals, common verbs and adjectives, etc. There appear to be two major strata: (a) items which are of common (pan-IE) distribution, even if they happen to be missing in some dialects, and (b) items of specifically 'Northwest European' provenance, i.e. attested only in the dialect-cluster Italic/Celtic/Baltic/Slavic/Germanic. These probably date from a (Bronze Age) period of common cultural contact and development. This second group contains roots that occur nowhere else in IE, as well as some that do, but have a highly specialized meaning in NWIE: e.g. the root in Go *freis*, Welsh *rhydd* 'free', which does appear elswhere, but apparently only with the sense 'beloved' (Skr *priya-*). I will be concerned here only with the uniquely distributed roots, not the complex question of semantic evolution.

(a) Common IE lexis. Many forms of this type have been cited earlier, but a collection in one place will give a better idea of the essential 'Indo-Europeanness' of the core Germanic lexicon. 'Foot' (Go *fōtus*, OHG *fuoz*, OIc *fótr*, L *pēs/pēdis*, Skr *pād-*, Li *pādas* 'sole'); 'eye' (Go *augō*, OE *ēage*, OIc *auga*, OCS *oko*, L *oculus*, Arm *aku*); 'mother' (OE *mōdor*, OIc *móðir*, L *māter*, OIr *mathir*, Li *móte*, Toch *mācar*); 'two' (Go *twai*, OE *twā*, OIc *tveir*, L *duo*, OW *dou*, Li *dvì*, OCS *dva*); 'sit' (Go *sitan*, OE *sittan*, OIc *sitja*, L *sedeō*, Li *sédmi*); 'bind' (Go *bindan*, OE *bindan*, OIc *binda*, L *(of-)fendix* 'fetter', Gr *peîsma* < */pénthsma/ 'bond'); 'full' (Go *fulls*, OE

---

[2] At least those presumed to come from the original settlement area (wherever exactly that was). Thus there is no general IE word for 'tiger', but there is one for 'bear' and 'salmon', and perhaps 'oak' or 'beech' – which may localize the original community within limits, i.e. as north-temperate. On the problems of localizing and even identifying particular species, however, see Campbell (1990), Friedrich (1970).

full, Li *pilnas*, OCS *plŭnŭ*, L *plēnus*, Skr *pūrṇá-*); 'new' (Go *niujis*, OE *niewe*, OIc *nyrr*, Li *naūjas*, OCS *novŭ*, L *nouus*). And so on.

(b) NWIE lexis. The specifically 'NW' vocabulary is also quite sizeable, consisting mainly of 'cultural' terms pertaining to agriculture and the like, as well as names for animals and plants endemic to this part of the IE world. The historical interpretation of these NW forms not found elsewhere in IE is difficult; some at least may be borrowings from neighbouring languages (now lost), developed independently in the languages of the NWIE cluster, or they may have been invented within the cluster: there is no way of telling. For instance, we can reconstruct a root */se-/ 'sow' as lying behind Go *saian*, OCS *sěti*, Li *sěti*, L *serō* (perf *sēuī*) 'sow', as well as forms with extensions (see §5.4) like L *sēmen*, OCS *sěmę*, OHG *sāt*, W *had* 'seed'. But is this a PIE root that happens not to survive elsewhere, a specifically NWIE root developed or invented in this group, or a root borrowed from some indigenous language into the language(s) of the IE invaders after they had settled down to agriculture? The same goes for the roots in L *far* 'spelt', *farina* 'flour', OIc *barr* 'cereals', Go *barizeins* 'made of barley'; in L *grānum* 'grain', OIr *grān*, Go *kaúrn*, OCS *zrŭno*; in OIr *aball* 'apple', OCS *ablŭko*, Li *óbùlas*, OE *æppel*; or OIr *eo*, OCS *jiva*, Li *ёva*, OIc *yr* 'yew'.[3] All of these and more could be accounted for in a number of ways, e.g. convergent loss in all non-NW dialects (methodologically dubious), borrowing, invention, etc.: though scholars have usually steered away from the idea of invention (see below under (iii)).

(ii) *Borrowings from non-Germanic IE*. These (fully integrated) loans are mainly from Celtic and Latin, the latter much more important. The most familiar Celtic borrowing is the root */ri:k-/ 'king', which appears in Go *reiks*, OS *-rīk*, OIc *-rík* (the latter two only as name-elements), Go *reiki* 'kingdom', OHG *rīhhi*, OE *rīce*. The PIE root (cf. L *rēx* < */re:g-s/) must be */re:g-/; but PIE */e:/ > */i:/ in Celtic (cf. Gaulish names like *Catu-rīges*, *Rīgo-magus*, etc.). If the Germanic forms were direct PIE inheritances, not by way of Celtic, we would expect Go **rēks*, etc. Another well-attested Celtic loan is the word for 'servant', Go *andbahts*, OHG *ambaht*, OE *ambeht* < Gaulish *ambactos*.

The Latin component is much larger, and consists mainly of items denoting cultural borrowings from Rome. Some typical ones are 'wine' (L *uīnum*, Go *wein*, OE *wīn*); 'trade, traffic' (L *caupō*, Go *kaupōn*, OE *cēapian*); 'oil' (L *oleum*, OE *oele*, OS, OHG *oli*); 'prison' (L *carcer*, Go

---

[3] This may be a Uralic loan, or go back to a putative 'Indo-Uralic' common language: note Finnish *juko(-puu)* 'yew-tree', Estonian *juka*, Cheremis *jakte* (a general conifer word). Some Uralists reconstruct a Proto-Uralic */joxi/ or */juwe/ and assume borrowing into IE; Indo-Europeanists reconstruct PIE */ejwo/ or something of the sort (cf. Campbell 1990: 168f).

karkara, OE *carcern* < root *carc-* + *ærn* 'house'; 'table' (L *mēnsa*, Go *mēs*, OHG *mias*); 'seal' (L *sigillum*, Go *sigljan* 'to seal', OE *-sigle* in compounds). These words are common stock in other languages as well, including non-IE ones: Finnish *viini* 'wine', *kauppias* 'salesman', *öljy* 'oil'. The majority of Latin loans in the individual Gmc dialects however are much later, via secondary contact with both spoken and written Latin after the christianization of the Germanic-speaking communities (§8.2.1).

(iii) *Uniquely Germanic items*. These show no apparent cognates outside of Germanic, either in IE or elsewhere, and must be assumed to be either borrowed or invented in PGmc. Their core status in many cases makes borrowing unlikely; but we are still faced with the odd problem of the relative stability over time of much of the rest of IE core lexis in the dialects ('mother', 'father', 'foot', 'cow', 'mouse' are virtually universal). Why should a number of quite common forms have been lost in Germanic, and required replacement (if that's indeed what happened)?[4] For some scholars, whatever the motivation, the only conceivable source is borrowing; the possibility of invention in PGmc seems not to arise. If a form has no IE cognates then it is a borrowing (so Lockwood 1966: 80). But if PGmc was incapable of lexical innovation more or less *ex nihilo*, it's unlike any attested language. In any case, lexical roots have to begin somewhere; they can't all be 'old' or 'original'. The question is in fact unanswerable, but the alternatives ought to be noted.

Here is a sample of important Germanic roots that seem to have no relations elsewhere in IE; some indeed are restricted to one branch of Germanic. The headword in each case is the modern English descendant.

(a) Common Germanic or NWGmc:

> BATH (OIc, OS *bað*, OE *bæþ*, OFris *beth*).
>
> BOAT (OE *bāt*, OIc *beit*; no other examples. All related forms, e.g. Fr *bateau* < *bat-el* (diminutive), It *battello*, W *bad* are loans from Germanic).
>
> DRINK (Go *drigkan*, OIc *drekka*, OE *drincan*, OHG *trinchan*).
>
> DRIVE (Go *dreiban*, OIc *drífa*, OE *drífan*, OS *dríban*).
>
> EVIL (Go *ubils*, OE *yfel*, OS *ubil*, OFris, MDu *evel*, OHG *ubil*). Some relation has been suggested to IE */up-/ 'exceeding', but this is uncertain. The root survives only in E, WGmc, which suggests PGmc origin, before the E/NW split.
>
> FINGER (Go *figgrs*, OIc *fingr*, OE *finger*; a connection has been suggested to */penk^w-/ 'five', but this is uncertain).

---

[4] The phenomenon however is not unknown in later periods. Yiddish has replaced some of its core Germanic lexis with Hebrew or Slavic loans: 'star' is *štern*, as might be expected, but 'moon' is *levone* from Hebrew, 'eye' is *ojg* (cf. G *Auge*), but 'mouth' is *pisk*, from Polish.

HAND (Go *handus*, OIc *hǫnd*, OE *hand, hond*, OHG *hant*. Probably the same root in Sw *hinna* 'reach' < */xinθ-/, and in older dialects Go *-hinþan* 'seize', strong verb III. These suggest an ablaut series */xenθ-, xanθ-, xunθ-/: the zero-grade /xunθ-/ gives Go *hunþ* 'plunder, booty' = 'that which is seized', OHG *hunda*, OE *hūþ* with Ingvaeonic nasal deletion and lengthening. The *o*-grade */xanθ-/ with accented suffix and Verner's Law gives *handus, hǫnd, hand*, etc.).

SEA (Go *saiws*, OIc *sær, sjár*, OE *sǣ*, OS *seu*, dat sg *sēwa*).

(b) West Germanic only:

BROOK (N) (OE *brōc*, MLG *brōk*, OHG *bruoh*).

PRICK (OE *pric(c)a, price, prician* 'to prick', MLG *pricke*, MDu *prikken*, OS *prekunga* 'pricking' = OE *pricung*. Unknown outside Invgaeonic except as a loan into NGmc (Icelandic *prike*)).

SHEEP (OE *scēap, scēp, scǣp*, OFris *skēp*, OS *scāp*, OHG *scāf*).

SOON (OE *sōna* 'immediately', OFris *sōn*, OS, OHG *sāno*; West Germanic only unless related to Go *suns* 'immediately').

Uniqueness to Germanic, or to one branch of Germanic, is not always clear; the following examples illustrate some classic difficulties:

EARTH (Go *aírþa*, OIc *jǫrþ*, OE *eorþe*, OHG *erda*). Apparently the root is */er-/ plus an extension */-θ-/, judging from OHG *ero* 'earth', OIc *jǫr-fi* 'gravel'. This may be common IE (possibly in Gr *éraze* 'on the ground', W *erw* 'field'); if these do contain the same root, then only the extended ō-stem noun */er-θ-o:/ is uniquely Germanic; MIr *ert* 'earth' is probably a loan from Germanic.

LITTLE (OE *lȳtel*, OS *luttil*, OHG *luzzil*) suggesting an ancestral root (or root-complex) */lu(:)t(t)-il-/. The root with this vocalism is unknown outside WGmc, but note Go *leitils*, OIc *lítil* with /i:/ and the same sense. Whether the roots are identical is problematic, as the vowels fail to match in any regular way.

(iv) *Inherited formations*. If a particular complex word (derivation, compound) shows up in all the old dialects, or at least in Gothic and either WGmc or NGmc, it can with some safety be attributed to PGmc (with certain caveats: see below). The problem is of course that given the productivity of compounding as a word-formation strategy, it is perfectly possible for a given compound to be reinvented more than once. There is no reliable measure of the probability of reinvention as opposed to inheritance; but a combination of (a) extremely wide distribution in the family, and (b) unlikelihood of independent invention (judged intuitively) suggests inheritance. There are at least some compounds in the dialects that can be taken as 'frozen' or lexicalized.

Very few specific compounds occur in all three major branches of Germanic; among them are are Go *man-leika*, OHG *manna-līhho*, OIc *mann-līkan* 'man-likeness' (i.e. effigy); Go *midjun-gards*, OE *middan-geard*, OIc *mið-garþr* 'middle-earth' (a mythological survival); Go *faíhu-gaírns*, OE *feoh-georn*, OIc *fé-gjarn* 'money-eager' (i.e. covetous). Some show up only in Gothic and NGmc, e.g. Go *fōtu-baúrd*, OIc *fōt-borþ* 'foot-board' (i.e. stool); Go *seina-gaírns*, OIc *sín-gjarn* 'his-eager', i.e. 'selfish, miserly'. This last is particularly interesting, as it's about the only attested compound with a personal pronoun as first element, which makes convergence highly unlikely. Those that occur only in Gothic and WGmc include Go *arbi-numja*, OHG *erpi-nomo*, OE *yrfe-numa* 'inheritance-taker' (heir); Go *auga-daúro*, OHG *ouga-toro*, OE *ēag-duru* 'eye-door' (window); for this last item NGmc has the type shown in OIc *vind-auga* 'wind-eye', the source of ModE *window*. The discontinuities and odd distributions should not be taken too seriously; we must recall how fragmentary the surviving material from Old Germanic is. Absence of a form in a dialect-group is suggestive, but not compelling.

What is more important of course is the TYPE of compound, i.e. the grammatical and semantic elements available, not the specific items (§8.3.2). The same holds for non-compound derivations; we have in fact (under the guise of looking at the inflectional morphology of nouns and verbs), already seen derivations of PGmc date, e.g. weak verbs, feminine abstracts in **/-iθo/* (§§7.3, 6.1.3).

8.2   Loans in Old English

8.2.1   Latin[5]

Loanwords can be identified in a number of ways. The easiest of course is when the loan is recent, and there is external evidence (like *sauna*, where the object itself, as well as the spelling, is Finnish and known to be so). In a textual tradition as old and incomplete as Old English, the problem can be more difficult, especially if the word itself is thoroughly 'nativized', i.e.

---

[5] For details, see standard sources like Serjeantson (1935: ch. 2), Campbell (1959: ch. 10), and the review and discussion in Kastovsky (1992).

shows no sign of its foreignness.[6] But we often (as in *rīce* above) have good phonological evidence: if for instance an OE form is very like a Latin one, but does not show the expected developments that it would if the two were independently inherited from PIE, we can identify it (a) as a loan, and (b) as one that came in after the processes involved ceased to be productive.

OE *pytt* 'pit, well' for example resembles (and indeed comes from) L *puteus*. But the skeleton /pVt-/ in both tells us that *pytt* is not Germanic (otherwise it would be **fyþþ* by Grimm's Law); and the L /u/ vs. OE /y/ tells us further that *pytt* has undergone *i*-umlaut, and that it must be from VL */putj-/ rather than the classic form, to provide both the IU environment, and the context for gemination of the final consonant. Thus *pytt* is a late vernacular Latin loan. On the other hand, using the same criteria, *tunece* 'tunic' < L *tunica* is late: otherwise it would be **tynece*. There may also be doublets, from borrowing at two different periods, which support this kind of argument: *celc* 'cup' < L *calix* shows IU and is therefore early, whereas the doublet *calic* (with /i/ retained and no IU) must be late.

Similarly, the source of a loan can be narrowed down in time by changes occurring in the donor language. In VL there was a lowering of the short high vowels /i, u/ to /e, o/: so OE *disc* < L *discus*, *must* 'must (incompletely fermented grape juice)' < L *mustum* are early, whereas *cest* 'box' < *cista*, *torr* 'tower' < *turris* are late.[7]

Germanic speakers had already met Latin on the continent; when Ingvaeonic speakers reached Britain in the fifth century, they came into contact with it again, mainly as one of the languages of the Romanized Celts. Later it became both a spoken and literary source through the influence of the church and Latin literature. Latin influence on post-settlement Old English is customarily divided into two main periods: early settlement, c. 450–600, and post-Christian, from after 650 or so until the eleventh century. Among the early loans are *stropp* 'strop' < *stroppus*, *forca* 'fork' < *furca*, *nunne* 'nun' < *nunna*, *mægester* 'master' < *magister*, *senap* 'mustard' < *sinapis*, *lafian* 'bathe' < *lauāre*. Nearly all of these are nouns; borrowings of verbs and adjectives are much rarer, as these tend to be produced by native word-formation strategies.

Many more loans came in during the later period, largely through the church. Christianity of course brought its own vocabulary, connected with its institutions: *abbod* < *abbat-em*,[8] *culpe* 'guilt' < *culpa*, *offrian* 'offer,

---

[6] Examples of 'foreignness' in this sense are the OE <ph> in *Seraphin* 'seraphim', *philosoph* 'philosopher', or the initial <z> and *-us* nominative ending in *zodiacus*. Loans like these presumably have the same status as ModE *object d'art*, *Weltanschauung*.

[7] The major late Latin changes and their relation to the dating of OE loans are treated in detail in Campbell (1959: §§545–64).

[8] If a Latin noun has stem-alternants (nom sg *abbas*, acc *abbat-em*), Germanic typically borrows the oblique form, probably because the oblique stems were at this time being

sacrifice' < *offerre, fers* 'verse' < *uersus.*[9] There were also numerous borrowings of plant names, like *lilie* < *lilium, rōse* < *rōsa, sigle* 'rye' < *secale,* and much other miscellaneous vocabulary.

The Benedictine reform (late tenth-century), produced many more loans, characteristically classical and/or scholarly, often giving doublets with older forms: *corona* 'crown' < *corōna* (earlier *coren*), *magister* (earlier *mægester*). Also *cruc* 'cross' < *cruc-em, paradīs* < *paradīsum, bibliopece* 'library' < *bibliotheca, declīnian* 'decline (a noun or adjective)' < *declīn-āre, paper* < *papyrus.*

The role of borrowing, as well as a curious fact about the IE obstruent system, is illustrated by the following: of the 186 words with initial /p/ listed in Holthausen (1963), nearly 49 per cent are Latin loans. Another 49 per cent are words with no cognates outside Germanic, and about 2 per cent are Celtic loans. There is not one OE word with a secure etymology involving IE initial */b-/, i.e. that can be taken as a firm IE inheritance. This is due to the very limited distribution of IE */b/ in general, which seems to have been the rarest of the consonant phonemes. So while it is true that the overall number of loans (of any provenance) in OE is quite low, compared to any modern Germanic language (about 3 per cent, as opposed to nearly 70 per cent in Modern English: Kastovsky 1992: 294), certain phonological categories are disproportionately Latinate.[10]

Latin also influenced the OE vocabulary in an indirect way through a large number of loan-translations. A **loan-translation** or **calque** is a morph-by-morph translation of a complex foreign original, creating a semantically transparent native compound in place of the opaque donor item. Since ME times English has tended to borrow opaque compounds and leave them untouched: OE, more typically for a Germanic language, tended to translate. So for instance English has the opaque *unicorn* < L

---

generalized in spoken Latin. Historical grammars (following the Romance philological tradition) give the 'source' as the accusative sg (hence *abbat-em*); though of course what is really borrowed is the stem-as-word, i.e. the source ought to be given as *abbat-*. In French itself however there is evidence that the accusative proper is the base: so *rien* 'nothing' /rjɛ̃/, whose nasal vowel is explicable only on the basis of Latin accusative *rem* 'thing' (nom *rēs*, stem *rē-*).

[9] The /f/ in *fers* (as also in *Fergilius* 'Virgil') shows that L initial /w/ (spelled <u>) had become /v/ by the time of borrowing. Since [v] was the foot-medial allophone of /f/ in OE (cf. §3.9.1), the initial [f] was apparently adopted. If the Latin initial had still been /w/, we would expect **wers*, etc. The /w/ > /v/ change enables us to separate two strata of Latin loans, early ones like *wīn* < *uīnum* (continental), *weall* 'wall' < *uallum, pāwa* 'peacock' < *pāuō, mealwe* 'mallow' < *malua* from later *fers, salfie* 'sage' < *saluia*, etc.

[10] In an etymological sense only of course, not a synchronic one. With respect to everyday or 'core' vocabulary such figures are misleading: much of the ModE loan-corpus consists of rare or technical items, and this is true of many OE loans as well. So the 'normal' loan-figures may be lower for both languages. Further, only a fragment of what must have been the total OE lexicon has survived: some 23–24,000 words.

uni-cornis 'one-horned', while Dutch, German and Swedish have calques (Du *een-horn*, G *Ein-horn*, Sw *en-hörning*); OE had *ān-hyrne*.

The abstract vocabulary of Old English is full of such calques, e.g.:

(8.1) 'mercifulness'
      L miser-i-   cord-   -ia
      mercy   heart   noun/abstract
      OE mild-   heort-   -ness

      'circumcise'
      L circum-   cid-   -ere
      around   cut   infinitive
      OE ymb-   snīþ-   -an

      'illumination'
      L il-   lumin-   -atiō
      in   light   noun/abstract
      OE in-   liht-   -nis

Other examples are *fore-sēon* 'foresee' < *pro-uidēre*, *prī-ness* 'trinity' < *trini-tas*.

The desire for transparency could lead to **folk-etymology**, the interpretation of opaque foreign elements as semantically plausible and phonologically similar native ones (as in ModE *Jerusalem (artichoke)* < It *girasole* 'sunflower'). A classic case is *mere-grot* 'pearl' = *mere* 'sea' + *grot* 'grain' < L *margarita* (cf. OHG *meri-griota*, where the second element = OE *grēot* 'gravel', presumably from the same root). A rather extreme example is *biscop-wyrt* 'marsh-mallow', literally 'bishop-wort' < L *hibiscum/-us*, where the non-element *-bisc-* seems to have been extracted.[11]

8.2.2   Scandinavian

England was invaded a number of times by NGmc speakers, and eventually settled (later ruled for a time) by them. The first invasions (small-scale Viking raids) began in the eighth century, and lasted until about 850. That year saw a massive Danish invasion, leading to the capture of major eastern centres like London, Canterbury and York. In the 870s the Danes turned their attention to Wessex, but were finally defeated by King Alfred at the Battle of Ethandun (Wiltshire) in 878.

---

[11] There is no ecclesiastical connection: the Latin word is < Gr *hibískos*, which has nothing to do with *epískopos* 'bishop'.

Under the terms of the Treaty of Wedmore, signed that year, the Danes abandoned Wessex, but were ceded most of England east of a line from Chester to London: this area was known as the Danelaw (the place where Danish law was in force).[12]

Invasions continued; there were some battles that re-established the *status quo ante* (in 937 King Athelstan defeated an army of Danes and Scots in the battle memorialized in the poem 'The Battle of Brunanburh', somewhere in Northumberland), but eventually the English lost. The invasions increased in scale, and eventually the Dane Cnut ('Canute') Sveinsson was crowned king in 1014. From then until 1042, when the throne passed back to the Wessex line with the accession of Edward the Confessor, England was politically a Danish province.[13]

During this period there must have been considerable English/NGmc bilingualism;[14] certainly a very large number of NGmc loans were taken in, and many later became core vocabulary. The great bulk of these however are not attested in OE sources, but only appear in the twelfth to thirteenth centuries.[15]

The identification of NGmc loans is often quite difficult. First, many words would have virtually the same phonological shape in North Germanic and Invgaeonic: e.g. OIc *ala* 'nourish' = OE *alan*, *bíta* 'bite' = *bītan*, *bera* 'bear' = *beran*, *dómr* 'judgement' = *dōm*, *snīða* 'cut' = *snīþan*, etc. So in principle OE could have borrowed a NGmc form with a shape like /do:m-r/, dropped the nom sg /-r/, and come out with /do:m/, and so on. The best evidence is from items that are widespread in NGmc but do not occur in WGmc – except in those dialects that have come into extensive contact with NGmc, or that appear in WGmc with meanings that seem to be NGmc.[16]

A good example of the first type is the late OE verb *tacan* 'take', which gradually superseded native *niman*. This is clearly a NGmc loan, since it is the usual NGmc word (OIc *taka*, Sw *ta*, pret *tog*, pp *tagit*), and appears only in those coastal WGmc dialects likely to have had Viking contacts

---

[13] The OE word *Dene* 'Danes' usually refers to Scandinavians of any kind; most of the invaders were indeed Danish (East Norse speakers), but there were Norwegians (West Norse) among them as well.

[13] For the history, see the brief outline in Lass (1987: §2.6) and references, and Kastovsky (1992: §5.2.3).

[14] It has even been suggested that the interaction was so intense that an 'Anglo-Norse creole' developed. This is supposed to have been the input to, and determined the essential character of, Middle English (so Poussa 1982).

[15] Of the 900 or so attested NGmc loans into English, only about 150 actually appear in OE. For more details see Kastovsky (1992: §5.2.3).

[16] There are some phonological criteria as well (e.g. non-palatalization of velars before front vowels: see §3.7); but these are applicable mainly to later loans, and are at best ambiguous.

(Frisian, Middle Dutch). Otherwise the WGmc verb for 'take' has the */nem-/ root (G *nehmen*, Du *nemen*).

An example of the second type – a phonological shape associated with a non-WGmc meaning – is OE *lagu* 'law'. This also displays beautifully the dangers of not knowing the conventions under which the handbooks operate, and the complex inferences required to evaluate an etymology. The usual etymon is 'Old Norse *lǫgr*'. There are a number of problems here. First, the apparently innocent 'Old Norse' is a mild lie: forms like *lǫgr* (and those given above) are not from any Old NGmc dialect that could conceivably have been the donor for Old English. They are in fact classical Icelandic orthographic forms (often normalized) from the twelfth to thirteenth centuries, which by common consent 'stand for' the unattested Old Danish or Old Norwegian that OE must actually have borrowed from.

This is harmless as long as the cited forms are very close to what OE must have borrowed; but in the case of *lagu/lǫgr* it's clear that the second could not – as such – have been the source of the first. Further, OE *lagu* is a feminine ō-stem (like *sagu* 'saying, saw'), whereas *lǫgr* is a masculine *u*-stem (like *magu* 'kinsman').

Now there is an OE masculine *u*-stem *lagu*; but it means 'sea, water', and is related to OS *lagu*, L *lacus* 'lake', OIr *loch*. *Lagu* 'law' on the other hand contains the same root as in *lecgan* 'lay' < */laɣ-j-/, i.e. the law is that which is 'laid down' (cf. the same semantics in G *Gesetz* which is related to *setzen* 'set'). So what is the source?

The etymology is transparent, if one looks for instance at the non-nominative forms of OIc *lǫgr*: gen sg/pl *lagar*, acc pl *lǫgu*. The <ǫ> /ɔ/ is from *u*-umlaut of */a/, and the original nom sg must have been */laɣ-u-z/, which would give *lǫgr* by normal West Norse sound changes. Therefore the ancestor of OE *lagu* is an unattested */laɡ-u/ < */laɣ-u-z/; 'Old Norse *lǫgr*' is not a source but merely a cognate. The gender and declensions are matters of internal OE restructuring (probably because feminine abstracts like this are more common than masculines). As long as one remembers all this, however, it is possible to talk intelligently about 'Norse' borrowings (mostly Old Danish, which sometimes makes things worse, as this is East, not West Norse).

Most Scandinavian loans (as the examples suggest) are phonologically nativized; it does not seem possible to identify any of the actual OE attestations solely by their shape. The clear identification is on semantic grounds: the correlation for instance of OE legal, military, administrative, maritime or other terms with well-localized Scandinavian ones. On that basis, we can identify among others the following ('sources' are Old Icelandic as described above):

(i) Legal and administrative. Aside from *lagu*, *fēo-laga* 'fellow, partner' (*fé-lagi*), *grið* 'peace, truce' (*grið*), *māl* 'lawsuit' (*mál*), *sac-lēas* 'innocent' (*sak-lauss*: note OE -*lēas* for cognate NGmc -*lauss* < PGmc **/lɑus-/*, suggesting an analysis part-way toward a loan-translation), *ūtlaga* 'outlaw' (*útlagr* 'outlawed').

(ii) Military/nautical. *Brynige* 'mail-shirt' (*brynja*), *cnīf* 'knife' (*knífr*), *lið* 'fleet' (*lið*), *cnear* 'small ship' (*knǫrr*), *barð* 'barque' (*barð* 'armed prow').

(iii) Other. *Becc* 'brook' (*bekkr*), *carl* 'man' (*karl*),[17] *hofding* 'chief, ringleader' (*hof-þingi* 'commander'), *loft* 'air' (*lopt*), *rōt* 'root' (*rót*), *scinn* 'skin, fur' (*skinn*), *wǣpen-getæc* 'wapentake, district' (*vápna-tak*).

As with Latin, few verbs are borrowed: among these are *ge-eggian* 'egg on, incite' (*eggja*), *serþan* 'rape, lie with' (*serþa* 'violate'), and *tacan* (*taka*) as above. Loan-translations are also quite common: *gold-wrecen* 'gold-wreathed' (*gull-rekinn*), *drince-lēan* 'entertainment given by a lord to his tenants' (*drekku-laun*), *land-cēap* 'fine on alienation of land' (*land-kaup*).

8.2.3 Celtic and French

Considering that the Ingvaeonic settlers invaded an essentially Celtic country,[18] the number of secure Celtic loans in OE is remarkably small. Only about a dozen or so are attested; most of these are from Brythonic Celtic, the dialect-group spoken by the larger number of British inhabitants (often 'Old Welsh' or 'Old British' in the handbooks). Among these are *binn* 'bin' *bannoc* 'bit, piece of cake', *dunn* 'dun, grey', *broc* 'badger', *bratt* 'cloak', *carr* 'rock', *luh* 'lake', *torr* 'rock', *cumb* 'deep valley, coombe'. As seems so often to be the case, borrowings from the languages of dispossessed and obviously not highly regarded groups tend to be semantically restricted, especially to toponymic (geographical name) elements.

Loans from Goidelic (the other Celtic subgroup) are even scarcer, and are associated not with the vernaculars of the local Celts, but with the church; these apparently were borrowed through contact with Irish missionaries. In this group are *drȳ* 'magician' < OIr *drúi* (cf. ModE *druid* < pl *druidh*), *ancor* 'hermit' < *anchara*, *stær* 'story' < *stoir* ultimately from L *historia*. We could also add *cros(s)*, which is very rare before

---

[17] Note the cognate (native) *ceorl*, presumably from *e*-grade of a root **/gVr-/* with a sense like 'mature' (NGmc has *o*-grade, hence PGmc **/ɑ/*). This root may also appear in Skr *járant-* 'old', Gr *gérōn* 'old man'.

[18] For the history of Germanic/Celtic relations in the early post-invasion period see Lass (1987: §2.3) and references, Kastovsky (1992: §5.2.4).

the eleventh century, and occurs only in place names; the usual OE word is *rōd* 'rood'.

The French element is miniscule, but of interest as the precursor of the post-1066 inundation. A small dribble of French words come in during the tenth to eleventh centuries, largely perhaps through the French-inspired religious revival of that period. The commonest of these is *prud, prut* 'proud'; it was clearly nativized, since it yields derivatives like *prutlic*, *pryto/prute* 'pride', and compounds like *world-pryde* 'worldly pride'. The /y/ in *pryto* is often taken as a sign of nativization: it is analogical, i.e. an indication that IU was morphologized, so that there were paradigms that could serve as models for loan-derivations as well (*prut/pryto* like *full* 'full'/*fyllo* 'fullness'). The variation of /u/ and /y/ in these forms however may not be due to a native morphological process at all, but to the fact that French /u/ had already begun to front to /y/ during this period (Pope 1934: §183). A few other loans appear in earlier texts (*sot* 'foolish', *capun* 'capon', *tumbere* 'dancer' < OF *tomber* 'fall'); but most are later (eleventh century and beyond), e.g. *gingifer* 'ginger', *bacun* 'bacon', *serfise* 'service', *prisun*, *castel*.

8.3   Word-formation

8.3.1   Typology and productivity

Word-formation (WF) is a general term for the creation of new lexemes. A **lexeme** is an abstract category ('headword') which may be manifested as one or more **word-forms**. E.g. OE had a lexeme FISC 'fish', whose (inflectional) forms were *fisc* (nom/acc sg), *fisces* (gen sg), *fiscas* (nom/acc pl), etc.[19] The simplest distinction between WF or **derivational morphology** and **inflectional morphology** is that the former creates new lexemes, whereas as the latter only produces forms of a given lexeme. So from FISC various derivational processes could produce the additional lexemes FISCAÐ 'fishing, fish-pond, fishing-rights', FISCERE 'fisher', FISCIAN 'to fish',[20] FISC-CYNN 'fish-tribe', FISC-MERE 'fish-pond', FISC-WYLLE 'full of fish', etc. Each of these in turn would of course have its own inflectional forms, e.g. FISCIAN has *fiscode* 'I fished', *fiscie* 'I fish', and so on.

---

[19] For more detail on these distinctions, see Bauer (1988: ch. 2), Matthews (1974: ch. 2). It is conventional to indicate lexemes in caps or small caps; I will not do this unless the theoretical distinction happens to be at issue. But 'word' in general is to be taken here in the sense of 'lexeme', and the examples in this section are just a reminder.

[20] More precisely, since class II -*ian* is an inflection (even if historically a derivational affix), and *fiscað* is a deverbal noun, the derivational sequence would be [N FISC] → [V FISC-IAN] → [N FISC-AÐ].

Broadly speaking three main types of WF strategies are of concern to us here: **compounding, affixation,** and **conversion** or **zero-derivation**. In compounding, new lexemes are created by putting together two or more others (FISC-MERE < FISC + MERE); in affixation, affixes (in Germanic usually suffixes) are added to base forms as in FISC-IAN, FISC-AÐ; and in zero-derivation an already existing form is adopted as a new lexeme, eg. OE RĀD 'riding, road' is in a sense a recruitment of the PRET$_2$ (or more accurately the PRET$_2$ stem) of the cl I strong verb RĪDAN 'ride'. (There are more subtle distinctions, which will come up later when the individual strategies are treated.)

One of the most striking features of the OE lexicon is the extensive involvement in WF, not only of transparent affixation, compounding, and conversion, but of other devices of varying ages: ancient ones like ablaut, and newer ones like *i*-umlaut. This results in what Kastovsky (1992: 294) calls 'large morphologically related word-families'; considerable portions of the lexicon 'cohere' in a rather special way, characteristic of older IE and to some extent more archaic modern languages like German, but quite alien to Modern English.

Here is an illustrative sample of the OE reflexes of the IE root */bhVr-/ 'carry, bear':

(a) *e*-grade: PRES of *ber-an* 'bear', including pres part *ber-ende*. By conversion, an adjective *ber-ende* 'fruitful', and the noun *ber-end* 'bearer', by affixation *ber-end-nes* 'fertility'.

(b) *o*-grade: PRET$_1$ of *beran*, *bær*; *bear-we* 'barrow, basket, bar-row' (with breaking of */æ/ < */ɑ/ < */o/); likewise *bear-m* 'lap, bosom'.[21]

(c) Lengthened *e*-grade: PRET$_2$ *bǣr-on*; the bare stem in *bǣr* 'bier' (for carrying corpses); affixation in *bǣr-e* 'manner, behaviour' (cf. ModE *bearing* in this sense), *(ge-)bǣr-an* 'conduct oneself', *-bǣr-e*, adjectival suffix in e.g. *lust-bǣr-e* 'desirable, pleasant' ('lust-carrying'); as a compound element in *bǣr-disc* 'tray', *bǣr-mann* 'porter'.

(d) Zero-grade: PART *boren*.[22] Directly, an element *-bor-a* 'carrier'. With IU of the earlier stem-vowel */u/ and a following dental element, *ge-byr-d(u)* 'birth', *byr-de* 'innate, natural' (= 'in-born'), *byr-ð-enn* 'burden'; hence compounds like *byrd-dæg* 'birthday'; with a different extension, *byr-ele* 'cup-bearer', and *byr-el-ian* 'pour' (i.e. 'be a cup-bearer').[23]

---

[21] The segmentations *bear-we*, *bear-m* are historically valid, but synchronically dubious. Still, one might imagine an OE speaker aware of patterns like *bearm/bær* but *weorþan/wearþ*, etc. relating *ber-* and *bear-*, even if by this stage the *-m-* has no meaning: certainly the semantic relation is clear. The IE affiliations of the post-radical element in *bearwe* are unclear: for *bearm* cf. Gr *phor-m-ós* 'carrying basket' (*phér-ō* 'I carry'), and the discussion in §8.3.3 below.
[22] IE */bhr̥-ó-no-s/ > */βur-ɑ-nɑ-z/, with lowering of */u/ > [o] by *a*-umlaut (§2.7).
[23] On the /-d-/ and /-l-/ elements see §8.3.3 below.

So with ablaut plus *a*-, *i*-umlaut, there are no fewer than five variant vocalisms for this one root; the interaction of processes and historical levels could be visualized like this:

(8.2)

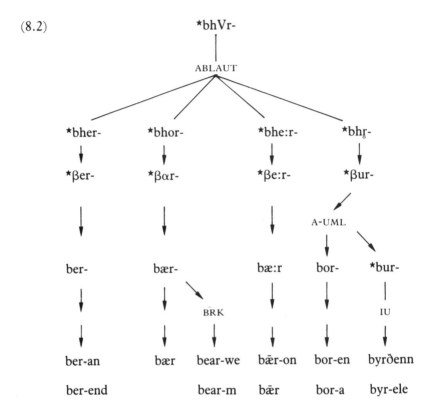

Processes of IE, PGmc, pre-OE date all appear to 'cooperate'; not of course synchronically, but they do leave traces, and presumably ones that in some sense might have been moderately transparent to speakers. However one interprets this complex historical layering, the important thing to note is the preservation of at least a root /bVr-/ with the sense 'carry'; and derived from this root, a set of alternant stems, which can serve both inflectional (as in strong verb tense-marking) and derivational purposes. What we have here is a type of morphology that can be called a **variable-stem** or **stem-based** system; unlike the ModE type, which is an **invariant-base** or **word-based** morphology.[24]

---

[24] The change from one to the other is the major typological shift in the evolution of English morphology. For discussion see Kastovsky (1990, 1992).

One problem of course (hinted at already) is that of **productivity**: to what extent are all (or any) of these formations and ones in similar word-families 'made' in OE – or better, 'makeable'? Or how far are they frozen or fossil formations, explicable not as the application of living rules, but simply as inherited lexicalized chunks dating back to a period of greater productivity?

Some WF strategies are apparently fully productive in OE, e.g. N+N compounding. It is however (generally: but see below) impossible to tell whether a given occurrence of any derived form represents an institutionalized lexical item, or whether it is a new formation. This is especially true of items that appear only once in the text corpus, e.g. *dæg-bōt* 'penance for a day' (Amos & Healy 1985: 30). This example is worth some discussion, as the general point is important.

First, N+N compounds of the form *dæg*-X are very common: *dæg-fæsten* 'a day's fast', *dæg-mǣl* 'day-marker, sundial', *dæg-sang* 'daily service', *dæg-feorm* 'a day's provision', *dæg-mete* 'daily food', *dæg-steorra* 'daystar', *dæg-tīma* 'daytime', *dæg-weard* 'day watchman'. Thus the pattern *dæg*-X = 'A day's X' or 'daily X' or 'X with respect to the/a day' is well-established. Further, in this case, *bōt* 'penance, compensation, atonement' is also common, and it too has compounds (*bōt-lēas* 'unpardonable') and derivatives (*bētan* 'atone, compensate, amend'). Therefore the option of inventing *dæg-bōt* on a single occasion would be open, and the context and WF rules of the language would make it intelligible.

In addition, given the fragmentary lexicon that has survived, there is no way of telling whether such a **hapax legomenon** (unique occurrence of a word) represents a fact about OE or a fact about the contingencies of survival. It is generally a fair assumption that a compound that occurs many times in different texts (like *dæg-mǣl*, with ten occurrences: Amos & Healey 1985: 30) is likely to be 'a word in the language'. The inverse assumption however is not safe.[25]

Other processes are more questionable: it is not clear whether for instance IU (in its morphologized form) is a productive process or just a relic of a time when it was productive because it was obligatory, and phonologically conditioned. For instance we could describe one way of forming causative verbs like this: given a strong verb with the sense S, produce a weak verb with the sense 'cause (X) to S' by using the PRET_1 stem as a base, and substituting the vowel that stands in the proper umlaut relation: so cl V *sittan* 'sit', PRET_1 *sæt* (stem /sæt-/) gives *settan* 'set'. But this

---

[25] By a compound that is 'in the language' I mean something like *bread-knife, fish-tank*: these are simply the ordinary names for these objects. As opposed to say *olive-knife, platypus-tank*, which I've just invented, but which can be processed on the model of the lexicalized ones.

is clearly not productive in a case like *rǣran* 'raise', even though it is historically a causative off the PRET₁ stem of *rīsan* 'rise', i.e. /rɑ:s-/. While the /ɑ:/ ~ /æ:/ relation is quite regular (*hāl* 'whole': *hǣlan* 'heal'), /s/ ~ /r/ is very sporadic; if we were to take this verb as a formation of OE date we would have to build rhotacism into the grammar as well! The question of productivity in a dead language can be answered only ambiguously;[26] but certainly ancient processes like ablaut and the umlauts, whose phonological environments have vanished, are not to be taken as 'active' in the same sense that perhaps breaking was. Our interest here is mainly historical; but the theoretical issue is an important one.

8.3.2   Compounding[27]

A compound is a lexeme made (in general) of two or more independent lexemes.[28] In the commonest and oldest IE nominal type, what the German tradition calls *echte Komposition* 'genuine compounding', the first element is a stem rather than a word-form proper. So Gr [[*hipp-ó-*] *damos*] 'horse-tamer' (IE *o*-stem *hipp-o-s*), Go [[*fōt-u-*] *baúrd*] 'stool' (*u*-stem *fōt-u-s*). During the evolution of Germanic (cf. the discussion of the thematic noun classes in chapter 6), the stem proper became more and more opaque, and few genuine stem compounds survive. Even in Gothic there are some whose first elements look like bare roots: beside the old type *gud-a-faúrhts* 'god-fearing' there is *arm-boug* 'arm-ring' (*guþ*, *arm* are both *a*-stems, so **arm-a-boug* might be expected).

In the newer *unechte* ('non-genuine') compounding, already apparent in Gothic and quite general in later dialects like OE, the first element may be simply the uninflected or zero-inflected form of a word, as in the *dæg*-X type discussed in the last section; or it may be an inflected noun-form, usually a genitive, as in [[*sunn-an*]-*dæg*] 'sun's day = Sunday', [[*dæg-es*]-*ēage*] 'day's eye = daisy'. Such compounds are 'non-genuine' because they can arise from syntactic phrases. Indeed, the line between genitival compounds and simple attributive phrases is fuzzy; the clearest evidence for lexicalization as a compound is non-compositionality of meaning, as in the two cases above: there is no real sense in which Sunday 'belongs to the sun' (indeed, in the culture in which OE was spoken it would be the Lord's day if anyone's), and a daisy is not the day's eye.

---

[26] It is not that easy with living languages either; for the problems, see the excellent discussion in Bauer (1988: ch 5).

[27] On compounding in general, see the overview in Marchand (1969); for Germanic see Carr (1939). OE compounds are covered nearly exhaustively in Kastovsky (1992).

[28] For older Germanic, we can limit compounds to two elements: the three-member type like OE *dæg-mǣl-scēawere* 'sundial-watcher', i.e. 'soothsayer, astrologer' is late, and seems to be an innovation.

Another type of structure also occurs, where a semantically and morphologically empty 'bridging element' or 'interfix' separates the two members, as in *stān-e-gella* 'kestrel' (lit. 'stone-yeller'),[29] where the *-e-* cannot be the genitive ending of the masculine *a*-stem *stān*. A similar phenomenon· occurs in German; in compounds like *Liebe-s-gedicht* 'love-poem', *liebe-s-krank* 'love-sick' the *-s-* cannot be a case-marker, since *Liebe* is feminine, and genitival *-s* in German as in OE belongs only to masculines and neuters.[30] Both these types are innovations; the earliest Germanic compound with an inflected first element appears to be the unique Gothic [[*baúrg-s*]-*waddjus*] 'city-wall', where *-s* is the nom sg affix.

The main topic here is the historical connections, the extent to which OE and Old Germanic in general reflect earlier (IE and PGmc) compound types, rather than the detailed semantic/syntactic structure of OE compounds in general.

A. Noun and adjective compounds

These are by far the commonest in IE generally as well as in Germanic. Three basic types seem to be ancient inheritances; these are often referred to in the literature by the names given them by the Sanskrit grammarians (indeed, a fine reflection of their IE antiquity), though other names are used. The main types are:

(i) **Dvandva** (Skr 'pair') or **Copulative**. The basic form is $[_N N_1 + N_2]$ or $[_{Adj} Adj_1 + Adj_2]$, and the general sense is '(object consisting of) $[X_1$ with/and $X_2]$'. The classic IE nominal type can be seen in Skr *putra-pautrāh* 'sons-(&)-grandsons'. The most widespread dvandvas in Germanic are the numerals 13–19: transparent in Go *fidwōr-taíhun* '4-(&)-10' = 14, somewhat opaque in OE *fēower-tēne* (see §8.4.3 below on the numerals). Adjectival dvandvas like Gr *leukó-melas* 'white-(&)-black', OIr *lethan-glas* 'broad-(&)-grey' do not seem to occur in Old Germanic, though there are modern ones like G *taub-stumm* 'deaf-(&)-dumb', E *bitter-sweet*. The ModE colour compounds like *blue-green*, etc. are probably not dvandvas but determinatives (type (ii) below), i.e. *blue-green* is not 'blue-(&)-green', but 'a kind of green, modified by blue'.

Aside from the numerals, the commonest Old Germanic dvandvas are kinship-collectives, like OE dat pl *āþum-sweoran* 'son-in-law(&)-father-in-law', *suhter-fædran* 'uncle-(&)-nephew'. Expanded forms of these types

---

[29] The usual definition of *stān(e)gella* is 'pelican'; this is an error based on a mistranslation of L *pellicanus* in some early glosses (the pelican was, after all, not a bird northern Europeans would be familiar with). The compound in fact survives in obscured form as ModE *staniel* 'kestrel'. See the interesting discussion in Bierbaumer (1985: 70f), which gives a useful insight into the way modern lexicographical errors can reflect ancient ones.

[30] Cf. the empty linking *-o-* in English forms like *aer-o-space, gastr-o-scope, soci-o-political, music-o-dramatic*.

occur in other WGmc languages: OS *gi-sun-fader* 'son-(&)-father' with the collective prefix *gi-*, OHG *suno-fatar-ungo* 'son-(&)—father' with a familial or tribal suffix *-ung-*, i.e. 'the son-and-father's people.

The question whether a particular compound is or is not a dvandva may be very subtle, even unanswerable. OE *were-wulf* 'werewolf' (*wer* 'man') could be interpreted as 'object that is both man-and-wolf'; or with *were-* as a modifier ('wolf, that is really a man': so Krahe & Meid 1967: §30). I prefer the former interpretation, and would take this to be as much a dvandva in the classic sense as ModE *panty-hose* (not hose which are also panties, but a double-purpose garment), or *Cadbury-Schweppes*.

The semantic uniqueness of dvandvas lies in the fact that neither element 'modifies' the other, or stands in any kind of 'case' relation to the other, nor is one element the head of the compound. In *āþum-sweoran* 'son-in-law' and 'father-in-law' are coequal constituting members of the 'object' named by this word; very different from the kind of relation in *fisc-nett*, where *nett* is clearly the head (a *fisc-nett* is a kind of *nett*), and *fisc-* has a 'determining' or modifying function ('a net, such that it is used for fish'). This latter type is far commoner, and we now turn to it.

(ii) **Tatpuruṣa** (Skr 'his servant') or **Determinative**. These are perhaps the commonest of all compound types. They have a head or **determinatum**, and another element that defines or modifies the head, a **determinant**. Virtually all Germanic compounds have the order determinant + determinatum, as in one view (Kastovsky 1992: 356) do all Germanic word-formations. So in *fisc-nett*, the determinatum or head is *nett*, and *fisc* tells us what kind of *nett* it is: similarly in a derivative like *ber-end* 'carrier', *-end* = 'one who does X', and *ber-* tells us what X is.[31] The most important structural types are:

(a) $[_N N_1 + N_2]$. IE type Skr *gṛhá-pati* 'house-master', L *aquae-ductus* 'aqueduct'. The relations between the two nouns are of many kinds: e.g. Go *auga-daúrō*, OHG *auga-toro*, OE *ēag-duru* 'eye-door, window' = 'door (for the use of an) eye'; NWGmc *sali-gastiz*, OE *sele-giest* 'hall-guest' = 'guest (who is in the) hall', OHG *brūti-gomo*, OIc *brúð-gumi*, OE *brýd-guma* 'bride-groom' = 'man (of the) bride', etc.

An interesting and important subtype is the 'tautological' or 'pleonastic' compound (especially common in poetry), where both elements are (close

---

[31] The modern type *kill-joy*, *pick-pocket* appears to be an exception. The determinatum here is surely connected with the action named by the first element (*kill-joy* = *joy-killer*). On the other hand these (which are an innovation) can be taken as exocentric or headless, and hence do not have internal determinata; in this they are rather like dvandvas, perhaps, or the type discussed in (iii) below. Some OE compounds appear to reverse the order too, e.g. *gāt-bucca* 'billy-goat', where *-bucca* is the determinant of *gāt* 'goat'. Kastovsky (1992: 366) likens these to derivatives with gender-marking suffixes, like *gyd-en* 'goddess'; but the fact remains that they are compounds with the wrong order.

to) synonymous. The type is ancient, as witnessed by Go *naudi-þaúrfts*, OHG *nōt-durft*, OE *nīed-þearf* 'compulsion, distress' = 'need-need' or 'compulsion-compulsion', 'hardship-need'; or OE *mōd-sefa* 'mind, spirit' = 'mind-mind' or 'spirit-spirit'.

One particularly common type has a deverbal noun for N_2: L *iū-dex* 'judge' = 'justice-sayer' (*-dex* < */-dik-s/, root as in *dic-ere* 'say'), or Greek *boó-kleps* 'cattle-thief' (*-kleps* < */klept-s/, root as in *klépt-ein* 'steal'). In Germanic these are always formed with one of two nasal suffixes: */-ɑn-/ or */-j-ɑn-/:

*/-ɑn-/: OHG *heri-zoho* 'army-leader', OE *folc-toga* 'folk-leader' (verb: *ziohan*, *tēon* 'lead, draw' = L *dūc-ere*); OHG *erpi-nomo*, OE *yrfe-numa* 'heir' = 'inheritance-taker' (verb: *niman* 'take'). Note that in these compounds N_2 always seems to be zero-grade (cf. OE past participles *tog-en*, *num-en*). The evidence for the original nasal suffix is the fact that these nouns are weak *n*-stems (cf. §6.1.3).

*/-j-ɑn-/. The second elements here are also formed from the zero-grade root, but show *i*-umlaut. A typical example is OIc *val-kyrja*, OE *wæl-cyr(i)ge* 'Valkyrie', lit. 'corpse-chooser' (OE *cēosan* 'choose', pp *coren* < */kuz-ɑn-/, hence *cyrge* < */kur-j-ɑn-/.

(b) [$_N$ Adj + N]. Type Gr *akró-polis* 'Acropolis, topmost city', L *angi-portus* 'narrow lane'. A widespread example is Go *midjun-gards*, OIc *mið-garðr*, OE *middan-geard* 'middle-earth'.

(c) [$_{Adj}$ N + Adj]. Type Gr *theo-eíkelos* 'godlike', OIr *cath-búadach* 'victorious in war'. These seem to be commonest with a past participle (weak or strong) as second element, the determinant often having an instrumental sense: Go *handu-waúrhts*, OE *hand-worht* 'hand-made', OHG *wīn-trunchan*, OE *wīn-druncen* 'wine-drunk', OIc *gull-hroðinn*, OE *gold-hroden* 'gold-adorned'.

(d) [$_{Adj}$ Adj$_1$ + Adj$_2$]. Type L *semi-uīuos* 'half-alive', OIr *dub-glas* 'dark-blue'. Adj$_1$ commonly has something to do with quantification, degree, or measure: OIc *al-hvitr*, OS *ala-hwīt*, OE *eall-hwīt* 'completely white', OHG *wīt-māri*, OE *wīd-mǣre* 'wide(ly)-famous', OHG *sāmi-quec*, OE *sam-cucu* 'half-alive'.

(iii) **Bahuvrīhi** (Skr 'having much rice') or **Exocentric**. An exocentric compound has no genuine internal head, even if the first element is in a sense the determinant of the second. The 'true' head is outside the compound, or the compound itself is interpretable only as predicated of some 'third party'. So in L *magn-animus* 'great-soul(ed)' or Gr *rhodo-dáktulos* 'rosy-finger(ed)' it is not the soul that is great or the fingers that are rosy *per se*, but someone/something that has a great soul or rosy fingers.

The basic types are (a) [$_{Adj}$ Adj$_1$ + N], and (b) [$_{Adj}$ Adj$_1$ + Adj$_2$], where Adj$_2$ is derived from a noun. Germanic examples for (a): OIc *ber-fœttr*, OE *bær-fōt* 'barefoot', OHG *glata-muati*, OE *glæd-mōd* 'glad-mind' = 'cheerful'. Examples of (b), so-called 'extended' bahuvrīhis with adjectival suffixes on the second element, are OS *gram-hugd-ig*, OE *gram-hyd-ig* 'hostile-mind-y' = 'hostile', OE *ān-ēage-de* 'one-eyed' (beside unextended *ān-eage*). (On the suffixes involved see §8.3.3 below.)

There is also a class of 'reversed' bahuvrīhis, i.e. [$_{Adj}$ N + Adj], but with the same interpretation as the opposite order; indeed, the two types may coexist with the same elements, as in OE *mōd-glæd* = *glæd-mōd*, OS *mōd-stark* 'fierce-minded' = *stark-mōd*.

B. Verb compounds

True verb compounds of the structural type [$_V$ N + V] (ModE *carbon-date*, *sky-dive*) or [$_V$ Adj + V] (*fine-tune*, *double-book*)[32] are doubtful for IE, and uncertain for PGmc.[33] There are however scattered early examples like Go *faíhu-geigan* 'money-lust' = 'lust after money', and OE has a few, like *morgen-wacian* 'morning-wake' = 'arise early', *ellen-campian* 'zeal-fight' = 'fight vigorously', *geþanc-metian* 'thought-ponder' = 'deliberate'. The more complex type like *cyne-helmian* 'to crown' can probably be taken as secondary derivations from compound nouns (*cyne-helm* 'crown').

There are many complex verbs with prefixed elements, which the German handbooks call *Präfix-Komposita* 'prefix compounds', suggesting a status somewhat ambiguous between true compounds and some other kind of derivational formation. One could separate those 'prefixes' that can appear as independent elements (e.g. *ofer* 'over', alone and in *ofer-stīgan* 'surmount') from those that are always bound to a stem (like collectivizing/perfective *ge-*); but these may be distinctions without a difference. Furthermore, many of these elements are not specific to verbs, but occur in nouns and adjectives as well; I will treat them all under the common heading of derivational prefixing (§8.3.3).

8.3.3   Derivation

In general, the older an IE language, the more transparent and complex its derivational morphology; and indeed, the more derived forms there appear to be, and the more central derivation appears to be to overall lexical structure. As Germanic evolved, this older derivational apparatus became increasingly opaque, and affixes often fused with stems leaving

---

[32] In ModE these are usually back-formations from compound nouns (*carbon-date*) or participial adjectives (*double-booked*).

[33] Unless the weak preterite (cf. §7.3.1) is itself a compound of the form [$_V$ N + V], where N is a verbal noun.

apparent simplex words. OE *leng-þu* 'length', *þīef-þu* 'theft' are clearly derivational formations, related via IU and an identifiable suffix to *lang*, *þēof*. But the same can't (quite) be said of *bearm* 'bosom' and *bær-* (PRET₁ stem of *beran*); and not at all of *hā-m* 'home' and *hīwan* 'family, household'. Semantic, morphological and phonological change have conspired to make these structures opaque (a bosom is only metaphorically a 'bearer', and though a home is where the family is, neither the OE vocalism nor any OE derivational pattern would relate these). The /m/ in these words is just 'the final consonant', not a formative.

In a wider IE perspective however many /-m/ reflect an important old derivational formative */-m-/; many apparently 'simplex' words descend from derivations with common IE formatives, buried word-formations from an earlier time. Yesterday's derivations are (or may be) tomorrow's unanalysable words.

Something of the complexity of these relations can be seen in some more OE words with final /-m/:

(i) *strēa-m* 'stream': Root */sreu-/. OHG *strou-m*, OIc *strau-m-r*, OIr *sru-ai-m*; Li *sra-véti* 'flow slowly', *sru-tà* 'liquid manure', OCS *stru-ja* 'current, flow', Gr *rhé-ein* 'flow', *rhoû-s* 'flood', Skr *srá-vati* 'it flows', *sru-tá-* 'flowing'.[34]

(ii) *sēa-m* 'seam': Root */seu-/. OE *si(o)w(i)an* 'sew', L *su-ere*, *sū-tu-s* 'sewn', *sū-tū-ra* 'suture, junction', Skr *sū-tra* 'string, set of aphorisms'.

(iii) *wear-m* 'warm'. Root */gʷhVr-/. L *for-m-us*, Gr *ther-m-é* 'heat', *thér-o-mai* 'become warm', OCS *gor-ĕti* 'it burns'.

(iv) *fæþ-m* 'fathom': Root */pɑt-/. OHG *fad-u-m*, OIc *faδ-m-r*, L *pat-ulus* 'open, spread out', Gr *pet-án-umi* 'stretch out', OW *etem* < */pet-e-mɑ/* 'fathom'. (The original sense of this root seems to be 'arms'-width' or 'embrace'.)

We could add many others to this small sample: *bearhtm* 'brightness', *ǽδm* 'breath', *botm* 'bottom', probably *besem* 'broom', *bosm* 'bosom'.

This is all in aid of a typological point that can now best be made with some numbers. Krahe & Meid (1967) list no fewer than 139 noun- and adjective-forming suffixes of IE/PGmc date, which can be uncovered in Old Germanic word-forms. Kastovsky (1992) recognizes for OE only 42

---

[34] IE */sr-/ > Gmc */str-/, Greek /hr/ (<ῥ>, transliterated <rh>). The same root and formative occur in later loans like *rhythm* < Gr *rhu-th-m-ós*; the root without the /-m-/ in *rheo(-stat)*, *(dia-)rrhoea*. With another root the formative occurs in *chris-m* < Gr *kri-s-m-a* < *kri-ein* 'anoint', ultimately by a tortuous history in *crea-m*.

(reasonably) productive ones. Nearly two-thirds of the inherited derivational suffixes have been lost or become opaque (similar figures emerge from the list of affixes in Quirk & Wrenn 1955: 109ff).

Not of course that OE was poor in WF strategies or derivatives: as the earlier discussion of 'bear' suggests, quite the reverse. But – as with inflections – it did its work with far less material than the older languages used, and in simpler structural configurations (cf. the attrition of nominal endings apparent in §6.1 and the figures for verb-forms in §7.1). Most importantly, this loss of material once again suggests a major evolutionary direction: from a root-and-stem framework towards a morphology where 'stem' and 'word' begin to coalesce, and derivational affixes are simply added to an invariant base, with no special stem-forming connectives, and little or no stem allomorphy.

Much derivational morphology is also buried in the inflectional system, as has been suggested before: major noun and weak verb classes contain historical WF material (cf. the discussion of the weak-verb classes in §7.3.2). Even the simplest looking nouns may be derivational in origin: e.g. a monosyllabic *a*-stem like *swan* 'swan' is probably a deverbal agent noun from the root */swVn-/ 'sing', e.g. */swɑn-ɑ-z/.[35] Hence the thematic */-ɑ-/ is actually (historically) a WF device here, not 'simply' a theme. Similar examples are common among the *n*-stems, e.g. agentives like *hunt-a* 'hunter', etc. which are *n*-derivations from verb roots. And in denominal verbs like *luf-ian* 'to love' (cf. *lufu* 'love') the old post-root material (*/-jo:-/), while defining a verb-class from the inflectional point of view, is actually (historically) derivational.

In the rest of this section we will look at a small selection of older WF affixes that are recognizable and important in OE, according to positional type: suffixes first, as these are the major device, then prefixes.

A. Suffixes, 1: noun and adjective

Many OE derivational suffixes seem to fall into (historical) families, with a basic consonantal element, which may have a preceding thematic vowel and/or a following vowel, and may appear in various ablaut grades. Some of the major ones are:

(i) The */-t-/ family. This includes noun-forming *-aþ*, *-þ(u)*, and adjective-forming *-t*, and continues an IE suffix complex with a */-t-/ base, occurring in both thematic and athematic forms. The simplex element can be seen in Skr *deva-śru-t-* 'audible to the gods' (= 'god-hear-suffix-'); an expanded */-to-/ occurs in L supines like *cap-tu-s* 'captured' = OE *hæf-t*

---

[35] This reflects a widespread IE tendency to name animals from typical attributes or activities. OE *fearh* 'pig' and *furh* 'furrow' are related this way: *o*-grade and zero-grade respectively of */pVrk-/ 'dig, furrow' (cf. L *porc-us* 'pig', *porc-a* 'field-drain').

'captive' (and cf. the discussion of the weak past participle in §7.3.1). An o-grade occurs as -ap ~ -op in fisc-ap 'fishing', hunt-op 'hunting', etc.; and a thematic PGmc */-iθ(u)/ is visible in pairs like fūl 'foul'/fȳl-þ 'filth', earm 'poor'/ierm-þu 'poverty'. Since IE */t/ did not undergo Grimm's Law and become /θ/ in clusters with */s/, it survives unshifted after /s/ in derivatives from adjectives in -lēas '-less': līf-lēas 'inanimate, dead'/līf-lēas-t 'death', slǣp-lēas-t 'sleeplessness'.

(ii) The */-l-/ family. This includes a number of noun and adjective suffixes, e.g. -el(e), -l(a), -ol, -els, with umlauting (< */-il-/) as well as non-umlauting types. Thematic */-ila-, -αlα, -ulα-/ yield a number of derivational patterns; one important group is deverbal adjectives in -ol, e.g. swic-ol 'deceitful' (swician 'deceive'), flug-ol 'swift' (PRET₂ stem of flēogan 'fly': cf. OIc svik-all, flog-all); the IE type can be seen in Gr nos-ē-l-ós 'ill' (< nós-o-s 'disease'). Other /-l-/ formations include agent nouns: bit-ela 'beetle' (zero-grade stem of bītan 'bite', i.e. 'the biter'): type in Skr pā-lá- 'guardian' (< pā- 'guard'); and deverbal instrument nouns: spin-el 'spindle' (spinnan 'spin'), scof-l 'shovel' (scūfan 'shove, push'). With an /-s/ extension, -els forms deverbal masculines: rǣd-els 'counsel' (rǣdan 'counsel, advise'), hȳd-els 'hiding-place' (hȳdan 'hide').

(iii) The */-r-/ family. This is structurally similar to the /-l-/ group. The major source is IE */-ro-/ (m), */-rα:-/ (f), Gmc */-rα-, -ro:-/. The commonest use is in deverbal adjectives: Skr cit-rá- 'visible' (cit- 'perceive'). The latter root + suffix also occur in OE hād-or, OHG heit-ar 'bright, clear'. Derivational connections are clear in bitt-er 'bitter' (zero-grade stem of bītan), slāp-or 'sleepy' (slǣpan), wac-or 'awake' (wac-ian 'awaken'); these often have /-l-/ variants, e.g. slāp-ol, wac-ol.

(iv) Nasal suffixes. Many n-stems are deverbal agent nouns formed with a suffix */-αn-, -o:n-/, as in Gr arēg-ōn 'helper' (aróg-ein 'help'). We have already looked at weak-verb derivatives like hunt-a 'hunter' (hunt-ian); there are also strong-verb ones like lid-a 'traveller' (PRET₂ stem of līþan 'travel', with Verner's Law), flot-a 'ship', i.e. floater (PRET₂ of flēotan 'float'). An extended suffix */-j-αn-/ gives masculine agent nouns with umlaut, as in myrðr-a 'murderer' (mordor 'murder'); feminine */-j-o:n-/ gives abstract deverbal nouns like ǣsce 'wish' (āscian 'ask').

The suffix */-i:n-/ (usually with following */-j-o:-/) gives feminine abstracts like ield-u 'old age' (eald 'old') < */αlð-i:n-j-o:/, streng-u 'strength' (strang 'strong'; beside streng-þ-u < */-iθo/). The nasal remains in some derivatives like byr-þ-enn 'burden', and (from a related suffix) feminines like fyx-en 'vixen' (m fox), gyd-en 'goddess' (god), etc. Unextended */-i:n-/ is commonest in Gothic, e.g. hauh-ei 'height', gen sg hauh-ein-s (hauh-s 'high').

(v) -ing/-ung. These originate in an IE /n/-formative + */-ko-/ (see (vi) below). Thus -ing < */-en-ko-/, -ung < */-n̥-ko-/. There is also evidence for an *o*-grade */-on-ko-/, as in L *hom-un-cu-lus* 'little man, homunculus'. The original sense is not certain, but the general model is X-*ing* = '(something) associated with, deriving from X'. The oldest Germanic uses seem to be in names, especially tribal: *Marouíngi* 'Merovingians' appears in second-century Greek sources. In the textual tradition both -*ing* and -*ung* occur as a kind of patronymic: OE *Scyld-ing-as*/-*ung-as* 'Scyldings, children of Scyld', L *Lotharingi*, OHG *Lutar-inga*, OE *Hloðer-ingan* 'Lotharingians, people of Lothar'.

OE seems to have two semantically differentiated suffixes from this one source, one always -*ing* (m), the other -*ing*/-*ung* (f). The first appears mainly in deadjectival formations like *ierm-ing* 'pauper' (*earm* 'poor'), *æþel-ing* 'nobleman' (*æþel* 'noble'), and in denominals like *hōr-ing* 'adulterer, fornicator' (*hōre* 'whore'). The second appears as a formative in deverbal nouns, e.g. *wun-ung* 'dwelling' (*wunian*), *gaderung* 'gathering' (*gæderian*). The -*ung* form, curiously, seems restricted almost exclusively to class II weak verbs as bases, as in the examples above.

(vi) -*ag*/-*eg* and their relatives: -*ig*, -*iht*/-*eht*. These are built on the IE */-ko-/ element as in -*ing* above. The commonest non-Gmc IE type is that in L *senex* 'old' (- /sene-k-s/: cf. Skr *sána-* 'old'), or the thematic version in *ant-i-cu-s* 'old' (*ante-* 'before'). The main Germanic type is that in Go *maht-eig-s*, OE *miht-ig* 'mighty' (*maht-s*, *meaht* 'might'), or OE *stān-eg* 'stony' OS *mōd-ag* 'brave' (OE has *mōd-ig*). A formation with IE */-to-/ gives the suffix in OE *stān-eht*/-*iht* 'stony', *þorn-eht*/*þyrn-iht* 'thorny'. As in other cases, the chaining of elements creates complex suffixes that by Germanic times have become unanalysable: again the principle of increasing opacity, where older WF material gets buried in chunks with no clear synchronic segmentation.

(vii) -*ness*. This is one of the most productive OE suffixes. It seems to arise from a complex of nasal formative + a basic shape */-Vssu-/, of uncertain antecedents (cf. Krahe & Meid 1967: §125). The nasal + suffix chain is clear in Go *gud-ji-nassus* 'priesthood', from the *n*-stem agent noun *gud-ja* 'priest' (*guþ* 'god'). The -*n*- appears originally to have been part of an *n*-stem nominal formation, later reanalysed as part of the suffix.

In WGmc numerous vowel-grades appear, as well as post-suffixed forms with */-ja-, -jo:/: the suffix leaves a trace in OS -*nassi*, -*nessi*, but is lost in OE. The original *jō*-stem formation however is dominant in WGmc generally, as suggested by the fact that such nouns are always feminine. In OE many different base types occur: -*ness* derivations may be deverbal (*forgif-ness* 'forgiveness' < *for-gifan* with present stem as base, *ge-coren-ness* 'chosenness' with the whole past participle of *cēosan* as base), or deadjectival (*biter-ness* 'bitterness', *clæn-ness* 'purity').

B. Suffixes, 2: verb

The main verb-forming suffixes have already been treated in §7.3.2; the formatives */-j-ɑn-/, */-o:(j-ɑ)n-/ for weak classes I, II respectively. The semantic and derivational types were discussed there. Because of the formal limitations on what constitutes a verb (since an infinitive is a necessary headword), there are few other suffixes; but there are a number that were used as extensions of the base. The commonest are:

(i) -s-ian. Many class II weak verbs have an /-s-/ formative: e.g. clæn-s-ian 'cleanse' (clǣne 'clean'), rīc-s-ian 'rule' (rīce 'kingdom'), milt-s-ian 'take pity on' (mild 'mild'). The source of the /-s-/ is not entirely clear, but it may well reflect the IE */-s-/ formative that appears in the s-aorist (L dic-ō 'I say', dīxī 'I said' = /di:k-s-i:/). Alternants with /-s-/ in a non-aspectual function do however appear in the ancient dialects (Skr bhā-s-ati 'it shines' ~ bhā-ti), and even within the same paradigm in the same aspect category (Gr aléks-ō 'I protect', infinitive all-alk-ein).[36]

(ii) -ett-an. This descends from the suffix seen in Greek verbs in -ázō, -ízō (líthos 'stone', lith-ázō 'I stone') plus the infinitive marker. The OE form derives from a Germanic type */-ɑt-jɑ-/. The meaning appears to be mainly 'frequentative or intensifying' (Kastovsky 1992: 391); though not always. There are some denominals (bōt-ettan 'remedy', cf. the noun bōt), but deverbals are commoner: blīc-ettan 'glitter' (blīcan 'shine'), hlēap-ettan 'leap up' (hlēapan 'leap').

(iii) -n-. An /-n-/ formative, reflecting an extended suffix */-in-o:n/, appears in a number of class II weak verbs, especially denominal and deadjectival: fæst-n-ian 'fasten' (fæst), for-set-n-ian 'beset' (for-settan 'hedge in, obstruct'), lāc-n-ian 'heal, cure' (lǣce 'physician'). The type is widespread in Germanic: cf. Go lēki-n-ōn, OHG lāhhi-n-ōn, OS lāk-n-ōn.

C. Prefixes

Since the same prefixes can occur on both nouns and verbs (cf. §4.2.3), I treat both categories together. Most of the productive prefixes are adjectival or adverbial elements of IE date, though in Germanic they are not always semantically transparent, or clearly related to their originals. A selection of the most important prefixal elements follows: where two OE forms are given, the first is the strong (stressed) allomorph, the second the weak.

(i) æf-, of- 'from, away': IE */ɑp-/, PGmc */ɑf-/. L ab, Gr apó. Go af-gaggan 'go away' (cf. L ab-īre), OE æf-þunca 'source of offense', of-þyncan 'displease' (cf. þyncan 'seem, appear').

---

[36] These verbs are treated exhaustively in Hallander (1966).

(ii) *on-* 'on, to, there, thither': IE, PGmc */ana-/. Gr *aná-*, Go *ana-*, Go *ana-qiman* 'approach' (cf. Gr *ana-baínein* 'ascend'); OHG *ana-sehan*, OE *on-sēon* 'behold, look upon'.

(iii) *and-*, *on-* 'against, away': IE */ant-í/, PGmc */anð-(α)-/. Gr *antí* 'against', Go *and(a)-*, OHG *ant-/int-*. Go *and-sakan*, OE *on-sacan* 'dispute, strive against', OE *and-saca* 'apostate'; Go *and-sitan*, OHG *int-sizzen*, OE *on-sittan* 'seat oneself, occupy'.

(iv) *for-*. This OE shape conflates two older prefixes: IE */par-/ 'before, for', as in Go *faúra-gagga*, OE *fore-geng(e)a* 'one who precedes'; and IE */pro-/ (Gr *pró-*) 'away, forth', often with a perfective or completive sense: Go *fra-liusan* 'lose', *fra-lusts* 'loss, perdition', OE *for-lēosan* 'abandon, destroy' (cf. *lēosan* 'lose').

(v) *ge-* (Go *ga-*, OHG, OS *gi-*). This is etymologically equivalent to L *con-* 'with', and has a wide range of related senses; it may also apparently be meaningless, or merely a morphological category marker. The oldest sense, that of 'association', can be seen in Go *ga-qiman* 'come together' = L *con-uenīre*, Go *ga-baíran* 'compare' = L *con-ferre* (simplex *baíran*, *ferre* 'carry'). Verbal *ge-* in OE is not always meaningful. In many cases it is simply coopted as a marker of the past participle (as now in German, Yiddish, Dutch and Afrikaans). Or a non-participial verb may appear in either form, with no apparent semantic difference: *(ge-)ādlian* 'be(come) ill', *(ge-)campian* 'fight'. When there is a clear sense, it is usually perfective or resultative: *ge-ærnan* 'gain by running' (*ærnan* 'run, ride, gallop'), *ge-āscian* 'gain by asking' (*āscian* 'ask'). In other cases the sense may be quite idiosyncratic, as in *ge-standan* 'endure' (*standan* 'stand').

On nouns, the sense seems to be collectivity or associativity: *ge-geng* 'body of fellow travellers', *ge-beorc* 'barking' (cf. *beorcan* 'bark'), *ge-fara*, *ge-fēra* 'fellow-traveller, companion', *ge-brōþor* 'brethren'. This use is also old: Go *ga-skōhi* 'pair of shoes', *ga-dragan* 'heap together', *ga-guþ-s* 'pious' (cf. *guþ* 'god', i.e. 'with god'), and remains in German (*Berg* 'mountain, *Ge-birge* 'mountain-chain').

(vi) *ofer-* 'over': IE */upár-/, PGmc */uβar-/ 'over, up'. Skr *upári*, Gr *hupér*, Go *ufar-*, OHG *ubar-*. Go *ufar-steigan*, OHG *ubar stīgan*, OE *ofer-stīgan* 'climb over, surmount' (cf. Gr *huper-steíkhein* 'go away over').

(vii) *ymb-* 'around': IE */ambhí-/, PGmc /umβi-/. Skr *abhí*, Gr *amphí*, L *amb-*. OHG *umbi-hwerban*, OE *ymb-hweorfan* 'turn around, revolve'; OHG *umbi-gangan*, OE *ymb-gān* 'go around' (cf. L. *amb-īre*).

(viii) *un-* 'negation': IE */-n̥-/, PGmc */un-/. This is the zero-grade of an old negative particle (cf. L *ne*, *n-ōn*). As a negative prefix, it shows up in different IE forms: Gr *á-gnotos*, L *i-gnōtus* 'unknown' = Go *un-kund*, OE *un-cūþ*, OIc *ó-kuðr* < */n̥-gn̥t-o-s/. The original sense of simple negation is perhaps the commonest (as above, and OE *un-æþele* 'un-noble, of low birth', *un-brād* 'un-broad, narrow'. In Germanic it also developed a perjorative sense, not a direct negation but *un*-X = 'bad, excessive (kind of) X': *un-dǣd* 'un-deed = bad deed'; this sort of meaning is still current in some WGmc languages, e.g. Afr *kruid* 'herb, plant', *on-kruid* 'un-plant = weed'. On verbs, the sense becomes reversative ('undoing of the result of a pre-action', Kastovsky 1992: 381): *un-bindan* 'unbind', *un-lūcan* 'unlock'.

8.4   Names, adverbs and numerals

8.4.1   Proper names

It may seem odd to treat personal names under the heading of a grammatical category like word-formation. Speakers of Germanic languages generally do not think of their names as having 'structure' (or meaning). There are of course obvious compounds (*Mary-Ann*), and some clear derivations with diminutive or feminizing suffixes (*Mari-etta* vs. *Mary*, *Marie*; *Joseph-ine* vs. *Joseph*), as well as names that seem to be simple non-onomastic lexical items (rare in English, but German *Wolf* 'wolf') or compounds (G *Wolfgang* 'wolf-path', *Gottlob* 'god-praise': but not perceived as such by speakers). The common run of names like *Alfred* or *Edith* however seem to be just unmotivated, arbitrary simple words, with no 'meanings'.

If however we look back at the OE forms of the last two, we see something quite different: *Ælf-rǣd*, *Ēad-gȳþ*. They are both compounds: the first consists of the elements of 'elf' and 'counsel'; the second of 'joy, blessing' and a derivative of *gēotan* 'pour'. *Alfred* is presumably a bahuvrīhi (§7.3.2) '(the one) counselled by the elves';[37] *Edith* is a determinative 'the pourer of blessings'.

Virtually all Old Germanic names are in fact either simplex lexemes or (more commonly) transparent word-formations of one kind or another; as an example, the personal names in the NWGmc runic corpus exhibit the following types:

(i) Bahuvrīhi compounds: *Glaaugiz* [[gla]-aug-i-z] 'bright-eye(d)'.
(ii) Determinative compounds: *Bidawarijaz* [[bid-a-]war-j-a-z] 'covenant-protector', *Widuhu(n)daz* [[wid-u-] hund-a-z] 'wood-dog' (= wolf?), *Ansugisalaz* [[ans-u-] gisal-a-z] 'gods'-hostage', *Skiþaleu-*

---

[37] 'Elves' here in the serious old (or Tolkien) sense of wise supernatural beings, not Santa's helpers.

baz [[skiþ-a-] leub-a-z] 'justice-lover', *Hadulaikaz* [[had-u-] laik-a-z] 'battle-dancer'.
(iii) Derivatives: *Har-j-a* 'warrior', *Har-i-so* 'female warrior', *Tan-ul-u* 'little enchantress', *Un-gand-i-z* 'un-beatable', *Hak-u-þ-u-z* 'crooked one', *Wig-i-z* 'warrior'.
(iv) Simplex nouns: *Haraban-a-z* 'raven'.

In other words, all the main Germanic word-formation types are represented in the NWGmc name-stock. Moreover, the structures are 'normal' and generally transparent, even to the extent of the first elements of determinative compounds showing the appropriate theme-vowels for their declension classes. At this stage names are 'words' like any others, more or less.

By attested OE times, the structural situation is much the same (except for a good number of borrowed names, mainly Celtic); but semantically things are rather different. While the name-elements or **themes** are still largely visible, and the different types of compounds are still identifiable, many names appear to be arbitrary collocations of themes. Bahuvrīhis like *Huaet-mod* 'brave-spirit' or determinatives like *Ælf-uini* 'Elf-friend'[38] reflect the principles seen in NWGmc names; but what are we to make of *Ælf-uulf* 'Elf-wolf', or even worse *Frið-hild* 'Peace-battle'? In fact as OE progressed, the principle of constructing **dithematic** names like these remained productive, but the themes themselves could become simply (nearly) meaningless elements, as in *Wulf-stān* 'Wolf-stone'; that is, names were in the early stages of becoming what we might call 'onomasticized', losing their lexical sense.[39]

Still, one could say that by and large OE names were still, if not necessarily 'meaningful', at least transparent; and that they still reflected standard Germanic WF strategies in the same way as ordinary lexical compounds or derivations. Here for instance is a sample of names from the ninth-century Northumbrian *Liber vitae* (Sweet 1885), a list of benefactors of the Durham church:

(i) Dvandvas (male): *Ead-bercht* 'blessed-bright', *Huaet-berht* 'brave-bright'.
(ii) Bahuvrīhis (male): *Ecg-bercht* '(sword)-edge-bright', *Ecg-heard* 'edge-hard', *Huaet-mod* 'brave-spirit(ed)', *uulf-hard* 'wolf-brave'.

---

[38] The non-classical spellings reflect the fact that these names come from very early sources (ninth century).
[39] On OE names see Clark (1992), Colman (1984, 1991b); the latter are classic studies in the importance of names as evidence, and the methodology and significance for historical linguistics of onomastics.

(iii) Determinatives: (a) male: *Aelf-uini* 'elf-friend', *Cyni-degn* 'royal-servant', *Berht-uulf* 'bright-wolf', *Isern-uulf* 'iron-wolf', *Gar-uulf* 'spear-wolf'; (b) female: *Cyni-ðryð* 'royal-power/majesty/glory', *Hildi-ðryth* 'battle-power', *Hroeð-gifu* 'glory-gift', *Frið-hild* 'peace-battle', *Uulf-hild* 'wolf-battle'.

(iv) Non-compound nouns and adjectives. (a) male: *Beorn* 'man, warrior', *Bercht* 'bright', *Snella* 'smart, strong one', *Huita* 'white one'; (b) female: *Cuoemlicu* 'comely', *Badu* 'battle', *Nunnae* 'nun'.

In a society in which female warriors (and warrior goddesses) were not unknown, the semantics of a compound name do not necessarily carry any gender implications (*Uulfhild* is no more 'feminine' than *Berhtuulf*, and *Aelfuini* could suggest desirable qualities for either sex). What does count however (at least in names with a nominal head) is simply the grammatical gender of the head noun: regardless of semantics *wolf* and *wine* (to give their later forms) are masculines, and *hild*, *giefu* are feminines.

8.4.2 Adverbs

This and the next category are somewhat 'mixed' in both origin and status, but can be treated more appropriately here than anywhere else. Adverbs are mainly inflectional in origin, but derivational by OE times; numerals (the topic of the next section) are partly inflected, but largely the product of WF processes (at least for ordinals and higher cardinals).

The IE adverb was not a distinct category; it seems rather that various kinds of morphological material could be used for signalling adverbial function. One widespread marker is the *o*-stem ablative sg */-o:-d/ < */-o-ed/ or its later *e*-grade */-e:-d/. The *o*-grade appears in Latin adverbs of the type *subit-ō* (see §6.3.2), perhaps in Greek adverbs in *-os*; in Germanic it is transparent in the type Go *ga-leik-ō* 'similarly', OS *gi-līc-o*, OHG *gi-līhh-o*. This is common in Gothic, and is the normal formation in OS and OHG.

In OE, this */-o:/ appears as /-α/, and only in a restricted class of adverbs from adjectives in */-inγ-, -unγ-/, e.g. *wēn-ing-a* 'perhaps', *dearn-ung-a* 'secretly'. The most widespread OE formation is in {-e}, probably from the *e*-grade of the ablative, corresponding to L {-ē} < */-e:-d/: L *facillim-ē* 'easily', whose ablative origin is clear in OL *facilum-ēd*. So OE *wīd* 'wide', adv *wīd-e*, *gelīc* 'similar', adv *ge-līc-e*, etc.

Since {-e} was typically added to adverbialize the extremely common adjectives in *-līc*, the complex {-līc-e} was reinterpreted during OE times as an adverbial ending in itself, and there were thus a number of doublets off the same base: from *heard* 'hard' the adverbs *heard-e*, *heard-līc-e*, from *hwæt* 'brave' *hwæt-e*, *hwæt-līc-e*. (Our ModE adverbial {-ly} is of course the descendant of {-līc-e}.)

Some OE adverbs appear to be distinguished from their corresponding adjectives by lack of umlaut: so *swōt-e* 'sweetly' (adj *swēte* 'sweet', Gmc base */swo:t-/), *clān-e* 'cleanly' (*clǣne*, base */klɑin-/). These may be original *u*-stems, which in their adjectival forms have gone over to *ja*-stem or another umlauting declension, while the adverb retained a *u*-stem base.

There are also some adverbs in {-a} of various origins: a significant type is illustrated by *fel-a* 'much' where {-a} is an oblique *u*-stem case form, as suggested by the nom/acc neuter form *feol-u* in Anglian dialects. This latter use reflects a common IE practice: the nom/acc neuter of an adjective could by itself have an adverbial function.

Other adverbs derive from special uses of particular adjective or noun case forms (cf. the ablative origins of {-a, -e} discussed above). So neuter gen sg in *eall-es* 'entirely', *dæg-es* 'by day', *niht-es* 'by night', *will-es* 'willingly'; this survives (synchronically reinterpreted as a plural) in expressions like 'he works *days/nights*', etc. There are also dative sg adverbs like *fācn-e* 'deceitfully' (*fācen* 'deceit'), *eall-e* 'entirely', and dative plurals like *gif-um* 'gratis' (*gi(e)fu* 'gift'), *hwīl-um* 'at times'. These seem to reflect metaphorizations or extensions of the basic semantics of the cases: there is a construction type sometimes called the 'genitive of respect' (cf. §9.4.2), where NP-gen = 'as for, with respect to NP'; and the dative often has an instrumental sense, which could be construed adverbially.

Comparison of adverbs is usually in {-or}, {-ost}, occasionally spelled <-ur, -ar, -ust-, -ast>; the comparative reflects a PGmc */-o:-z/ (Go *-ōs*). By normal WGmc sound changes (as in the *a*-stem nom sg */-ɑ-z/), the /r/ should have disappeared in OE; it is most likely retained by analogy to adjectival comparison.

The superlative has the same vowel, but with the presumably adjectival superlative suffix */-st-/; in many cases there is an */-m-/ formative as well, giving a double superlative: *inne-m-est* 'inmost', *ūte-m-est* 'outmost' (cf. *inne* 'inside', *ūte* 'outside'). The simplex type can be seen in *for-m-a* 'first' (cf. *for-e* 'in front', and the discussion of ordinal numerals in §8.4.3), *hinde-m-a* 'last' (*hinder* 'behind'). This */-m-/ occurs in Gothic as well (*fru-m-ist-s* 'first'), though not elsewhere in West Germanic; it is an old IE marker, and can be seen in the Latin parallel to *for-m-a*, *fru-m-ist-s*, i.e. *pri-m-u-s* 'first'.

8.4.3   Numerals

The IE numerals are a kind of hybrid category: virtually all the dialects reflect an original system where the cardinals 1–4 and 100 carry case/ gender inflections (so are noun- or adjective-like), and the rest are indeclinable, or have very limited inflection. The numerals are one of the most cross-dialectally coherent IE subsystems; with few exceptions, nearly all the languages show the same structures and materials, at least up to 60. I will first treat the cardinals 1–4, then 5–10, then the teens, decades, hundreds, thousands and ordinals.[40]

A. Cardinals 1–4

1. OE *ān*, Go *ain-s*, OIc *einn*. These and the reflex types in L *ūnus* < OLat *oinos*, Skr *eka-*, Gr *oi(w)os* 'single' suggest an IE base */oi-/, with extensions */-n-, -k-, -w-/. 'One' is usually a thematic adjective, i.e. *oinos* = {oin-o-s}, etc. The /-n-/ extension, the sole Gmc one, may reflect a deictic suffix */-no-/; PGmc must have had */αin-α-z/ < */oi-n-o-s/. When used adjectivally, the declension usually follows that of the strong adjective (§6.3.1).

2. This shows a reasonably full paradigm, with gender differentiation only in nom/acc:

(8.3)		Go	OE	OIc
nom	m	twai	twēgen	tveir
	n	twa	twā	tvau
	f	twōs	"	"
acc	m	twans	twēgen	tvá
	n	twa	twā	tvau
	f	twōs	"	tvær
gen		twaddje	twēg(e)a	tveggia
dat		twaim	twǣm	tveim(r)

IE */d(u)wo:/ (m), */d(u)woi/ (f, n): Skr *d(u)va, d(u)ve*, Gr *dúo*, L *duo*; all Gmc forms descend from the */dw-/ alternant, e.g. OE *twā* < */twαi/ < */dwoi/. The genitive in Go and OIc shows a change called the Germanic **Verschärfung** 'intensification' or **Holtzmann's Law**: PGmc */-jj-, -ww-/ under certain conditions became geminate obstruents in N, EGmc. So */-jj-/ > /-dd-/ in EGmc, > */-γγ-/ < /-gg-/ in NGmc, and */-ww-/ > */-γγ(w)-/ in E and NGmc. The Go, OIc genitives show */-jj-/ (< */twαjj-o:/); for */-ww-/, */triww-α-/ 'true' > Go *triggw-s*, OIc *trygg-r*.[41] The original continuants remain in WGmc, as in OE *twēg(e)a*, OHG *zweiio* < */twαjj-o:/, OHG *triuwi*, OE *trēow* 'true'. The *-gen-* in *twegen* appears to be by anaology to *bē-gen* 'both', and may reflect a deictic base */(j)en-/, as in

---

[40] For detailed treatment of the IE numeral system see Szemerényi (1989: ch. 8, §5) and his exhaustive bibliography; on Germanic, see Prokosch (1938: §§99–100).

[41] On Holtzmann's Law, see Lehmann (1965). Lehmann attributes the hardening of the old continuants to a contiguous laryngeal.

geon-d 'through', Go *jain-s* 'that' (so Prokosch 1938: §93); or an IE 'distributive' numeral base */-noi/ as in L *bī-nī* 'two-by-two, double', *ter-nī* 'three each'.

3. Like '2', this is marked for gender only in nom/acc; the attested forms are:

(8.4)		Go	OE	OIc
nom	m	þreis	þrī(e)	þrír
	n	þrija	þrēo	þriú
	f	–	"	þriár
acc	m	þrins	þrī	þriá
	n	þrija	þrēo	þriú
	f	þrins	"	þriár
gen		þrije	þrēora	þriggia
dat		þrim	þrim	þrim(r)

IE had three gender forms, */trejes/ (m), */t(r)isres/ (f), */tri:/ (n), as seen in Skr *trayas, tisras, tri*; most dialects however only show two bases, as in L *trēs, tria*. The original paradigm has been extensively remodelled. The IE genitive was apparently of the type */tri(j)o:m/ (hence OIc *þriggia*, with *Verschärfung*). ModE *three* must descend from the n/f *þrēo*.

4. OE *fēower*, Go *fidwōr*, OIc *fiórer*. IE */kʷetwores/ (m), */kʷetsres/ (f), */kʷetwo:r/ (n): Skr *catvaras*, Gr *téttores* (IE */kʷ/ regularly > /t/ before front vowels), L *quattuor*. The original paradigm is generally lost; when '4' is inflected, it follows a noun or adjective pattern. The initial Gmc /f/ may seem puzzling; this ought to presuppose IE */p/ by Grimm's Law (§2.3). But there is a common development where */kʷ/ > /p/ in the presence of another labial in the word (Krahe 1963: §60 Anm.); since this precedes Grimm's Law, and Grimm's Law precedes Verner's Law, Go *fidwōr* transparently reflects an original */kʷetwó:r/.[42] The other Gmc forms are less clear, except that OE probably continues the masculine, or at least the skeleton */kʷe__w__r/ and OIc probably a feminine. Prokosch (1938: §99) suggests an IE alternant */kʷekʷó:r/, with */-kw-/ > [-ɣw-] by Verner's Law, which > /-w-/.

B. Cardinals 5–10

5. OE *fíf*, Go *fimf*, OIc *fimm*. IE */penkʷe/: Skr *pañca*, Gr *pénte*, L *quinque* (*qu*- either by assimilation to the medial, or analogy to *quattuor*: see below under '7' and '9' for more analogical forms). OE shows Ingvaeonic

---

[42] On the other hand, there may be an analogy to 'five' with initial IE */p-/; cf. the discussion of '6–9' below.

nasal loss and compensatory lengthening as expected: OIc shows nasal-cluster assimilation (cf. *tǫnn-r* 'tooth' < */tɑnθ-/, OE *tōþ*).

6. OE *seohs*, *siex*, Go *saíhs*, OIc *sex*. IE */s(w)eks/*: Skr *sas-*, L *sex*, Gr *héks* (Delphic *wéks*), Welsh *chwech*. The */s-/* (cf. OPr *uschts* 'sixth') may reflect an old analogy to '7' (Szemerényi 1989: ch. 8, §5). The earlier OE vocalism /eo/ derives from breaking before /xs/ (*/sexs/ < */seks/), and the later *siex* from WS raising before /x/.

7. OE *seofon*, Go *sibun*, OIc *siau*. IE */septm̥/*: Skr *saptá*, Gr *heptá*, L *septem*. Go, OE show loss of /-t-/, probably early enough so we can reconstruct PGmc */sefún/ > */seβún/, which would give the attested forms. OIc *siau* is problematic, but may be an analogical formation after '8', NGmc */ɑːttɑu/ < */ɑxtɑu/ (see below).

8. OE *eahta*, Go *ahtau*, OIc *átta*. IE */okto:(u)/*: Skr *astāu*, Gr *oktṓ*, L *octō*. PGmc */ɑxtɑu/ is expected, and the reflexes are normal.

9. OE *nigon*, Go *niun*, OIc *nió*. IE */newn̥/*: Skr *náva*, G *(en)néa*, L *nouem*. L *nouem* has its /-m/ after *decem* '10', another pairwise analogy in the numeral system. The medial /-ɣ-/ <g> in OE is difficult; the best guess is that there were two PGmc forms, */niwun/ and */niɣun/, the latter restricted to Ingvaeonic (cf. OS *nigun*, Dutch *negen*). Such doublets are not uncommon, and in this case both places of articulation are velar.

10. OE *tīen* (WS), *tēn(e)* (Angl), Go *taíhun*, OIc *tió*. IE */dekm̥(t)/*: Skr *dáśa*, Gr *déka*, L *decem*. Assuming PGmc */texun/, OE shows breaking, raising, and deletion of medial /x/; OIc has an analogical form after '9'. The final /-ɑn/ in some dialects (OS *tehan*, OHG *zehan*) suggests an IE alternant */dekom/. ModE *ten* is from shortening of Anglian *tēn(e)*.

C. Cardinals 11–12

OE *en(d)leofan*, *twelf*, Go *ainlif*, *twalif*, OIc *ellefo*, *tolf*. This formation is unique to Germanic and Baltic: cf. Lith *vienúo-lika*, *dvy-lika*. It seems to be a quasi-compound of the numerals '1', '2' with a suffix from IE */likʷ-/, the zero-grade of */leikʷ-/ 'leave' as in Gr *leíp-ō*, L *li-n-qu-ō* (with nasal infix, cf. pp. *lic-tus*). The original sense is apparently something like '(ten-and) one/two left over', but this must be opaque except in Gothic and perhaps OHG (*einlif*, *zwelif*) where at least the first numeral is transparent.

D. The teens

(8.5)

	Go	OE	OIc
13	–	þrītēne	þrettán
14	fidwōrtaíhun	fēowertēne	fiog(or)tán
15	fimftaíhun	fiftēne	fimtán
16	–	siextēne	sextán
17	–	seofontēne	siaut(i)án
18	–	eahtatēne	áttián
19	–	nigontēne	nítián

These are (dvandva) compounds defined by the arithmetic operation of addition: the interpretation is '(the sum) {N + 10}'. Gothic is the most transparent, and we could safely reconstruct the missing *saíhstaíhun, etc. The pattern is common IE, cf. Skr cátur-dasa-, L quattuor-decim '{4 + 10} = 14', etc. The OE -tēne appears to be an inflected form of */texun-/ '10'.

E. The decades 20–60

(8.6)

	Go	OE	OIc
20	twai tigjus	twentig	tuttugu
30	þrije tigiwe (gen)	þrītig	þrír tiger
40	fidwor tigjus	fēowertig	fiórer tiger
50	fimf tigjus	fiftig	fimtigi
60	saíhs tigjus	sixtig	sextigi

Gothic shows the original structure most clearly: a cardinal numeral + the plural of 'decade', probably a derivative of */dekm̥t/, with the Germanic form */texúnð-/. In Go and OIc (probably because of the /-u-/), this was declined as a u-stem, and Go developed a new analogical nominative, tigjus. OIc tuttugu is probably an accusative dual, with various internal changes due to the presence of an original /w/ and nasal (cf. Go acc twans tigjus, and the effect of a preceding /w/ in '12', OE twelf but OIc tolf). The original structure is that of a simple numerical adjective phrase, 'n decades'; but in OE the plural noun has been reduced to a suffix, which is probably as opaque as ModE -ty.

F. *The decades 70–120; 1000*

(8.7)

	Go	OE	OIc
70	sibuntēhund	hund seofontig	siau tiger
80	ahtautēhund	hund eahtig	átta tiger
90	niuntēhund	hund nigontig	nió tiger
100	taíhuntēhund	hund teontig,	tió tiger
		hund hundred	
110	–	hund endleofantig	ellefo tiger
120	–	hund twelftig,	
		hundtwentig	hundraþ
1000	þūsundi	þūsend	þúsund '1200'

Wright & Wright (1925: §234) remark that 'many attempts have been made to explain the decades 70–120, but no satisfactory explanation of their morphology has ever yet been given'. Sixty-five years later one could still say pretty much the same. While it is not even certain how the Gothic forms are to be segmented (*sibun-tēhund* or *sibuntē-hund* or *sibunt-ē-hund?*), the origin of *hund* anyhow is clear: it must be the IE word for '100', */kṃt-óm/ (Skr *satám*, L *centum*, Gr *he-katón*). This may be from */d(e)kṃt-/ '10 decades', and would give Gmc */xunð-/.

The real problem is the sense of *hund* in the OE numerals, and the related Old Saxon equivalents like *ant-sibunta*, *ant-ahtoda*, where *ant-* = reduced *hund*.[43] One interpretation might be something like '(special) hundred made of (groups of) sevens', etc., i.e. the higher decades are taken to be something more like lower hundreds (in our sense). In OE this principle for 70–90 was apparently in conflict with the old '*n tigjus*' one, which led to double formations, with both *hund* and reduced *-tig*; and it is notable that the complex forms were already varying with simple *seofontig*, etc. in early WS.

The original *-tig* formation operated in OE through 120, which ought to have led (sensibly!) to ModE *tenty, *eleventy, *twelfty; but during the OE period neuter *hund* alone, or the obscured compound *hund-red* (where *-red* = the root of Go *raþjo* 'number', cf. L *ratiō*) came to be used for the tenth decade. The later hundreds were generally (multiplicatively) prefixed by cardinals, e.g. *fēower hund* '400', etc. Thus the teens had additive structures: *fēower-tēne* = {4 + 10}; but the decades and hundreds, etc. were multiplicative: *fēowertig* = {4 × 10}.

The word for '1000' appears to be from */tu:-s-kṃti:/ 'power hundred', with a prefix */tu:-/ 'be strong, swell' (cf. L *tū-me-ō* 'swell'); the expected

---

[43] This still persists in a further reduced form in Netherlandic '80': Dutch *tachtig*, Afrikaans *tagtig*, where the /t-/ is all that's left of *ant-*.

forms would be Go *pūs-hundi, etc., but early obscuration of the compound led to the loss of /x-/ in */xunð-/.

The Scandinavian use of hundraþ for '120', þúsund for '1200', etc. requires some comment. Though PIE used a decimal system (as do all its descendants overall, except for traces of a 20-based one in a few languages like French and Danish), there is some evidence for an early duodecimal system, perhaps due to contact with Babylonia. Older Germanic legal texts preserve a distinction between a common 'hundred' = 100 and a so-called 'great hundred' = 120 (12 × 10 rather than 10 × 10). In NGmc especially this carries on well into the counting series, e.g. OIc tvau hundraþ '240', þriú hundraþ '360', þúsund '1200'.

G. The ordinals 1st–3rd

These, unlike the rest of the ordinals (see (H) below) are suppletive or semi-suppletive, and involve a variety of different IE formations.

1st. Go fruma, OE forma. This is from a base */pr-/ meaning 'before', plus the superlative suffix */-mo-/ (§8.4.2 above), i.e. it has precisely the sense 'foremost'. Similar forms occur in other IE dialects, e.g. Gr prá-mo-s, Li pìr-ma-s. There is an alternative type with the superlative */-ista-/, e.g. OE fyrst < */fur-ist-/, which of course comes down as ModE first, OIc fyrst-r.

2nd. Go anþar, OE ōþer, OIc annarr. This is apparently from a root with a sense like 'different, distinct', which appears in Skr ántaraḥ 'distinct from', Li añtras 'the other'. In later times this was replaced in some dialects by a more regular form, as in G zweite (cf. zwei '2'), Du twede (twee). In English it was replaced as well, but by a borrowing: second < OF second(e) < L secundus 'following' (the same root */sek^w-/ as in sequ-or 'follow'). The original form has tended to split semantically, and now keeps its old sense in mod E other, G ander.

3rd. Go þridja, OE þridda, OIc þriþe. This is not entirely suppletive, as it still obviously contains the root for '3'. But the formation is different from that of the other ordinals, involving a suffix */-tjo:-/ (cf. L ter-ti-us). The E, WGmc forms must go back to a variant with an accented suffix, hence the voiced dental from Verner's Law. ModE third is metathesized from þridda (cf. bird < OE bridd, dirt < OSc drit).

H. The rest of the ordinals

(8.8)

	Go	OE	OIc
4th	–	fēorþa	fiorþe
5th	fimfta	fifta	fimte
6th	saíhsta	siexta	sétte
7th	–	seofoþa	siaunde
8th	ahtuda	eahtoþa	átte
9th	niunda	nigoþa	níonde
10th	taíhunda	tēoþa	tíonde
11th	–	enlefta	ellepte
12th	–	twelfta	tolfte

The basic formation is that of an adjective in */-to-/, as in L *quar-tu-s* '4th', Gr *tétar-to-s*, etc.; in the ancient dialects this held for 4–6 (L *quin-tu-s*, *sex-tu-s*), but beyond that the numerals were turned into thematic adjectives (L *septim-u-s*, etc.). In Germanic however the */-to-/ (> */-θα-/) formation was extended to 7–12 as well. These are declined as weak adjectives.

From 13 on, IE had a {units + tens} construction, as in L *tertius decimus* '13th', Gr *trítos kaì dékatos* (*kai* 'and'); this still occurs in Go and OHG, e.g. *fimfta taíhunda* '15th', *dritto zehanto* '13th'. The originals of these were probably suffix-accented, as Go, OIc /d/ suggest (Verner's Law); the /t/ in 5th, 6th is due to assimilatory devoicing, and the /t/ in OE, OIc 11th, 12th to dissimilation in fricative clusters.

From 20 on, NGmc and OE have the */-to-/ formation, and OHG an adjectival */-o:st-/: OE *twentigoþa*, OHG *zweinzigosto*. These numerals have not survived in Gothic or OS, so we can only guess what they might have looked like.

9   Topics in OE historical syntax: word-order and case

9.1   Reconstructed syntax?

Morphology, as we have seen, poses problems for historical reconstruction that make straightforward storytelling difficult. There are no 'regular morph-changes' quite like 'regular sound-changes' (except of course insofar as changes of morph-shape reflect regular changes in constituent phonemes). In addition, analogy and semantics are constantly interfering with what might otherwise be reasonably 'regular' developments. Syntax poses these problems as well, in addition to special ones of its own.

The 'vocabulary' (set of elements) is much more complex than those for phonology or morphology, and the idea of 'ancestry' is conceptually difficult. Since syntax is the 'creative' part of grammar, we do not normally think of a given sentence in a language as the 'descendant of' an equivalent sentence in an earlier stage, itself the descendant of some yet older sentence. It makes sense to say that OE *cyning* is the descendant of WGmc */kuninɣ/, which descends in turn from PGmc */kuninɣ-α-z/. But it appears not to make the same kind of sense to say that the OE sentence *se cyning þās word gehīerde* 'the king heard those words' is the descendant of the Proto-Gmc sentence */se kuninɣαz θαis worðu ɣαxαuziðα/.

It shouldn't be hard to see why, in a general way. Given sentences' high specificity of meaning, their embedding in discourses, texts, etc. – as well as the fact that the 'set of sentences' in a language is at least indefinitely large – we would not expect this kind of descent. Anymore than we'd expect discourses or texts to be ancestral to others (barring special cases like successive translations or utterances of a ritual or scripture, or prefabricated chunks like proverbs or idioms). Sentences can be (and probably are) largely 'fashioned anew' for specific utterance-occasions; this is not however true of the materials they're made of, like morphemes or phonemes. So while we can say that *cyning* 'descends from' */kuninɣαz/, and that each phoneme in it is a descendant of a particular phoneme in Ingvaeonic, West Germanic, NWGmc, Proto-Gmc . . . , we can't apparently make the same kind of claims about syntax.

Or can we? While a particular sentence does not have an 'ancestry', this is not the case for a particular construction. Take for example a word-order pattern. Here the possibilities for history open out a bit. Surely *þās word gehīerde* could be a 'descendant' of an older object-Verb construction, which we might try to project back to an earlier stage, even PGmc. To take another example, if we find a particularly widespread use of an 'unexpected' government relation (e.g. certain classes of verbs or prepositions taking objects in cases we would not expect), we might make this too a candidate for historical exploration and perhaps reconstruction.

In this chapter we will explore, in a preliminary way, two aspects of Old English syntax that can be interpreted as continuations or developments of older Germanic (and Indo-European) patterns. This will be a brief outline of what for want of a better term we might call an 'etymological syntax': because of limitations of space I will restrict myself to two main issues: word-order, and the syntax of the cases.[1]

The point is that it appears to be possible, under certain conditions, to attribute a construction type to a protolanguage, or to see it as a descendant of another, more or less in the way we do phonological or morphological reconstruction. For example, if all the daughters of a protolanguage agree in some 'arbitrary' feature (one that is not necessary or even highly likely), there's no objection to reconstructing this for the immediate parent. And if the same structure or a very similar one shows up in more distant sister languages, this gives us an even wider time-scale. The reverse however does not hold – at least not in detail. For instance, the Old Germanic dialects show such a variety of relative clause formations that we cannot recover a single ancestral construction. But this does not mean that NWGmc or PGmc or IE had no relative clauses: indeed it is virtually impossible for this to have been the case. All it means is that the change has been so deep and idiosyncratic that we have no material for recovering an earlier stage.[2]

9.2   Basic constituent order

Virtually all languages have numerous word-order possibilities; but most have a **basic** or **dominant** order of major constituents. It is customary to

---

[1] There are many other topics just as interesting and important, and perhaps just as accessible to historical investigation: e.g. tense and aspect, subordination, concord. But the complications here are enormous, and in some cases beyond my competence. For convenience and (relative) brevity I will confine myself to just these two. At least they will help to clear up some obscurities, and give an idea of how such issues might be handled.

[2] The literature on syntactic reconstruction is enormous, consisting both of articles on how to do it, and ones saying it can't be done. A good beginning would be some of the papers in Fisiak (1984), especially those by Hamp, Harris, Pilch, Gerritsen, Rudes, and Winter.

think of languages as falling into broad order types with respect to the major clause constituents Subject, (direct) Object, Verb; and into subtypes with respect to other clause-internal orders, e.g. whether modifiers in general precede or follow their heads, or what kind of adpositions the language has: prepositions (as in English **with** *John*) or postpositions (as in Finnish *Juha-n* **kanssa** 'John-gen with').[3]

A basic order in this sense is not exclusive. ModE is clearly an SVO language overall, in terms of neutral or unmarked order in simple declarative main clauses (the usual criterion): *John loves Mary*, but not **John Mary loves* (SOV), **Loves John Mary* (VSO), etc. But other orders do exist: e.g. OSV (*this book I hate*). Similarly, ModE is a Modifier + Noun language (*these cats, red shoes, three mice*); but there are postmodifying constructions as well (*Soldiers Three, Prometheus Bound*).

It seems likely that PIE was basically SOV,[4] though the daughter languages show a wide variety of orders, including SVO and VSO (the later particularly in Celtic). PGmc is usually taken as continuing this order, though there is of course considerable debate.[5] As I remarked earlier, we can't reconstruct syntax by strict comparative method the way we do phonology or morphology; but in the case of Old English we do have at least fragments of an ancestor: the NWGmc runic corpus (third to seventh centuries AD). This corpus is small and often obscure; there are not that many inscriptions, and some are damaged, partly illegible, or uninterpretable. But it is a precious resource: it brings us as close as we can get to the foundations of Germanic, and contains the earliest pieces of Germanic syntax we have. (The oldest inscriptions predate the Gothic text corpus by some three centuries.) It is, despite its small size, rich enough to suggest reasonable ancestors for some major OE construction types, and gives us some material for constructing a syntactic history of the murky period between the two traditions.

Here are some examples of the major construction types (S, O, V marked):[6]

[3] See Greenberg's classic paper (1966a), and the discussions in Comrie (1981), Hawkins (1983), Croft (1990).
[4] This is contentious, and not accepted by all scholars. For the basic arguments see Lehmann (1974).
[5] On PGmc syntax see Lehmann (1972), Hopper (1975), and the discussion in Gerritsen (1984).
[6] Texts from Antonsen (1975). I have capitalized proper names, but have left vowel length unmarked, as is conventional.

(9.1)   (i) ek erilaz Ansugislas em Uha haite (Kragehul spearshaft, c.
                 300)
                 S   V S V
                 I messenger Ansugislaz-gen/sg am Uha am-called
                 'I am the messenger of Ansugislaz, I am called Uha'
           (ii) ek erilaz Sawilagaz hateka (Lindholm amulet, c. 300)
                 S   V
                 I messenger Sawilagaz am-called
          (iii) ek Hlewagastiz Holtijaz horna tawido (Gallehus horn 2, c.
                 400)
                 S   O   V
                 I Hlewagastiz Holtijaz horn make-pret/1/sg
                 'I H.H. made (this) horn'
          (iv)   [me]z Woduride staina þrijoz dohtriz dalidun (Tune stone,
                 c. 400)
                           O   S   V
                 me-dat Woduridaz-dat/sg stone-acc/sg three daughters
                 make-pret/3/pl
                 'For me, Woduridaz, three daughters made (this) stone'
           (v)   runo fahi ragina-kudo tojeka (Noleby stone, c. 400)
                 O   V
                 rune suitable divine do-1/sg
                 'I make (the) suitable, divine rune'
          (vi)   runoz waritu (Järsberg stone, c. 450)
                 O   V
                 rune-acc/pl write-1/sg
                 'I write (these) runes'
         (vii)   makija maridai Ala (Vimose chape, c. 250–300)
                 O   V   S
                 sword decorate-pret/1/sg Ala
                 'Ala decorated (the) sword'
        (viii)   ek Wiwaz after Woduride witada-hlaiban worahto (Tune
                 stone, c. 400)
                 S   V
                 I Wiwaz after Woduridaz-dat/sg guard-loaf make-pret/1/sg
                 'I Wiwaz for Woduridaz (the) loaf-ward wrought (this)'
          (ix)   ek Hagustaldaz hlaaiwido mago minino (Kjølevik stone, c.
                 450)
                 S   V   O
                 I Hagustaldaz bury-pret/1/sg son-acc/sg my-acc/sg
                 'I Hagustaldaz buried my son'

(x) ek wiz Wiwio writum runo (Eikeland clasp, c. 450)
    S   V   O
    I we Wiwio write-pret/pl rune
    'I-and-my-fellows (descendants of) Wiwio wrote (this) rune'

(xi) Hariuha haitika fara-uisa gibu auja (Sjælland bracteate 2, 450–500)
    S   V   V   O
    Hariuha I-am-called travel-wise give-1/sg luck
    'Hariuha I am called, (the) travel-wise, I give luck'

(xii) aiwuida t Uha (Darum bracteate 3, 450–500)
    V   O S
    make-right-pret/1/sg it Uha
    'Uha made it right'

(xiii) tawo laþodu (Trollhättan bracteate, c. 450–500)
    V   O
    prepare-1/sg invitation
    'I prepare the invitation'

(xiv) wate hali hino horn hala skaþi haþu ligi (Strøm whetstone, c. 450)
    V   O   S   S   V   S   V
    wet stone this horn scythe scathe mown-down lie
    'Wet this stone, horn! Scythe, scathe! (That which is) mown down, lie!'

About 70 per cent of the transitive clauses in this corpus are OV (mainly SOV, with one OVS: vii); less than 20 per cent are SVO, and the rest V-initial (imperatives as expected for IE generally, otherwise topicalized verbs: see the analysis of the whole corpus in Antonsen 1975: §7.9). As far as adpositions go, only prepositions appear (and this is true for the early NGmc inscriptions as well).

Evidence for other parameters is somewhat thin, but it seems clear that NWGmc is basically postmodifying: N + Modifier constructions of all types (adjectives, determiners) outnumber Modifier + N by about 4:1. The main exceptions appear to be quantifiers; at least the one quantified NP in the data (in *prijoz dohtriz*, (9.1, iv)) is preposed. There is also a systematic distinction in genitive modifiers depending on the animacy of the head noun: genitives precede inanimate heads (*Hnabdas hlaiwa* 'Hnabdaz-gen grave', Bø stone, c. 500), and follow animate heads (*erilaz Ansugislas* 'messenger Ansugislaz-gen' (9.1, i)). It is also worth noting that the one early EGmc inscription with a modified noun has a prenominal genitive with an inanimate head (*gutanio wih-hailag* 'Gothic-women's consecrated, sacred (object)', Pietroassa ring, c. 300–400). This may then represent a very old pattern.

So it looks as if the earliest attested ancestor of OE (and a language not all that far removed from PGmc itself) is basically SOV, if with SVO and V-initial orders as alternants. It is prepositional and largely postmodifying, though premodification occurs as well.[7] How does this square with the properties of attested OE, and what might we deduce about syntactic evolution in the interim?[8]

The very earliest OE texts (c. 700–800) present a syntax not far removed from NWGmc, though with a somewhat different distribution of certain order types. A number of 'signatures' of the familiar type show OV order, e.g. a gold ring from Lancashire (c. 800?: Page 1987: 42) in mixed runes and roman letters says *Æðred me ah Eanred mec agrof* 'Æðred me owns, Eanred me carved', and there are a number of others of this sort. On the other hand, VO transitive clauses appear too, as in the eighth–ninth century Thornhill grave inscription (Page 1987: 39):

(9.2)   jilsuiþ arærde æft[er] berhtsuiþe bekun on bergi
      S   V   O
      Jilsuiþ raised after Berhtsuiþ-dat beacon on mound-dat
      'J. raised (the) beacon on (the) mound in memory of B.'

Verb-initial imperatives are common too, as in the second line of the above inscription, *gebiddaþ þær saule* 'pray for her soul', or the Lancaster slab inscription (c. 700), *gibidæþ foræ Cynibalþ* 'pray for C.'. Verb-initial also occurs in topicalizations, as in:

(9.3)   (i)   foeddæ hiæ wylif in romæcæstri (Franks casket, eighth c.)
            V   O   S
            raised them she-wolf in Rome
            '(a) she-wolf raised them in Rome'
     (ii) bismæradu uŋker men (Ruthwell Cross, eighth c.)
            V   O   S
            mocked-pl us-two men
            'men mocked both of us'
     (iii) alegdun hiæ hinæ limwoerigne (Ruthwell Cross)
            V   S   O
            lay-pl they him limb-weary-acc-sg
            'they laid him, limb-weary'

---

[7] Postmodifying prepositional SOV languages are rare; SOV tends to imply premodification, and most such languages are postpositional.

[8] Considering the small corpus and specialized register (most of the inscriptions are funerary, ritual, or 'signatures'), one might doubt its representativeness. Indeed, it probably does not present spoken NWGmc, but an archaizing formal variety. If so, this is all to the good, as it shows us an older stage. At any rate it's all the pre-OE, non-Gothic syntax we have, and nothing in it is out of line with later developments.

The bulk of the OE material in fact presents a picture either consistent with or easily derivable from an ancestor that looked like NWGmc. Both OV and VO orders are common in transitive clauses (the latter increasing later on: see below). OE is largely premodifying (especially in later prose), but postmodification is not uncommon. It is basically prepositional, though postpositions do appear.[9]

Fortunately, from the mid-eighth century on there are surviving texts of greater length, which give us a more detailed idea of the syntactic resources available as input to later periods, and the kind of changes that must have preceded the emergence of OE as a recognizable dialect tradition. One of the earliest texts of any size displays these properties clearly: the Northumbrian version of Cædmon's Hymn (Moore MS, c. 734–7; Smith 1968):

1 Nu syclun hergan hefaenricaes uard
  Now must-we praise heaven-kingdom's guardian
2 medudæs maecti end his modgidanc
  god's might and his mind-thought
3 uerc uuldurfadur sue he uundra gihuaes
  work glory-father-s how he of-wonders each
4 eci dryctin or astelidae.
  eternal lord beginning ordained
5 He aerist scop aelda barnum
  He first made men-of children-for
6 heben til hrofe haleg scepen,
  heaven for/as roof holy creator
7 tha middungeard moncynnæs uard
  then middle-earth mankind's guardian
8 eci dryctin æfter tiadæ
  eternal lord after made
9 firum foldu frea allmectig.
  men-for earth lord all-mighty[10]

Constituent order here is interesting; of the four main clauses, two are VO and two OV (already a notable shift from the 20 per cent VO of NWGmc):[11]

---

[9] On the status of postpositions in OE, see the exhaustive discussion in Colman (1991a).

[10] A rough prose translation: 'Now we must praise heaven-kingdom's guardian, God's might and his mind-thought, the work of the glory-father, how he, eternal lord, ordained the beginning of all wonders. He first made for the children of men heaven as a roof, the holy creator; then mankind's guardian, eternal god, lord all-mighty afterward made earth for men'.

[11] One must of course be careful with these figures: the statistics of a single text are not

(9.4)   VO:
        Nu scylun hergan hefaenrices uard (1)
              V   O
        he aerist scop . . . heben til hrofe (5–6)
        S   V   O

        OV:
        sue he uundra gihuaes . . . or astelidae (3–4)
           S   O V
        tha middungeard . . . tiadæ (7–8)
              O   V

The last clause in fact shows both OV and VO orders, if we look at the second object of *tiadæ*:

(9.5)   tha middungeard . . . eci dryctin æfter tiadæ, firum foldu
              O   S   V   O

In fact, rightward movement of an object is one of the major sources of the later dominant VO order of English (see §9.3 below).

   Both original modifier orders occur, but premodification is dominant:

(9.6)   PREMODIFIED: hefaenricaes uard (1), metudaes maecti (2), his modgidanc (2), eci dryctin (4, 8), heleg scepen (6), moncynnæs uard (7)
        POSTMODIFIED: uerc uuldurfadur (3), uundra gihuaes (3), frea allmectig (9)

The ratio is nearly 2:1 in favour of premodification, as opposed to the NWGmc 4:1 in favour of postmodification. The older dominance pattern has clearly receded, but both options are still current (though the NWGmc segregation of genitives according to the animacy of the head no longer operates).

   The earliest prose texts show a similar picture, but also the beginnings of certain tendencies that were to develop fully later. Some of these patterns are illustrated in these examples from the ninth-century Martyrology fragment (Sweet 1885):

strictly comparable with those of a multi-text corpus (even a small one). But the tendencies illustrated here seem to be characteristic, and that's what counts for our purposes here. For OE word-order and its development in general, see Bean (1983), Traugott (1992: §4.6), Stockwell & Minkova (1991), Minkova & Stockwell (1992).

(9.7)   i. Adrian se casere hine ðrēatede ðæt hē Crīste wiðsoce
       S   O   V   S   O   V
      A. the emperor him pressed that he Christ deny
      'A. the emperor pressed him to deny Christ'
   ii. mīne englas ðec lædað in hiofonlican Hierusalem
       S   O   V
      my angels thee lead in heavenly Jerusalem
  iii. hē geðrowade eft in Rome martyrdom for Crīste
       S V   O
      he suffered again in Rome martyrdom for Christ
  iv. gemyne ðū mec on ðǣre ēcean reste
       V   S O
      remember thou me in eternal rest

In this early text, the figures for OV vs. VO transitive clauses (excluding imperatives, which are always V-initial) are 17 OV to 14 VO, a ratio of roughly 1.5:1, as opposed to the NWGmc 4:1. We can already see a drift away from dominant OV order.

As OE developed, a strong tendency arose to restrict OV to subordinate clauses; we have no data for NWGmc on this, but the development in general is not surprising in a language with a 'mixed' word-order. In Alfredian and post-Alfredian prose, perhaps the majority of main clauses without topicalization are VO (in particular verb-second, which we will look at in the next section), and subordinate clauses tend to be OV. Or to put it another way, the verb tends to come early in main clauses and late in subordinate clauses, and the overall pattern is reminiscent of the dominant order in modern German or Dutch. This is not however an original Germanic pattern, but the result of later developments.

9.3   The clausal brace and verb-second order

Modern English is an SVO language, which is not the same as being verb-second. In SVO English, a sequence XSVO (where X = any non-subject constituent, like an adverb) is allowed; in a language with a main clause verb-second (V-2) constraint, like German or Swedish, if anything other than the subject occupies the initial slot in a main clause, the verb moves to second position. (This is traditionally called 'subject-verb inversion'.)[12]

---

[12] For a detailed synchronic and diachronic study of the Germanic V-2 rule, see Weerman (1989).

(9.8)   *English*
I *go* to London tomorrow
S V   X
Tomorrow I *go* to London
X   S V

German
Ich *fahre* morgen nach London
S   V   X
Morgen *fahre* ich nach London
X   V   S
*Morgen ich *fahre* nach London
X   S   V

A tendency toward this V-2 order is already apparent in the earliest OE texts, as well as in OS, OHG from the ninth century, especially after temporal conjunctions, but also after topicalized objects (verbs in italics):

(9.9)   *Old English*
(i) ðā *cwōm* godes engel of hiofonum (*Martyrology*, ninth c.)
then *came* God's angel from heaven-dat pl
(ii) ðā *heht* se casere gesponnan (*Martyrology*)
then *commanded* the emperor to-be-harnessed

Old High German
(i) so *inprinnant* die perga (*Muspilli*, ninth c.)
then burn-3/pl the mountains
(ii) Thō *nam* er godes urlub (*Ludwigslied*, ninth c.)
then *received* he God's permission
(iii) Einan kuning *weiz* ih (*Ludwigslied*)
one king *know* I

Old Saxon
(i) Gabriel *bium* ic hētan (*Heliand*, tenth c.)
Gabriel *be*-1 sg I called
(ii) Thō *quam* frōd gumo ūt fon them alaha (*Heliand*)
Then *came* (the) wise man out of the temple

This tendency was never as strict in OE as it later became in the other Germanic languages (except of course English); but it is a major feature of OE and other Germanic word-orders, which does not at first sight have obvious antecedents in the NWGmc materials. But as we will see, there are historical and other clues that suggest a reconstructable history.

A second important phenomenon, appearing in all the old WGmc dialects, seems to be related: the so-called **clausal brace** (G *Satzklammer*). In this construction, if a main clause contains a finite auxiliary and a non-finite main verb (infinitive, participle), the auxiliary appears in second position (as with the V-2 rule above); the main verb however is not contiguous to it, but comes at the end of the clause. The auxiliary and the main verb thus form a 'brace' around the rest of the clause-constituents. Examples from modern German:[13]

(9.10)   Ich *habe* das Buch *gelesen*
        S Aux   O   MV
        I *have* the book *read*-pp = 'I (have) read the book'

        Ich *werde* das Buch *lesen*
        S   Aux O   MV
        I *will* the book *read*-inf = 'I will read the book'

This seems to be an exclusively WGmc development (at least it is vanishingly rare in early NGmc); examples appear as early as the eighth to ninth centuries in all the WGmc traditions:

(9.11)   *Old English* (Ruthwell Cross, eighth c.)
        he *walde* on galgu *gistiga*
        S Aux   MV
        he *wished* on (the) gallows *to-ascend*

        Old High German (*Muspilli*, ninth c.)
        denne *scal* manno gilîh fona deru moltu *arstên*
            Aux S   MV
        then *shall* men's bodies from the earth *arise*

The OHG example shows the cooperation between the V-2 constraint and the brace; a non-topicalized version would presumably have been *manno gilîh scal denne . . . arstên*.

There is much speculation and debate about how these two phenomena, V-2 and the brace, arose (see e.g. Stockwell 1977, 1984 and Vennemann 1984). But it is barely possible that they are unrelated. One likely connection is that they both reflect a phenomenon known as **Wackernagel's Law** (Wackernagel 1892): the tendency (certainly early IE, perhaps cross-linguistic) for clitics to gravitate to second position in a main clause. ('Clitics' would include genuine enclitic particles, and other unaccented,

---

[13] For discussion, examples, and an attempt at historical reconstruction, see Vennemann (1984).

'light' elements like pronominal objects and later certain classes of verbs: see below.)

Most of the original IE clitics are gone by Germanic times, but there are some suggestive remnants in Gothic. For example *uh* 'and/intensifier', *u* 'question'. These tend to appear as clitics to the first autonomous element in the clause: *uz-uh-iddja* 'out-and-go-pret/3/sg' = 'and he went out', *ni-u-andhafjis* 'neg-Q-answer-2/sg' = 'dost thou not answer?'

An extension of the principle would allow other elements to enter this position: in particular 'light' verbs, e.g. copulas or tense/aspect auxiliaries, which typically do not carry phrase or clause accent. This results – contrary to the old neutral verb-final order in main clauses – in a finite verb in position 2, with the (non-finite) lexical main verb remaining in its original final position.

If we now assume that (as is typical for OV languages), auxiliaries normally followed the main verb, we can see the brace developing this way (v = Aux, V = Main Verb):

(9.12)   S   O   V   v   >   S   v   O   V

A further extension of the principle would then allow non-auxiliary verbs to enter this position, giving rise to the V-2 order in main clauses:

(9.13)   (a)   S   O   V   v   >   S   v   O   V

          (b)   S   O   V   >   S   V   O

After this, a strong and widespread tendency for co-constituents of a phrase to remain together ('Behaghel's First Law') could have prompted a reapplication to structures of the type in (9.13a), bringing the auxiliary and main verb together in second position, as is now typical of English and largely of Yiddish.

By another development (cf. Vennemann 1974), the subject slot is reinterpreted as a 'topic' position, rather than exclusively a place for subjects, and other items are allowed to move into it (e.g. adverbs); at this point the structure is reinterpreted as Topic-V-X rather than S-V-X.

The Wackernagel's Law account of the brace seems fairly solid; but there is an alternative view of the origin of V-2 order. This is that V-2 was not built on the 'opening up' of the Auxiliary slot, but originated in a different construction type entirely. Stockwell (1977) suggests that V-2 arises from verb-initial sentences introduced by a topicalized adverb. We know that V-1 orders were not uncommon in old Germanic (cf. §8.2); so given VS(O), say, movement of an adverb produces AdvVS(O), which is already verb-second by default.[14] This structure then serves as the model for V-2, and is later generalized. The two accounts are not mutually exclusive; it seems not unlikely that both are partly right, since we would not in fact expect single causes for anything as complex as a word-order shift.[15]

9.4   The syntax of the OE cases in historical perspective

9.4.1   Overview: form, function and syncretism

Recall (§6.1.2) that PIE probably had an eight-case system, with distinct nominative, vocative, genitive, dative, ablative, locative, instrumental and accusative. Pre-Germanic IE, then distributed the possible range of grammatical/semantic functions among eight relatively independent categories; Germanic had to cover the same range with just four. A non-exhaustive but useful list of the major relational categories that would have to be expressed by the case system of a highly inflecting language would include at least these:

(i) Grammatical: subject, direct object, possessor, experiencer, receiver.
(ii) Other: location-in/-on/-at, movement-to/-from, movement-across, movement-into/-out of, comitative (with-X), instrument, cause, partitive.

Given a reduced array consisting of nominative, accusative, genitive and a 'fourth case' for everything else, it seems at first as if the dispositions should be predictable: the old nominative will keep its subject function,

---

[14] For a further development of this view, and a consideration of the possible effects of (archaic) V-1 verse-order on OE prose word-order, see Stockwell & Minkova (1992).
[15] The development of SVO from SOV is most often thought of as resulting mainly from rightward movement of elements originally to the left of the verb, or from 'afterthoughts' inserted at the right edge of the clause, after the object. But the Wackernagel's Law scenario has good support outside Germanic; see the discussion in Hock (1991: ch. 13), with examples from Romance, Baltic and Slavic as well. The rightward movement account is however valid and important for later periods in the history of Old English (Stockwell 1977, Gerritsen 1984).

the accusative will mark direct objects, the genitive possessors and probably partitive; all the rest (which in some sense could be viewed as 'prepositional' relations) would in principle be assigned to the dative. Since this is the conflation of old dative, locative, ablative and instrumental, it would be the natural dustbin for all left-over relations.

But this is not in fact the result (nor is it in other IE languages with reduced case arrays, as we will see); the grammatical relation 'object' for instance may be coded on cases other than accusative, and certain prepositions may take accusative or genitive instead of expected dative. But these 'irregularities' often prove to have order hidden behind them, and provide interesting insights into what the semantics of the original IE case system must have been like. We will see in fact that languages as far apart as Greek and Old English show detailed similarities in case usage; some of these may be due to the natural semantics of particular categories, while others are persistent reflections of ancient pan-IE patterns. I begin with one typical example that will lead into all kinds of useful byways.

As we've seen throughout this book, certain synchronic facts, given the proper perspective, have great historical significance. Consider the case-government properties of two OE prepositions, *on* and *ofer*. (I refrain from giving precise glosses to them for reasons that will become apparent when we look at the data.) The examples here are all taken from *Beowulf*, so we can see the system at work in a single 'speaker':

(9.14) (a) *on* + Dative
    i. Bēo ðū *on ofest-e* (386)
    Be thou in haste-dat/sg
    ii. *on him* byrne scan (405)
    on him (the) mailshirt shone
    iii. beornas *on blanc-um* (856)
    men on steed-dat/pl

    (b) *on* + Accusative
    i. Ðā mec sǣ oþbær . . . *on Finna land* (578–9)
    then me sea bore . . . on Finn-gen/pl land-acc/sg
    'then the sea bore me . . . up onto the land of the Finns'
    ii. þā ic *on holm* gestāh (632)
    then I on sea-acc/sg set out-pret/sg
    'then I set out across/over the sea'
    iii. hȳ *on holt* bugon (2598)
    they on wood-acc/sg fled
    'they fled into the wood'

(c) *ofer* + Dative
i. *ofer þæm* hongiað hrinde bearwas (1363)
over it-dat/sg hang frosty groves
'frosty groves hang over it'
ii. Nihthelm geswearc *ofer dryhtgum-um* (1789–90)
night-helm darkened over retainer-dat/pl
'night darkened over the retainers'
iii. mæst hlifade *ofer* Hrōðgāres *hordgestrēon-um* (1898–9)
mast towered over Hrothgar's treasure-dat/pl
'the mast towered over H's treasures'

(d) *ofer* + Accusative
i. Gewāt þā *ofer wægholm* (217)
depart-pret/3/sg then over sea-acc
'then he departed over the sea'
ii. þanon hē gesōhte sūð-Dena folc *ofer ȳða gewealc* (463–4)
thence he sought South-Danes' folk over waves' rolling
'From there he sought the South-Danish folk over the rolling waves'
iii. gang *ofer grund-as* (1404)
(a) path over (the) ground-acc/pl

Essentially, for both of these prepositions the dative uses involve (more or less) static location (mailshirt on a man, a mast towering); while the accusatives imply motion of some kind (coming into a place, departing over the sea). This is not a purely English idiosyncracy; it has a clear IE background, and may also reflect some deeper properties of the way case systems tend to work.

Consider the Latin equivalent (and cognate) of *on*, and the Greek of *ofer*:[16]

(9.15) (a) L *in* + Ablative
i. *in silu-īs* abditī latēbant (BG 2, 19, 6)
in wood-abl/pl hidden lie hidden-imperf/3/pl
'they were lying hidden in the woods'
ii. *in spē* uictoriae (BG 3, 26, 4)
in hope-abl/sg victory-gen/sg
'in hope of victory'

---

[16] Latin examples from Hale & Buck (1903, 1966), Greek from Goodwin (1894/1965); BG = Caesar, *De bello Gallico*, Il = *Iliad*, Od = *Odyssey*.

(b) L *in* + Accusative
i. cum *in castr-a* contenderunt (BG 4, 37, 1)
when in camp-acc/pl hurry-pres/3/pl
'when hurrying into camp'
ii. ut *in Galli-am* uenīrent (BG 4, 16, 1)
that in Gaul-acc/sg come-pres/subj/3/pl
'in order that they might come into Gaul'

(c) Gr *hupér* + Genitive
stê *hupèr kephal-ês* (Il 2, 29)
stand/aorist/3/sg over head-gen/sg
'it stood over his head'

(d) Gr *hupér* + Accusative
hupèr oud-òn ebéseto dōmatos (Od 7, 135)
over threshold-acc/sg step-aor/3/sg house-gen/sg
'he stepped over the threshold of the house'

For the moment we can disregard the fact that the 'static' or locative examples here are ablative in Latin and genitive in Greek (we will see why below). What is important is that (a) location and motion tend to[17] govern different cases, and (b) that the latter tends to take the accusative and the former some other case – as in Old English. And indeed elsewhere in Germanic, and not just in the ancient languages; in German, where case-marking of a sort remains, we get the same distribution:

(9.16)   G *in, über* + Dative
i. Ich wohne *in dies-em* Haus
'I live in this (dat) house'
ii. Ein Flugzeug kreiste *über dem* Haus
'A plane circled over the (dat) house'

G *in, über* + Accusative
i. Ich ging *ins* Eßzimmer
'I went *into-the* (acc) dining-room'
ii. Ich ging *über die* Brücke
'I went over the (acc) bridge'

---

[17] 'Tend to' because case choices are not completely fixed for all instances (even if they are non-arbitrary). It is generally true that cases are 'used with a certain degree of freedom, which enables speakers to choose among different formal means to convey the same meaning' (Luraghi 1987: 356). The examples given in this section are 'majority' or 'normal' uses.

The import of this data appears to be that case-government by prepositions is not a purely syntactic matter (e.g. a rule 'Prep X governs case Y'): the precise sense of the preposition is also involved. The uneven results (Latin ablative vs. Greek genitive vs. OE dative for the locative functions) are due to differential mergers or **syncretisms** in the different languages. If we look at the original IE case system and what (in general) fell together with what in Greek, Latin and Old English, we find that the patterns of syncretism, while not identical, are largely similar:

(9.17)

IE	Latin nom	gen	dat	abl	acc	Greek nom	gen	dat	acc	Old English nom	gen	dat	acc
nom	x					x				x			
gen		x					x				x		
dat			x	x				x				x	
abl				x			x					x	
loc				x			x	x				x	
inst				x			x					x	
acc					x				x				x

At first glance the 'grammatical' cases (nom, gen, acc) have remained more or less intact, but the 'concrete' ('local' and 'movement') cases have had their functions redistributed. Germanic has chosen the simplest solution: virtually everything has collapsed into dative; the situation in Latin and Greek is much more complicated.[18]

But we note that the collapse of local/motional cases in Greek, Latin and Old English excludes the coding of motion-into/across: this is quite generally handled by accusative. One might have thought that accusative was a 'dedicated' or quintessentially grammatical case, marking the syntactic function direct object; but it appears from the data (and this holds as well for Sanskrit, Lithuanian and Slavic) that this motional function is pan-IE, and therefore probably ancient.

This suggests a more refined and less limited notion of what 'a case' is. On one interpretation (e.g. Kuryłowicz 1964: ch. 8), all the IE cases have at least two sets of functions: 'core' or primary and non-core or secondary, with the latter derivable from the former. (This may in fact be generally true of case systems.) For grammatical cases like the accusative or genitive, the syntactic functions are primary; but there are motivated

---

[18] But not irrational. For the logic behind the various syncretisms see Kuryłowicz (1964: ch. 8), and the lucid account in Luraghi (1987).

secondary functions as well, growing out of these in a reasonably natural way.

We can for instance reconstruct the IE accusative as primarily the direct object case; but it has a set of extended meanings, having to do with 'attainment of a goal' (a natural move from coding the result of the action of a transitive verb). From this there develop senses coding what one has to do to achieve a goal, e.g. the traversal of space; and from this traversal of time. Thus the accusative marks not only movement (as a derivative of 'goal'), but 'extent' in space or time as well.

Another example involves two apparently rather different issues: the syncretism of ablative and genitive in Greek, and the development of non-possessive uses of the genitive in IE generally. The genitive originally marks possession and similar notions (but see the next section); the ablative separation or movement from a reference-point. How are they connected? We note that the genitive can also mark 'origin' (cf. *'Germany's* greatest composer'); and since origin in a sense equals 'extraction of X out of Y', this associates also with ablative of separation. Here the genitive/ ablative syncretism in Greek is at least partly motivated: if Greek is to dump the ablative, what case would be the most natural sub-stitute, on the grounds of already having some of the right semantic associations?[19]

Similarly, the partitive use of the genitive may also flow from the semantics of certain kinds of possessives: 'one of *Germany's* greatest composers', 'the *box's* contents', 'the greatest composer *of the nineteenth century*', 'the contents *of the box*'. It's no accident that *of*, which is originally an ablative preposition (in fact the weak form of *off*: the two are not orthographically distinguished until after the sixteenth century) codes both ablative and possessive relations.[20]

A given case-category then can be best visualized, not as a tightly bounded entity with one specific 'meaning', or 'function', but rather as a kind of 'region' in linguistic and/or conceptual space: a core surrounded by a constellation of attracted related senses and metaphorical extensions. This notion will help us understand some of the more 'irregular' case-usages in Old English (and elsewhere), which we turn to in the next section.

It is important however to remember that there are also 'irrational' or unmotivated syncretisms as well, and that these are not in fact uncommon. For instance, in modern Finnish the genitive and accusative singular have

---

[19] Germanic of course made a different choice: but the parameters defining the (eventual) Germanic dative (motion and location) are also a natural grouping.

[20] Note that in calling *of the nineteenth century* a 'genitive' in English, the emphasis is on the semantic values associated with a case-category, not its formal manifestation.

the same marker, /-n/, but absolutely no semantic or syntactic common features. This is not an original condition but a syncretism, and one motivated on a completely different linguistic level. The accusative was originally marked by /-m/, and the genitive as now by /-n/; Finnish developed a prohibition against final /-m/, which caused merger of /-m/ and /-n/. Thus a purely phonological restructuring as it were 'subverted' the syntax and morphology.[21]

But in general we can say that in syncretism or other kinds of system-restructuring, languages will tend to group semantically related functions in the same morphological categories; and as we saw with the accusative of motion, these groupings can remain remarkably stable over long periods of time (though what precisely this stability really means is another matter, which I return to below). In the next section I present a brief historically based account of some of the major case-usages in Old English.

9.4.2   Historical persistence or natural semantics? IE remains in OE case syntax[22]

In this section we consider certain uses of the case-forms that are (whatever else) historically motivated. For instance, even though the accusative is the prototypical direct object case, there are numerous apparently transitive verbs in OE that take genitive or dative objects. These verbs tend (to some extent) to fall into coherent semantic classes, and the same classes often show similar case-government behaviour in Greek and/or Latin.

This strongly suggests a reconstructable ancestral state of affairs: at the evolutionary stage represented by OE we could say for any verb V_i taking a genitive object, for example (where i is either a particular verb or a semantic class) that:

V_i takes a genitive object in OE because V_i takes a genitive object in Latin, Greek . . . And V_i takes a genitive object in Latin, Greek . . . because $*V_i$ took a genitive object in Proto-IE.

Now it is possible (and in many cases in fact likely) that there are (synchronic) semantic reasons for just why this should be so in Greek,

---

[21] Syncretisms of this kind (formal but not semantic) are of course common in English as well: e.g. the collapse of unstressed vowels at the end of the OE period caused merger of most of the case forms of many classes of nouns (e.g. nom *sunu*, gen *suna*, dat *sune* all collapse in *sune*, etc.; see further chapter 10).

[22] For a rewarding and insightful but difficult treatment of the IE case sytem and its developments, see Kuryłowicz (1964: ch. 8). This account is particularly nice because of its insistence on establishing semantic connections, and it has influenced my discussion here. On case in OE see van Kemenade (1987), Traugott (1992: §4.4).

Latin, PIE . . . But the historical inertia of linguistic systems may well override this; we have no way of telling whether V_i takes a genitive in OE because of its semantics and the semantics of the OE genitive, or simply as a residue of what the situation was in the past. (For this book the former would be a bonus, but not really a necessary part of the description.)

The issue is an important one, similar to that of transparency and productivity in word-formation (cf. §8.3.1). How do we assess the status of an apparent (and known to be historical) semantic motivation at a given time? For instance, no normal English speaker now sees the relation (mentioned in the last section) between *of* and *off*, any more than they interpret *offal* as *off-fall* 'that which has fallen off (in the course of butchering, etc.)'[23] Therefore it's anachronistic to analyse *offal* as if it were motivated or transparent (whatever its history, and however clear this looks to the historian); being as ignorant as we are about OE speakers' intuitions the safest bet would be to regard phenomena like genitive objects as relics.[24] I will not however be too scrupulous about this distinction, though it can be taken as there in the background.

As illustrations of the complex historical developments of the senses of the IE cases and their syntax, we will look at some of the main uses of the OE genitive and dative.

A. Genitive

The genitive appears at first to have mainly an 'adjectival' function, since the prototype genitive is a noun modifier: *meotod-es meahte* 'God's might', *þis-es godspell-es geendung* 'this gospel's ending'. Such constructions appear to express a simple 'X possesses Y' relation: one could derive *meotodes meahte* from *meotod hæfð meahte* 'God has might', etc.

But this analysis fails with genitives like *ent-a geweorc* 'giant's work', where the work is rather made by the giants than their possession; or *weard Scylding-a* 'guardian of the Scyldings', where the Scyldings are recipients rather than possessors of guarding. Considerations of this kind have led some scholars (e.g. Kuryłowicz 1964: ch. 8) to argue that the genitive is an underlyingly (or historically) 'sentential' case: in its **adnominal** (modifying) function it derives from possessive sentences, and in

---

[23] Cf. Afrikaans *afval* 'offal', which looks more transparent: *af* 'off, from', *val* 'to fall'. But speakers seem not to recognize this either; the compound has been lexicalized as an uninterpretable or opaque chunk, regardless of what the elements look like from the outside.

[24] Not perhaps dative objects (see below). There is a good case to be made for a living distinction in OE between the senses of dative and accusative as cases for objects of the same verb, whether or not this has a historical basis (it seems that it partly does): see discussion in Plank (1983).

the two uses indicated above from other kinds of either 'underlying' or historically prior syntactic constructions.

The potential sources of these non-possessive genitives can suggest (via a fairly intricate kind of argument) why at least some verbs in later periods commonly take genitive objects. All the IE languages display the two non-possessive genitive types above, called **subject(ive)** and **object(ive)** genitive respectively. In a subject genitive the 'possessor' is construable as the subject of an implicit verb (e.g. *enta geweorc* < 'giants made (the) work'); in an object genitive the possessor is an object (*weard Scyldinga* < 'X guards the Scyldings').[25] Similar constructions occur in Latin and Greek:

(9.18)   Caesar-ī aduentus 'Caesar's coming' < 'Caesar came'
          Pausaní-ou mīsos 'hatred of Pausanias' < 'X hates P'

If these genitives are reduced sentences, the well-attested possibility of subject/object ambiguity arises naturally: L *hostis occisio* 'the enemy's killing' could arise via *X hostem occidit* 'X killed the enemy' or *hostis occiditur* (*a X*) 'the enemy is killed (by X)'.[26]

If certain classes of genitive have a syntactic source, then syntactic argument is open to us for explicating others. Some verb types with preferentially genitive objects can then be interpreted as arising through other syntactic operations. In particular, verbs of perception may take genitive objects through 'suppression' of an accusative (Kuryłowicz 1964: 185f), i.e. they are only 'secondarily' direct objects. Thus the construction *hīeran X-gen* (also for Go *hausjan*) 'to hear something' might have arisen via a type *'to hear [noise-acc] of-something', where the accusative object is lost and the (originally partitive or separative) genitive remains.

In other instances the syntactic origin is not nearly so clear; but whatever the ultimate cause, the semantic classes of verbs taking genitive objects are quite consistent across IE. Some of the most important are:

(i)   Verbs of perception, mental state, desire: Go *gaírnjan* 'long for', *lustōn* 'desire'; OE *gyrnan, wilnian* 'desire', *wundrian* 'admire', *hogian*

---

[25] On this interpretation, the example cited above (*þises godspelles geendung*) could be ambiguous between possessive and subject genitive: related to or derived from either 'this gospel has an end' or 'this gospel ends'.

[26] Examples abound in ModE as well, depending of course on the nature of the lexical items involved. *The president's assassination* is most likely object, *the president's speech* most likely subject; but *the president's shooting* could refer either to someone shooting him or his marksmanship. Many (unrelated) languages also have the possessive/subject/object distinction, and the same kind of potential ambiguity (e.g. Finnish).

'intend'; OIc *kenna* 'know', *minnask* 'remember'; L *cupīre* 'desire', *oblīuīscor* 'forget', *meminī* 'remember', *miror* 'admire'; Gr *epithumeîn* 'long for', *memnêsthai* 'remember', *aisthánesthai* 'perceive'.

(ii) Verbs of deprivation, separation: Go *ga-hrainjan* 'cleanse', *ga-þarban* 'abstain'; OE *bedǣlan* 'deprive', *berȳpan* 'despoil'; OIc *sakna, missa* 'lose'; L *leuāre* 'relieve', *dēsinere* 'cease from'; Gr *apestéresthai* 'deprive'.

The second group probably reflect the ablative-like function of the genitive (cf. the previous section); though ablative and genitive merged in Greek, the merger of ablative and dative in Germanic and the continuing distinction of ablative from other cases in Latin suggests that verbs of this type are 'original' genitive-object classes. There may also be a connection with the original partitive function in some of the other verbs: unlike 'ordinary' transitive verbs like 'kill', 'push', etc., mental state verbs do not 'completely affect' their objects (if indeed they affect them at all); thus genitive after verbs like 'love', 'remember', etc. may reflect something like 'unaffectedness' or 'partial affectedness' or 'non-completion'. (It may be of interest that in Finnish verbs of this type characteristically take not accusative but partitive objects.)[27]

Partitivity is of course directly reflected in constructions like *ān hiora* 'one of-them' (cf. L *eōrum una pars* 'of-them one part'). One other widespread use of the genitive is worth mentioning here, the so-called 'genitive of respect', in which the genitive codes something like 'that respect in which its head possesses some quality': OE *mǣr-es līf-es man* '(a) man of glorious life', cf. L *integer uit-ae* '(one) upright of-life' = 'a man of upright life'.

B. Dative

Since the Germanic dative is the syncretism of the IE dative, ablative, locative and instrumental, we should expect a rather heterogeneous set of categories to be represented in its syntax: in fact virtually all location or movement categories except movement-into/across, which as we saw earlier is generally the province of the accusative.

The IE dative itself may well be a secondary formation; according to this view, the dative is 'nothing else than an offshoot of the loc. used with personal nouns' (Kuryłowicz 1964: 190). Formally the relation is reasonably clear: the original dative/locative ending was *$/$-ei$/$, which then

---

[27] Other categories coded by genitive objects in IE (but less consistently in Germanic) include verbs of reigning/ruling, eating/drinking/enjoying. See Kuryłowicz (1964: 184) for examples.

split into full-grade dative */-ie ~ -oi/, and zero-grade locative */-i/.
The 'personal' property is clear in the 'dative of possession', which
is a widespread IE construction:

(9.19)   L *mihi* sunt bis septem nymphae
          to-me are twice seven nymphs = 'I have twice seven nymphs'

          Gr eisìne-*moi* ekeî ksénoi
          are-to-me there friends = 'I have friends there'

          OE *him* on þæt hēafod
          to-him on the head = 'on his head'

Here 'possession' is construed not as mediated by a verb of 'having', but as
location-at the possessor (cross-linguistically a very common strategy).

The 'personal reference' (location with respect to a person) sense of the
dative is also a natural source for its use in (apparent) subjects of so-called
'impersonal' verbs: e.g. OE *þyncan* 'seem', *mislimpan* 'fail', *gespōwan*
'succeed', L *persuadēre* 'persuade', Gr *dei* 'have need':

(9.20)   L *hīs* persuadērī nōn poterat
          to-them to-be-persuaded neg be able-perf/3/sg
          'they could not be persuaded'

          Gr deî *moi* toúton
          have need/3/sg *to-me* this-gen/sg
          'I have need of this'

          OE *mē* ðyncð betre
          to-me seem-pres/3/sg better
          'it seems better to me'

With verbs of this kind, as the parsing suggests, the 'real' subject is an
abstract 3 person neuter singular; such 'dative subjects' are of course really
locatives, not true (grammatical) subjects. Constructions of this kind still
remain, especially in German: *mir scheint* 'to-me seems' = 'it seems to
me', etc.

The dative also serves as direct object of a large number of rather
heterogeneous verbs, especially those involving separation: OE *ætwindan*
'escape', *linnan* 'cease', corresponding to Latin ablative objects for verbs
like *carēre* 'lack', *abdicāre* 'abdicate'. Also verbs of serving, confiding,
trusting: OE *þegnian* 'serve', *betǣcan* 'entrust', L *seruāre* 'serve', *fidere*,
confidere 'trust', *nitor* 'rely on'.

Because of its composite origin, the Germanic dative is the pre-eminent prepositional case (indeed this might be a better name than 'dative'). Most prepositions not strictly of the accusative (motion-into) type normally govern dative; and the case itself, with or without prepositions, marks a host of local and movement functions: e.g. locative (*wīc-um wunian* 'to dwell in the houses'), instrumental (*hrēran mid hond-um* 'to stir with (one's) hands'), comitative (*lȳtl-e werod-e* 'with a small troop'). The locative function is also clear in the frequent use of noun datives as adverbs, e.g. *hwīl-um* 'at times', *stycce-mǣl-um* 'piece-meal, little-by-little'.

One other use is worth noting: the **dative absolute**. This corresponds to the Latin ablative absolute and Greek genitive absolute, and to the Sanskrit locative absolute (unsurprisingly, given the syncretisms discussed earlier).[28] An 'absolute' construction in this sense is a kind of loose adverbial adjunct to another construction, normally with a perfective or progressive (location-in-time) sense, encoding notions like 'after X happened', 'while X was the case'. The typical absolute construction involves a participle (past or present) and an NP in subject or object relation, both in the appropriate case, with no finite verb in evidence:

(9.21)   Gr taût' eprákhē *Kónon-os stratēgoûnt-os*
          these things happened *Konon-gen/sg being-general-gen/sg*
          'these things happened while K. was general'

          L *omni-bus rē-bus comparāt-īs* diem dīcunt
          all-abl/pl thing-abl/pl ready-abl/pl day-acc/sg say-3/pl
          'all things being ready, they appoint a day'

          OE *him sprecend-um* hī cōmon
          he-dat speaking-dat they come-pret/pl
          'while he was speaking they came'

This construction (which is not common) is often thought to be non-native; Quirk & Wrenn (1955: §111) say that it 'is modelled directly on the Latin ablative absolute'. Indeed it frequently occurs in translations in just this way (the example above translates *eō loquente ueniunt* 'he-abl speaking-abl they came'). But there are original examples, and the presence of absolutes in oblique cases that can be seen to be historically related in Latin and Greek (and the Greek genitive absolute especially, which seems to presuppose an original ablative) suggests that it is inherited, not

---

[28] For an interesting discussion of the Sanskrit locative absolute, and the semantics of the construction generally, see Whitney (1889: §303).

borrowed (even if Latin does of course, as a prestigious literary language, reinforce its use).

The complex interaction of cases described in this and the last section suggests once again the view of case-categories as (somewhat fuzzy) 'regions' rather than 'points' in structure. The Germanic results (like those in the other older IE languages) are consistent with a core/periphery model, in which certain sense-overlaps allow for both syncretism and not fully determined (even alternating) usages in the later languages. We could perhaps end this discussion by representing the relations among the IE dative, locative, genitive and ablative this way:

(9.22)

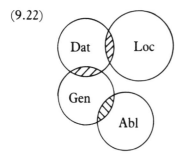

The shaded areas represent the intersections of the case-functions/senses, i.e. those overlaps which could later be reapportioned among different cases, and which could serve as 'attractors' for syncretisms.

Part V:

Historical postlude

I returned, and saw under the sun, that the race is not to the strong, nor
the battle to the strong, neither yet bread to the wise, nor yet riches to
men of understanding, nor yet favour to men of skill; but time and
chance happeneth to them all.

Ecclesiastes 9:11

10   The dissolution of Old English

10.1   Stasis, flux, transition[1]

The decay and transformation of a given language system are as much part
of its history as its origin and development. In this book the focus is of
course on origins and persistences; dissolution, and the rebuilding of the
remains into a new system are really more part of the next phase, say 'the
origins of Middle English'. Still, the picture is not complete without at
least a glance at the other end. This chapter presents a sketch of what
happened at the end of the OE period, and how it led on to what followed;
in particular, the dissolution of some of the major structures we saw either
as continuations of or emergences from IE and PGmc. Like all emergences, Old English was of limited duration. But the precise way in which
it turned into its descendant, Middle English, is of considerable interest,
at least as a pendant to our concerns with Old English itself; and we can
see in the transition the germs of the major typological features of later
English, and the flowering of directions of change already implicit in Old
English itself.

A major part of the historian's craft is juxtaposing successive language-
states, and constructing good stories out of the observed (or reconstructed)
transitions between states. 'Language-state' is of course a fairly gross
idealization: no language is ever (absolutely) static or homogeneous, there
is always some change going on, some variation present that may (or may
not) be the prelude to change.

But at certain points in a history the ever-present flux intensifies, and
variation appears to take on a new direction. At such points we feel
ourselves watching the birth of a new order, often in the guise of the
dissolution of the old. Such 'transitional' states are of particular interest to
the historian; they tend to define the boundaries between 'epochs' in a
history, phase-transitions between relatively clear-cut and definable traditions that by contrast to the transition-zones are recognizable 'states'.

[1] For detailed discussion of the topics sketched in this chapter, and references, see Lass
(1992b), especially §§2.1–3, 2.8–10.

Even during the Old English period itself, many of the main structures appear to be breaking down, and late MSS begin to show a somewhat chaotic picture with respect to certain structural features, as old systems (at all grammatical levels) change and new ones begin to be born. There are texts that are prototypically Old English, and others just as clearly Middle English; nobody would doubt for instance that these two versions of Matthew 8:20 are in those two languages respectively:[2]

> (a) Foxas habbað holu, and heofonan fuglas nest; sōþlīce mannes sunu næfð hwær hē hys hēafod ahylde.
> (b) Foxis han dennes, and briddis of heuene han nestis, but mannus sone hath not where he schal reste his heed.

But there are problematical texts, where assignment to 'Old' or 'Middle' is debatable. Here is a sample from one such text, the *Peterborough Chronicle*, which is usually found in anthologies of 'Early Middle English', and is customarily taught as one of the first examples of the 'new' language. This extract will introduce the main themes of this chapter; given a knowledge of (relatively) 'classical' Old English, and some idea of what Middle English looks like, what is this in fact written in?[3]

> 1 On þis gære for se king henri ouer sæ æt te lammasse.
>   in this year travelled the king Henry over the sea at Lammas
> 2 & ð oþer dei þa he lai an slep in scip.
>   and the second day when he lay and slept in ship
> 3 þa þestrede þe dæi ouer al landes
>   then darkened the day over all lands
> 4 & uuard þe sunne suilc als it uuare thre niht ald mone.
>   and became the sun as if it were a three-night old moon
> 5 an sterres abuten him at middæi
>   and stars about it at midday
> 6 Wurþen men suiðe ofuundred & ofdred
>   became men very amazed and terrified
> 7 & sæden ð micel þing schulde comen herefter.
>   and said that a great thing should come hereafter
> 8 sua dide. for þat ilc gær warth þe king ded.
>   and so it did for that same year became the king dead

---

[2] The OE text is from the West Saxon Gospels (c. 1000); the ME from a late Wycliffite version (c. 1400). Both cited from Görlach (1974: 154).
[3] Text from Hall (1920: 6). I have left the abbreviations and punctuation in the text as printed, but have substituted <&> for the 'Tironian' sign in the original.

While much of the syntax is clearly of the OE type (V-2 after an adverbial,: 1, 3, etc.), and many forms are virtually unchanged (*for, sæ, æt, oþer, þa, sunne*), there are some major differences:

(a) The allophones [f, v] of /f/ (cf. §3.9.1) have become phonemicized; or at least [v] is perceived as worth representing independently: *ouer* for *ofer*.[4]

(b) Original /æj/ is now apparently interpreted as a diphthong rather than a /-VC/ sequence: *dei, lai* for *dæg, læg*.

(c) Some unstressed vowels appear to be undergoing merger: *þestrede* (3) for *þēostrode* (cl II *þēostrian* 'darken'); this also shows monophthongization of original /eo/.

(d) Some endings have been lost: *scip* (2) for *scip-e* (dat sg).

(e) Some nouns have begun to shift declension toward the *a*-stem target (§6.1.3): *sterr-es* for *steorr-an* (*n*-stem: nom sg *steorra*).

(f) As a result of (c), some morphological endings have merged: *sæd-en* (7) for *sægd-on*, with *-on* now merged with *-en*; similarly *com-en* for *cum-an*.

Such changes were in fact already beginning a century earlier, for instance in Wulfstan's *Sermo ad Anglos* (1014; MS virtually contemporary, see Whitelock 1963). This text shows some merger (or as the handbooks often say 'confusion') of endings, e.g. *-an* for pret pl *-on* (*scylan, dydan, brǽcan*), and *-an* for dat pl *-um* (*suman, gehwylcan, þysan*); as well as occasional *-e-* for *-o-* in preterites of class II weak verbs (*clumedan* 'they mumbled', *geswugedan* 'they kept silent', expected *clumedon, geswugedon*). So what the *Peterborough Chronicle* shows is not entirely new: there's just much more of it. Or to put it another and perhaps equally interesting way, much less of the 'classical'.

These developments show in embryo the kinds of things that were to pick up speed later, and result in the creation of a virtually 'new' language. From this little bit of evidence it seems that the most important new developments involve (a) monophthongization of old diphthongs and creation of new ones; (b) certain vowel mergers in stressed syllables; and (c) major collapses of formerly distinctive vowels in weak syllables, with potentially profound implications for morphology.

---

[4] In most mediaeval traditions (and occasionally even in OE) word-medial [v] is spelled <u>; a famous early example is *Beowulf* 1799 *hliuade* 'it towered' for *hlifade*.

10.2   Monophthongization and merger

Some of the most important phonological changes in the late OE period involve the diphthongs and the low vowels /ɑ, æ, æ:/. In about the eleventh century the old diphthongs (both short and long) began to monophthongize, producing in one case merger with existing nuclei, and in the other a new category. By this time we can assume general loss of the <ie> diphthongs in WS, and a diphthong inventory for all dialects of short and long /æɑ/ and short and long /eo/. The developments are:

(10.1)   (a)   ǣɑ   æɑ
                     æ ———→ æ   æ: ———→ æ:

         (b)   ĕo ———→ ø   eo ———→ ø:

The changes (a) simply merge the old diphthongs with nuclei already present in the system; (b) create a new vowel, restoring an old system type with two front-rounded vowels (cf. §3.8.2).

Recall that the creation of the unique OE diphthong types (§3.6.2) was a harmonic process: the second elements came to agree in height with the first. These late monophthongizations are also harmonic; in the case of the /æɑ/ diphthongs, the second mora now assimilates in backness as well. For /eo/ the assimilation is bidirectional: the first mora takes on the rounding of the second, and the second the backness of the first.

The import of this is that e.g. *eall* 'all', *rætt* 'rat' now have the same vowel /æ/, and *bēam* 'beam' and *glǣm* 'gleam' have /æ:/; for the /eo/ diphthongs, *heofon* 'heaven' has /ø/ and *bēo* 'bee' /ø:/.

Either shortly after these changes, or partially overlapping with them, /æ/ (now itself a conflation of old /ǣɑ, æ/) underwent merger with /ɑ/. But this time, instead of one of the old qualities remaining, the output is a new type, the low front vowel /a/.[5] The whole pattern then for the short low front vowels is:

(10.2)   eall   ǣɑ
         rætt   æ ———→ æ ———→ a   all, rat, cat[6]
         catte   ɑ ———————— ɑ

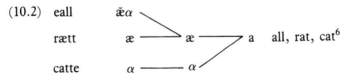

---

[5] For evidence and argument see Lass (1976: ch. 4). The value /a/ remains until the seventeenth century, when the vowel raises again to /æ/ (hence modern /æ/).
[6] The long back vowel in *all* is due to later changes: diphthongization of ME /a/ to /au/ before dark /l/, and later monophthongization.

The result is a short vowel system reminiscent of the older type with only one low vowel; there is a kind of cyclic evolution from PIE to late OE:

(10.3)   i u   i u   i u   i u   i u
         e o > e   > e o > e o > e o
         α   α   α   æ α   a
         PIE   PGmc   WGmc   OE   lOE

(I omit the front-rounded /y, ø/ here; see §3.8.2 for discussion.) The late OE type of system remains stable until the later seventeenth century. At this point lowering of the reflex of OE /o/ (as in *lot* < *hlott*) to [ɒ] creates the modern (and recreates the OE!) type of short vowel system with both front and back low vowels: ModE /æ, ɒ/ = OE /æ, α/. And some varieties (especially Irish and US) later unrounded /ɒ/, so that there are now systems exactly like the OE one, with /æ, α/.

As might be expected, these developments ushered in a period of highly unstable spelling, e.g. in the *Peterborough Chronicle* the reflex of OE *hēafod* 'head' is spelled *heaued, hæued, heued*; *eorl* 'earl' is *eorl, erl, æorl*; *eall* 'all' is *ælle, alle*.

10.3   The new diphthongs

While the old diphthongs were monophthongizing, a series of quite new ones was being created; these, unlike the OE type, were not height harmonic, but closing, i.e. the second elements were higher than the first, in fact either /-i/ or /-u/. This again is a return to the original pre-OE (in fact Indo-European) type; another example of the constant cycling between alternative systems and return to 'centres of gravity' (Lass 1977) or 'preferred' system-types characterizing the long-term history of English.

In a nutshell, what happened is this: from the eleventh century to c. 1250, new diphthongs arose from two sources, at first sporadically, but gradually taking over all available environments. The two sources are:

(a) 'Middle English Breaking': /i/ or /u/ are inserted in certain /-VC/ environments, creating /ViC/ or /VuC/ sequences. So OE [eç] > [eiç]: *fehtan* 'fight' > ME *feighten*, and OE [ox] > [ɔux]: *dohtor* 'daughter' > ME *doughter*.

(b) 'Vocalization': certain consonants vocalize to /i/ or /u/ after certain vowels, so that /VC/ > /Vi/ or /Vu/. So OE /æj/ > /ai/: *dæg* > ME *dai*, and [oɣ] > [ɔu]: *boga* 'bow' > ME *bowe*.

In (a), a vowel is inserted with the same place of articulation as the preceding one (or as the following allophone of /x/, which is conditioned by the preceding vowel), and /x/ remains. In (b), a postvocalic fricative becomes a high vowel ('one step down' in degree of stricture), with the same place of articulation (palatal [j] > [i], velar [γ] > [u]). Vocalization of this kind is a quite new source of diphthongs; before, they were either original vowel-clusters as far back as one could reconstruct, or developed from the breaking of monophthongs.

The details of these diphthongizations are complex and not entirely relevant here; but the general principles are important, as these processes have three major systemic effects: (a) creation of a new set of 'old-type' diphthongs; (b) restriction of /j/ to syllable onsets and complete loss of [γ]; and (c) destruction of the diphthongal length contrast. The latter comes about by merger of OE /V:x/ and /Vx/ sequences: e.g. the reflexes of both *dohtor* with /ox/ and *sōhter* 'sought' with /o:x/ have /ɔux/; ME apparently allowed only two types of nuclei, with no possibility of a short bimoric one.

The various diphthongizations resulted in an early seven-member system, which later collapsed to five. Some of the major sources are:

(10.4)

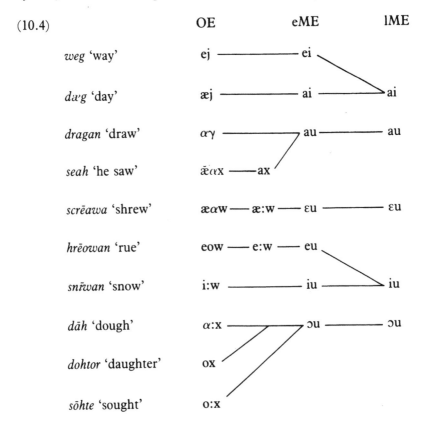

	OE	eME	lME
weg 'way'	ej	ei	
dæg 'day'	æj	ai	ai
dragan 'draw'	αγ	au	au
seah 'he saw'	ǽɑx — ax		
scrēawa 'shrew'	æɑw — æ:w — ɛu		ɛu
hrēowan 'rue'	eow — e:w — eu		
snīwan 'snow'	i:w	iu	iu
dāh 'dough'	α:x	ɔu	ɔu
dohtor 'daughter'	ox		
sōhte 'sought'	o:x		

No new diphthong types appeared in English until the seventeenth century, when diphthongization before /r/ led to centring diphthongs with /-ə/ as second element, e.g. in /diːr/ [diːə] 'dear'.

10.4   Quantity adjustment[7]

Throughout OE and most earlier periods, vowel-length was relatively 'free': the material following an accented vowel had little controlling effect on its length. But toward the end of the OE period, a new type of conditioning began to emerge, in which the postvocalic environment became a major determinant of length. In particular, late OE and early ME developed both lengthening and shortening rules responsive to following segmental and prosodic environments. The changes of interest here are:

(a) **Homorganic Lengthening.**[8] By about the tenth century (if not earlier), short vowels begin to lengthen before clusters of sonorant + homorganic voiced obstruent, e.g. /-rd, -rn, -ld, -nd, -mb/; so modern long nuclei (long vowels or diphthongs) in words like *child* < *cĭld*, *climb* < *clĭmban*, *field* < *fĕld*.

(b) **Pre-Cluster Shortening I.** At some point during the OE period (later rather than earlier) long vowels shorten before clusters of three consonants, as in *gŏd-spell* 'gospel' < *gōd-spell*, *nǣddre* 'adder' < *nǣddre*. This accounts for the failure of lengthening (a) in *children* < *cildru*.

(c) **Trisyllabic Shortening I.** At about the same time, long vowels shortened before clusters of two consonants in stressed antepenults: *blĕtsian* 'bless' < *blētsian*, *Hlămmæsse* 'Lammas' < *Hlāf-mæsse*.

Later on, in about the eleventh century, changes (b, c) were generalized to more extensive environments:

(d) **Pre-Cluster Shortening II.** Long vowels now shorten before clusters of two (rather than three) consonants (except of course those that cause homorganic lengthening). So *cĕpte* 'kept' < *cēpte*, *mĕtte* 'met' < *mētte*. Since the present systems of such verbs did not have the relevant clusters (*cēpan*, *mētan*), these kept the long vowel, hence the ModE length alternations in *keep* vs. *kept*, *meet* vs. *met*, etc.

---

[7] See Lass (1974) for an early treatment of these phenomena, and a somewhat more sophisticated account in Lass (1992b: §2.5.2). The whole subject of quantity adjustment (including later ME developments) is exhaustively and challengingly treated in Ritt (forthcoming). The names given to the sound changes discussed here (as well as the term 'quantity adjustment') first appeared as far as I know in Lass (1974), but are fairly widely used.

[8] The unity of this change has been challenged by Minkova & Stockwell (1992), who argue that there are a number of unrelated subchanges; in particular that the clusters involving /l/ illustrate a quite different mechanism from those involving nasals.

(e) **Trisyllabic Shortening II**. Long vowels now shorten in antepenults before one consonant (rather than two): *sŭþerne* 'southern' < *sūþerne*, hence a long nucleus in ModE *south* < *sūþ*, but a short one in *southern*.

These changes not only mark a shift in the locus for conditioning of syllable weight, and impose considerable restrictions on the applicability of the /V/ vs. /V:/ contrast; they introduce a quite new kind of morphophonemic alternation, based on quantity rather than just quality.[9] And they also produce new variant allomorphy in places where it did not exist before: thus in addition to the alternations in *keep/kept*, etc. produced by pre-cluster shortening, verbs like OE *sellan* 'sell', *tellan* 'tell', pret *sealde*, *tealde* end up (by homorganic lengthening) with short vowels in the present and long vowels in the past: early ME *sĕllen*, *tĕllen*, pret *sālde*, *tālde* (hence by later changes ModE *sold*, *told*).

10.5   Weak vowel collapse and the new morphology[10]

As we saw in §10.1, the erosion of morphologically important qualitative distinctions was beginning as early as the eleventh century (Wulfstan's mergers of *-on/-an*, *-um/-an*, etc.). In fact (cf. §4.3.1) many such distinctions had already been lost in pre-OE times, so the principle is nothing new. But the extent of collapse in later times is much greater, and has a radical systemic effect.

In a *Peterborough Chronicle* sample (entries for 1132, 1135, 1137–9), for instance, the preterite plural (OE *-on*) appears mainly as *-en* (81 per cent of occurrences); but there are 16 per cent *-on*, and a scatter of *-an* and *-æn* spellings as well. Similarly, the infinitive ending appears mainly as *-en* (85 per cent), but there are still 8 per cent original *-an*, and nearly 10 per cent 'impossible' *-on*. Staying with nasal suffixes, adverbial *-an* (OE *befor-an* 'before') is exclusively *-en*, as is dative pl *-um*; the strong pp *-en* appears mainly as *-en* (92 per cent), but *-an* also occurs.

So the incipient mergers we saw in Wulfstan have proceeded to such a point that any /-Vn/ suffix can be written three ways (or even four, counting the unhistorical *-æn*, which is of course probably a spinoff of the /æ/-/ɑ/ merger); this shows clearly that weak vowels before nasals are no longer distinct. Therefore the grammatical information carried by these endings is no longer as specific as it was in OE, since they are no longer in

---

[9] The qualitative differences in *keep* vs. *kept*, *south* vs. *southern* are due to much later changes occurring in the fifteenth to seventeenth centuries.

[10] The classic treatment of the post-OE history of vowels in weak syllables is Minkova (1991), which surveys the previous literature in detail, and corrects numerous bits of mistaken mythology, as well as providing a coherent overall account.

opposition; a generalized <-Vn> occurs for infinitive, pret pl, dat pl, etc.; and only context tells which is meant.

The same is true for other unstressed syllables, where the majority writing is <-e->, regardless of history, though other vowel-graphs can appear (e.g. *hungær* 'hunger' < *hungor, sunu/sune* 'son' < *sunu*). Generalizing, OE weak <e> can be written <e, o, a, æ>, weak <u> is <u, e>, and weak <a> is <a, o, e>. The only weak vowel that is uniformly distinct from the others is /i(:)/ < -*ig* (*bodi, mani, hali* 'holy' < *bodig, mænig, hālig*).

The structural consequences of these developments are enormous: overall, no grammatical contrast underwritten solely by a distinction in unstressed vowels survives beyond the twelfth century. This means that by c. 1150 the following formerly contrastive categories (among others) are no longer viable:[11]

(a) The internal morphology of noun declensions with vocalic endings (e.g. *u*-stems, *ō*-stems). Contrasts like *u*-stem nom sg -*u* vs. gen sg -*a* vs. dat sg -*e*, etc. vanish (*sun-e* stands for original *sun-u, sun-a, sun-e*).

(b) All dat pl (whatever the declension) are the same as all oblique cases (except gen pl) of *n*-stem nouns. So *a*-stem dat pl *stān-um* > *stan-en*, jut as *n*-stem gen sg, dat sg, nom/acc/dat pl are -*en*: a form like *tungen* could be any of these forms of 'tongue' (OE *tunge, -an, -um*). Only the *n*-stem gen pl -*ena* remains distinct as -*ene*.

(c) All gen pl in -*a* merge with dat sg in -*e* (e.g. *stān-a, stān-e* are both *stan-e*). Similarly *a*-stem gen sg -*es*, nom/acc pl -*as* merge in -*es* so that *stan-es* can be either.

(d) Pres 3 sg -*eþ* and 3 pl -*aþ* merge in -*eþ*; preterite subjunctive plural -*en* and indicative -*on* are no longer distinct.

In summary, only three types of endings survive reliably into Middle English: generalized -*e* representing older -*e, -a, -u*; generalized -*en* representing older -*en, -on, -an*; and generalized -*es* representing older -*es, -as*.[12] It takes just a little reflection to see what is going to happen; this language has to build itself a quite new kind of morphology, more like that

---

[11] If what follows is a bit congested, have a look again at the noun and verb paradigms in chapters 6–7.

[12] One far-reaching general effect of these changes is the gradual dissociation of case and number. In OE these were generally 'cumulated' on single morphs, so that e.g. *a*-stem -*as* = {nom/acc, pl}, but there is no ending that is just {pl} (like e.g ModE nominal-*s*). What eventually happened is that number, as a 'prototype' noun category, gradually won out over case, gender, etc.; just as in the verb tense won out over person and number. (For details of these later developments see Lass 1992b: §§2.9.1, 2.9.2.1–4.)

of ModE. Without going into detail, one might predict from this that the endings most likely to remain stable are those marked by specific consonants, which do not get lost as easily as vowels in weak syllables; indeed, the most likely candidate for a 'target' for noun-inflection is the *a*-stem masculine, with its salient plural in /-s/; this is already attracting some masculines during the OE period, and later begins to attract feminines as well, as the purely vocalic inflection of the *ō*-stems becomes less and less useful. At the very least we can say that any language that looks like this does not look a whole lot like Old English as we know it, but does begin resembling the language we speak now. And this is as good a place as any to stop.

Glossary

This glossary contains major technical terms that may be unfamiliar or vaguely familiar to some readers, and either are not defined in the text, or are frequent and/or important enough so that a shorter definition would be useful. Terms in **boldface** within an entry are defined elsewhere in the glossary; those in *italics* are subsidiary or related. Section numbers in [ ] after an entry refer to discussion in the text; other useful references will be included here as well. The definitions are not exhaustive, but rather keyed to the context of this book. For more detailed treatment, or definitions of terms not in the glossary, Crystal (1985) is useful. Some of the definitions here have been taken almost intact from an earlier glossary of mine (Lass 1987).

ablative A case or expression encoding the notion 'away from'.
ablaut A set of Indo-European vowel **alternations**, ancestral to those in e.g. *ride/rode/ridden*. [chapter 5]
accent see **stress**
accusative A case typically marking the direct object of transitive verbs, and in some instances notions like motion-toward, motion-into, duration.
active see **voice (1)**
adposition A grammatical item typically marking relations of locality, direction, etc., with respect to a noun or NP (its object). Adpositions preceding their objects are *prepositions*; those following are *postpositions*.
affix A grammatical form, normally incapable of standing alone (i.e. **bound** or attached to a full word or **stem**, its *base*); one preceding its base is a *prefix*, one following is a *suffix*; one inserted into a base is an *infix*.
affricate An articulation consisting of a **stop** closure followed by a **homorganic fricative** release, e.g. [tʃ] in *church*.
agentive A form expressing the notion 'agent/doer of an action', e.g. *hunter* is an agentive or *agent noun*, {-er} is an agentive suffix.

allomorph   A particular realization of a **morpheme**, or member of the class of forms constituting the morpheme, e.g. the phonologically different plural endings in *cat-s, dog-s, fish-es.*

allophone   A particular realization of a **phoneme**, or member of the class of phonetic segments constituting the phoneme, e.g. [t^h] in *tick*, [t] in *stick* are allophones of /t/.

alternation   A situation in which two or more linguistic elements (e.g. **allophones, allomorphs, morphemes**) have their distribution controlled by some rule assigning one to a given environment, the other(s) to other(s).

alveolar   Of segments made with the tip or blade of the tongue against the alveolar ridge (behind the upper incisors), e.g. [t, s].

analogy   Formation according to some given pattern, hence a general term for 'irregular' or sporadic processes of change that lead to regularities of one kind or another, by altering forms in the direction of more regular or typical 'targets'. So ModE *son-s, nut-s, book-s* were created by analogical extension of the *a*-**stem** plural in *-s* to nouns that originally formed their plurals quite differently: OE *sunu/suna, hnutu/ hnyte, bōc/bēc.*

Anglo-Frisian   The presumed early (pre-fifth-century) speech community consisting of the ancestors of Old English and Frisian; the language spoken in this community; the period of presumed unity before the split of the ancestor of Old English.

Anglo-Frisian Brightening (AFB)   The early sound change by which WGmc */ɑ/ was fronted to [æ], as in *dæg* 'day' vs. Go *dags*. [§3.5]

antepenult   The third-from-last syllable of a word.

aorist   A 'punctual past' (pastness with no particular marking for **aspect**), as opposed to a **perfect** or **imperfect** or other types.

aorist present   A type of **strong verb** whose present system does not show the vowel which it would have if it were the descendant of an IE present, but rather that associated with a historical aorist. [§7.2.1]

approximant   A segment produced with approximation of articulators but neither closure nor friction, e.g. [j, w].

aspect   A time-related category distinct from tense, encoding a view of an action with respect to its temporal contour. E.g. indicating such properties of an action or state as completeness, duration, being-in-process-of, habitualness, etc. Both *I read* and *I am reading* are 'present', but the first carries habitual aspect, and the second progressive. [See Lass 1987: §4.5.2]

aspirated   Of a consonant (most often a **stop**) released before the onset of **voice** on a following vowel, and thus producing a period of [h]-coloured friction before voicing begins, e.g. [t^h] in *tick*.

assimilation   Any process in which a segment becomes phonetically similar or identical to another in its vicinity. If a segment changes so as to become more like a following one, the assimilation ⊙ *regressive* (right-to-left); if it changes so as to become more like one before it, the assimilation is *progressive* (left-to-right).

a-**stem**   A noun or adjective whose **stem** was formed with a historical **thematic** vowel */-α-/ added to the **root**, like *dæg* < */ðαγ-α-z/. This class also contained nouns with /-w-/ or /-j-/ before the theme vowel (*wa*-stems, *ja*-stems), like *bearu* 'grove' < */βαr-wα-z/, *here* 'army' < */xαr-jα-z/. [§6.1.3]

athematic   see **thematic**

attributive   The position of an adjective within the same phrase as the noun it modifies (*the* **good** *boy*); as opposed to predicate position, where it is separated by a **copula** or similar verb (*the boy is* **good**).

back   Loosely, a phonetic term referring to any segment whose maximal stricture is in the vicinity of some structure in the rear of the vocal tract (velum, uvula, rear wall of pharynx). Of **velar, uvular, pharyngeal** consonants and vowels like [u, o, α]. A segment with a primary nonback articulation but a secondary back one (e.g. a **dark** [ɫ]) may also be treated as back).

back-formation   A type of **derivation** in which an apparently complex form is (erroneously) split up, and a (previously nonexistent) simple form is produced, which looks like what the complex one might be derived from. Thus the noun *burglar* existed in English from the seventeenth century, but the verb *burgle* (as if *burglar* = *burgle* + -*er*) was formed in the nineteenth.

backness   The position of a segment on the **front/back** axis of the vocal tract.

back umlaut   An early OE sound change in which **front** vowels /i, e, æ/ diphthongize before a **back** vowel in a following syllable, e.g. *heofon* 'heaven' < */xefon/. [§3.6.3]

bahuvrīhi   A type of **compound** in which the **head** does not appear within the word itself, but the compound as a whole is predicated of a 'third party': e.g. *barefoot* is not a kind of foot but characterizes a person (who has bare feet). [§8.3.2]

bilabial   Of a consonant produced with the upper and lower lips as articulators, e.g. [p, m].

bimoric   see **mora**

bound   (As opposed to free). Of an item that cannot appear independently, but only attached to some other: e.g: plural {-s}, {cran-} in *cranberry*.

brace   Also clausal brace, *Satzklammer*. A West Germanic construction in which a **finite** auxiliary is separated from the main verb of the clause by all other (non-subject) clause material. [§9.3]

breaking   An early OE sound change, in which **front** vowels diphthongize before certain **back** consonants, e.g. *seah* 'he saw' < */sæx/. [§3.6]

breathy voice   A form of phonation in which the vocal folds vibrate for only part of their length, with a chink open at the posterior part through which **voiceless** non-vibrating air passes simultaneously, giving a 'breathy' or 'sighing' effect. ModE /h/ between vowels (as in *aha!*) is usually breathy voiced (but voiceless initially as in *ha!*). The transliterations <bh, dh, gh> in loans from Indic languages (*bhaji, Gandhi, ghee*) normally indicate breathy voiced stops.

calque   Also loan-translation. A (virtually) literal piece-by-piece translation of a foreign item: e.g. OE *ymb-snīþan* rendering L *circum-cidere* 'circumcise' = 'around-cut'. [§8.2.1]

causative   A type of verb expressing the notion 'cause X to Y', e.g. *set* is a causative of *sit* (= 'cause X to sit').

central   Of a vowel articulated toward the centre of the vowel-space, i.e. neither **front** nor **back**, like [ə].

centralized   Of a vowel whose articulation has been shifted from a peripheral (**front** or **back**) locus to a **central** or at least less peripheral one.

clitic   A grammatical item, essentially an independent word rather than an **affix**, but attached to and forming a phonological unit with some other word, its *host*. E.g. *-n't* in English contracted negatives like *wouldn't*, where the full word *not* is phonologically reduced and attached to the verb. A clitic attached to the right of its host is *enclitic*, one attached to the left is *proclitic*.

cluster   Any sequence of segments normally forming (part of) a major syllable constituent. Most often in reference to consonants (e.g. /ts/ in *cats*), but sometimes also for vowel-sequences (/aɪ/ in *my*).

coarticulation   The formation of more than one articulatory gesture at the same time; e.g. an English **dark** /l/, which has an **alveolar lateral** articulation as in some sense 'basic', also has the back of the tongue raised toward the **velum**.

coda   The constituent of a syllable following the **nucleus**, e.g. /-ts/ in *cats* /kæts/. [§3.2]

cognate   Having the same ancestor (< L *co-gnātus* 'allied by birth'). German and English are cognate languages (their relationship mediated via Proto-IE, Proto-Germanic, NWGmc, WGmc); and any two forms in a pair or n-tuple of languages with a common ancestor that descend from the same original are cognate forms (or cognates).

comparative   A term applied to any process by which ancestral forms are extrapolated through comparing attested forms (comparative reconstruction). Thus in the simplest possible case comparison of the initial consonants of IE words meaning 'mouse' (L *mūs*, OE *mūs*, etc.) leads to the **reconstruction** of an ancestral initial consonant */m-/. In a more complex case, the initials of L *porcus* 'pig', OE *fearh*, OIr *orc* and many similar sets lead to reconstruction of an ancestor or **protoform** with */p-/.

compensatory lengthening   Lengthening of a vowel attendant on loss of a following consonant, so that the **weight** of a syllable remains constant. Schematically, a **rhyme** /-VCC/ > /-VVC/ when the first consonant is lost. E.g. the long vowel in OE *gōs* 'goose' reflects an earlier /VN/: cf. OHG *gans*.

complement   (a) The **noun phrase** following a **copula**, as in *John is a teacher*; (b) a subordinate clause in noun function, e.g. the bracketed clause in *I said [I was sick]*.

complementary distribution   A situation where two items occur in mutually exclusive environments, and hence cannot **contrast**, e.g. the **aspirated** and unaspirated **allophones** of /k/ in *cat* and *scat* respectively.

complex   Of any linguistic unit consisting of more than one element or constituent. A **diphthong** or long vowel /VV/ is a complex **nucleus**, an inflected form like *walk-s* is a complex word, etc.

compositionality   The property of a complex item (e.g. word, phrase, etc.) whereby its total meaning is purely the sum of the meanings of its component parts.

compound   A word consisting of at least two other words (or **stems**), treated grammatically as a unit: *blackboard*, *bitter-sweet*. [§8.3.2]

compound stress rule   The rule assigning an overall **stress** contour to **compounds** in English and other Germanic languages. In OE as well as ModE, this involves (in general) assignment of primary stress to the first element, and secondary stress to the second (as in *bláckbìrd*). [§4.2]

conditioning   The factors inducing some specific **realization** of an element. Conditioning may be **phonological** (e.g. /æ/ lengthens to /æ:/ before **voiced stops** in some dialects of English), **morphological** (e.g. *house* has the **allomorph** /hauz/ before {plural} as in *houses*), or **lexical** (only certain words in English take plural *-im*, e.g. *seraph*, *kibbutz*).

conjugation   (a) The set of forms belonging to a particular verb; (b) a class of verbs with same (type of) conjugation in the first sense.

consonantism   The consonant(s) associated with some particular category or form; e.g. one might refer to the '/r/-consonantism' of verbal forms like *were*, as opposed to the '/z/-consonantism' of *was*.

consonant-stem   Also athematic root noun. A noun formed with no **thematic** element, but with endings added directly to the **root**, e.g. L *uox* /woks/ 'voice' = {wok-s}. [§6.1.3]

context-sensitive Of a phonological rule or change that requires a specific environment (e.g. some following segment or position in the word) to operate; as opposed to *context-free.*

continuant Of any segment made without a complete closure, whose articulation is capable of being (virtually) indefinitely sustained: e.g. **fricatives** and all **sonorants**.

contract verb One whose medial consonant has been deleted, giving a /-VV-/ sequence from original */-VCV-/: e.g. OE *slēan* 'slay' /slæɑn/ < */slɑxɑn/.

contrast Distinctive difference, i.e. ability to signal difference in meaning. The English phonemes /p/, /t/ are in contrast by virtue of the distinctions *pit* vs. *tit*, *pip* vs. *tip*, etc.

conversion Also zero-derivation. The use of an item originally belonging to one grammatical category as a member of another, without change of form; the simplest possible kind of word-formation. E.g. the conjunction *but* used as a verb and a noun in *but me no buts*.

copula A verb typically having a 'linking' function, whose subject and **complement** have the same status. Especially of verbs expressing notions like equality or identity, classically the verb 'to be'.

correspondence A regular (because historical) relationship between a segment in one language and one in another: e.g. English /t/ and German /ts/ in *tongue/Zunge*, *to/zu*, *two/zwei*, etc.

dark Having a **back coarticulation**; particularly of **velarized** /l/.

dative (a) A case or expression coding the notion 'movement toward', typically used for indirect object; (b) a general term for the Old Germanic 'fourth case', in which IE dative, **ablative**, **locative**, and other cases are merged.

daughter A language descended from another (its mother); Latin and Old English are both daughters of Proto-Indo-European.

deadjectival Formed from an adjective or adjectival **root**; OE *bieldan* 'encourage' is a deadjectival formation from the root of *beald* 'bold'.

declension (a) The set of forms of a noun, pronoun, or adjective; (b) a class of nouns, etc. with the same (type of) declension.

deictic   see **deixis**

deixis The reflection in linguistic form of the orientation of discourse participants and their spatial and temporal environments, normally with reference to the speaker. The dimensions *proximal* (toward the speaker) and *distal* (away from the speaker) are the fundamental deictic poles. Thus *I*, *me*, *this*, *here* and present tense are deictically proximal, *you*, *he*, *that* and past are deictically distal. [Lass 1987: §4.4]

demonstrative A **deictic** pronoun or adjective like *this*, *that*, *these*, *those*.

denominal Of a derived item formed from a noun or nominal **root**.

dental Formed with the tongue-tip or blade against the upper incisors, e.g. [θ, ð]. Also a general cover-term for articulations in the dental/ **alveolar** region.

derivation Word-formation by use of **affixes** or other processes, typically excluding formation of **compounds**. The set of such word-formation processes in a language is its *derivational morphology*. [§8.3.3]

determinant (1) Also *determinative, extension*. An element of uncertain status added to an IE **root**, creating a number of possibilities for semantically related and formally similar, but not identical, items. E.g. the IE **root** */wVr-/ 'turn' has a /-t-/ extension in L *uertō* 'turn', an /-m-/ extension in *uermis* 'worm'. [§5.5]

determinant (2) That element of a **compound** that modifies the other (the **head**, also called the *determinatum*), e.g. *black-* in *blackbird*. [§8.3.2]

determinative Or *tatpuruṣa*. A **compound** where one element (the determinatum) is modified by another (the **determinant** (2)), e.g. *fish-net*. [§8.3.2]

determinatum see **determinant** (2)

determiner An article, **demonstrative**, etc. that defines the overall semantic character of a noun phrase.

deverbal Of a derived item formed from a verb or verbal **root**.

diacritic A graphic device that signals a modification of some letter. E.g. the dieresis <¨> above a letter as in German <ü, ö> indicates the opposite backness value from what the unadorned segment has; the <e> at the end of an English monosyllable like *fate* (cf. *fat*) is a signal of vowel length.

digraph A sequence of two letters used as a unit symbol (e.g. for a particular **phoneme**), like <æ, th, ee>.

diphthong A syllable **nucleus** with two detectable different vowel-qualities; phonologically **complex**, consisting of two vowel-slots, e.g. /aɪ/ in *bite*.

diphthongization A process by which a **monophthong** becomes a diphthong.

Diphthong Height Harmony (DHH) The early OE process in which the second element of a diphthong comes to agree in height with the first, e.g. /eo/ in OE *cēosan* 'choose' /tʃeosɑn/ < */keusɑn/. [§3.6.2]

dissimilation A process by which two segments become unlike (the opposite as it were of **assimilation**); e.g. /r . . . r/ > /l . . . r/ in French, as in L *peregrīnus* > *pèlerin* 'pilgrim'.

distal see **deixis**

distribution The total set of contexts in which an element may appear; e.g. the distribution of English /h/ is 'syllable-initial position'.

dithematic see **theme (2)**

dual A number category expressing the notion 'two and two only', as opposed to plural ('more than two' in a language with a dual).

durative An **aspect** coding the notion of continuous action; virtually the same as **progressive**.

dvandva A **compound** whose elements are coequal, not in any modifying relation to each other, e.g. *panty-hose*. [§8.3.2]

e-**grade** (a) That **ablaut-grade** of an Indo-European **root** having /e/ as its nuclear vowel: e.g. L *teg-ō* 'I cover', root */tVg-/; (b) the **reflex** of an IE *e*-grade in some later language, regardless of whether it actually has /e/. So OE *bītan* 'bite' is 'an old *e*-grade' because its nuclear /i:/ is from */ei/ (the root is */bheid-/ 'split'). [chapter 5]

enclitic see **clitic**

epenthesis The insertion of a segment (vowel or consonant); adjective *epenthetic*.

exbraciation 'Movement' of a constituent out of a clausal **brace**. [§9.3]

exocentric Of a construction not having an internal **head**, e.g. a **bahuvrīhi** compound.

extension see **analogy, determinant (1)**

extrametrical Of an item at the edge of some domain that is 'invisible' to or disregarded by stress and similar rules. [§4.2.3]

extraposition 'Movement' of a constituent to a position outside the boundaries of a clause, e.g. the shift from SOV to SVO order where the object is extraposed to the right.

finite Of a verb marked for tense, number, person or at least tense, as opposed to *nonfinite* verbal forms (**infinitive, participle**, etc.).

folk-etymology The reanalysis of a (normally simple) semantically **opaque** (i.e. uninterpretable) item as a **transparent** complex one, i.e. one whose component parts appear to mean something, and whose combination has a reasonable interpretation, e.g. *Jerusalem (artichoke)* < It *girasole* 'sun-flower'. [§8.2.1]

foot A rhythmic unit consisting of a **strong** or stressed syllable plus any **weak** (unstressed) syllables to its right. [§4.2]

formative A general term for any **morph** that appears in processes building a complex word-form, without necessarily specifying its status. E.g. the /-s-/ in OE *clǣn-s-ian* 'cleanse' (cf. *clǣne* 'clean').

front Loosely, of any segment with a non-**back** place of articulation; more commonly and specifically, of vowels produced with a maximal stricture (roughly) opposite the hard palate, e.g. [i, e, æ].

fronting Articulatory shift of a segment from a **back** to a **front** place of articulation.

geminate A double or long segment analysed as a sequence of two identical short ones. E.g. [t:] = [tt], [i:] = [ii]. The process of lengthening under this interpretation is *gemination* (the term is more usually applied to consonants than to vowels).

genitive A case or expression typically coding 'possession' or 'origin'.

Germanic Stress Rule (GSR) The Germanic innovation whereby **stress** comes to fall on the first syllable of the lexical **root**. [§4.2.2]

glottal Of any segment where the vocal folds are the articulators, e.g. [h].

government In traditional usage, the determination of particular case forms of nouns or pronouns by their 'governing' verbs or prepositions: e.g. while perhaps the majority of OE transitive verbs govern **accusative** (impose this case on their objects), some govern **genitive** or **dative**.

grade (a) The vowel that a form has as a result of **ablaut**; (b) derivatively, the **vocalism** associated with a tense form of a **strong verb** (so 'present grade', etc.).

grammaticalization 'Downgrading' or 'bleaching' of a form from full-word status to that of an ending or grammatical marker: e.g. the **weak** past ending was probably once a form of (the ancestor of) the verb *do*, but was grammaticalized into a tense-marker.

Grimm's Law A major transformation of the Indo-European **obstruent** system, which accounts for correspondences like Germanic */f/ = L /p/ in *father: pater*, and many others. [§2.3]

hardening The change of a **fricative** to a **stop**. [§3.9.3]

harmony A kind of **assimilation**, in which all members of some phonological category (most often vowels) within some domain (e.g. the word) come to agree in particular articulatory features like backness, rounding, etc. Harmony may be progressive (left-to-right) as in **Diphthong Height Harmony**, or regressive (right-to-left) as in the various kinds of **umlaut**.

head (a) An obligatory and characteristic constituent of a complex category, e.g. the noun in a noun phrase, the **nucleus** of a syllable, the **strong syllable** of a **foot**; (b) the item modified by an adjective or other modifier; (c) the **determinatum** of a **compound**: the element that determines the compound's part of speech and gender, and is marked for case, number, etc.

heavy syllable One whose **rhyme** contains at least one complex or branching category: e.g. rhymes of the types /-VV(C)/, /-VCC/ are heavy in Germanic. [§3.2]

height The position of a vowel on the vertical axis of the vocal tract.

heteroclite A noun belonging to two **declensions**, specifically in Indo-European with **stems** in both /-n/ and /-r/. [§6.1.3]

hiatus The abutting of two vowels in adjacent syllables as in *neon, bias, my own*.

high vowel   One with maximal possible stricture between the tongue and the upper part of the oral cavity, e.g. [i, u].

Holtzmann's Law   Also *Verschärfung*. An early Germanic change in which certain **geminate sonorants** become **obstruents**, e.g. *[-ww-] > [-gg-]. [§8.4.3]

homorganic   Having the same point of articulation.

imperative   A verbal category (**mood**) expressing commands or orders.

imperfect   A combined **tense/aspect** category indicating **progressive aspect** in the past: Fr *je disais*, E *I was saying*.

inchoative   An **aspect** expressing the notion 'entering into an action, beginning'.

indicative   A **mood** expressing assertion.

infix see **affix**

inflected   Carrying an **affix** or other marker of grammatical function; e.g. *walk-ed*, *rode* are in their different ways inflected for past tense, *cat-s*, *mice* for plural number.

inflectional   Of that part of a language's **morphology** not used in word-formation, but for the marking of grammatical categories.

Ingvaeonic   Also *North-sea Germanic*. The ancient Germanic-speaking community whose language is ancestral to Old English, Old Frisian, Old Saxon; the language of that community; the period (early Christian era) in which that community was presumably (relatively) unified.

instrumental   A case of expression encoding the notion 'means by which something is done'.

intervocalic   Appearing between vowels.

***i*-stem**   A noun or adjective whose **stem** is formed with a historical **thematic** element */-i/ added to the **root**, e.g. *wine* 'friend' < */win-i-z/. [§6.1.3]

***i*-umlaut (IU)**   An early Germanic change in which **back** vowels were **fronted** and nonlow front vowels raised before a following /i, j/. [§3.8]

***ja*-stem** see *a*-stem

***jō*-stem** see *ō*-stem

labial   Of a consonant articulated with one or both lips; either a cover-term for both **bilabial** and **labiodental**, or if not, bilabial only.

labiodental   Of a consonant produced with the upper teeth against the lower lip, e.g. [f, v].

laryngeal   (a) Consonants produced within the larynx, i.e. with no oral articulation (= **glottal**); (b) a specific category of consonants, some at least laryngeal properly speaking, reconstructed for Indo-European on various complex grounds. [chapter 5]

lateral   Of a consonant produced with the airstream escaping on one of both sides of the tongue, rather than along the centre of the oral tract, e.g. [l].

length Duration used as a linguistically significant parameter of **contrast**.

lengthened grade (a) That **ablaut-grade** of an Indo-European **root** with a nuclear long vowel, e.g. L *tēgula* 'tile' (root */tVg-/); (b) the **reflex** of an IE lengthened grade in some later language, e.g. OE *bǣron* 'they carried' < */bhe:r-/. [chapter 5]

lexeme An abstract 'headword' category, serving as a cover-term for a set of *word-forms*, its members. Thus the lexeme SING underlies the word-forms *sing, sings, sang, sung, singing,* etc.

lexical (a) Referring to 'dictionary' or basic meaning (not grammatical meaning); (b) of a word or group of words characterized in some way as idiosyncratic.

lexis The vocabulary of a language; the level of analysis dealing with words and their relations.

light syllable One whose **rhyme** contains a short vowel alone or a short vowel plus no more than one consonant. [§3.2]

liquid A **sonorant** but non-**nasal** consonant; usually applied to /r, l/, but also extended (as in this book) to the 'glides' or 'semivowels' /j, w/.

loan-translation see **calque**

locative A case or expression denoting 'location in'.

lowering The movement of a vowel from **high** to **mid** or from mid to **low**.

low vowel Also open. One with maximally open tongue position, e.g. [æ, ɑ].

merger The falling together of two formerly distinct categories, at any level of linguistic analysis.

metanalysis Also *false separation*. Detaching a segment in (usually) a two-word group from its original position and attaching it to the other constituent: e.g. Elizabethan *nuncle* 'uncle' < *mine uncle*, conversely *adder* < OE *nǣddre* as if *a nadder* > *an adder*.

metathesis The inversion of segments: e.g. /rV/ > /Vr/ in OE *þridda* > ModE *third*.

middle see **voice (1)**

mi-**present** A class of Indo-European present-tense formations in which the first-person singular had */-mi/ rather than the more usual */-o:/, e.g. Gr *ei-mí* 'I am'; the Germanic continuations of such verbs.

mid vowel One that is neither **high** nor **low**; a cover-term for the two non-polar heights *half-close* or higher mid [e, o] and *half-open* or lower mid ([ɛ, ɔ].

minimal pair see **phoneme**

modality A grammatical category encoding notions having to do with speaker's attitude toward or state of knowledge with respect to a proposition. The class of auxiliary verbs expressing notions like ability, obligation, possibility, necessity, etc.; e.g. *can, may, must, might,* are called *modal auxiliaries* or *modals*.

modifier The class of items including adjectives, adverbs, **genitives** and **determiners**.

monophthong A steady-state vowel (long or short).

monophthongization The change from a **diphthong** to a monophthong.

mood The grammatical category encoding modality, e.g. notions like possibility, necessity, real vs. unreal state, assertion vs. question, orders, etc., e.g. **subjunctive, indicative**.

mora (Pl *morae*). A unit of quantity or **weight**, e.g. a short vowel or one element of a long vowel (interpreted as a /VV/ sequence) or a diphthong, or a single consonant in a syllable **rhyme**.

morph A piece of linguistic material at the **phonetic** or **phonological** level, which cannot be analysed into any smaller parts without loss of meaning. A morph may (but does not have to) realize a **morpheme**. E.g. the *-ed* in *climb-ed* realizes a morpheme ({past}), but the *-o-* in *aer-o-space* apparently does not.

morpheme The grammatical equivalent (loosely) of **phoneme**; a minimal piece of grammatical or lexical material which may or may not correspond to a single morph. E.g. the morpheme (= 'category') {past} is represented in *walk-ed* by a suffix, in *rode* by the vowel (or by a vowel 'change' from the present *ride*), and in *fit* by zero.

morphologization A reinterpretation or status-change that may occur when the phonological environment conditioning an **alternation** is destroyed, leaving the alternation free to extend to other environments.

morphology (a) The subdiscipline of linguistics concerned with word-structure (i.e. deployment of **morphemes** in words); (b) the set of devices a language has for **inflection** and **derivation**, and its rules for word-formation.

morphophonemic Also mor(pho)phonological. Pertaining to **alternations** of **phonemes** in (mainly) morphological contexts in a language; e.g. **ablaut**, or the vowel-alternations in OE *dōm* 'judgement' vs. *dēman* 'to judge'. The set of such alternations in a language is its morphophonemics or morphophonology.

morphophonological see **morphophonemic**

nasal Of any consonant or vowel produced with a lowered velum (soft palate), allowing passage of air through the nasal cavity, e.g. [m, ẽ].

nasalization The addition of **nasal** resonance to a vowel.

neutralization The loss of **contrast** between two or more linguistic categories.

nominal A noun or noun-like category, e.g. noun, pronoun, adjective.

nominative The case typically coding the grammatical function of **subject**.

nonfinite Of a verb-form not marked for tense, person, or number.

North Germanic (NGmc) (a) The branch of Germanic comprising the Scandinavian languages; (b) the language spoken before the split into East and West Norse. [§1.2]

Northwest Germanic (NWGmc) (a) The Germanic subgroup to which **North** and **West** Germanic belong; (b) the language spoken before the split into North and West groups, previously thought to be unattested. Now taken by many scholars to be an attested tradition, the language of the bulk of the early **runic** inscriptions. [§1.4]

Northwest Indo-European (NWIE) A group of IE subfamilies including Italic, Celtic, and Germanic, forming a **Sprachbund** in NW Europe in the Bronze Age. [§8.1]

noun phrase (NP) A construction whose **head** is a noun or **nominal**, and which has the typical distribution and functions of a noun.

***n*-stem** Also weak noun. A noun formed with a historical **thematic** element containing */-n-/ added to the **root**, e.g. *guma* 'man' < */ɣum-ɑn-/. [§6.1.3]

nucleus (a) The constituent of a syllable **rhyme** giving the main output of acoustic energy, typically a vowel, but also a syllabic consonant; (b) a general term for the members of a language's vowel system, covering both simple vowels and diphthongs.

oblique With respect to case forms, all non-**nominatives**.

obstruent The class of consonants comprising **stops**, **fricatives** and **affricates**.

***o*-grade** (a) That **ablaut grade** of an Indo-European **root** with /o/ as its nuclear vowel: e.g. L *toga* 'toga', root */tVg-/; (b) the **reflex** of an IE *o*-grade in some later language, regardless of whether the vowel is actually /o/: OE *bær* 'he carried' is 'an old *o*-grade' because it descends from PGmc */βar-/ which descends from IE */bhor-/, root */bhVr-/ 'carry'. [chapter 5]

onomastic Pertaining to names.

onset (a) The syllable-constituent preceding the **rhyme**, e.g. /k-/ in *cats* /kæts/; (b) the first element or **mora** of a diphthong.

opaque see **transparent, folk-etymology**

opposition A systematic **contrast**, e.g. /p/ vs. /b/, **voiceless** vs. **voiced**, present vs. past.

optative A **mood** expressing wishing.

orthographic Pertaining to spelling (*orthography*).

ō-stem   A noun or adjective formed with a historical **thematic** element
*/-o:-/ added to the **root**, e.g. *giefu* 'gift' < */γeβ-o:/. This class also
contains forms with a /-j-/ or /-w-/ element (*jō*-stems, *wō*-stems): *synn*
'sin' < */sun-jo:/, *beadu* 'battle' < */βað-jo:/. [§6.1.3]

palatal   Articulated with the front of the tongue against or approaching
the hard palate; most strictly of consonants like [ç, j], but also of
(especially **high**) **front** vowels. In a looser but often useful sense, the
term includes **palato-alveolars** as well: [i, ç, ʃ] could all count as
palatal.

Palatal Diphthongization (PD)   A dubious OE sound change in which
front vowels supposedly diphthongized after **palatal** consonants. [§3.7]

palatalization   (a) The imposition of **palatal** or [i]-colouring on any
consonant; (b) the articulatory shift of a non-palatal consonant in a
palatal direction, e.g. /k/ > [tʃ], /t/ > [tʃ].

palato-alveolar   Articulated toward the rear of the **alveolar** ridge, with
the body of the tongue raised toward the palate, e.g. [ʃ, tʃ].

paradigm   The set of forms belonging to a particular word-class or
member of a word-class.

parameter   Any set of related values along which a given one can be
situated; e.g. 'glottal state' is a parameter whose values or settings are
voiced, voiceless, breathy-voiced, etc.

partitive   A case or expression coding the notion 'part of a whole',
'portion', e.g. constructions with *some (of)*.

passive   see **voice (1)**

past   see **preterite**

penult   The next-to-last syllable of a word.

perfect   An **aspect** or aspect-like category encoding notions like 'completion', 'present relevance': *he has written* (as opposed to **aorist** or
preterite *he wrote*).

perfective   Expressing the notion 'completion of an action', e.g. non-
perfective *to eat*, perfective *to eat up*.

peripheral   see **central**

pharyngeal   Articulated in the pharynx, usually with the tongue-root as
active articulator.

phoneme   A minimal, **segment**-sized **phonological** unit serving a contrastive function, i.e. capable of distinguishing meaning. A classic test
for phonemic status is the existence of *minimal pairs* (word-pairs
differing only in one **segment**): e.g. /t/ and /d/ are phonemically distinct
in English by virtue of *tip* vs. *dip*, etc. See also **contrast**.

phonemicization   see **phonologization**

phonetic   Pertaining to the realization in substance (= sound) of a
phonological category or unit, or to the physical and/or perceptual

aspects of the sound-structure of a language.

phonological Pertaining to the structure and 'deeper' or more 'abstract' organization of the sound sytem of a language; a language's phonology is its inventory of **phonemes** and the rules for their combination, distribution, etc.; in short all the 'grammatical' or structural aspects of the sound level. In a wider sense, phonology could be said to subsume phonetics as its 'surface' aspect.

phonologization Also *phonemicization*. Shift of a former allophonic **alternation** to a phonemic **contrast**, through loss or alteration of the environment that conditioned it.

phonotactic Pertaining to the distribution and grouping of **phonemes** in a language; e.g. English has a phonotactic rule that the maximal syllable-initial consonant cluster has three members, and that the first must be /s/ (as in *spring, string, scrape*, etc.).

phrase A construction type defined by possessing a **head**, and which typically has the same overall distribution as its head.

postmodifying Having modifiers after their **heads**, e.g. *the Church Militant*.

postposition see **adposition**

prefix see **affix**

premodifying Having modifiers before their **heads**, e.g. *good boy*.

preposition see **adposition**

preterite A simple past tense or **aorist**, e.g. *walked, rode*.

preterite present A type of Germanic verb whose present system is historically (and formally) a **strong verb** past tense, e.g. OE *cann* 'I/he can'. [§7.4.1]

principal parts A set of forms (particularly of a verb) from which the entire **paradigm** can be constructed.

progressive (1) see **assimilation**

progressive (2) An **aspect** coding 'ongoing action', e.g. *I am reading* as opposed to simple or habitual present *I read*.

prosodic Pertaining to **suprasegmental** phenomena, especially **stress**.

protoform An unattested (reconstructed) ancestral form.

protolanguage An unattested (reconstructed) language presumed to be ancestral to some later one(s).

proximal see **deixis**

quantifier An item expressing general (not numerical) quantity; E.g. *some, any, all, each*.

quantity see **weight**

raising The movement of a vowel from **low** to nonlow (**mid** or **high**).

reduplication An **inflectional** or **derivational** device in which a syllable or portion of a syllable is copied, e.g. Greek **perfect** formation as in present *leípō* 'I leave', perfect *lé-loipa*. [§7.2.2]

reflex   The historical descendant of some earlier item: e.g. OE /æ/ is a reflex of PGmc */ɑ/, OE *dæg* 'day' is a reflex of PGmc */ðɑɣɑz/.

resolution   The metrical or prosodic phenomenon whereby two **light syllables** count as one **heavy syllable**. [§4.3]

resonant   see **sonorant**

Restoration of [ɑ]   An OE sound change in which [æ] < [ɑ] by **Anglo-Frisian Brightening** is retracted to [ɑ] before **back** vowels, e.g. *faran* 'go' < */færɑn/. [§3.5]

retraction   Movement of the place of articulation of any segment toward the rear of the vocal tract, e.g. [æ] > [ɑ].

retroflex   Produced with the tongue-tip curled back behind the **alveolar** ridge.

rhotacism   A change in which *[z] < */s/ becomes /r/: e.g. OE *curon* 'they chose' < */kuzún/ < */kusún/.

rhyme   The syllable-constituent comprising the **nucleus** and **coda**, e.g. /-æts/ in *cats* /kæts/.

root   (a) In the strict sense, a minimal string of segments carrying a particular sense; not a 'word', but a 'base' for word-building. E.g. L *dom-*'house' as in *dom-u-s* (nom sg), *dom-u-m* (acc sg), etc. See also **stem**. (b) In a looser historical usage, the source of a word or group of related words in a later language. Thus the Greek root *kard-* 'heart' appears in *cardiac, electrocardiogram*, etc., and the Latin root *cord-* with the same meaning in *cordial, record*; whereas the IE root */kVrd-/ lies behind all of these, as well as *heart*, G *Herz*, etc. [§§5.3–4, 6.1]

root noun   see **consonant-stem**

rounded   Pronounced with the lips protruded or compressed, or narrowed in some non-neutral attitude, e.g. [w, u, y].

runic   The alphabet used by Germanic speakers before they turned to roman or other writing systems. Also of languages surviving only in this alphabet, e.g. 'Runic Northwest Germanic'.

***s*-mobile**   An IE prefix-like */s-/ which appears in some forms of certain **roots** and not others. [§5.4]

sandhi   Phonetic changes occurring at the junction of **morphemes** or words: e.g. *have to* > *hafta* (assimilation of /v/ to voiceless /t/).

schwa   A term from Hebrew grammar referring to an unstressed, 'neutral' or 'obscure' vowel, normally **mid** and **central**; e.g. the vowels in the first and third syllables of *abandon*.

segment   A cover-term for any consonant or vowel.

sibilant   A **fricative** or **affricate** with high-frequency 'hissing' friction, e.g. [s, z, ʃ].

sonorant   A non-**obstruent** segment, e.g. a **nasal** or **liquid** or vowel; also in some usages **resonant**.

split The development of one category into two or more: e.g. WGmc
*/ɑ/ splits into OE /æ/ and /ɑ/.

Sprachbund (Plural *Sprachbünde*). A group of languages (not necessarily
genetically related and often not) spoken in a given area, and influenc-
ing one another to the extent that the group is characterized by certain
common features. [§1.4]

stem In a language of the older IE type, a **root** (sense (a)) plus a
stem-formative or **thematic** element. In languages without a clear
root/stem distinction, we generally refer only to stems; e.g. OE *fōt-es*
'foot' (gen sg) has the stem *fōt-*. [§6.1.1]

stop A consonant produced with complete closure between two articulators, e.g. [p, b].

stress Prominence assigned to a particular syllable in a word. In
particular, prominence whose main acoustic correlate is not pitch
movement. Also *accent*. [§4.2.1]

strong adjective The form of the Germanic adjective carrying maximum
categorial information, i.e. relatively clear marking for case, number,
gender. [§6.3]

strong syllable One bearing (relatively) greater **stress** than an adjacent
one; the stressed syllable or **head** of a foot. [§4.2.1]

strong verb One forming its tenses by means of **ablaut** rather than
suffixation, e.g. OE *rīdan/rād* as opposed to (**weak**) *lufian/luf-od-e*. Does
not include verbs with internal vowel-change plus suffixation, like
þencan 'think': this is weak, given past *þōh-te*. [§7.2]

subjunctive A **mood** typically coding notions like 'unreality', 'doubt',
etc.; in Latin and some Germanic languages also a marker of subordinate clauses.

suffix see **affix**

superheavy syllable One whose **rhyme** contains a long vowel or diphthong plus two or more consonants, i.e. /-VVCC/.

supine A kind of past participle, normally with a **perfective** sense, e.g.
L *cap-tu-s* 'having been captured'.

suppletive Of an **alternation** in which the alternating forms are not
phonologically related, e.g. *go/went, bad/worse* as opposed to non-
suppletive or 'regular' *walk/walk-ed, big/bigg-er*.

suprasegmental Referring to phonological properties best described as
not having a locus in particular **segments**, e.g. **stress**. [§4.1]

syncope Also *syncopation*. Deletion of a word-internal vowel. [§4.3.2]

syncretism Falling together of grammatical categories, especially cases;
e.g. the **merger** of IE dative, ablative and others in the Germanic
dative. [§9.4]

tatpuruṣa   see **determinative**

thematic   Of a **root** followed by some **formative** (usually a vowel), making a **stem** to which endings are added; this formative is a theme or thematic element. As opposed to an **athematic** form, where endings are added directly to the root. [§6.1.1]

theme (1)   see **thematic**

theme (2)   An element in a compound name, e.g. *Wulf-* 'wolf', *-stān* 'stone' in *Wulfstān*. Such a name is *dithematic*, as opposed to a *monothematic* one like *Wulf*. [§8.4.1].

topicalized   Of a syntactic constituent moved from its 'normal' position to the front of a sentence, for purposes of emphasis or focus; e.g. *this book* in *this book I like* as opposed to non-topicalized order in *I like this book*.

transparent   Of any complex structure whose morphology and/or meaning are interpretable on the basis of segmentation, i.e. analysis into parts: e.g. *blackbird* is segmentable as *black + bird*. As opposed to *opaque*, i.e. not segmentable. OE *hlāf-weard* 'loaf-guardian' is transparent, whereas its later version *hlāford* 'lord' is at best semi-transparent (the 'loaf' element is visible, but the rest opaque); while the still later development *lord* is completely opaque. See also **folk-etymology**.

umlaut   A type of **assimilation** (specifically a **harmony**) in which a vowel is influenced by another vowel or vowel-like element to its right.

unrounded   Pronounced with the lips neutral or spread, e.g. [i, æ, t].

***u*-stem**   A noun or adjective with a historical **thematic** */-u-/ added to the **root**, e.g. *sunu* 'son' < */sun-u-z/. [§6.1.3]

uvular   Produced with the back of the tongue against the uvula, e.g. French /r/ [ʁ].

velar   Produced with the back of the tongue against the velum (soft palate), e.g. [k, x]; in an extended sense, of higher **back** vowels like [u, o].

velarized   With superimposed **velar** colouring, as in *dark* /l/ [ɫ].

verb-second rule   The constraint in Germanic languages whereby the **finite** verb appears in second position in a main clause. [§9.3]

Verner's Law (VL)   An early Germanic change in which voiceless **fricatives** become voiced if they are not immediately preceded by an accented vowel. This leads to **alternations** such as /θ ~ d/ in OE *weorþan* 'to become' vs. *wurdon* 'they became' etc. [§2.4]

Verschärfung   see **Holtzmann's Law**

vocalism   The vowel-quality associated with a particular item or category.

vocalization   The change of a non-vowel to a vowel.

vocative   A case or expression of 'direct address'.

voice (1)   A category of the verb, involving primarily an opposition of *active* (subject 'acting on' the verb) and *passive* (subject 'acted on'). Many languages have a third voice, *middle*, which mainly codes action performed for or on behalf of the subject. [§7.1]

voice (2) Vibration of the vocal folds. Segments with such vibration (e.g. vowels, [d, z, m]) are voiced; those without it (e.g. [p, t, s]) are voiceless.

Wackernagel's Law The tendency in ancient IE languages for certain 'light' elements like **clitics** to gravitate to second position in a main clause. [§9.3]

wa-**stem** see *a*-**stem**

weak adjective The form of the Germanic adjective carrying relatively minimal categorial information, as opposed to the **strong** adjective. [§6.3]

weak noun see *n*-**stem**

weak syllable One with relatively low prominence relative to an adjacent one; the unstressed syllable in a **foot**.

weak verb One forming its past tense by a suffix containing a **dental** element, e.g. *walk, walk-ed*, as opposed to a **strong** verb. [§7.3]

weakening Also lenition. Any change involving (a) opening of articulatory stricture (e.g. **stop** > **fricative**); (b) increasing output of periodic acoustic energy (e.g. **voiceless** > **voiced**); or (c) loss of articulation, when a consonant with an oral articulation becomes **glottal** (e.g. [x] > [h]). [Lass 1984: ch. 8]

weight Or quantity. A structural property of syllables, dependent on the **mora**-count of the **rhyme**, and the presence or absence of branching configurations within the rhyme. Syllables may be **light, heavy,** or **superheavy.** [§3.2]

West Germanic (a) The subgroup of Germanic containing English, Dutch, Frisian and German among others; (b) the language spoken by the ancestral group during the presumed period of unity, before the split into distinct subgroupings. [§§1.2, 1.4]

word-form An actual word (**inflected** or not) that is a member of a **lexeme.**

wō-**stem** see *ō*-**stem**

zero-derivation see **conversion**

zero-grade (a) That **ablaut-grade** of an Indo-European **root** where the nuclear vowel has been deleted, e.g. Gr *pt-* in *pt-éron* 'wing' (root */pVt-/; (b) the **reflex** of an IE zero-grade in a later language, regardless of whether it actually has 'zero': e.g. OE *wurdon* 'they became' is 'an old zero-grade' because /-ur-/ is from */-r̥-/. [chapter 5]

zero-syllable An 'empty' but potentially fillable syllable-slot in a **foot**; a construct devised to account for the rhythmic behaviour of monosyllabic words in certain types of languages.[§4.2]

References

Abercrombie, D. 1964. Syllable quantity and enclitics in English. In Abercrombie et al. 1964: 216–22

Abercrombie, D., Fry, D. B., McCarthy, P. A. D., Scott, N. C., Trim, J. L. M. 1964. *In Honour of Daniel Jones. Papers contributed on the occasion of his eightieth birthday 12 September 1961*. London: Longmans

Adamson, S., Law, V., Vincent, N., Wright, S. (eds.) 1990. *Papers from the 5th International Conference on English Historical Linguistics*. Amsterdam: Benjamins

Allen, W. S. 1951. Some prosodic aspects of retroflexion and aspiration in Sanskrit. *BSOAS* 13. 939–46. Reprinted in Palmer 1970: 82–90

    1965. *Vox Latina*. Cambridge: Cambridge University Press

    1973. *Accent and rhythm*. Cambridge: Cambridge University Press

Amos, A. C. and Healey, A. D. 1985. The Dictionary of Old English: the letter "D". In Bammesberger 1985: 13–38

Anderson, J. M. 1988a. The great Kentish collapse. In Kastovsky & Bauer 1988: 97–108

    1988b. The status of voiced fricatives in Old English. In Anderson & Macleod 1988: 90–112

Anderson, J. M. and Macleod, N. (eds.) 1988. *Edinburgh studies in the English language*, 1. Edinburgh: John Donald

Anderson, J. M. and Jones, C. 1974. *Historical linguistics. Proceedings of the First International Conference on Historical Linguistics, Edinburgh, 3–7 September 1973*. 2 vols. Amsterdam: North-Holland

Antonsen, E. A. 1975. *A concise grammar of the older runic inscriptions*. Tübingen: Niemeyer

Árnason, K. 1980. *Quantity in historical phonology. Icelandic and related cases*. Cambridge: Cambridge University Press

Baldi, P. 1983. *An introduction to the Indo-European languages*. Carbondale & Edwardsville: Southern Illinois University Press

Bammesberger, A. 1984. *English etymology*. Heidelberg: Winter

    1985. *Problems in Old English lexicography. Studies in memory of Angus Cameron*. Eichstätter Beiträge, 15. Regensburg: Verlag Friedrich Pustet

    1986. *Der Aufbau des germanischen Verbalsystems*. Heidelberg: Winter

    1990. *Die Morphologie des urgermanischen Nomens*. Heidelberg: Winter

Bauer, L. 1988. *Introducing linguistic morphology*. Edinburgh: Edinburgh University Press

Bean, M. C. 1983. *The development of word order patterns in Old English*. London: Croom Helm

Beekes, R. S. P. 1990. *Vergelijkende taalwetenschap. Tussen Sanskrit en Nederlands.* Utrecht: Aula

Bennett, W. H. 1972. Prosodic features in Proto-Germanic. In van Coetsem & Kufner 1972: 99–116

Benveniste, E. 1935. *Origines de la formation des mots indo-européens*. Paris: Klincksiek

Bierbaumer, P. 1985. Research into Old English glosses: a critical survey. In Bammesberger 1985: 65–78

Bierbaumer, P. 1988. Slips of the ear in Old English texts. In Kastovsky & Bauer 1988: 127–38

Birnbaum, H. and Puhvel, J. (eds.) 1966. *Ancient Indo-European dialects. Proceedings of the Conference on Indo-European linguistics held at the University of California, Los Angeles April 15–27, 1963*. Berkeley and Los Angeles: University of California Press

Blake, N. F. (ed.) 1992. *The Cambridge History of the English Language. I, 1066–1476*. Cambridge: Cambridge University Press

Bomhard, A. R. 1986. The aspirated stops of Proto-Indo-European. *Diachronica* III.1, 67–80

Brunner, K. 1965. *Altenglische Grammatik. Nach der angelsächsischen Grammatik von Eduard Sievers*. 3rd edn. Tübingen: Niemeyer

Campbell, A. 1959. *Old English grammar*. Oxford: Clarendon Press

Campbell, L. 1990. Indo-European and Uralic tree names. *Diachronica* VII:2. 149–80

Carr, E. H. 1939. *Nominal compounds in Germanic*. London: Oxford University Press

Clark, C. 1992. Onomastics. In Hogg 1992a: 452–89

Collinge, N. E. 1970. *Collectanea linguistica*. The Hague: Mouton

Colman, F. 1983. Old English /ɑ/ ≠ /æ/ or [ɑ] ~ [æ]? *Folia Linguistica Historica* IV/2.117–37

1984. Anglo-Saxon pennies and Old English phonology. *Folia Linguistica Historica* V./1.91–144

1985. OE *ie*: Quid est? *Lingua* 67. 1–23

1991a. What positions fit in? In Kastovsky 1991: 51–102

1991b. *Money talks: reconstructing Old English*. Berlin: Mouton de Gruyter

1992a. *Evidence for Old English. Material and theoretical bases for reconstruction. Edinburgh Studies in the English Language, 2*. Edinburgh: John Donald

1992b. A touch of (sub-)class? Old English 'preterite-present' verbs. In Rissanen et al. 1992: 241–61

Comrie, B. 1976. *Aspect*. Cambridge: Cambridge University Press

1981. *Linguistic universals and language typology*. Oxford: Blackwell

1985. *Tense*. Cambridge: Cambridge University Press

Corbett, G. 1991. *Gender*. Cambridge: Cambridge University Press

Croft, W. 1990. *Typology and universals*. Cambridge: Cambridge University Press

Crystal, D. 1985. *A dictionary of linguistics and phonetics*. 2nd edn. Oxford: Blackwell

Daunt, M. 1939. Old English sound changes reconsidered in relation to scribal tradition and practice. *Transactions of the Philological Society*, 108–37

Davenport, M. Hansen, H., Nielsen, H. F. (eds.) 1983. *Current topics in English historical linguistics*. Odense: Odense University Press

Dolgopolsky, A. 1989. Cultural contacts of Proto-Indo-European and Proto-Indo-Iranian with neighbouring languages. *Folia Linguistica Historica* VIII/1–2, 2–36

Dresher, B. E. and Lahiri, A. 1991. The Germanic foot: metrical coherence in Old English. *Linguistic Inquiry* 22. 251–86

Duncan-Rose, C. and Venemann, T. (eds.) 1988. *Rhetorica Phonologica Syntactica. A Festschrift for Robert P. Stockwell from his friends and colleagues*, 221–32. London: Routledge

Elliott, R. W. V. 1963. *Runes. An introduction*. Manchester: Manchester University Press

Fisiak, J. (ed.) 1978. *Recent developments in historical phonology*. The Hague: Mouton

 (ed.) 1984. *Historical syntax*. Berlin/New York/Amsterdam: Mouton

 (ed.) 1985. *Papers from the 6th International Conference on Historical Linguistics*. Amsterdam: Benjamins

Fleming, H. C. 1987. Toward a definitive classification of the world's languages. *Diachronica* IV:1/2. 159–224

Friedrich, P. 1970. *Indo-European trees: the arboreal system of a prehistoric people*. Chicago: University of Chicago Press

Gamkrelidze, T. and Ivanov, V. V. 1973. Sprachtypologie und die Rekonstruktion der gemeindg. Verschlüsse. *Phonetica* 27. 150–6

Gerritsen, M. 1984. Divergent word-order developments in Germanic languages: a description and a tentative explanation. In Fisiak 1984: 107–36

Giegerich, H. 1985. *Metrical phonology and phonological structure. German and English*. Cambridge: Cambridge University Press

Goldsmith, J. 1989. *Autosegmental and metrical phonology*. Oxford: Blackwell

Goodwin, W. W. 1894. *A Greek grammar*. 2nd edn. London: Macmillan. Reprint 1965. New York: St Martin's Press

Görlach, M. 1974. *Einführung in die englische Sprachgeschichte*. Heidelberg: Quelle & Meyer

Greenberg, J. 1966a. Some universals of grammar with particular reference to the order of meaningful elements. In Greenberg 1966b: 73–113

 (ed.) 1966b. *Universals of language*, 2nd edn. Cambridge, Mass: MIT Press

Hale, W. G. and Buck, C. D. 1966. *A Latin grammar*. Reprint (first published 1903). University, Alabama: University of Alabama Press

Hall, J. 1920. *Selections from early Middle English 1130–1250*. 2 vols. Oxford: Clarendon Press

Hallander, Lars-G. 1966. *Old English weak verbs in -sian*. Stockholm: Almqvist & Wiksell

Hamp. E. P. 1984. The reconstruction of particles and syntax. In Fisiak 1984: 173–82

Harris, M. B. 1984. On the strengths and weaknesses of a typological approach to syntax. In Fisiak 1984: 183–98

Hawkins, J. A. 1983. *Word order universals*. New York: Academic Press

Hock, H. H. 1991. *Principles of historical linguistics*. 2nd edn. Berlin: Mouton de Gruyter

Hockett, C. F. 1959. The stressed syllabics of Old English. *Language* 35. 575–97

Hodge, C. T. 1986. Indo-European consonant ablaut. *Diachronica* III.2. 143–62

Hogg, R. M. 1988. On the impossibility of Old English dialectology. In Kastovsky & Bauer 1988: 183–204

(ed.) 1992a. *The Cambridge History of the English Language. I, The beginnings to 1066.* Cambridge: Cambridge University Press

1992b. Phonology and morphology. In Hogg 1992a: 67–167

1992c. *Old English grammar.* Oxford: Basil Blackwell

Hogg, R. M. and McCully, C. B. 1987. *Metrical phonology: a coursebook.* Cambridge: Cambridge University Press

Holthausen, F. 1963. *Altenglisches etymologisches Wörterbuch.* 2nd edn. Heidelberg: Winter

Hopper, P. J. 1973. Glottalized and murmured occlusives in IE. *Glossa* 7.141–66

Hopper, P. J. 1975. *The syntax of the simple sentence in Proto-Germanic.* The Hague: Mouton

Howell, R. B. 1991. *Old English breaking and its Germanic analogues.* Tübingen: Niemeyer

Joseph, B. D. 1985. Proto-Indo-European consonantism: methodological and further typological concerns. In Fisiak 1985: 313–21

Kastovsky, D. 1990. The typological status of Old English word-formation. In Adamson et al. 1990: 205–24

(ed.) 1991. *Historical English syntax.* Berlin: Mouton de Gruyter

1992. Semantics and vocabulary. In Hogg 1992a: 290–408

Kastovsky, D. and Bauer, G. (eds.) 1988. *Luick revisited. Papers read at the Luick-Symposium at Schloß Leichtenstein, 15.–18.9.1985.* Tübingen: Gunter Narr Verlag

Kastovsky, D. and Szwedek, A. (eds.) 1986. *Linguistics across historical and geographical boundaries. In honour of Jacek Fisiak on the occasion of his fiftieth birthday.* 2 vols. Berlin: Mouton de Gruyter

Katamba, F. 1989. *An introduction to phonology.* London: Longman

Keyser, S. J. and O'Neil, W. 1985. *Rule generalization and optimality in language change.* Dordrecht: Foris

King, A. 1992. You say [æjðər] and I say [æjhwæðər]? Interpreting Old English written data. In Colman 1991a: 20–43

Kiparsky, P. 1973. The inflectional accent in IE. *Language* 49. 794–949

Kiparsky, P. and Halle, M. 1977. Towards a reconstruction of the IE accent. In L. M. Hyman, *Studies in stress and accent,* 209–38. Los Angeles: University of California Press

Klaiman, M. H. 1991. *Grammatical voice.* Cambridge: Cambridge University Press

Koerner, E. F. K. 1985. The place of Saussure's *Mémoire* in the development of historical linguistics. In Fisiak 1985: 323–46

Krahe, H. 1963. *Germanische Sprachwissenschaft. I, Einleitung und Lautlehre.* Berlin: de Gruyter

1965. *Germanische Sprachwissenschaft. II, Formelehre.* Berlin: de Gruyter

Krahe, H. and Meid, W. 1967. *Germanische Sprachwissenschaft. III, Wortbildungslehre.* Berlin: de Gruyter

Kufner, H. 1972. The grouping and separation of the Germanic languages. In van Coetsem and Kufner 1972: 71–98

Kuhn, S. 1961. The syllabic phonemes of Old English. *Language* 37.522–38

Kuhn, S. and Quirk, R. 1953. Some recent interpretations of Old English digraph spellings. *Language* 29.372–89

Kuryłowicz, J. 1927.ǝ indo-européen et *h* hittite. In *Symbolae grammaticae in honorem Ioannis Rozwadowski*, I, 95–104. Cracow: Drukarnia Uniwerstetu Jagiellońskiego

1964. *The inflectional categories of Indo-European*. Heidelberg: Winter

Laanest, A. 1975. *Einführung in die ostseefinnischen Sprachen*. Hamburg: Buske

Lass, R. 1974. Linguistic orthogenesis? Scots vowel quantity and the English length conspiracy. In Anderson & Jones 1974, II: 311–52

1976. *English phonology and phonological theory. Synchronic and diachronic studies.* Cambridge: Cambridge University Press

1977. 'Centres of gravity' in language evolution. *Die Sprach* 23.11–19

1980. *On explaining language change.* Cambridge: Cambridge University Press

1983. Velar /r/ and the history of English. In Davenport et al. 1983: 67–94

1984a. *Phonology. An introduction to basic concepts.* Cambridge: Cambridge University Press

1984b. Quantity, resolution and syllable geometry. *Folia Linguistica Historica* 4.151–80

1986. Words without etyma: Germanic 'tooth'. In Kastovsky & Szwedek 1986, I: 473–82

1987. *The shape of English. Structure and history.* London: J. M. Dent

1988. The 'Akzentumsprung' of Old English *ēo*. In Duncan-Rose & Venemann 1988: 221–32

1990. How to do things with junk: exaptation in language evolution. *Journal of Linguistics* 26.79–102

1991. On data and 'datives': Ruthwell Cross *rodi* again. *Neuphilologische Mitteilungen* 92.395–403

1992a. Front-rounded vowels in Old English. In Colman 1992a: 88–116

1992b. Phonology and morphology. In Blake 1992: 23–155

Forthcoming. Phonology and morphology. To appear in R. Lass (ed.), *The Cambridge History of the English Language. III, 1476–1776.* Cambridge: Cambridge University Press

Lass, R. and Anderson, J. M. 1975. *Old English phonology.* Cambridge: Cambridge University Press

Lehmann, W. P. 1965. Germanic evidence. In Winter 1965: 212–23

1966. The grouping of the Germanic languages. In Birnbaum & Puhvel 1966: 13–28

(ed.) 1967. *A reader in nineteenth-century historical Indo-European linguistics.* Bloomington: Indiana University Press

1972. Proto-Germanic syntax. In van Coetsem & Kufner 1972: 239–68

1974. *Proto-Indo-European syntax.* Austin: University of Texas Press

Lehnert, M. 1965. *Altenglisches Elementarbuch.* Berlin: de Gruyter

Li, C. (ed.) 1977. *Mechanisms of syntactic change.* Austin: University of Texas Press

Lockwood, W. B. 1966. *Indo-European philology.* London: Hutchinson

Lucas, P. J. 1987. Some aspects of the interaction between verse grammar and metre in Old English poetry. *Studia Neophilologica* 59. 145–75

Luick, K. 1914/41. *Historische Grammatik der englischen Sprache.* Leipzig: Tauchnitz. Repr. 2 vols. 1965: Oxford: Blackwell

Luraghi, S. 1987. Patterns of case syncretism in Indo-European languages. In Ramat et al. 1987: 355–72

McCully, C. B. 1992. The phonology of resolution in Old English word-stress and metre. In Colman 1991a: 117–41

Marchand, H. 1969. *The categories and types of present-day English word-formation. A synchronic-diachronic approach.* Munich: C. H. Beck'sche Verlagsbuchhandlung.

Markey, T. L. 1976. *A North-Sea Germanic reader.* Munich: Fink

Matthews, P. H. 1974. *Morphology.* Cambridge: Cambridge University Press

Mayrhofer, M. 1972. *A Sanskrit grammar.* Tr. G. B. Ford. University, Alabama: University of Alabama Press

Minkova, D. 1991. *The history of final vowels in English. The sound of muting.* Berlin: Mouton de Gruyter

Minkova, D. and Stockwell, R. P. 1992. Homorganic clusters as moric busters in the history of English: the case of *-ld, -nd, -mb*. In Rissanen et al. 1992: 191–206

Mitchell, B. 1985. *Old English syntax.* 2 vols. Oxford: Clarendon Press

Moore, S. and Knott, T. 1955. *The elements of Old English.* Ann Arbor: Wahr

Moulton, W. G. 1972. The Proto-Germanic non-syllabics (consonants). In van Coetsem & Kufner 1972: 141–74

Møller, H. 1880. Review of F. Kluge, *Beiträge zur Geschichte der germanischen Conjugation* (1879). *Englische Studien* 3.

Murray, R. W. & Vennemann, T. 1983. Sound change and syllable structure: problems in Germanic phonology. *Language* 59. 514–28

Nielsen, H. F. 1985. *Old English and the continental Germanic languages. A survey of morphological and phonological interrelations.* 2nd edn. Innsbruck: Innsbrucker Beiträge zur Sprachwissenschaft, 33

1989. *The Germanic languages. Origins and early dialectal interrelations.* Tucsaloosa: University of Alabama Press

Page, R. 1987. *Runes.* London: British Museum Publications

Palmer, F. R. (ed.) 1970. *Prosodic analysis.* London: Oxford University Press

Palmer, L. R. 1972. *Descriptive and comparative linguistics. A critical introduction.* London: Faber & Faber

Pilch, E. 1984. Syntactic reconstruction. In Fisiak 1984: 383–92

Plank, F. 1983. Coming into being among the Anglo-Saxons. In Davenport et al. 1983: 239–78

Polomé, E. C. 1965. The laryngeal theory so far: a critical bibliographical survey. In Winter 1965: 9–78

1972. Germanic and the other Indo-European languages. In van Coetsem & Kufner 1972: 43–70

Pope, M. K. 1934. *From Latin to modern French.* Manchester: Manchester University Press

Poussa, P. 1982. The evolution of early standard English: the creolization hypothesis. *Studia Anglica Posnaniensia* 14. 70–85

Prokosch, E. 1938. *A comparative Germanic grammar.* Baltimore: Linguistic Society of America

Quirk, R. and Wrenn, C. L. 1955. *Old English grammar.* London: Methuen

Ramat, A. G., Carruba, C., Bernini, G. (eds.) 1987. *Papers from the 7th International Conference on Historical Linguistics*. Amsterdam: Benjamins

Renfrew, C. 1988. *Archaeology and language*. Cambridge: Cambridge University Press

Rissanen, M., Ihalainen, O., Nevalainen, T., Taavitsainen, I. (eds.) 1992. *History of Englishes. New methods and interpretations in historical linguistics*. Berlin: Mouton de Gruyter

Ritt, N. Forthcoming. *Adjustments of vowel quantity in early Middle English*. Cambridge: Cambridge University Press

Rudes, B. 1984. Reconstructing word order in a polysynethic language: from SOV to SVO in Iroquoian. In Fisiak 1984: 471–508

Ruhlen, M. 1987. *A guide to the world's languages. I, Classification*. Stanford: Stanford University Press

Saussure, F. de. 1879. *Mémoire sur le système primitif des voyelles dans les langues indo-européennes*. Leipzig: B. G. Teubner

Serjeantson, M. 1935. *A history of foreign words in English*. London: Routledge & Kegan Paul

Smith, A. H. 1968. *Three Northumbrian poems*. London: Methuen

Steponavičius, A. 1987. *English historical phonology*. Moscow: Vysšaya Škola

Stockwell, R. P. 1977. Motivations for exbraciation in Old English. In Li 1977: 291–316

1984. On the history of the verb-second rule in English. In Fisiak 1984: 575–92

Stockwell, R. P. and Barritt, C. W. 1951. Some Old English graphemic-phonemic correspondences: æ, ea, a. *Studies in Linguistics*, Occasional Papers, 4.

1955. The English short digraphs: some considerations. *Language* 31. 373–89

Stockwell, R. P. and Minkova, D. 1991. Subordination and word order change in the history of English. In Kastovsky 1991: 367–408

1992. Poetic influence on prose word order in Old English. In Colman 1992a: 142–54

Forthcoming. Syllable weight in the history of English. Paper delivered at the 7th ICEHL, Valencia 1992.

Streitberg, W. 1963. *Urgermanische Grammatik*. Heidelberg: Winter

Sweet, H. 1885. *The oldest English texts*. EETS, 83. London: Oxford University Press

Szemerényi, O. 1985. Recent developments in Indo-European linguistics. *Transactions of the Philological Society*, 1–72

1989. *Einführung in die vergleichende Sprachwissenschaft*. Darmstadt: Wissenschaftliche Buchgesellschaft

Tops, G. 1978. The origin of the Germanic dental preterite: von Friesen revisited. In Fisiak 1978: 349–72

Traugott, E. C. 1992. Syntax. In Hogg 1992a: 168–289

van Coetsem, F. and Kufner, H. (eds.) 1972. *Toward a grammar of Proto-Germanic*. Tübingen: Niemeyer

van Kemenade, A. 1987. *Syntactic case and morphological case in the history of English*. Dordrecht: Foris

Vennemann, T. 1974. Topics, subjects and word order: from SXV to SVX via TVX. In Anderson & Jones 1974: 339–76

1984. Verb-second, verb late, and the brace construction in Germanic: a discussion. In Fisiak 1984: 627–36

Verner, K. 1875. Eine Ausnahme der ersten Lautverschiebung. *Zeitschrift für Vergleichende Sprachforschung auf dem Gebiete der Indogermanischen Sprachen* 23.2, 97–130. Translation in Lehmann 1967: 132–63

Wackernagel, J. 1892. Über ein Gesetz der idg. Wortstellung. *Indogermanische Forschungen* 1.333–436

Weerman, F. 1989. *The V-2 conspiracy – a synchronic and diachronic account of verbal positions in Germanic languages.* Dordrecht: Foris

Whitelock, D. 1963. *Sermo Lupi ad Anglos.* London: Methuen

Whitney, W. D. 1889. *Sanskrit grammar.* 2nd edn. Cambridge, Mass: Harvard University Press

Winter, W. (ed.) 1965. *Evidence for laryngeals.* The Hague: Mouton

1984. Reconstructing comparative linguistics and the reconstruction of the syntax of undocumented stages in the development of languages and language families. In Fisiak 1984: 615–25

Wright, J. 1899. *A primer of the Gothic language.* 2nd edn. Oxford: Clarendon Press

Wright, J. and Wright, E. M. 1925. *Old English grammar.* London: Oxford University Press

Index of names

Subject index

Boldface entries indicate primary or more extensive discussions of particular topics.

ablative
  absolute 239
  IE 127
  in adverbs 208–9
ablaut **105–9**
  conditioning 107–9
  e-grade vs. *o*-grade vs. zero-grade vs.
    lengthened grade 106–9
  in word-formation 191–2
  qualitative vs. quantitative 107
  types of zero grade 116–18
  verbal 108–9
absolute *see* dative, ablative, genitive,
    locative
accent
  Greek 87
  Indo-European 21, 87–8
  Latin 88
  Sanskrit 87
Accent Shift **21–2**
accusative
  IE 233
  plural 129
  prepositional objects 229–31
  of motion 233, 234
  of extent 233
adjective
  comparison 149–50
  deverbal 201
  Germanic strong vs. weak **146–9**
  IE stem-types 146
  pronominal elements 147
adposition order 218, 220
  OE 222
adverb **207–8**
affixation 191
affixoids 94n
affricates
  origins in Old English 56–8

Afrikaans
  consonant-stem plurals 136
  number '80' 213
  velar fricative 75
  /y/ 2
'afterthoughts' 228n
agentives 134, 200, 201
analogy
  numerals 210, 211
  reflexes of WGmc */ɑ/ 43
  strong past participle 118, 162
Anatolian 11
Anglian 161
  adverbs 208
  forms of 'be' 171
Anglo-Frisian Brightening **42–4**, 105, 156
aorist
  IE 151–2
  lengthened grade 109
  sigmatic 109
  zero-grade 108, 154
Armenian 11
a-stems 46, **129–30**
  HVD 102, 125
  masculine in IE 128
  medial syncope 130
  neuters 130
  source of {-s} plural 129
a-umlaut **26–7**
  in word-formation 191n
athematic nouns 125, **135–6**
athematic (root) verbs 170–2
$\bar{æ}_1$, vs. $\bar{æ}_2$ 64–5

back-formation 198n
backness accommodation 56–7
back umlaut 50, **51–2**
Baltic 11
  numbers '11', 12' 211

Index of Old English words and affixes

Headwords are given in the usual 'standard' (West Saxon) orthography; alternative spellings are listed after the headword. Inflexional forms of nouns, pronouns, verbs and adjectives are given under the nominative singular and infinitive respectively. Citations of paradigms (complete or partial) are in boldface. All non-past forms of the verb 'to be' are listed (inaccurately but conveniently) under *bēon*. Alphabetization: <þ, ð> form a separate listing after <t>, and <æ> after <a>; <u> is alphabetized with <w> when it represents /w/, as in *uulf = wulf*. In cases of forms that differ only in vowel length (e.g. *lim* vs. *līm*), the short vowel form is first. PN = proper name. Bound morphs generally are unglossed; prefixes are indicated by a following hyphen (e.g. *of-*), suffixes by a preceding hyphen (e.g. *-an*), and infixes and other word-internal morphs by paired hyphens (e.g. *-o-*).